Rick Steves'
GREAT BRITAIN
& IRELAND
1998

John Muir Publications
Santa Fe, New Mexico

Other JMP travel guidebooks by Rick Steves
  Asia Through the Back Door (with Bob Effertz)
  Europe 101: History and Art for the Traveler (with Gene Openshaw)
  Mona Winks: Self-Guided Tours of Europe's Top Museums
   (with Gene Openshaw)
  Rick Steves' Best of Europe
  Rick Steves' Europe Through the Back Door
  Rick Steves' France, Belgium & the Netherlands (with Steve Smith)
  Rick Steves' Germany, Austria & Switzerland
  Rick Steves' Italy
  Rick Steves' Russia & the Baltics (with Ian Watson)
  Rick Steves' Scandinavia
  Rick Steves' Spain & Portugal
  Rick Steves' Phrase Books for: German, Italian, French,
   Spanish/Portuguese, and French/German/Italian

Thanks to my wife, Anne, for making "home" my favorite travel destination.
Thanks also to Roy and Jodi Nicholls for their research help, to our well-traveled
readers for their input, and to the local friends listed in this book who put the
"Great" in Britain.

John Muir Publications, P.O. Box 613, Santa Fe, NM 87504

Printed in the United States of America
Second printing April 1998

Previously published as *2 to 22 Days in Great Britain* copyright © 1986, 1987,
1989, 1991, 1992, 1993, 1994

For the latest on Rick's lectures, guidebooks, tours, and public television series,
contact Europe Through the Back Door, Box 2009, Edmonds, WA 98020,
tel. 425/771-8303, fax 425/771-0833, Web site: www.ricksteves.com, or
e-mail: rick@ricksteves.com.

ISSN 1090-6843
ISBN 1-56261-387-1

Europe Through the Back Door Editor Risa Laib
John Muir Publications Editors Krista Lyons-Gould, Chris Hayhurst
Research Assistant for Ireland Roy Nicholls
Production Janine Lehmann, Nikki Rooker
Design Linda Braun
Cover Design Janine Lehmann
Maps Dave C. Hoerlein
Typesetting Melissa Tandysh
Printer Banta Company
Cover Photo Big Ben, London, England; Leo de Wys./Dave and Les Jacobs

Distributed to the book trade by
Publishers Group West
Berkeley, California

The Best Destinations in Great Britain and Ireland

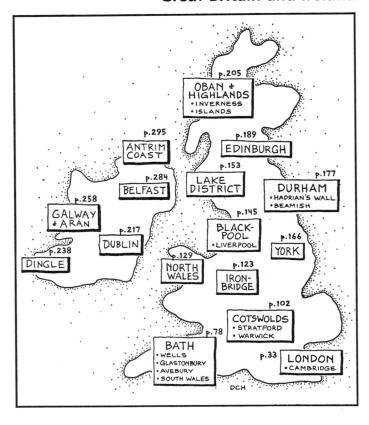

p.205 OBAN & HIGHLANDS
• INVERNESS
• ISLANDS

p.295 ANTRIM COAST

p.189 EDINBURGH

p.284 BELFAST

p.153 LAKE DISTRICT

p.177 DURHAM
• HADRIAN'S WALL
• BEAMISH

p.258 GALWAY & ARAN

p.217 DUBLIN

p.145 BLACK-POOL
• LIVERPOOL

p.166 YORK

p.238 DINGLE

p.129 NORTH WALES

p.123 IRON-BRIDGE

p.102 COTSWOLDS
• STRATFORD
• WARWICK

p.78 BATH
• WELLS
• GLASTONBURY
• AVEBURY
• SOUTH WALES

p.33 LONDON
• CAMBRIDGE

DCH

CONTENTS

INTRODUCTION

This book breaks Britain and Ireland into its top big-city, small-town, and rural destinations. It gives you all the information and opinions necessary to wring the maximum value out of your limited time and money in each of these destinations. If you plan a month or less for Britain and Ireland, and have a normal appetite for information, this lean and mean little book is all you need. If you're a travel info fiend, this book sorts through all the superlatives and provides a handy rack upon which to hang your supplemental information.

Experiencing the British and Irish cultures, people, and natural wonders economically and hassle-free has been my goal for more than 20 years of traveling, tour guiding, and travel writing. With this new edition I pass on to you the lessons I've learned, updated for your 1998 trip.

Rick Steves' Great Britain & Ireland is a personal tour guide in your pocket. Places covered are balanced to include a comfortable mix of exciting big cities and great-to-be-alive-in small towns. While covering the predictable biggies (such as Big Ben, Stratford, bagpipes, and the Book of Kells), the book also mixes in a healthy dose of Back Door intimacy (nearly edible Cotswold villages, Gaelic folk pubs, angelic boys' choirs, and windswept Roman lookouts). I've been selective. On a short trip, visiting both Oxford and Cambridge is redundant; I cover just the best (Cambridge). There are plenty of great countryside palaces; again, I recommend just the best (Blenheim).

The best is, of course, only my opinion. But after more than two busy decades of travel writing, lecturing, and tour guiding, I've developed a sixth sense for what tickles the traveler's fancy. The places featured in this book will knock your spots off.

This Information Is Accurate and Up-to-Date

Most publishers of guidebooks that cover a country from top to bottom can afford an update only every two or three years, and then it's often by letter. Since this book is selective, covering only the top month of sightseeing, I'm able to update it each year. (Don't tell my publisher, but I'm so committed to this book, I'd do it for free.) Even with an annual update, things change. But if you're traveling with the current edition of this book, I guarantee you're using the most up-to-date information available. This book will help you have an inexpensive, hassle-free trip.

Use this year's edition. I tell you, you're crazy to save a few bucks by traveling on old information. If you're packing an old book, you'll learn the seriousness of your mistake . . . once you start your trip. To rescue those of you who will inevitably travel with a two-year-old edition of this book (and realize your mistake too late), I've sent the latest edition to my lead B&Bs in each town for you to transcribe over breakfast. Your trip costs about $10 per waking hour. Your time is valuable. This guidebook saves lots of time.

Planning Your Trip

This book is organized by destinations, each one a mini-vacation on its own, filled with exciting sights and homey, affordable places to stay. In each chapter, you'll find:

Planning Your Time, a suggested schedule with thoughts on how to best use your limited time.

Orientation, including tourist information, city transportation, and an easy-to-read map designed to make the text clear and your entry smooth.

Sights with ratings: ▲▲▲—Don't miss; ▲▲—Try hard to see; ▲—Worthwhile if you can make it; No rating—Worth knowing about.

Sleeping and **Eating** with addresses and phone numbers of my favorite budget hotels and restaurants.

And **Transportation Connections** to nearby destinations by train and **Route Tips for Drivers**.

The Appendix is a traveler's toolkit with information on history, architecture, TV for sightseers, climate, telephoning, and a British–Yankee vocabulary list.

Browse through this book, choose your favorite destinations, and link them up. Then have a great trip! You'll travel like a temporary local, getting the absolute most out of every mile, minute, and dollar. You won't waste time on mediocre sights because, unlike other guidebooks, I cover only the best. Since your major financial pitfall is lousy, expensive hotels, I've worked hard to assemble the best accommodations values for each stop. And as you travel the route I know and love, I'm happy you'll be meeting some of my favorite British and Irish people.

Trip Costs

Five components make up your trip costs: airfare, surface transportation, room and board, sightseeing, and shopping/entertainment/miscellany.

Airfare: Don't try to sort through the mess. Find and use a good travel agent. A basic, round-trip, U.S.A.-to-London flight costs $500 to $1,000, depending on where you fly from and when. Always consider saving time and money in Europe by flying "open-jaws" (into one city and out of another; for instance, into London and out of Dublin).

Surface Transportation: For a three-week whirlwind trip of all my recommended British destinations, allow $450 per person for public transportation (train pass and key buses), or $500 per person (based on two people sharing) for a three-week car rental, gas, and insurance. About $150 more covers the ferry to Ireland and train and bus connections to its major sights. Car rental is cheapest if arranged from the U.S.A. Train passes are normally available only outside of Europe. You may save money by simply buying tickets as you go (see Transportation, below).

Room and Board: You can thrive in Britain and Ireland on $60 a day per person for room and board. A $60-a-day budget allows $10 for lunch, $15 for dinner, and $35 for lodging (based on two people splitting the cost of a $70 double room that includes breakfast). That's doable. Students and tightwads do it on $40 ($15–$20 per bed, $20 a day for meals and snacks). But budget sleeping and eating require the skills and information covered below (and in greater detail in my book, *Rick Steves' Europe Through the Back Door*).

Sightseeing: In big cities, figure $5 to $10 per major sight (Imperial War Museum-$7, Edinburgh Castle-$9), $2 for minor ones (climbing church towers), $10 for guided walks and $25 for bus tours and splurge experiences (Welsh and Scottish folk evenings). An overall average of $15 a day works for most. Don't skimp here. After all, this category directly powers most of the experiences all the other expenses are designed to make possible.

You will be tempted to buy the British Heritage Pass, which gets you into over 500 British Heritage and National Trust properties (£28 for seven days, £39 for 15 days, £54 for 30 days; sold at airport information desks and the British Travel Centre on Regent Street in London). Of the 500 sights included (a list comes with the pass), here are the sights I describe and recommend for a three-week tour of Britain, along with their adult admission prices. A typical sightseer with three weeks will probably pay to see nearly all of these: Tower of London-£8.50 (London); Shakespeare's Birthplace and Anne Hathaway's Cottage-£5.50 (Stratford); Warwick Castle-£9 (near Stratford); Blenheim Palace-£8 (near the Cotswolds and Oxford); Roman and Medieval Baths-£6 (Bath); Stonehenge-£3.50 (near Bath); Caerphilly Castle-£2.20 and Tintern Abbey-£2.20 (South Wales); Caernarfon Castle-£3.80 (North Wales); Wordsworth's Dove Cottage-£4.30 (Lakes District); Housesteads Roman Fort-£2.50 (Hadrian's Wall); Edinburgh Castle-£5.50, Georgian House-£4, Gladstone's Land-£2.60, and Holyrood Palace-£5.30 (Edinburgh); Culloden Battlefield-£2 (near Inverness); and Urquhart Castle-£3 (near Loch Ness). Your pass also saves you £1 on all Guide Friday bus tours (you'll probably take four). This totals nearly £82—and takes the pain out of all these admissions with one big pill.

Shopping/Entertainment/Miscellany: This can vary from nearly nothing to a small fortune. Figure $1 per postcard, tea, or ice-cream cone; $2 per beer; and $10 to $30 for evening entertainment. Good budget travelers find that this category has little to do with assembling a trip full of lifelong and wonderful memories.

Exchange Rates

I list prices in pounds (£) throughout this book.

1 British pound (£1) = about $1.60

1 Irish pound (£1) = about $1.60

Britain: The British pound sterling (£), also called a "quid," is broken into 100 pence (p). Pence means "cents." You'll find coins ranging from 1p to £1 and bills from £5 to £50. For a rough approximation, multiply British prices by 1.5 to convert pounds to dollars: £6 is $9, £4.50 is about $7, and 80p is $1.20. Scotland and Northern Ireland issue their own currency in pounds, worth the same as an English pound. English, Scottish, and Northern Ireland's Ulster pounds are technically interchangeable in each region, although Scottish and Ulster pounds are "undesirable" in England. Banks in any of the three regions will convert your Scottish or Ulster pounds into English pounds at no charge.

Ireland: The Irish-English money relationship is like the Canadian-American one. The Irish call their pound a "punt." While their relative values fluctuate, currently both the British

and Irish pounds are worth about the same. Use Irish, not
English money on the Emerald Isle. Ireland is a different
country—treat it that way.

Prices, Times, and Discounts

The prices in this book, as well as the hours and telephone
numbers, are accurate as of late 1997. The economy is flat and
inflation is low, so these prices should be pretty accurate in
1998. Britain and Ireland are always changing, and I know
you'll understand that this, like any other guidebook, starts to
yellow even before it's printed.

In Britain and Ireland you'll be using the 24-hour clock.
After 12:00 noon, keep going—13:00, 14:00. . . . For anything
over 12, subtract 12 and add p.m. (14:00 is 2:00 p.m.).

This book lists peak-season hours for sightseeing attractions (July and August). Off-season, roughly October through
April, expect shorter hours, more lunchtime breaks, and fewer
activities. Some places are open only on weekends or closed
entirely in the winter. Confirm your sightseeing plans locally,
especially when traveling between October and April.

While discounts (called "concessions" in Britain) are not
listed in this book, nearly all British and Irish sights are discounted for seniors (loosely defined as anyone retired or willing to call themselves a "senior"), youths (ages 8–18), students,
groups of ten or more, and families.

When to Go

July and August are peak season—my favorite time—with very
long days, the best weather, and the busiest schedule of tourist
fun. Prices and crowds don't go up as dramatically in Britain as
they do in much of Europe. Still, travel during "shoulder season" (May, early June, September, and early October) is easier
and a bit less expensive. Shoulder-season travelers get minimal
crowds, decent weather, the full range of sights and tourist fun
spots, and the joy of being able to just grab a room almost
whenever and wherever they like—often at a flexible price.
Winter travelers find absolutely no crowds and soft room
prices, but shorter sightseeing hours. The weather can be cold
and dreary, and nightfall draws the shades on sightseeing well
before dinnertime. While England's rural charm falls with the
leaves, city sightseeing is fine in the winter.

Plan for rain no matter when you go. Just keep going and

take full advantage of "bright spells." In Ireland, rainy weather is called "nice and soft." Conditions can change several times in a day, but rarely is the weather extreme. Daily averages throughout the year range between 42 and 70 degrees Fahrenheit. Temperatures below 32 or over 80 degrees are cause for headlines (see the climate chart in the Appendix). July and August are not much better than shoulder months. May and June can be lovely. While sunshine may be rare, summer days are very long. The summer sun is up from 6:30 until 22:30 (10:30 p.m.). It's not uncommon to have a gray day, eat dinner, and enjoy hours of sunshine afterwards.

Sightseeing Priorities

Depending on the length of your trip, here are my recommended priorities.

Britain:

3 days:	London
5 days, add:	Bath, Cotswolds, Blenheim
7 days, add:	York
9 days, add:	Edinburgh
11 days, add:	Stratford, Warwick, Cambridge
14 days, add:	North Wales, Wells/Glastonbury/Avebury
17 days, add:	Lake District, Hadrian's Wall, Durham
21 days, add:	Ironbridge, Blackpool, Scottish Highlands
24 days, add:	South Wales

(The Whirlwind Tour map on page 9 and suggested three-week itinerary on page 8 include everything in the above 24 days. With 30 days you could slow down or add a five-day swing through Ireland.)

Ireland:

3 days:	Not worth the trouble
5 days, add:	Dublin, Dingle Peninsula
7 days, add:	Galway and a day in Belfast
9 days, add:	County Clare/Burren
11 days, add:	Northern Ireland's Antrim Coast
15 days, add:	Aran Islands, Wicklow area

Itinerary Tips

Most people fly into London and remain there for a few days. Instead, consider a gentler small-town start in Bath, and visit

London at the end of your trip. You'll be more rested and ready to tackle Britain's greatest city. Heathrow Airport has direct connections to Bath and other cities.

To give yourself a little rootedness, minimize one-night stands. It's worth a long drive after dinner to be settled into a town for two nights. B&Bs are more likely to give a good price to someone staying more than one night.

Many people save a couple of days and a lot of miles by going directly from the Lake District to Edinburgh, skipping the long joyride through Scotland. I consider Wales, rather than Scotland or Ireland, the best quick look at Celtic Britain.

Ireland, because of its nature and the expense and headaches involved in getting there, is not worth a very quick visit. It requires a minimum of five days. Don't overlook the handy ferry connections from Belfast to Scotland and from southeast Ireland to France. If you ask the Irish about ferries, they'll say, "I don't believe in them. But they're there."

Red Tape and Taxes

You need a passport, but no visa or shots, to travel in Britain and Ireland.

Sales Tax: Britain's and Ireland's sales tax, the "value added tax" or VAT, is built into the price of nearly everything you buy. Tourists can get this VAT refunded on souvenirs they take out of the country. But unless you buy something worth at least $100, your refund won't be worth the trouble. Before you make a substantial purchase of merchandise, ask the store clerk if you will be able to get a VAT refund. You'll likely get a "Tax-Free Shopping Cheque" which is redeemable for cash or credit-card credit at virtually any European airport before you fly home.

Banking

Credit or debit cards are widely accepted in Britain and Ireland (and are necessary for renting a car and handy for booking rooms and theater and transportation tickets over the phone). For cash advances you'll find that Barclays, National Westminster, and places displaying an Access or Eurocard sign accept MasterCard. Visa is accepted at Barclays and Midland banks. In general Visa is far more widely accepted than American Express.

Many travelers also carry an ATM card. They get you a

Best Three-Week Trip in Britain By Car

Day	Plan	Sleep in
1	Arrive in London, bus to Bath	Bath
2	Bath	Bath
3	Pick up car, Avebury, Wells, Glastonbury	Bath
4	South Wales, St. Fagans, Tintern	Stow/Chipping
5	Explore the Cotswolds, Blenheim	Stow/Chipping
6	Stratford, Warwick, Coventry	Ironbridge
7	Ironbridge Gorge, Llangollen	Ruthin
8	Highlights of North Wales	Ruthin
9	Liverpool, Blackpool	Blackpool
10	Southern Lake District	Keswick area
11	Northern Lake District	Keswick area
12	Drive up west coast of Scotland	Oban
13	Highlands, Loch Ness, Scenic Drive	Highlands/ Edinburgh
14	More Highlands or Edinburgh	Edinburgh
15	Edinburgh	Edinburgh
16	Hadrian's Wall, Beamish, Durham	Durham
17	York Moors, York, turn in car	York
18	York	York
19	Early train to London	London
20	London	London
21	London	London
22	Side trip to Cambridge, London	Whew!

While this three-week itinerary is designed to be done by car, it can be done by train and bus or, better yet, with a rail 'n' drive pass (best car days: Cotswolds, North Wales, Lake District, Scottish Highlands, Hadrian's Wall). For three weeks without a car, I'd probably cut back on the recommended sights with the most frustrating public transportation (the Cotswolds, South and North Wales, Ironbridge Gorge, the Highlands). With more time, everything is workable without a car.

Whirlwind Three-Week Tour of Great Britain

better exchange rate than traveler's checks and are as common-place in Britain and Ireland as they are in the U.S.A. Be certain your PIN is only four numbers long.

Traveler's checks work fine in Britain and Ireland. Many people traveling exclusively in Great Britain buy traveler's checks in pounds sterling. While policies vary, some British banks favor various traveler's checks by waiving the commission fee (Barclays and Visa checks at Barclays banks, American Express checks at Lloyds banks, Thomas Cook checks at Midland banks or Cook offices). American Express exchange offices don't charge a commission on their checks or any others. This can save you around 2 percent. But don't let this cloud your assessment of that bank's exchange rates. Save time and money by changing plenty of money at a time. (Bank charges often exceed £4.)

On my last trip, I bought all my pounds in cash from a good American foreign exchange service, stowed them safely in my money belt, and never needed a bank. Even in jolly old England and friendly Ireland you should use a money belt. Thieves target tourists. A money belt (call 425/771-8303 for our free newsletter/catalog) provides peace of mind. You can carry lots of cash safely in a money belt—and, given the high bank fees, you should.

Bank holidays bring most businesses to a grinding halt on Christmas, December 26, New Year's Day, Good Friday, Easter, the first and last Monday in May, and the last Monday in August.

Travel Smart

Upon arrival in a new town, lay the groundwork for a smooth departure. Reread this book as you travel, and visit local tourist information offices. Buy a phone card and use it for reservations and confirmations. You speak the language; use it! Enjoy the friendliness of the local people. Ask questions. Most locals are eager to point you in their idea of the right direction. Pack along a pocket-size notebook to organize your thoughts, and practice the virtue of simplicity. Those who expect to travel smart, do. Plan ahead for banking, laundry, post office chores, and picnics. Mix intense and relaxed periods. Every trip (and every traveler) needs at least a few slack days. Pace yourself. Assume you will return.

As you read this book, make note of festivals, colorful market days, and days when sights are closed. Sundays have pros and cons, as they do for travelers in the U.S.A. (special events, limited hours, closed shops and banks, limited public transportation, no rush hours). Saturdays are virtually weekdays. Popular places are even more popular on weekends—especially sunny weekends, which are sufficient cause for an impromptu holiday in this soggy corner of Europe.

Consider making the travel arrangements and reservations listed below before your trip or within a few days of arrival.

Before You Go
• Reserve a room for your first night.
• If you'll be traveling in July and August, and want to be sure of my lead listings, book the B&Bs on your route (and the Ruthin Medieval Banquet) as soon as you're ready to commit to a date.
• Confirm car rental and pick-up plans with your rental agency.
• If you'll be attending the Edinburgh Festival (August 16–September 5 in 1998), call the festival office at 0131/225-5756 to book a ticket by credit card (Visa, MasterCard, Amex) after April 1. And while you're at it, book your Edinburgh room.
• Write to Ceremony of Keys, H.M. Tower of London, London EC3 N4AB, at least five weeks in advance, with an international reply coupon (available at U.S. post offices), requesting an invitation to the "Ceremony of the Keys" (the nightly 21:30 pageantry-filled changing of the keys in the Tower of London, small group of visitors allowed). Say which night or nights you can come (it's free). While they request five weeks' notice, you might try for an appointment near the end of your trip by sending a stamped envelope addressed to your London hotel once you arrive.

Within a Day or Two of Arrival
• If you'll be in London the last night of your trip, reserve a room and book tickets for a London play or concert.
• If the Royal Shakespeare Company will be performing at the Stratford Theater when you're in Stratford, book a ticket (tel. 01789/295-623).

Tourist Information
In Britain, virtually every town has a helpful tourist information center (abbreviated "TI" in this book) eager to make your visit as smooth and enjoyable as possible. Take full advantage of this service. Arrive (or telephone) with a list of questions and a proposed sightseeing plan. Pick up maps, brochures, and walking-tour information. In London you can pick up everything you'll need for Britain in one stop at the National Tourist Information Centre.

In Ireland the tourist information centers have lost their government funding and are now little more than sales outlets for the various hotels and gimmicky new attractions. They have little of value to give you except flyers printed by whoever wants your money.

Avoid the room-finding service offered by TIs throughout Britain and Ireland (bloated prices, fees, no opinions, and they take a cut from your host).

Each country's national tourist office in the U.S.A. is a wealth of information. Before your trip, request any information you may want (such as city maps and schedules of upcoming festivals).

British Tourist Authority: 551 5th Ave., 7th floor, New York, NY 10176-0799, tel. 800/462-2748 or 212/986-2200, web site: www.visitbritain.com. Their free London and Britain maps are excellent (and the same maps are sold for £1.20 each at TIs in Britain).

Irish Tourist Board: 345 Park Ave., 17th floor, New York, NY 10154, tel. 800/223-6470 or 212/418-0800, fax 212/371-9059, web site: www.ireland.travel.ie.

Recommended Guidebooks

You may want some supplemental travel guidebooks, especially if you're traveling beyond my recommended destinations. I know it hurts to spend $25 or $35 on extra books and maps, but when you consider the money they'll save you and the improvements they'll make in your $3,000 vacation, not buying them would be penny-wise and pound-foolish.

While this book offers everything you'll need for the structure of your trip, each place you will visit has plenty of great little guidebooks to fill you in on local history. For cultural/sightseeing background in bigger chunks, Michelin and Cadogan guides to London, England, Britain, and Ireland are good. The best budget travel guides to Britain and Ireland are the Lonely Planet and Let's Go guidebooks. Lonely Planet's guidebook is more thorough and informative. Let's Go is youth-oriented with good coverage of nightlife, hosteling, and cheap transportation deals.

Rick Steves' Books and Videos

Rick Steves' Europe Through the Back Door (John Muir Publications, 1998) gives you budget-travel skills such as minimizing jet lag, packing light, planning your itinerary, traveling by car or train, finding beds without reservations, changing money, avoiding rip-offs, outsmarting thieves, hurdling the language barrier, staying healthy, taking great photographs, and much more. The book also includes chapters on 37 of my favorite "Back Doors," eight of which are in Great Britain and Ireland.

Rick Steves' Country Guides (John Muir Publications, 1998) are a series of eight guidebooks covering Europe, France/Belgium/Netherlands, Italy, Spain/Portugal, Germany/Switzerland/Austria, Scandinavia, and the Russia/Baltics, just as this one covers Britain and Ireland. These are updated annually and come out each January.

Europe 101: History and Art for the Traveler (John Muir Publications, 1996, co-written with Gene Openshaw), gives you the story of Europe's people, history, and art. Written for smart people who were sleeping in their history and art classes before they knew they were going to Europe, *101* really helps Europe's sights come alive. To be honest, this book is more applicable to travel on the European continent than to travel in Britain.

Mona Winks (John Muir Publications, 1996, also co-written with Gene Openshaw), provides fun, easy-to-follow, self-guided tours of Europe's top 20 museums. In London *Mona* leads the way through the British Museum, the National Gallery, and the Tate Gallery.

My television series, *Travels in Europe with Rick Steves* (52 shows which air nationally on public television), includes eight half-hour shows on Britain and Ireland. A new series of 13 shows is airing in 1998 and earlier shows are still airing on both public television and the Travel Channel. These are also available in information-packed home videos, along with my two-hour slideshow lecture on Britain (call us at 425/771-8303 for our free newsletter/catalog).

Maps

The maps in this book, designed and drawn by Dave Hoerlein, are concise and simple. Dave, who is well-traveled in Britain and Ireland, has designed the maps to help you locate recommended places and get to the tourist office, where you'll find more in-depth maps of the city or region (cheap or free).

Maps to buy in England: Train travelers can do fine with a simple rail map (such as the one that comes with your train pass) and city maps from the TI as you travel. If you're driving, get a road atlas (3 miles to 1 inch) covering all of Britain. Ordnance Survey, AA, and Bartholomew editions are available for about £7 in TIs, gas stations, and bookstores. Drivers, hikers, and bikers may want much more detailed maps for the Cotswolds, North Wales, Lake District, and West Scotland.

Tours of Britain and Ireland

Your travel agent can tell you about all the normal Britain tours. But they won't tell you about ours. At ETBD we offer 21-day Britain tours and 14-day Ireland tours featuring the all-stars covered in this book (call us at 425/771-8303, ext. 217, for details). And ETBD tour guide Roy Nicholls leads his own garden tours and south England tours in his spare time (call Roy in England at 44/1373-831-311, e-mail: brittours@online. rednet.co.uk).

Transportation in Britain and Ireland

By Car or Train?

Cars are best for three or more traveling together (especially families with small kids), those packing heavy, and those scouring the countryside. Trains and buses are best for solo travelers, blitz tourists, and city-to-city travelers.

Britain has a great train-and-bus system, and travelers who don't want (or can't afford) to drive a rental car can enjoy an excellent tour using public transportation. Britain's 100-mph train system is one of Europe's best. (For a free BritRail map and schedule, contact BritRail in the U.S.A. at 800/677-8585, 126 Westchester, White Plains, NY, 10604.) Buses pick you up when the trains let you down.

My choice is to connect big cities by train and to explore rural areas (Cotswolds, North Wales, Lake District, and Highlands) footloose and fancy-free by rental car. You might consider a BritRail/Drive pass, which gives you various combinations of rail days and car days to use within a month's time.

Deals on Rails, Wheels, and Wings in Britain

Regular tickets on Britain's great train system (15,000 departures from 2,400 stations daily) are the most expensive per mile in all of Europe. Those who go round-trip (leaving after 9:30), buy in advance, or ride the bus save big.

Buying Train Tickets in Advance: Either go direct to any station or call and book your ticket with a credit card. To book ahead, call 0345/484-950 (from the States call 011/44/345/484-950) to find out the schedule and best fare for your journey; then you'll be referred to the appropriate number to call—depending on the particular rail company—to book your ticket. Here are a few of the many deals. **Super Apex** fares offer the

Cost of Public Transportation

1998 BRITRAIL CLASSIC PASS

	Adult first class	Adult standard	Over 60 first class	16-25 youth standard
8 consec. days	$375	$259	$319	$205
15 consec. days	575	395	489	318
22 consec. days	740	510	630	410
1 month	860	590	730	475

"Standard" is the polite British term for "second" class. No over 60 2nd class pass discount. If traveling with tots 5-15, ask about the "BritRail Kids Pass." Groups of 3 or 4 can now get a 20% to 25% "party" discount on any BritRail pass. See your travel agent for exact prices.

1998 BRITRAIL FLEXIPASS

	Adult first class	Adult standard	Over 60 first class	16-25 youth standard
4 days in 1 month	$315	$219	$269	$175
8 days in 1 month	459	315	390	253
15 days in 1 month	699	480	590	N/A
15 days in 2 months	N/A	N/A	N/A	385

Note: overnight journeys begun on your BritRail pass or Flexipass's final night can be completed the day after your pass expires--only BritRail allows this trick. A bunk in a twin sleeper costs $40.

BRITRAIL PLUS CAR PASS

	First class	First class over 60	Standard class
Any 3 days by rail + 3 days by car in 1 month:	$393	$360	$325
Any 6 days by rail + 7 days by car in 1 month:	740	689	634

BritRail Plus Car gives you rail travel throughout England, Scotland and Wales and use of a Hertz car. Prices listed are per person for a manual shift 2-door economy car. An additional adult pays $221 (1st cl)/$153 (2nd cl) for a 3+3 pass, or $340/$234 for a 6+7 pass. Add about $50 per person for a compact car, and another $40 for an intermediate car. Possible to add any number of car days, but no rail days. Drivers must be 25 or older. No over 60 discounts for standard class.

Britain & Ireland:
Point-to-point 1-way 2nd class fares in $US by rail (solid line) and bus (dashed line). Add up fares for your itinerary to see whether a railpass will save you money.

greatest savings, but must be booked at least 14 days in advance and apply only to journeys of about 250 miles (i.e., London–Edinburgh). **Apex** fares must be booked at least seven days in advance for journeys of about 100 miles (i.e., London–York) or longer. (You can book Apex and Super Apex tickets as early as six to eight weeks before your journey; be

BritRail Routes

KEY: ✳ MAP NOT TO SCALE   LONDON AIRPORTS: ✈
LONDON STATIONS: A- HEATHROW   B- GATWICK

1 VICTORIA - S · SE ENG, CONN TO PARIS & BRUSSELS
2 CHARING CROSS - SE ENG
3 WATERLOO - S ENGLAND PARIS + BRUSS (CHUNNEL)
4 LIVERPOOL ST. - EAST ANGLIA, AMSTERDAM
5 KING'S CROSS - MIDLANDS, NE ENG, E SCOTLAND
6 ST. PANCRAS - E MIDLANDS
7 EUSTON - MIDLANDS, N WALES, NW ENG, W SCOT
8 PADDINGTON - W ENG, S WALES

━► RAIL ---BUS
⋯⋯ FERRY WITH
(6H) CROSSING TIME
NOTE: FASTER ENGLISH
CHANNEL CROSSINGS WITH
HOVERCRAFT & HYDROFOIL
ON SOME RUNS CHECK!
THE CHUNNEL IS
FASTER STILL...

DCH

warned that cheap fares go fast in summer, tickets are non-refundable, and that you'll need to pin down dates and times.) To save a few pounds, get a **Super Advance** ticket (for any journey for any day) by buying your ticket before 14:00 on the day prior to your journey. If you buy a ticket the same day you want to travel, leave after 9:30, and avoid traveling on Friday or summer Saturdays, you'll save a little with a **Super Saver** ticket. There can be up to 30 different prices for the same journey. A clerk at any station (or the helpful folks at tel. 0345/484-950, 24 hours daily) can figure out the cheapest fare for your trip. Savings can be significant. For a London–Edinburgh round-trip, the regular fare is £73.50, Super Apex is £34, Apex is £48, Super Advance is £60, and Super Saver is £64. For a York–London round-trip, the regular fare is £59, Apex is £36, Super Advance is £43, and Super Saver is £49.

Railpasses: Consider getting a railpass. The BritRail pass comes in "consecutive day" and "flexi" versions, with price breaks for second class ("standard" class), youths, and seniors. BritRail passes cover England, Scotland, and Wales. There are now Scotland passes, England/Wales passes, and BritRail-Drive passes, which allow you to take a day of rail here and a day of car rental there. (Hertz seems to have more offices than Avis.) Any Brit pass or Eurailpass gives a discount on the Eurostar train that zips you to continental Europe under the English Channel. These passes are sold outside of Europe only. For specifics, contact your travel agent or Europe Through the Back Door (tel. 425/771-8303).

Buses: Although trains are twice as fast as buses, they're also 50 percent more expensive. Round-trip bus tickets usually cost no more than one-way fares. And buses go many places that trains don't. Budget travelers can save a wad with a **bus pass**. The National Express sells Tourist Trail bus passes (over the counter, tel. 0990/808-080): three consecutive days (£49), five days out of ten (£79), eight days out of 16 (£119), 15 days within 30 days (£179). Their U.S.A. sales agent offers passes as well as individual tickets for trips within Britain and into the continent (tel. 540/298-1395). In Britain, bus stations are normally at or near train stations. The British distinguish between "buses" (for local runs with lots of stops) and "coaches" (long-distance express runs).

There are several **backpacker's bus circuits**. These hop-on-and-hop-off bus circuits take mostly youth hostelers around

Public Transportation in Ireland

the country super cheap and easy. For instance, **Slow Coach** does a 1,600-kilometer circle connecting London, Bath, Stratford, the lakes, Edinburgh, York, Cambridge, and London hostels (open-ended pass-£99, tel. 01249/891-959). **Haggis Backpacker** offers a similar deal, with daily hop-on, hop-off buses circling Scotland (1,000 km: Edinburgh, Inverness, Skye, Fort William, Glencoe, Oban, Edinburgh; tel. 0131/557-9393) for £75. Anyone is welcome.

Flights: For reasonable flights, try **British Midland Airline**. If you've got more money than time, don't buy a ticket for a long train trip without considering a BM flight such as Heathrow–Dublin (10/day, 70 min, £95) and Heathrow–Edinburgh (8/day, 75 min, £85 one-way, £74 stand-by). For 24-hour recorded schedule info, call 0181/745-7321. For reservations, call 0345/554-554, or in the U.S.A., 800/788-0555.

BM also offers good fares on flights to Frankfurt, Amsterdam, Brussels, Paris, and Nice.

Transportation within Ireland

Ireland's train system matches its sparse population. Trains work like spokes, connecting Dublin with each corner of the country (Rosslare in the southeast, Cork in the south, Limerick and Tralee in the southeast, Galway in the west, and Belfast in the north). Between the bus and train systems you can get around the Emerald Isle quite handily. Departures are not as frequent as the European norm.

Irish Explorer Passes make a public bus and train tour of Ireland inexpensive. All can be purchased easily and cheapest in Ireland at major stations (Dublin information tel. 01/836-6111).

Rail only: in the Republic, any five days in 15 (£60); in all of Ireland, any five days in 15 (£75).

Bus only: in the Republic, three days in eight (£28), eight days in 15 (£68), and 15 days in 30 (£98).

Rail and bus: in the Republic, eight days in 15 (£90); in all of Ireland, eight days in 15 (£105) and 15 days in 30 (£180).

Car Rental

Car rental for this tour is cheapest if arranged in advance through your hometown travel agent. The best rates are weekly with unlimited mileage, or leasing (possible for "rentals" of over three weeks). You can pick up and drop off just about anywhere, any time. For a trip covering both Britain and Ireland you're better off with two separate car rentals. If you pick up the car in a smaller city, such as Bath, you'll more likely survive your first day on the British roads. If you drop it off early or keep it longer, you'll be credited or charged at a fair, prorated price. Big companies have offices in most cities. (Ask to be picked up at your hotel.) Small local rental companies can be cheaper but aren't as flexible.

The Ford 1.3-liter Escort-category car costs about $50 per week more than the smallest cars but feels better on the motorways and safer on the small roads. Remember, minibuses are a great budget way to go for five to nine people.

For peace of mind, spring for the CDW insurance (Collision Damage Waiver, about $15 per day), which gives a zero (or low)-deductible rather than the standard value-of-the-car "deductible." A few "gold" credit cards cover CDW insurance; quiz your credit card company on the worst-case senario.

Driving

Your U.S.A. license is all you need to drive in Britain and Ireland. Set your car up for a fun road trip. Establish a cardboard-box munchies pantry. Buy a rack of liter boxes of juice for the trunk. Buy some Windex and a roll of paper towels for cleaner sightseeing.

Britain: Driving in Britain is basically wonderful—once you remember to stay on the left and after you've mastered the "roundabouts." But be warned: Every year I get a few cards from traveling readers advising me that, for them, trying to drive British was a nerve-racking and regrettable mistake. To get a little slack on the roads, drop by an auto shop and buy the red "L" sign which student drivers ("learners") put in their windows.

A British Automobile Association membership comes with most rentals. Understand its towing and emergency road service benefits. Gas (petrol) costs about $3 per gallon and is self-serve. Green pumps are unleaded. Seat belts are required by law. Speed limits are 30 mph in town, 70 mph on the motorways, and 60 mph elsewhere. (I "went with the flow," speeding for a month on my last trip and never saw a car pulled over.) The national sign for 60 mph is a white circle with a black slash. Avoid big cities whenever possible. Most have modern ring roads to skirt the congestion. The shortest distance between any two points is usually the motorway. Road signs can be confusing, inconsistent, and too little, too late. Study your map before taking off. Miss a motorway exit and you can lose 30 minutes. A Britain road atlas (sold at gas stations and book stores) is $10 very well spent.

Parking is confusing. One yellow line marked on the pavement means no parking Monday through Saturday during work hours. Double yellow lines mean no parking at any time. Broken yellow lines mean short stops are okay, but always look for explicit signs or ask a passerby. White lines are good news.

Even in small towns, rather than fight it, I just pull into the most central and handy "pay and display" car park I can find. Rates are reasonable by U.S.A. standards. Locals love to share "pay and display" stickers. If you stand by the machine, invariably someone on their way out with time left on their sticker will give it to you. I keep a bag of 10p and 20p coins in the ashtray for parking meters.

Ireland: In Ireland you'll be dealing with the same left-hand drives and roundabouts. Traffic and parking are rarely a problem. Ireland's roads, while getting much better with the financial help of the European Union, are still among the worst in Europe. There simply aren't enough people to justify big, slick roads. Except for rush hour in the big cities, traffic is wonderfully sparse. But roads are so narrow, every car or truck that passes you can give you a slight adrenaline rush. Take things slowly. If you rush you'll wear yourself out, hit a pothole, and blow a tire—or worse. Distances are short. Enjoy the scenery.

A single yellow sign means parking is regulated (look for a street sign explaining the hours or limits on that street). A double yellow line means parking is not permitted at any time. Some towns require a disk which you can buy at the TI or newsstands. Parking lots are cheap and central. While theft is rare in Ireland, tourists' cars are likely targets. Don't tempt thieves needlessly.

Telephones and Mail

Use the telephone routinely. You can make long-distance calls directly, cheaply, and easily, and there's no language barrier. Call ahead to reserve or reconfirm rooms, check opening hours, confirm tour times, and reserve theater tickets.

To call long distance, you'll need the correct area code. Britain and Ireland have about as many area codes as we have prefixes. For long distance, you'll find area codes listed by city on phone booth walls, from directory assistance (free and happy to help, dial 192 in Britain), and throughout this book. For more telephone tips, see the Appendix.

The British telephone system is great. Easy-to-find public phone booths are either coin- or card-operated. Phones take any coin from 10p to £1, and a display shows how your money supply's doing. Only completely unused coins will be returned, so put in biggies with caution. (If money's left over, you can make another call.) The more convenient phone card booths are common only in cities. Buy a £2, £5, or £10 phone card at newsstands, hotels, tourist offices, or post offices and use it for ease and economy. Ignore the Mercury phone booths and stick with the dominant British Telecom system. Some "credit card phones" have a slot that will take—but not accept—your BT phone card. You need a "phone card" booth. Phone cards are your key to easy telephoning in Ireland as well.

The only tricky phones you'll use are the expensive Mickey Mouse coin-op ones in bars and B&Bs. Some require money before you dial and others only after you've connected. Many have a button you must push before you begin talking. But all have clear instructions. Long distance in Britain is most expensive from 8:00 to 13:00 and cheapest from 17:00 to 8:00. A short call across the country is quite inexpensive. Don't hesitate to call long distance.

Direct Dialing: When calling long-distance within either Britain or Ireland, dial the area code (which starts with zero) then dial the local number. When dialing internationally, dial the international access code (of the country you're calling from), the country code (of the country you're calling to), the area code (without the initial zero), and the local number. For example, London's downtown area code is 0171. To call one of my listed London B&Bs from New York, I dial 011 (U.S.A.'s international access code), 44 (Britain's country code), 171 (London's area code without the zero), then 727-7725 (the B&B's number). To call it from old York, dial 0171/727-7725.

To call my office from Britain, I dial 00 (Britain's international access code), 1 (U.S.A.'s country code), 425 (Edmond's area code), then 771-8303. For a listing of international access codes and country codes, see the Appendix.

USA Direct Services: Calling the U.S.A. from any kind of phone is easy if you have an AT&T, MCI, or Sprint calling card. Each card company has a toll-free number in each European country which puts you in touch with an English-speaking operator. The operator takes your card number and the number you want to call, puts you through, and bills your home phone number for the call (at the cheaper U.S.A. rate of $3 for the first minute then $1 per minute plus a $2.50 service charge). You'll save money on calls of three minutes or more. Calling an answering machine is an expensive mistake. Use a small-value coin or a British or Irish phone card to call home for five seconds—long enough to say "call me," or to make sure an answering machine is off so you can call back using your USA Direct number. European time is six/nine hours ahead of the east/west coast of the U.S.A. For a list of calling card operators, see the

Appendix. Avoid using USA Direct for calls between European
countries; it's much cheaper to call direct using coins or a British
or Irish phone card.

Mail: To arrange for mail delivery (allow ten days for a
letter to arrive), reserve a few hotels along your route in
advance and give their addresses to friends, or use American
Express Company's mail services (available to anyone who has
at least one Amex traveler's check). Phoning is so easy that I've
dispensed with mail stops all together.

Sleeping
In the interest of smart use of your time, I favor accommodations (and restaurants) handy to your sightseeing activities.
Rather than list hotels scattered throughout a city, I choose
two or three favorite neighborhoods and recommend the best
accommodations values in each, from $12 bunk beds to fancy-
in-my-book $140 doubles.

I've described my recommended hotels and B&Bs with a
standard code. Prices listed are for one-night stays in peak season, include a hearty breakfast, and assume you're going direct
and not through a tourist information office. Prices may be
soft for off-season and longer stays. While many places have
larger rooms and offer families special deals, Britain is peculiar
in its insistence on charging per person rather than per room.
Because of this, small groups usually pay the same for a single
and a double as they would for a triple. All rooms have sinks.
Any room without a bathroom has access to a free bath or
shower on the corridor. In Britain and Ireland, rooms with private plumbing are called *en suite*; rooms that lack private
plumbing are *standard*. As more rooms go *en suite*, the hallway
bathroom is shared with fewer standard rooms.

Almost every place has three floors of rooms, steep stairs,
and no elevator. Offhand, I can't think of a single elevator
among my recommended places. If you're concerned about
stairs, call and ask about ground-floor rooms.

Sleep Code
To give maximum information with a minimum of space, I use
this code to describe accommodations listed in this book. *Prices
in this book are listed per room, not per person.* Breakfast is
included.

S = Single room, or price for one person in a double.

D = Double or twin room. (I specify double- and twin-bed rooms only if they are priced differently, or if a place has only one or the other.)

T = Three-person room (often a double bed with a single).

Q = Four-person room (adding an extra child's bed to a T is usually cheaper).

b = Private bathroom with toilet and shower or tub.

t = Private toilet only. (The shower is down the hall.)

s = Private shower or tub only. (The toilet is down the hall.)

CC = Accepts credit cards (**V** = Visa, **M** = MasterCard, **A** = American Express). If CC isn't mentioned, assume you'll need to pay cash.

No smoking—While most places allow smoking in the sleeping rooms and not in the breakfast room, many are going entirely smoke-free. I'll note these, as well as places that smell musty.

Family deal—Indicates that parents with young children can easily get a room with an extra child's bed or a discount for larger rooms.

According to this code, a couple staying at a "Db-£30, CC:VM" hotel would pay a total of £30 (about $45) per night for a room with a private toilet and shower (or tub). The hotel accepts Visa, MasterCard, or cash.

Bed and Breakfasts (B&Bs)

Thank God Britain and Ireland have such lousy hotels, because the bed-and-breakfast alternative gives you double the cultural intimacy for half the price.

I'm assuming you have a reasonable but limited budget. Skip hotels. Go the B&B way. If you can use a telephone and speak English, you'll enjoy homey, friendly, clean rooms at a great price by sticking to my listings. Always call first.

If you're traveling beyond my recommended destinations, you'll find B&Bs where you need them. Any town with tourists has a tourist information office (TI) that books rooms or can give you a list and point you in the right direction. In the absence of a TI, ask people on the street for help.

B&Bs range from large guest houses with 15 to 20 rooms to small homes renting out a spare bedroom. The philosophy of the management determines the character of a place more than its size and facilities offered. Avoid places run as a business by absentee owners. My top listings are run by couples who enjoy welcoming the world to their breakfast table.

The B&Bs I've recommended are nearly all stocking-feet comfortable and very "homely," as they say in England. I look for a place that is friendly (that enjoys Americans); located in a central, safe, quiet neighborhood; clean, with good beds, a sink in the room, and shower down the hall; a good value; not mentioned in other guidebooks (therefore, filled mostly by English or Irish travelers); and willing to hold a room until 16:00 or so without a deposit (though more and more places are requiring a deposit or credit-card number). In certain cases my recommendations don't meet all these prerequisites. I'm more impressed by a handy location and a fun-loving philosophy than a checklist of facilities.

I promised the owners of the places I list that you will be reliable when you make a telephone reservation; please don't let them (or me) down. If you'll be delayed or won't make it, simply call in. Americans are notorious for "standing up" B&Bs. Being late is no problem if you are in telephone contact.

A few tips: B&B proprietors are selective as to whom they invite in for the night. Risky-looking people (two or more single men are often assumed to be troublemakers) find many places suddenly full. If you'll be staying for more than one night you are a "desirable." Sometimes staying several nights earns you a better price—ask about it. If you book through a TI it'll take a 10 percent commission. If you book direct, the B&B gets it all (and you'll have a better chance of getting a discount).

If my listings are full, ask for guidance. (Mentioning this book can help.) Owners usually work together and can call up an ally to land you a bed.

B&Bs are not hotels. If you want to ruin your relationship with your hostess, treat her like a hotel clerk. Americans often assume they'll get new towels each day. The British and Irish don't, and neither will you. Hang them up to dry and reuse. Nearly all B&Bs have plenty of stairs. Expect good exercise and be happy you packed light.

In Britain and Ireland you'll pay £18 to £30 ($27–$45) per person for a B&B in 1998. Small places (with a gross income of under £46,000) don't have to pay a 17 percent tax and can offer cheaper prices. Small places don't have hired help and can skimp on safety regulations, allowing them to operate cheaper yet. Prices include a big cooked breakfast. How much coziness, tea, and biscuits are tossed in varies tremendously.

"Twin" means two single beds, and "double" means one double bed. If you'll take either one, let them know or you might be needlessly turned away. "Standard" rooms come with just a sink. More and more are going *en suite*, meaning with a private shower/tub and a loo. Many better places have a basic room (with a shower down the hall) that they don't even advertise.

The British Tourist Board rates hotels and B&Bs with a crown system. B&Bs are rated as follows: no crowns (basic, clean, one bath per 12 people, safe); one crown (no nylon bed linen, a sink in the room, one bath per eight people); two crowns (tea and coffee in room on request, TV in room or lounge, luggage help); three crowns (hot evening meals, one-third of rooms with bathroom); four crowns (three-fourths of rooms with bathroom, nearly a hotel); five crowns (all with private bathroom, valet, porters, virtually a high-class hotel). Some idealistic guest-house proprietors are refusing to bow to the pressure to fill their B&Bs with all the gimmicks and extras. They continue to offer just a good bed with a shower down the hall, a traditional breakfast, and a warm welcome. So while unlisted by the tourist board, they are an excellent value.

Realizing that the facilities-based crown system was too impersonal, the tourist board added a rating measuring the cozy, personal, intangible touches (commended, highly commended, deluxe).

While many put great stock in the various tourist board ratings, most of my favorites have dropped out altogether and aren't even listed. Being "listed" is supposed to be a mark of quality. In practice it's a mark of paying your dues and playing by the materialistic rules that the tourist board sets and changes as it likes.

The Irish equivalent of the crown system is the posted tourist-board shamrock. This shamrock implies quality, but I find that it means only that the place sporting it is working with the tourist board. It really has nothing to do with value. Ignore the shamrocks.

Making Reservations

It's possible to travel at any time of year without reservations, but given the high stakes, erratic accommodations values, and the quality of the gems I've found for this book, I highly recommend calling ahead for rooms a day or two in advance as you travel. When tourist crowds are down, you might make a habit of calling between 9:00 and 10:00 on the day you plan to arrive, when the hotel knows who'll be checking out and just which rooms will be available. I've taken great pains to list telephone numbers with long distance instructions (see Telephones and Mail, above; also see Appendix). Use the telephone and the convenient telephone cards. A hotel receptionist will trust you and hold a room until 16:00 without a deposit, though some will ask for a credit-card number. Honor (or cancel by phone) your reservations. Long distance is cheap and easy from public phone booths. Call and cancel if for some reason you won't be able to show up. Don't needlessly confirm rooms through the tourist office; they'll take a commission.

If you know exactly which dates you need and really want a particular place, reserve a room before you leave home. To reserve from home, call, fax, or write the hotel. Phone and fax costs are reasonable. To fax, use the form in the Appendix. If you're writing, add the zip code and confirm the need and method for a deposit. A two-night stay in August would be "2 nights, 16/8/98 to 18/8/98"—European hotel jargon uses your day of departure. You'll often receive a letter back requesting one night's deposit. Your credit-card number and expiration date will usually be accepted as a deposit, though you may need to send a signed traveler's check or a bank draft in the local currency. If your credit card is the deposit, you can pay with your card or cash when you arrive; if you don't show up, you'll be billed for one night. Reconfirm your reservations a day in advance for safety (or you may be bumped—really).

Hostels

Britain and Ireland have more than 400 hostels of all shapes and sizes. They can be historic castles or depressing huts, serene and comfy or overrun by noisy children. Unfortunately, many of the international youth hostels have become overpriced and, in general, I no longer recommend them. The only time I do is if you're on a very tight budget and want to cook your own meals, or if you're traveling with a group that doesn't have much money and likes to sleep on bunk beds in big rooms. The informal private hostels are often more fun, easygoing, and cheaper. These alternatives to the IYHF hostels are more common than ever. If you're traveling alone, hosteling is the best way to conquer hotel loneliness. Hostels are also a tremendous source of local and budget travel information. If you hostel selectively, you'll enjoy historical and interesting buildings.

You'll pay an average of £8 for a bed, £1 for sheets, and £2 for breakfast. Anyone of any age can hostel in Britain and Ireland. While there are no membership concerns for private hostels, IYHF hostels require membership. If you don't have a hostel card, IYHF hostels sell one-night guest memberships for £1.50.

Forte Travelodge in Britain

The Forte Travelodge chain has 120 freeway-friendly motels throughout Britain. These are superconvenient, offering simple, clean, and comfortable rooms for up to four for £34.50 (each with a double bed, a single bed, a 5-foot trundle bed, private shower, WC, and TV). Each hotel has an attached restaurant, a 24-hour staffed reception desk, and good security. You can reserve by credit card (CC:VMA, tel. 01384/78884 or toll-free tel. 0800-850-950 in Britain, web site: www.travelodge.co.uk/index.htm) and pay when you check in (any time after 15:00, as late as you like). When you're ready to go (before noon), you just drop off the key, Lee. Of course they are as cozy as a Motel 6, but they're great for families, and many travelers love them.

Eating

I don't mind English food. But then, I liked dorm food. True, England isn't famous for its cuisine and probably never will be, but we tourists have to eat. If there's any good place to cut corners to stretch your budget in Britain and Ireland, it's in eating. Here are a few tips on budget eating:

The traditional "fry" is famous as a hearty way to start the day. Also known as a "heart attack on a plate," the breakfast is especially feasty if you've just come from the land of the skimpy continental breakfast across the Channel. Your standard fry gets off to a healthy start with juice and cereal or porridge. (Try Weetabix, a soggy English cousin of shredded wheat. Scotland serves great porridge.) Next, with tea or coffee, you get a heated plate with a fried egg, lean Canadian-style bacon, a bad sausage, a grilled tomato, and often a slice of delightfully greasy pan toast and sautéed mushrooms. Toast comes on a rack (to cool quickly and crisply) with butter and marmalade. Order kippers (filleted herring smoked in an oak fire). This meal tides many travelers over until dinner. Order only what you'll eat. A B&B hostess, your temporary local mother, doesn't like to see food wasted. And there's nothing un-British about skipping the "fry"—few locals actually start their day with this heavy traditional breakfast.

These days, the best coffee is served in a *cafetiere* (also called a "French Press"). When your coffee has steeped as long as you like, plunge down the filter and pour. To revitalize your brew, pump the plunger.

Many B&Bs don't serve breakfast until 8:30. If you need an early start, ask politely if it's possible. While they may not make you a cooked breakfast, they can usually put out cereal, toast, juice, and coffee.

Picnicking saves time and money. Try boxes of orange juice (pure by the liter), fresh bread (especially Irish soda bread), tasty English cheese, meat, a tube of Colman's English mustard, local eatin' apples, bananas, small tomatoes, rice crackers, gorp or nuts, plain "Digestive Biscuits" (the chocolate-covered ones melt), and any local specialties. At open-air markets and supermarkets you can get food in small quantities. (Three tomatoes and two bananas cost me 50p.) Decent sandwiches (£2) are sold everywhere. I often munch a relaxed "meal on wheels" in a car, train, or bus to save 30 precious minutes.

British restaurants are fairly expensive, but cheap alternatives abound: fish-and-chips joints, Chinese and Indian take-outs, cafeterias, pubs (see below), B&Bs that serve evening meals, and your typical, good old greasy-spoon cafés. Bakeries have meat pies (and microwaves), pastries, yogurt, and cartons of "semi-skimmed" milk—ideal for fresh, fast, cheap lunches.

People of leisure punctuate their day with a "Cream Tea." You'll get a pot of tea, two homemade scones, jam, and thick, creamy-as-honey clotted cream. For maximum pinky-waving taste per calorie, slice your scone thin.

Pasties (past-eez) are "savory" (not sweet) meat pies that originated in mining country. They had big crust handles so miners with filthy hands could eat them and toss the crust. Today you'll find them in bakeries and cafés. They make a quick, cheap, hot lunch.

Pub Grub and Beer

Pubs are a basic part of the British and Irish social scene, and whether you're a teetotaler or a beer guzzler they should be a part of your travel here. Pub is short for "public house." It's an extended living room where, if you don't mind the stickiness, you can feel the pulse of Britain and Ireland. Most traditional atmospheric pubs are in the countryside and smaller towns. Unfortunately, many city pubs have been afflicted with an excess of brass, ferns, and video games. In any case, smart travelers use the pubs to eat, drink, get out of the rain, and make new friends.

Pub grub gets better each year. It's Britain's and Ireland's best eating value. For £5, you'll get a basic budget hot lunch or dinner in friendly surroundings. The *Good Pub Guide*, published annually by the British Consumers Union, is excellent. Pubs attached to restaurants often have fresher food and a chef who knows how to cook.

I recommend certain pubs, but food can spoil, and your B&B host usually takes pride in being right up-to-date on the best neighborhood pub grub. Ask for advice (but adjust for nepotism and cronyism, which run rampant). Locals will rarely recommend a rough pub that's a local hangout. If you want this experience (the food will be cheaper but not very good), ask for a "spit-and-sawdust" place. Big-city spit-and-sawdust places may not welcome tourists. Rural and village ones will. They are the most interesting.

Pubs generally serve assorted meat pies such as steak and kidney pie or shepherd's pie, curried dishes, fish, quiche, vegetables, and (invariably) chips and peas. Better pubs let you substitute a "jacket potato" (baked potato) for your fries. Servings are hearty, service is quick, and you'll rarely spend more than £4 to £6 ($6–9). Your beer or cider adds another pound. Free tap water is always available. In Britain a "ploughman's lunch" is a modern "traditional English meal" that nearly every tourist tries . . . once. Pubs that advertise their food and are crowded with locals are less likely to be the kind that serve only lousy microwaved snacks.

The British and Irish take great pride in their beer. They think that drinking beer cold and carbonated, as Americans do, ruins the taste. At pubs, long "hand pulls" are used to pull the traditional rich-flavored "real ales" up from the cellar. These are the connoisseur's favorites: fermented naturally, varying from sweet to bitter, often with a hoppy or nutty flavor. Notice the fun names. Experiment with the obscure local microbrews. Short "hand pulls" at the bar mean colder, fizzier, mass-produced, and less interesting keg beers. Mild beers are sweeter with a creamy malt flavoring. Stout is dark and more bitter, like Guinness. For a cold, refreshing, basic American-style beer, ask for a "lager." Try the draft cider (sweet or dry) . . . carefully. English ladies like a half-beer and half-lemonade "shandy." Teetotalers can order a soft drink. Drinks are served by the pint or the half-pint. (It's almost feminine for a man to order just a half; I order mine with quiche.) There's no table service. Order drinks and meals at the bar. Pay as you order and don't tip.

Pub hours vary. The strictly limited wartime hours finally ended a few years ago, and now pubs can serve beer from 11:00 to 23:00, and Sunday from noon to 22:30. Children are served food and soft drinks in pubs, but you must be 18 to order a beer. A cup of darts is free for the asking. People go to a "public house" to be social. They want to talk. Get vocal with a local. Pubs are the next best thing to relatives in every town.

Stranger in a Strange Land

We travel all the way to Europe to enjoy differences—to become temporary locals. You'll experience frustrations. There are certain truths that we find God-given and self-evident, such as cold beer, ice in drinks, bottomless coffee cups, hot showers, and driving on the right side of the road. One of the benefits of travel is the eye-opening realization that there are logical, civil, and even better alternatives. A willingness to go local ensures that you'll enjoy a full dose of European hospitality.

Send Me a Postcard, Drop Me a Line

If you enjoy a successful trip with the help of this book and would like to share your discoveries, please fill out and send the survey at the end of this book to me at Europe Through the Back Door, Box 2009, Edmonds, WA 98020. I personally read and value all feedback. Thanks in advance—it helps a lot.

For our latest travel information, tap into our web site: www.ricksteves.com. My e-mail address is rick@ricksteves.com. Anyone can request a free issue of our newsletter.

Judging from the happy postcards I receive from travelers, it's safe to assume you're on your way to a great vacation—independent, inexpensive, and with the finesse of an experienced traveler. Thanks, and happy travels!

BACK DOOR TRAVEL PHILOSOPHY
As Taught in *Rick Steves' Europe Through the Back Door*

Travel is intensified living—maximum thrills per minute and one of the last great sources of legal adventure. Travel is freedom. It's recess, and we need it.

Experiencing the real Europe requires catching it by surprise, going casual . . . "Through the Back Door."

Affording travel is a matter of priorities. (Make do with the old car.) You can travel—simply, safely, and comfortably—anywhere in Europe for $60 a day plus transportation costs. In many ways, spending more money only builds a thicker wall between you and what you came to see. Europe is a cultural carnival, and time after time you'll find that its best acts are free and the best seats are the cheap ones.

A tight budget forces you to travel close to the ground, meeting and communicating with the people, not relying on service with a purchased smile. Never sacrifice sleep, nutrition, safety, or cleanliness in the name of budget. Simply enjoy the local-style alternatives to expensive hotels and restaurants.

Extroverts have more fun. If your trip is low on magic moments, kick yourself and make things happen. If you don't enjoy a place, maybe you don't know enough about it. Seek the truth. Recognize tourist traps. Give a culture the benefit of your open mind. See things as different but not better or worse. Any culture has much to share.

Of course, travel, like the world, is a series of hills and valleys. Be fanatically positive and militantly optimistic. If something's not to your liking, change your liking. Travel is addicting. It can make you a happier American, as well as a citizen of the world. Our Earth is home to nearly 6 billion equally important people. It's humbling to travel and find that people don't envy Americans. They like us, but with all due respect, they wouldn't trade passports.

Globetrotting destroys ethnocentricity. It helps you understand and appreciate different cultures. Travel changes people. It broadens perspectives and teaches new ways to measure quality of life. Many travelers toss aside their hometown blinders. Their prized souvenirs are the strands of different cultures they decide to knit into their own character. The world is a cultural yarn shop. And Back Door travelers are weaving the ultimate tapestry. Come on, join in!

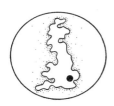

LONDON

London, more than 600 square miles of urban jungle with 7 million struggling people, many of whom speak English, is a world in itself, a barrage on all the senses. On my first visit, I felt very, very small. London is much more than its museums and famous landmarks. It's a living, breathing, thriving organism.

London has changed dramatically in recent years, and many visitors are surprised to find how "un-English" it is. Whites are now a minority in major parts of the city that once symbolized white imperialism. Arabs have nearly bought out the area north of Hyde Park. Chinese take-outs outnumber fish-and-chips shops. Many hotels are run by people with foreign accents (who hire English chambermaids), while outlying suburbs are home to huge communities of Indians and Pakistanis. London is learning—sometimes fitfully—to live as a microcosm of its formerly vast empire. With the English Channel Tunnel complete, many see more foreign threats to the Britishness of Britain.

With just a few days here, you'll get no more than a quick splash in this teeming human tidepool. But, with a quick orientation, you'll get a good taste of its top sights, history, and cultural entertainment, as well as its ever-changing human face.

Have fun in London. Blow through the city on the open deck of a double-decker orientation tour bus, and take a pinch-me-I'm-in-Britain walk through downtown. Ogle the crown jewels at the Tower of London, hear the chimes of Big Ben, and see the Halls of Parliament in action. Hobnob with the tombstones in Westminster Abbey, duck WWII bombs in Churchill's underground Cabinet War Rooms, and brave the earth-shaking Imperial War Museum. Overfeed the pigeons at Trafalgar Square. Visit with Leonardo, Botticelli, and Rembrandt in the National Gallery. Whisper across the dome of St. Paul's Cathedral and rummage through our civilization's attic at the British Museum. Cruise down the Thames River. You'll enjoy some of Europe's best people-watching at Covent Garden and the Buckingham Palace Changing of the Guard. Just sit in Victoria Station, at a major tube station, at Piccadilly Circus, or in Trafalgar Square, and observe. Spend one evening at a theater and the others catching your breath.

Planning Your Time

The sights of London alone could easily fill a trip to Britain. But on a three-week tour of Britain, I'd give it three busy days. If you're flying in, consider starting your trip in Bath and making London your British finale. Especially if you hope to enjoy a play or concert, a night or two of jet lag is bad news.

Here's a suggested three-day schedule:

Day 1: 9:00, Tower of London (Beefeater tour, crown jewels); 12:00, Picnic on Thames while cruising from Tower to Westminster Bridge; 13:00, Big Ben, Halls of Parliament, Westminster Abbey, walk up Whitehall, and visit the Cabinet War Rooms; 16:00, Trafalgar Square and National Gallery; 17:30, visit National Tourist Information Centre near Piccadilly, planning ahead for your trip; 18:30, Dinner near Piccadilly. Take in a play?

Day 2: 9:00, Spend 30 minutes in a phone booth getting all essential elements of your trip nailed down. If you know where you'll be and when, call those B&Bs now; 9:30, Take the Round London bus tour (consider hopping off for the 11:30, Changing of the Guard at Buckingham Palace); 12:30, Covent Gardens for lunch and people-watching; 14:00, Tour British Museum; 17:30, Visitor's Gallery in Houses of Parliament (if in session); 19:00, Take in a play, concert, or evening walking tour.

Day 3: Choose among these activities for the day: some serious shopping at Harrods or open-air markets, Museum of the Moving Image, Imperial War Museum, Tate Gallery, cruise to Greenwich or Kew, tour St. Paul's Cathedral, Museum of London, a walking tour, or an early train to your next destination.

If heading to Bath on the 18:15 train, you'll check into your B&B at about 19:30.

After considering nearly all of London's tourist sights, I have pruned them down to include only the most important (or fun) for a first visit. You won't be able to see all of these, so don't try. You'll keep coming back to London. After 20 visits myself, I still enjoy a healthy list of excuses to return.

Orientation
(downtown tel. code: 0171, suburban: 0181)
To grasp London comfortably, see it as the old town without the modern, congested sprawl. Most of the visitor's London lies between the Tower of London and Hyde Park—about a 3-mile walk.

Tourist Information
London Tourist Information Centres are located at Heathrow Airport's Terminal 3 (daily 8:00–18:00, most convenient and least crowded), at Victoria Station (daily 8:00–19:00, shorter hours in winter, crowded and commercial), and at Waterloo International Terminal Arrivals Hall (daily 8:30–22:30). Like the LTICs, the handier National Tourist Info Centre (described below) covers London.

Bring your itinerary and a checklist of questions. Pick up these publications: *London Planner* (a great, free BTA monthly listing all the sights with latest hours and events), walking-tour brochures, the "Silver Jubilee Walkway" (a free map charting a 12-mile walk past 400 historic sights in London), theater guide, Thames River cruise schedules, a Britain map (£1.20), and a London map (£1.20). The fine £1.20 London map rivals the £4 maps sold in newsstands (free from BTA in the U.S.A., tel. 800/462-2748 or 212/986-2200, 551 5th Ave., 7th floor, New York, NY 10176-0799, web site: www.bta.org.uk). The TIs sell BT phone cards, passes for the tube (subway), long-distance bus tickets and passes, Great British Heritage Passes, individual admissions to various London sights (saving a wait in line at the sight), and tickets to plays (if you don't mind a booking fee of 15 percent or more, depending on the play). They'll book you a room for a £5 booking fee—save money and call direct. Smelling a new source of profit, London TIs are pushing a 50p-per-minute telephone information service. Avoid it.

The National Tourist Information Centre makes gathering information easy (9:00–18:30, Saturday and Sunday 10:00–16:00). It's just off Picadilly Circus—to the southwest—on Lower Regent Street (tel. 0181/846-9000). The Scottish Tourist Centre, a block away at 19 Cockspur Street, will also be moving nearby; call for new address before heading out (tel. 0171/930-8661).

Check out the National Tourist Information Centre's well-equipped London/England desk, Wales desk (tel. 0171/409-0969), and Ireland desk (tel. 0171/839-8416 or 0171/493-3201). At the center's extensive book shop, gather whatever books, maps, and information you'll need for your entire trip. Consider getting the *Michelin Green Guide to Britain* (£9). Train travelers can pick up *Let's Go: Britain and Ireland* (£15, 50 percent higher than the U.S. price) and hostelers may want the *Youth Hostel Association 1998 Guide* (£5). To cover the highlights in this book, consider these maps (or their equivalents): Cotswolds Wyedean Official Tourist Map (Tintern to Coventry); the Lake District Touring Map (entire region or just the northwest corner, Ordnance Survey); the Wales Tourist Map; and the Leisure Touring Map of Scotland. Drivers will need a *Britain Road Atlas* (£10). Stock up. You are your own guide. Be a good one.

Helpful Hints

Theft Alert: Be on guard in London more than anywhere else in Britain for pickpockets and thieves, particularly on public transportation and in places crowded with tourists. Tourists, considered naive and rich, are targeted.

Changing Money: Standard transaction fees at banks and exchange desks are £3 to £4. American Express Offices offer a good rate and change any brand of traveler's checks for no fee. There are several offices (Heathrow Terminal 4 tube station and at 6 Haymarket near Piccadilly, Monday–Friday 9:00–17:30, Saturday 9:00–16:00, Sunday 10:00–16:00, tel. 0171/930-4411).

Telephones: In London dial 999 for emergency help and 192 for directory assistance (free from phone booths only). The area code for any downtown London phone number is 0171, for suburban London, 0181. All numbers listed in this chapter with an area code of 0171 can be dialed directly (without the area code) within London. Beware of the many 0839 toll numbers.

These will connect you to recorded information—usually slow moving and very expensive. At any newsstand, TI, or post office, buy a handy BT phone card (£2, £5, or £10). It's a big city. If you call sights before heading out, you'll travel more smooth and plan for special events or tours.

What's Up: For the best listing of what's happening (plays, movies, restaurants, concerts, exhibitions, protests, walking tours, shopping, and children's activities), pick up a current copy of *What's On* (£1.30, fine for tourists) or *Time Out* (50p more, more theater reviews, more hip) at any newsstand. The TI's free monthly *London Planner* lists sights, plays, and events at least as well.

Children: Call 0171/222-8070 for a taped rundown on "Children's London" (Monday–Friday 16:00–18:00). The TI has a free brochure "Where to Take Children in London."

Sunday Morning Activities: Few London sights are open on Sunday before 14:00. (Major museums are usually open Sunday afternoons.) Some Sunday morning activities: a church service at St. Paul's, Westminster Abbey, or the Tower of London chapel; Original London Sightseeing Tour by bus; a Thames cruise; Tate Gallery; Cabinet War Rooms; Imperial War Museum; Museum of the Moving Image; Kew Gardens and Palace; Madame Tussaud's; a walking tour; open-air markets at Petticoat Lane and Campden Market; and the Victoria and Albert Museum. "Speaker's Corner" in Hyde Park gets going at noon.

Arrival in London

By Train: London has eight train stations, all connected by the tube (subway), all with exchange offices and luggage storage. From any station, enter the tube and head to the stop nearest your hotel.

By Bus: The bus station is next to Victoria Station, which has a TI and tube entrance.

By Plane: For detailed information on getting from London's airports to downtown London, see Transportation Connections near the end of the chapter.

Getting Around London

London's taxis, buses, and subway system make a private car unnecessary. In a city this size, you must get comfortable with public transportation. Don't be timid.

By Taxi: Big, black, carefully regulated cabs are everywhere. I never met a crabby cabbie in London. They love to talk and know every nook and cranny in town. Rides start at £1.40 and cost about £1.50 per tube stop. Often legitimate charges are added on, but for a short ride, three people in a cab travel at tube prices. If a cab's top light is on, just wave it down. If that doesn't work, ask for directions to a nearby taxi stand. Telephoning is unnecessary; taxis are everywhere. Stick with the metered cabs. I take a cab a day just to get my general London questions answered.

By Bus: London's extensive bus system is easy to follow if you have a map listing the routes. Get a free map from a TI or tube station. Signs at stops list routes clearly. Conductors are terse but helpful. Ask to be reminded when it's your stop. Just hop on, tell the driver where you're going, pay what he says, grab a ticket, take a seat, and relax. (Go upstairs for the best view.) Rides start at 90p. If the driver is not taking money, hop in, grab a seat, and the conductor will eventually sell you a ticket. If you have a transit pass, get in the habit of hopping buses for quick little straight shots (even just to get to a metro stop). Buses and taxis are miserable during rush hours: 8:00 to 10:00 and 16:00 to 19:00.

By Tube: London's subway is one of the planet's great people-movers and the fastest (and cheapest) long-distance transport in town. Any ride in the Central Zone (on or within the Circle Line, including virtually all my recommended sights and hotels) costs £1.20. You can avoid ticket-window lines in metro stations by buying tickets from coin-op machines; practice a few fares on the punchboard to see how the system works. (Note: These tickets are valid only on the day of purchase.)

Every city map includes a tube map with color-coded lines and names. Pick up a free tube map at any station window and keep it handy. The lines each have a name (such as Circle, Northern, or Bakerloo). At every metro station, you'll have a choice of two platforms per line, served by trains heading in opposite directions. Navigate by signs leading to the platforms (usually labeled north, south, east, or west) that clearly list the stops served by each line, or ask a local or an orange-vested staff person for help. Some tracks are shared by several lines, and electronic signboards announce which train is next. Each train has its final destination or line name above its windshield. Read the system notices clearly posted at the platform; they explain the tube's latest flood, construction, or bomb scare. Ask questions of locals and watch your wallet. Bring something to do to pass the waits productively, especially on the notoriously tardy Circle Line. And always . . . mind the gap.

When leaving the system you'll need your ticket to get through the turnstiles. Save time by choosing the best street exit (look at the maps on the walls). Remember, "subway" means pedestrian underpass in "English." For tube and bus information, call 0171/222-1234.

London Tube and Bus Passes: These deals, valid on both the tube and buses, are worth considering. The "Travel Card," covering Zones 1 and 2, gives you unlimited travel for a day, starting after 9:30, for £3.20. The "LT Card" offers the same benefits, without any time restriction, for £4.30. Families should ask about the one-day "Family Travel Card." The "Weekend Travel Card," for £4.80, costs 25 percent less than two one-day cards. The "7 Day Travel Card" costs £13, covers Zone 1, and requires a passport-type photo (cut one out of any snapshot and bring it from home). All passes are available for more zones, and are purchased as easily as a normal ticket from any station. If you figure you'll take three rides in a day, get a day pass.

If you want to travel a little each day or if you're part of a group, consider buying a "carnet" for £10: You get ten separate tickets for tube travel in Zone 1 and you save 20 percent over the cost of buying individual tickets.

Tours of London
▲▲**Hello London Walk**—Catch a bus to Westminster Bridge (#12 from Notting Hill Gate or #211 from Victoria Station). Sit on the top deck and relax until the first stop east of the bridge. Allow an hour for the following 1.5-mile walk from Westminster Bridge to Piccadilly Circus (includes walking and gawking, not eating or sightseeing).

From Westminster Bridge, walk downstream along the Jubilee Promenade (along the eastern riverbank) for a capital view. Then, for that "Wow, I'm really in London!" feeling, cross the bridge for a close-up view of the Houses of Parliament and Big Ben (floodlit at night). If you ride the tube instead of the bus, the Westminster stop is right at Big Ben. Walk halfway across the bridge for the great view. (Then look for Westminster Pier, offering Thames River cruises, north of the bridge on the Big Ben side.)

London Underground

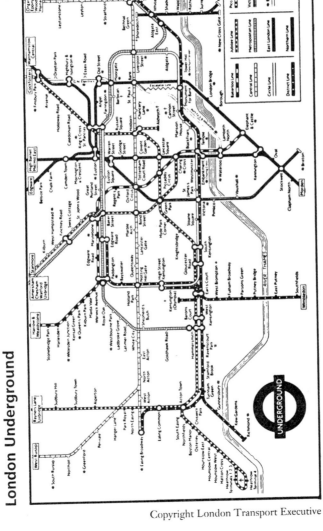

Central London

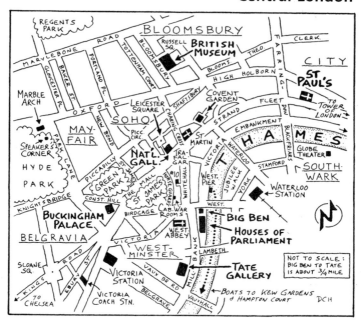

To thrill your loved ones (or bug the envious), call home from a pay phone near Big Ben at about three minutes before the hour. You'll find a phone on Great George Street, across from Parliament Square. As Big Ben chimes, stick the receiver outside the booth and prove you're in London: ding dong ding dong . . . dong ding ding dong.

Cross Parliament Street to say hello to Churchill in the park. (He's electrified to avoid the pigeon problem that stains so many other great statues.) To his right is Westminster Abbey with its two stubby, elegant towers.

Walk north up Parliament Street (which turns into White-hall) toward Trafalgar Square. As you stroll along this center-of-government boulevard, you'll see the thought-provoking cenotaph in the middle of the street, reminding passersby of Britain's many war dead.

Stop at the barricaded and guarded little Downing Street to see the British "White House" at #10, home of the prime minister. Break the bobby's boredom—ask him a question.

Nearing Trafalgar Square, look for the "Queen's Life Guard" (horse guards) behind the gated fence, and the 17th-century Banqueting Hall across the street (details below).

Just before Trafalgar Square, drop into the Clarence Pub for a reasonable meal or pint of whatever you fancy. (Cheaper cafeterias and eateries are on the same block.)

The column topped by Lord Nelson marks Trafalgar Square. The stately domed building on the far side of the square is the National Gallery (free) with its classy café (upstairs in the Sainsbury wing). To the right of the National Gallery is St. Martin-in-the-Fields Church and its Café in the Crypt (see Eating, below).

To get to Piccadilly from Trafalgar Square, take Cockspur Street to Haymarket (passing American Express at 6 Haymarket) then take a short left on Coventry Street.

On colorful Piccadilly, the classy Criterion Brasserie is an affordable splurge for lunch. The National Tourist Information Centre and theaters are nearby, and the Rock Circus and frenetic Pepsi Trocadero Center are within a block (details below). Leicester Square (with its half-price ticket booth for plays) thrives just a few blocks away. For seediness, walk through Soho (north of Shaftesbury Avenue) up to Oxford Street. From Piccadilly or Oxford Circus, you can taxi, bus, or tube home.

▲▲▲Original London Sightseeing Tour—This 90-minute, once-over-lightly, double-decker bus tour drives by all the most famous sights, providing a stressless way to get your bearings and at least see the biggies. You "hop on and hop off" at any of the 25 stops and catch a later bus (runs about every ten minutes in summer, every 20 minutes in winter). Some buses have a tape-recorded narration (your choice of eight languages), and others come with a much-more-fun, English-only, live guide (roughly every third bus has a guide). An inexpensive form of transport as well as an informative tour, it's worth the £12. There are daily departures from 9:30 until early evening from Victoria Street (1 block north of Victoria Station), Marble Arch, Piccadilly Circus, Trafalgar Square, and so on (reservations unnecessary; ticket good for all the next day if purchased after 14:00, tel. 0181/877-1722). Bring a sweater and extra film. Note: If you pick up the bus at Victoria at 9:30, you can hop off near the end of the 90-minute loop at the Buckingham Palace stop, a five-minute walk from the Palace and the Changing of the Guard at 11:30. The many copycat tours offer about the same service and value.

▲▲**Walking Tours**—Several times every day top-notch local guides lead small groups through specific slices of London's past. While the TI and many hotels have the various fliers, only *Time Out* and *What's On* list all scheduled walks, enabling you to choose according to your schedule and interests. Simply show up at the announced location, pay £4.50, and enjoy two chatty hours of Dickens, the Plague, Shakespeare, Legal London, the Beatles, Jack the Ripper, or whatever is on the agenda. Evenings feature organized pub crawls and ghost walks. "London Walks" is the dominant company (for recorded schedule, tel. 0171/624-3978, web site: london.walks.com.) Chris Salaman offers private walking tours for as little as £3 per person (tel. 0181/871-9048).

▲▲**Cruise the Thames**—Boat tours with an entertaining commentary sail regularly between Westminster Pier (north of the base of Westminster Bridge on the Big Ben side) and the Tower of London (£4.20, round-trip £5.40, three tours hourly from 10:20–21:00 in peak season, 30-minute cruise, tel. 0171/930-4097). Similar boats leave the Westminster Pier for Greenwich (£5.60, round-trip £6.70, two hourly from 10:00–17:00, 50 minutes) and Kew Gardens (£6, round-trip £10, seven tours per day, 90 minutes, tel. 0171/930-2062). For pleasure and efficiency, consider combining a one-way cruise with a tube ride back.

Sights—Central London

Note: Summer hours are listed. Sights close early off-season. Students and seniors should ask for "concessions" (discounts). Since many places run sporadic tours, make a habit of telephoning first.

▲▲**Westminster Abbey**—England's historic coronation church is a crowded collection of famous tombs (including the tomb of the unknown soldier). Like a stony refugee camp waiting outside St. Peter's gates, this English hall of fame is thought-provoking but a bit overrated. Its tombstone history is thick with Richards, Annes, Henrys, Marys, Elizabeths, Poet's Corner, and so on. The most Gothic-looking decor (like the fine choir in the center) is 19th-century neo-Gothic. At the high altar you'll see the historic coronation throne (£4, Monday 9:30–16:45, Tuesday–Friday 9:00–16:45, Saturday

London

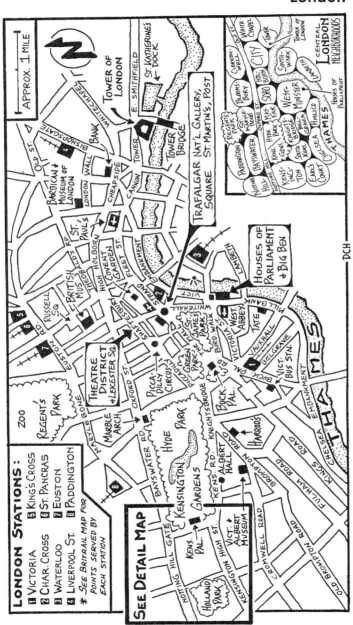

9:00–14:45 and 15:45–17:45, additional hours on Wednesday 18:00–19:45—the only time photography is allowed; last admission 45 minutes before closing; tube: Westminster, tel. 0171/222-5152). Praying is free—use separate entrance.

Walkman tours of the abbey cost £6 (offered until 15:15 weekdays or until 13:15 Saturday). Guided "super tours" are £7 and must be booked in advance (up to six per day, 90 minutes, tel. 0171/222-7110 to book and get times). These "super tours," a historic rundown on the tombs and memorials, are led by a verger (church equivalent of a bat boy). While the £4 entry gets you a brochure with all the basics for a self-guided tour, if you have 90 minutes to spare the live tour is worth the extra £3.

Evensong is on Monday, Tuesday, Thursday, and Friday at 17:00, Saturday and Sunday at 15:00; and an organ recital is held Sunday at 17:45. If you've got that urge to rub a knight, the cloister sports a brass-rubbing center.

▲▲**Houses of Parliament** (Commons and Lords)—These are too tempting to terrorists to be opened wide to tourists, but if Parliament is in session you can view debates in either house (Monday, Tuesday, and Thursday 14:30–22:00 with long waits until 18:00, Wednesday and Friday 9:30–14:00, use St. Stephen's entrance, tube: Westminster, tel. 0171/219-4272). The House of Lords has more pageantry, shorter lines, shorter hours, and less-interesting debates (tel. 0171/219-3107 for schedule).

If you request a "card of entry" from the American Embassy three to four months in advance, you can avoid the line (or "jump the queue") at the House of Commons and see the opening ceremony. Write to: American Embassy, 24 Grosvenor Square, W1A 1AE London; then pick up your card(s) at the American Embassy in London. You can request up to four cards (free). For more information call the embassy at 0171/499-9000; once in their phone tree press 0 to get an operator, then ask for Protocol.

Notice Westminster Hall on the left as you go through security. The Houses of Parliament are located in what was once the Palace of Westminster, long the palace of England's medieval kings before it was largely destroyed by fire in 1834. The impressive Westminster Hall dates from the 11th century (its famous hammer-beam roof was added in 1397). The palace was rebuilt in Victorian Gothic style after the fire (a move away from neoclassicism back to England's Christian and

medieval heritage, true to the Romantic Age). Completed in
1860, only a few of its 1,000 rooms are open to the public.

The clock tower (315 feet high) is named for its 13-ton
bell, Ben. The light above the clock is lit when the House of
Commons is sitting. For a hip HOP view, walk halfway over
Westminster Bridge.

▲▲Cabinet War Rooms—This is a fascinating walk
through the underground headquarters of the British government's fight against the Nazis in the darkest days of the Battle for Britain. The nerve center of the British war effort was
used from 1939 through 1945. Churchill's room, the map
room, and so on, are just as they were in 1945. For all the
blood, sweat, toil, and tears details, pick-up the headsets at
the entrance and follow the included 45-minute Walkman
tour (£4.40, daily 9:30–18:00, on King Charles Street just off
Whitehall, follow the signs, tube: Westminster, tel.
0171/930-6961).

Horse Guards—The Horse Guards have a 11:00 inspection
Monday through Saturday (at 10:00 on Sunday) and a colorful
dismounting ceremony daily at 16:00. The rest of the day is
terrible for camcorders (on Whitehall, between Trafalgar and
#10 Downing Street, tube: Westminster).

▲Banqueting Hall—England's first Renaissance building
(designed by Inigo Jones around 1620) and one of the few
London landmarks spared by the 1666 fire, the Hall is the
only surviving part of the original Palace of Whitehall. Don't
miss its Rubens ceiling which, at Charles I's request, drove
home the doctrine of the legitimacy of the divine right of
kings. In 1649, divine right ignored, Charles I was beheaded
on the balcony of this building by a Cromwellian parliament.
Admission includes a fine 20-minute audiovisual history, an
interesting-only-to-history-buffs 35-minute tape-recorded
tour, and a look at a fancy banqueting hall (£3.25, Monday–
Saturday 10:00–17:00, last entry at 16:30, subject to closure
for government functions, aristocratic WC, immediately
across Whitehall from the Horse Guards, tube: Westminster,
tel. 0171/930-4179).

▲▲Trafalgar Square—London's central square is a thrilling
place to just hang out. Lord Nelson stands atop his 185-foot-
tall fluted granite column, gazing out to Trafalgar where he
lost his life but defeated the French fleet (part of the 1842
memorial is made from the melted-down cannons of his

victims at Trafalgar). He's surrounded by giant lions, hordes of people, and even more pigeons. (When bombed, resist the impulse to wipe immediately—it'll smear. Wait for it to dry and flake off gently.) The square is the climax of most marches and demonstrations (tube: Charing Cross).

▲▲**National Gallery**—Newly renovated, displaying Britain's top collection of European paintings from 1250 to 1900—works by Leonardo, Botticelli, Velazquez, Rembrandt, Turner, van Gogh, and the Impressionists—this is one of Europe's classiest galleries. Don't miss the "Micro Gallery," a computer room even your dad could have fun in (closes 30 minutes earlier than museum). You can study any artist, style, or topic in the museum and even print out a tailor-made tour map. (Free, Monday–Saturday 10:00–18:00, Wednesday until 20:00, Sunday 12:00–18:00, free one-hour tours weekdays at 11:30 and 14:30 and Saturday at 14:00 and 15:30, on Trafalgar Square, tube: Charing Cross or Leicester Square, tel. 0171/839-3321.) Ask about the Walkman tours (free, but donation requested).

The National Portrait Gallery, around the corner, is as exciting as somebody else's yearbook (free, Monday–Saturday 10:00–18:00, Sunday 12:00–18:00, tel. 0171/306-0055).

▲▲**Piccadilly Circus**—London's touristy "Town Square" is surrounded by fascinating streets and swimming with youth on the rampage. The new Rock Circus offers a very commercial but serious history of rock music with Madame Tussaud wax stars. It's an entertaining hour under radio earphones for rock 'n' roll romantics (£8, daily 10:00–20:00, plenty of photo ops, many enter with a beer-buzz and sing happily off-key under their headphones—nearly as entertaining as the exhibit itself, tube: Piccadilly Circus). For overstimulation, drop by the shiny new Pepsi Trocadero Center's "theme park of the future" for its virtual reality games, including SegaWorld, Imaginator, and Virtuality, along with a nine-screen cinema (admission to Trocadero is free; individual attractions cost £2–8; combined "Adrenalin Ticket"-£10; between Coventry and Shaftesbury, just off Piccadilly). Chinatown, to the east, has swollen since Hong Kong lost its independence. Nearby Shaftesbury Avenue and Leicester Square teem with fun-seekers, theaters, Chinese restaurants, and street singers.

Soho—North of Piccadilly, Soho isn't as sleazy as it used to be, but it's still worth a gawk. This is London's red-light district

National Gallery Highlights

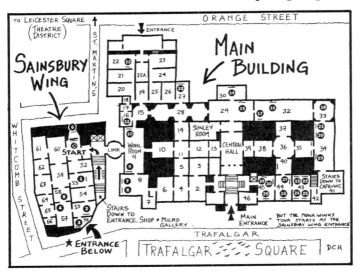

TO LEICESTER SQUARE
(THEATRE DISTRICT)

ORANGE STREET

ENTRANCE

SAINSBURY WING

MAIN BUILDING

WHITCOMB STREET

START

WOHL ROOM 9

LINK

SUNLEY ROOM

CENTRAL HALL

STAIRS DOWN TO CAFE+WC

STAIRS DOWN TO ENTRANCE, SHOP + MICRO GALLERY

MAIN ENTRANCE

BUT THE MONA WINKS TOUR STARTS AT THE SAINSBURY WING ENTRANCE

★ ENTRANCE BELOW

TRAFALGAR

TRAFALGAR SQUARE

DCH

Medieval and Early Renaissance
1. Wilton Diptych
2. UCCELLO—Battle of San Romano
3. VAN EYCK—Arnolfini Marriage
4. CRIVELLI—Annunciation With St. Emidius
5. BOTTICELLI—Venus and Mars

High Renaissance
6. LEONARDO DA VINCI—Virgin and Child (cartoon)
7. MICHELANGELO—Entombment
8. RAPHAEL—Pope Julius II

Venetian Renaissance
9. TINTORETTO—Origin of the Milky Way
10. TITIAN—Bacchus and Ariadne

Northern Protestant Art
11. VERMEER—Young Woman Standing at a Virginal
12. Hoogstraten Peepshow
13. REMBRANDT—Self-Portrait

Baroque
14. RUBENS—The Judgment of Paris
15. VAN DYCK—Charles I on Horseback

16. VALÁZQUEZ—The Rokeby Venus
17. CARAVAGGIO—Salome Receiving the Head of John the Baptist

French and Later Italian
18. CLAUDE LORRAIN—Seaport
19. TURNER—Dido Building Carthage
20. BOUCHER—Pan and Syrinx
21. TIEPOLO

British
22. CONSTABLE—The Hay Wain
23. TURNER—The Fighting Téméraire
24. TURNER—Rain, Steam, Speed

Impressionism and Beyond
25. MONET—Gare St. Lazare
26. RENOIR—The Umbrellas
27. DEGAS—La La at the Cirque Fernando
28. MANET—The Waitress (La Servante de Bocks)
29. SEURAT—Bathers, Asnieres
30. VAN GOGH—Sunflowers
31. CÉZANNE—Bathers
32. PICASSO—Bowl of Fruit, Bottle of Water
33. MONET—Water Lilies

where "friendly models" wait in tiny rooms up dreary stairways and scantily clad con artists sell strip shows. Anyone who goes into any one of these shows will be ripped off. Every time. Even a £3 show comes with a £100 cover or minimum (as it's printed on the drink menu) and a "security man." The door has no handle until you pay.

▲**Covent Gardens**—This boutique-ish shopping district is a people-watcher's delight with cigarette-eaters, Punch 'n' Judy acts, food that's good for you (but not your wallet), trendy crafts, sweet whiffs of pot, hair that's two-tone (neither natural), and faces that could set off a metal detector. For the best lunch deals walk a block or two away from the eye of this touristic tornado. It's hard to go wrong in a little tea-and-sandwich deli (vegetarians like #2 Neal's Yard, off Neal Street, tube: Covent Gardens).

▲▲▲**British Museum**—This is the greatest chronicle of our civilization anywhere. Visiting this immense museum is like hiking through Encyclopedia Britannica National Park. After an overview ramble, cover just two or three sections of your choice more thoroughly. The Egyptian, Mesopotamian (Assyrian), and Greek (Parthenon) sections are highlights.

The huge winged lions (which guarded Assyrian palaces 800 years before Christ) guard the museum's three great ancient galleries. For a brief tour, connect these ancient dots:

Start with the Egyptian. Wander from the Rosetta Stone past the many statues, side-tripping into small rooms on the right for more intimate peeks at pharoahs' art. At the end of the hall, climb the stairs to mummyland.

Back at the winged lions, wander through the dark, violent, and mysterious Assyrian rooms. The Nimrud Gallery is lined with royal propaganda reliefs and wounded lions.

The most modern of the ancient art fills the Greek section. Find room #1 behind the winged lions and start your walk through Greek art history with the simple and primitive Cycladian fertility figures. Later, painted vases show a culture really into partying. The finale is the Elgin Marbles. The much wrangled over bits of the Athenian Parthenon (from 450 B.C.) are much more impressive than they look. To better appreciate these ancient carvings, read through the orientation material in the tiny intro rooms between rooms 7 and 8. (Free, Monday–Saturday 10:00–17:00, Sunday 14:30–18:00, least crowded weekday mornings, tube:

Tottenham Court Road; guided 90-minute £6 tours offered daily—three per day on Sunday, two per day in winter—call museum for times, tel. 0171/636-1555.) As of March '98, the British Library (notable for its manuscripts) will no longer be in the British Museum (see below).

British Library—Wander through the manuscripts that have enlightened and brightened our lives for centuries, from the Magna Carta, Bibles, and Beethoven, to the Beatles (free, Monday–Saturday 9:30–18:00, Sunday 11:00–17:00, 96 Euston Road, tube: King's Cross or Euston, tel. 0171/412-7000). Note: The library will open in March '98.

▲**Buckingham Palace**—In order to pay for the restoration of the fire-damaged Windsor Castle, the royal family is opening its lavish home to the public until 2000 (£9 to see the state apartments and throne room; open August and September only; daily from 9:30–16:30; limited to 8,000 visitors a day—come early to get an appointed visit time; tube: Victoria, tel. 0171/930-4832). If the flag is flying (or you see her yellow Toyota), the queen is home.

▲**Changing of the Guard at Buckingham Palace**—Overrated but almost required. The guard changes daily from April through July at 11:30 and every other day August through March (no band when wet). Join the mob at the back side of the palace (the front faces a huge and very private park). The pageantry and parading are colorful and even stirring, but the actual changing of the guard is a non-event. It is interesting to see nearly every tourist in London gathered in one place at the same time. Hop into a big black taxi and say, "To Buckingham Palace, please." For all the color with none of the crowds, see the Inspection of the Guard Ceremony at 11:00 in front of the Wellington Barracks, east of the palace on Birdcage Walk. Afterwards, stroll through nearby St. James' Park. For today's schedule, call 0171/930-4832. (Tube: Victoria, St. James' Park, or Green Park.)

▲▲**Tate Gallery**—One of Europe's great art houses, the Tate specializes in British painting (14th-century through contemporary), pre-Raphaelites, Impressionism, and modern art (Matisse, van Gogh, Monet, Picasso). Learn about the mystical watercolorist Blake and the romantic, nature-worship art of Turner (free, daily 10:00–18:00; free tours weekdays 11:00, 12:00, 14:00, and 15:00; Saturday at 15:00; tube: Pimlico; call to confirm schedule, tel. 0171/887-8000).

Sights—West London

▲**Hyde Park**—London's "Central Park" has more than 600 acres of lush greenery, a huge man-made lake, the royal Kensington Palace (not worth touring), and the ornate neo-Gothic Albert Memorial across from the Royal Albert Hall. Early afternoons on Sunday, Speaker's Corner (tube: Marble Arch) offers soapbox oratory at its best. "The grass roots of democracy" is actually a holdover from when the gallows stood here and the criminal was allowed to say just about anything he wanted to before he swung. I dare you to raise your voice and gather a crowd—it's easy to do.

▲**Victoria and Albert Museum**—A gangly but surprisingly interesting collection of costumes, armor, furniture, decorative arts, and much more from the West as well as from Asia and Islam. Walk through centuries of aristocratic living rooms and follow the evolution of fashion in England (through 40 fascinating and well-described display cases) from 1600 to today (£5, Monday 12:00–18:00, Tuesday–Sunday 10:00–18:00, tube: So. Kensington, pleasant garden café, tel. 0171/938-8500).

Kew Gardens—For a fine park and a palatial greenhouse jungle to swing through, take the tube or the boat to every botanist's favorite escape, Kew Gardens (£4.50, Monday–Saturday 9:30–18:00, Sunday 9:30–19:00, galleries and conservatories close a half-hour earlier, tube: Kew Gardens, tel. 0181/940-1171). For tea, consider the Maids of Honor (280 Kew Road, near garden entrance, tel. 0181/940-2752).

Sights—East London, "The City"

▲▲**The City of London**—When Londoners say "the City," they mean the 1-square-mile business, banking, and journalism center that 2,000 years ago was Roman Londinium. The outline of the Roman city walls can still be seen in the arc of roads from Blackfriars Bridge to Tower Bridge. Within the City are 24 churches designed by Christopher Wren. It's a fascinating district to wander, but since nobody actually lives there, it's a ghost town on Saturday and Sunday. An hour in the city's Central Criminal Courts, known as "Old Bailey," is always interesting (Monday–Friday 10:30–13:00 and 14:00–16:00, quiet in August, no cameras or bags, no cloakroom, at Old Bailey and Newgate St., tube: St. Paul's, tel. 0171/248-3277).

▲▲**St. Paul's Cathedral**—Wren's most famous church is the great St. Paul's, its elaborate interior capped by a 365-foot

dome. St. Paul's was Britain's World War II symbol of resistance, as Nazi bombs failed to blow it up. (There's a memorial
chapel to the heroic firefighters who kept watch over it with
hoses cocked.) The crypt (free with admission) is a world of
historic bones and memorials, including Admiral Nelson's
tomb and interesting cathedral models. This was the wedding
church of Prince Charles and the late Princess Diana. Climb
the dome for a great city view and some fun in the whispering
gallery. Whisper sweet nothings into the wall and your partner
(and anyone else) on the far side can hear you. (£4 entry, £3.50
extra to climb dome; daily 9:30–16:30; free on Sunday but
restricted viewing due to services; allow an hour to climb up
and down the dome; £3.50 for 90-minute cathedral and crypt
tours: with a guide at 11:00, 11:30, 13:30, and 14:00 or £3 for a
Walkman anytime; Sunday services at 8:00, 8:45, 11:00, and
15:15; tube: St. Paul's, tel. 0171/236-4128.)

▲**Museum of London**—Stroll through London history—
from pre-Roman times to the Blitz up through today (£4, free
after 16:30; Tuesday–Saturday 10:00–18:00, Sunday
12:00–18:00, usually closed Monday but open on bank-holiday
Mondays; tube: Barbican or St. Paul's, tel. 0171/600-3699).
This regular stop for the local schoolkids gives the best
overview of London history in town.

▲▲**Tower of London**—William I, still getting used to his
new title of "the Conqueror," built the stone "White Tower"
(1077–1097) to keep the Londoners in line. The tower served
as an effective lookout for invaders coming up the Thames.
His successors enlarged it to its present 18-acre size. Because
of the security it provided, over the centuries it has served as
the Royal Mint, the Royal Jewel House, and a prison. You'll
find more bloody history per square inch in this original tower
of power than anywhere in Britain. Don't miss the entertaining
50-minute Beefeater tour (free, leaving regularly from inside
the gate, last one usually at 15:30) of this historic fortress,
palace, prison, and host to more than 3 million visitors a year.
Britain's best armory and most lovely Norman chapel (St.
John's Chapel, 1080) are in the White Tower. The crown jewels, which date from the Restoration (Cromwell sold or melted
down the earlier jewels), are the best on earth. The long midday summer lines are made almost enjoyable by museum displays along the way. To avoid the crowds arrive at 9:00 and go
straight for the jewels, doing the tour and tower later. (£8.50;

tower hours: Monday–Saturday 9:00–18:00, with last entry at 17:00, Sunday 10:00–18:00; the long but fast-moving line is worst on Sundays; tube: Tower Hill, tel. 0171/709-0765.) Visitors are welcome on the grounds to worship in the Royal Chapel on Sunday (free, 11:00 service with fine choral music).

Every night at 21:30, with pageantry-filled ceremony, the Tower of London is locked up (as it has been every night for the last 700 years). To attend this free event, you need to request an invitation at least five weeks before your visit. Write to: Ceremony of Keys, H.M. Tower of London, London EC3N 4AB. Include your name, number of people (up to seven), requested date, alternative dates, and an international reply coupon (buy at a U.S. post office). Although five week's notice is requested, you might try for an appointment near the end of your trip by sending a stamped envelope addressed to your London hotel once you arrive.

Sights Next to the Tower—The best remaining bit of London's Roman Wall is just north of the tower (at the Tower Hill tube station). **Tower Hill Pageant**, a 15-minute, high-tech, historical amusement ride, takes you through 20 centuries of London history followed by a small but fine exhibition of Roman and Saxon artifacts uncovered during the recent riverside development. It's worthwhile for rich kids with time to kill (£6.95, daily 9:30–17:30, until 16:30 off-season, across the street from the Tower turnstile, tel. 0171/709-0081). Freshly painted and restored, **Tower Bridge** has an 1894–1994 history exhibit (£5.70, daily 10:00–18:30, last entry at 17:15, good view, poor value, tel. 0171/403-3761). **St. Katherine Yacht Harbor**, chic and newly renovated, just east of the Tower Bridge, has mod shops and the classic old Dickens Inn, fun for a drink or pub lunch.

Sights—South London

▲▲**Imperial War Museum**—This impressive museum covers the wars of this century, from heavy weaponry to love notes and Varga Girls, from Monty's Africa campaign tank to Schwarzkopf's Desert Storm uniform. You can trace the development of the machine gun, watch footage of the first tank battles, hold your breath through the gruesome WWI trench experience, and buy WWII-era toys in the fun museum shop. Rather than glorify war, the museum does its best to shine a light on the powerful human side of one of mankind's most persistent traits (£4.70, daily 10:00–18:00, free after 16:30, 90 minutes is enough time for most visitors, tube: Lambeth North, tel. 0171/416-5000).

▲▲**Museum of the Moving Image**—This high-tech, inter-active, hands-on museum traces the story of moving images from a caveman's flickering fire to modern TV. There's great footage of the earliest movies and TV shows. Turn-of-the-century-clad staff speak as if silent films are the latest marvel. You can make your own animated cartoon. Don't miss the speedy 50-year montage of magic MGM moments. Brit movie buffs will enjoy the 90-minute film of British cinematic highlights (£5.95, daily 10:00–18:00, tube: Waterloo; or tube: Embankment, then walk across the Thames pedestrian bridge, tel. 0171/928-3535).

More Sights

▲▲**National Maritime Museum in Greenwich**—Today's museums are contained in a royal shell. The Tudor kings pre-ferred Greenwich to their other palaces. Henry VIII was born here. Later kings commissioned Inigo Jones and Chris Wren to beautify the place. In spite of its architectural and royal treats, this is England's maritime capital, and visitors go for things salty.

Crawl through the *Cutty Sark*, the last of the great clipper ships. Launched in 1869, she was queen of the seas. With 32,000 square feet of sail, she could blow with the wind 300 miles in a day (£3.50, daily 10:00–17:00, from noon on Sunday, tel. 0181/858-3445). Moored nearby, the little *Gipsy Moth IV* is the 53-foot sailboat Sir Francis Chichester used for his solo voyage around the world in 1967 (£1).

Straddle the zero meridian, set your wristwatch to Green-wich mean time at the Old Royal Observatory, and relive four centuries of Britannia-rules-the-waves history at the National Maritime Museum (£5.50, £4 for observatory only; daily 10:00–17:00; tel. 0181/858-4422). Only two galleries of the Maritime Museum are open (because the museum is being refurbished for the year 2000 celebration) so you'll likely be sold a combined ticket that includes the Maritime Museum, Royal Observatory, and Queen's House.

Getting to Greenwich is either a joy (cruise down the Thames from central London's piers at Westminster, Char-ing Cross, or Tower of London) or a snap (tube to Island

Gardens in Zone 2, free with tube pass, then walk under pedestrian Thames tunnel; or catch the train from Charing Cross station to Maze Hill). Greenwich tourist information: tel. 0181/858-6376.

Thames Barrier—East of Greenwich the world's largest movable flood barrier welcomes visitors with an informative and entertaining exhibition (£3.40, Monday–Friday 10:00–17:00, weekends 10:30–17:30; catch 70-minute boat from Westminster Pier, or take 30-minute boat from Greenwich pier, or train from London's Charing Cross station to Charlton then walk 15 minutes; tel. 0181/854-1373).

Honorable Mention—**Madame Tussaud's Waxworks** is expensive but dang good (£8.95, children £5.95, daily 9:00–17:30, buy ticket at TI to save a little money and get in with no wait, Marylebone Road, tube: Baker Street, tel. 0171/935-6861; combined ticket for Tussaud's and Planetarium is £10.95 for adults, £6.95 for kids). At **Geffrye Decorative Arts Museum** you can walk through British front rooms from 1600 to 1960 (free, Tuesday–Saturday 10:00–17:00, Sunday 14:00–17:00, closed Monday, tube: Liverpool Street, then bus 22A or 22B north, tel. 0171/739-9893). Architects love the quirky **Sir John Soane's Museum** (free, 10:00–17:00, closed Sunday and Monday, tube: Holborn).

Shopping in London

▲**Harrods**—Artfully mixing big and classy, Harrods is filled with wonderful displays, elegant high teas, and fingernail-ripping riots during its July sales. Harrods has everything from elephants to toothbrushes. Need some peanut butter? The food halls are sights to savor (with reasonable cafeterias; 10:00–18:00; until 19:00 on Wednesday, Thursday, and Friday; closed Sunday; tel. 0171/730-1234). For royal window-shopping, cruise nearby King's Road in Chelsea. Most stores close around 18:00 but stay open until 20:00 on Wednesday or Thursday, depending on the neighborhood.

▲**Street Markets**—If you like garage sales and people-watching, hit a London street market. The tourist office has a complete, up-to-date list. The best are Portobello Road (Saturday 8:30–17:00, antique and flea market, near recommended B&Bs, tube: Notting Hill Gate) and Camden Market (Saturday and Sunday 10:00–17:00; a huge, trendy arts and crafts festival; tube: Camden Town). There's some good early morning market activity somewhere any day of the week. Warning: Street markets attract two kinds of people—tourists and pickpockets.

Famous Auctions—London's famous auctioneers welcome the curious public. For schedules (most weekdays, closed mid-summer), telephone Sotheby's (tel. 0171/493-8080, tube: Oxford Circus) or Christie's (tel. 0171/839-9060, tube: Green Park).

Entertainment and Theater in London

London bubbles with top-notch entertainment seven nights a week. Everything's listed in the monthly *Time Out* or *What's On* magazines, available at most newsstands. You'll choose from classical, jazz, rock, and far-out music, Gilbert and Sullivan, dance, comedy, Bahai meetings, poetry readings, spectator sports, film, and theater.

London's theater rivals Broadway's in quality and beats it in price. Choose from the Royal Shakespeare Company, top musicals, comedy, thrillers, sex farces, and more. Performances are nightly except Sunday, usually with one matinee a week. Matinees (Wednesday, Thursday, or Saturday, listed in a box in *What's On*) are cheaper and rarely sold out. Tickets range from about £8 to £25.

Most theaters, marked on tourist maps, are in the Piccadilly–Trafalgar area. Box offices, hotels, and TIs have a handy "Theater Guide" brochure listing what's playing.

The best and cheapest way to book a ticket is simply to call the theater box office directly, ask about seats and dates available, and book by credit card. You can call from the U.S.A. as easily as from England (photocopy your hometown library's London newspaper theater section). Pick up your ticket 15 minutes before the show.

Getting a ticket through a ticket agency (at most tourist offices or scattered throughout London) is quick and easy but prices are inflated by a standard 20 to 25 percent booking fee. Ticket agencies are scalpers with an address. Agencies are worthwhile only if a show you've got to see is sold out at the box office. They scarf up hot tickets, planning to make a killing after the show is sold out. U.S.A. booking agencies get their tickets from another agency, adding even more to your expense by involving yet another middleman.

Cheap theater tricks: Most theaters offer cheap returned tickets, standing room, matinee, and senior or student stand-by deals. These "concessions" are indicated with a "conc" or "s" in the listings. Picking up a late return can get you a great seat at a cheap-seat price. Standing room costs only a few pounds. If a show is "sold out," there's usually a way to get a seat. Call and ask how. The famous (but overrated) "half-price booth" in Leicester (pronounced "Lester") Square sells cheap tickets to shows on the push list the day of the show only (Monday–Saturday, 14:30–18:30). I usually buy the second-cheapest tickets directly from the theater box office. Many theaters are so small that there's hardly a bad seat. After the lights go down, "scooting up" is less than a capital offense. Shakespeare did it.

Royal Shakespeare Company—If you'll ever enjoy Shakespeare, it'll be here. (But lo, I've tried and failed.) The RSC splits its season between the Royal Shakespeare Theatre in Stratford (tel. 01789/295-623) and the Barbican Centre in London (daily 9:00–20:00; credit-card booking, they mail out schedules; tel. 0171/638-8891, or for recorded information call 0171/628-9760). Tickets range in price from £5 (preview) to £24. The best way to buy is direct, by telephone and credit card. You can pick up your ticket at the door; £6 stand-by tickets are sold at 9:00 the day of the show. For a complete schedule, write to the Royal Shakespeare Theatre, Stratford-upon-Avon, Warwickshire, CV37 6BB.

Shakespeare at the New Globe Theater—To see Shakespeare in an exact replica of the theater for which he wrote his plays, check out the Globe. This thatch-roofed, open-air, round theater does the plays as Shakespeare intended (with no amplification). Curtain times are usually at 14:00 and 19:30, May through September. You'll pay £5 to stand and up to £20 to sit (on a backless bench). Allow time to explore the historic exhibit about the bard and his work. The theater and exhibit are open to tour when there are no plays (£5, daily 10:00–17:00, includes guided 30-minute tour offered on the half hour; if a play is scheduled, the museum is open only 9:00–12:30; on the south bank directly across the Thames from St. Paul's, tube: Mansion House, tel. 0171/928-6406).

Music—For a fun classical event, attend a "Prom Concert." This is an annual music festival with almost nightly concerts in the Royal Albert Hall from July through September at give-a-peasant-some-culture prices (£3 standing-room spots sold at the door, tel. 0171/589-8212). Look into the free lunchtime concerts popular in churches (especially Wren's St. Bride's

London Area

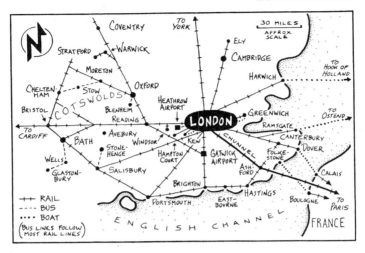

Church, tel. 0171/353-1301; and St. Martin-in-the-Fields, weekdays except Thursday at 13:00, tel. 0171/930-1862).

Day Trips from London

You could fill a book with the many easy and exciting day trips from London (Earl Steinbicker did: *Daytrips in Britain by Rail, Bus or Car from London and Edinburgh*). Several tour companies take London-based travelers out and back every day. Some offer bus tours that can be used by those without a car as a "free" way to get to Bath or Stow-on-the-Wold (saving you, for instance, the £28.50 London–Bath train ticket). Evan Evans' tours leave from behind Victoria Station at 9:00 (with your bag stowed under the bus), include a full day of sightseeing with £5 to £10 worth of admissions, and leave you in Bath or Stow before returning to London (£29.50 for Stonehenge and Bath; £45 for Salisbury, Stonehenge, and Bath; and £42.50 for Oxford, Blenheim, Burford, and Stow; tel. 0181/332-2222). Greenline does a tour of Bath and Stonehenge for £24 (tel. 0181/668-7261 or stop by the Greenline office in Fountain Square directly south of Victoria Station).

The British rail system uses London as a hub and normally offers round-trip fares (after 9:30) that cost virtually the same as one-way fares. "Day return" tickets are best (and cheapest) for day trips. Sometimes you can save money if you purchase "Super Advance" tickets before 14:00 on the day before your trip.

For more ideas, see BritRail's handy "Day Trips from London" booklet (available in the U.S.A. for $17 postpaid, CC:VMA, tel. 800/677-8585). But given the high cost of big-city living and the charm of small-town England, I'd see London and get out.

Sleeping in London
(£1 = about $1.60, tel. code: 0171)
Sleep Code: **S**=Single, **D**=Double/Twin, **T**=Triple, **Q**=Quad, **b**=bathroom, **t**=toilet only, **s**=shower only, **CC**=Credit Card (**V**isa, **M**asterCard, **A**mex). Unless otherwise noted, prices include a big English breakfast.

London is expensive but there's no need to spend a fortune or stay in a depressing dump. Plan on spending £50 to £60 ($80–95) for a basic, clean, reasonably cheery double in a usually cramped, cracked-plaster building, with a hearty English (as opposed to continental) breakfast. Rather than mess with a dorm or hostel, I'd spend £35 for a sleepable double with breakfast in a safe, clean, tiny, dreary place where the landlords are absent and service is minimal. (Hang up your towel to dry and reuse). My London splurges, at £70 to £130, are spacious, thoughtfully appointed places you'd be happy to entertain or make love in. TVs are nearly standard in rooms (those without usually have an inviting TV lounge).

I reserve my London room in advance with a phone call direct from the States. Assure the manager you'll arrive before 16:00, and leave your credit-card number as security. If you must send a deposit, ask if you can send a signed $100 traveler's check. (Leave the "pay to" line blank and include a note explaining that you'll be happy to pay cash upon arrival. That way they can avoid bank charges.)

Sleeping in Victoria Station Neighborhood, Belgravia
The streets behind Victoria Station teem with budget B&Bs. It's a safe, surprisingly tidy and decent area without a hint of the trashy touristy glitz of the streets in front of the station. The first three listings are on Ebury Street, between the train and coach stations, proudly part of Belgravia. Even with

London, Victoria Neighborhood

Margaret Thatcher living around the corner (you'll see the policeman standing outside #73 Chester Square), this is a classy and peaceful place to call home in London. Decent eateries abound (see Eating section, below). The cheaper listings are relatively dumpy. Don't expect £50 cheeriness in a £34 room. Those traveling on a shoestring off-season save a few pounds by arriving late without a reservation and checking around. Competition is fierce and prices in this area are often soft (especially for multi-night stays). Especially for Warwick Way hotels (and in the summer when you'll want the window open at night), request a quiet back room. All hotels are within a five-minute walk of the Victoria tube, bus, and train stations. There's a £8-per-day garage and a nearby launderette (self-serve or full-serve, 3 Westmoreland Terrace, tel. 0171/821-8692).

At **Woodville House** the quarters are tight, showers are down the hall, and several rooms are noisy on the street, but this well-worn place is a good value with lots of travel tips and endless tea, coffee, and friendly chat (especially about the local rich and famous) from Rachel Joplin (S-£39, D-£58; bunky family deals for three, four, or five in a room; easy credit-card reservations, 107 Ebury Street, SW1W 9QU; tel. 0171/730-1048, fax 0171/730-2574).

Lime Tree Hotel is enthusiastically run by David and Marilyn Davies. The thoughtfully decorated public areas and rooms are more spacious than most in this area and guests are welcome in the peaceful garden—ask where the entrance is. The renovated rooms offer the best value (Sb-£65–75, Db-£85–100, Tb-£110–120, family room-£120–140, David will deal in slow times, CC:VMA, 135 Ebury Street, SW1W 9RA, tel. 0171/730-8191, fax 0171/730-7865). Each room comes with a TV, phone, hair dryer, safe, and coffee pot.

Cherry Court Hotel, run by the friendly Patel family, offers small rooms and good prices on a quiet street very close to the station (Sb-£35, Db-£40, Tb-£60, CC:VMA, pleasant garden, 23 Hugh Street, SW1V 1QJ, tel. 0171/828-2840, fax 0171/828-0393, e-mail: cherryc@globalnet.co.uk).

Cedar Guest House, across the street, is a minimal place with eight rooms at near-youth-hostel prices. It's run by a Polish organization to help Poles afford London, but all are welcome (D-£30–32, T-£46, 30 Hugh Street, SW1V 1RP, tel. 0171/828-2625).

Elizabeth Hotel has a gracious feel, offering a large lobby, small but pleasant rooms, and free access to the private park overlooks (S-£36–40, Sb-£55, D-£62, Ds-£66, small Db-£70, Db-£80, Tb-£96, Qb-£106, Quint/b-£115, 37 Eccleston Square, SW1V 1PB, tel. 0171/828-6812). Either traveler's checks or personal checks are accepted as a deposit.

Limegrove Hotel, run by harried Joyce, is a little smoky and has only two toilets and two showers for seven rooms, but is a fine value with full English breakfast served in your room (S-£28, small D-£36, D-£38, Db-£50, T-£48, Tb-from £60, cheaper off-season or for stays of six days or more, 101 Warwick Way, SW1V 4HT, tel. 0171/828-0458). Back rooms are quieter.

Astoria Hotel, a formerly elegant 1835 building, has faded but spacious rooms with soft prices for longer stays (Sb-£60, Db-£70, Tb-£75, Qb-£85, CC:VM, all with CNN on the

TV, 39 St. Georges Drive, SW1V 4DG, tel. 0171/834-1965, fax 0171/834-1977, run by Ahmed).

Rubens at the Palace has a classy lobby and comfortable, if slightly worn, rooms. The American owners plan to remodel. Prices are soft—ask (Sb-£125, Db-£145, Tb-£185, suites available, CC:VMA, 2 blocks north of the station, close to Buckingham Palace, tel. 0171/834-6600, fax 0171/828-5401; from the U.S.A., tel. 800/424-2862).

"South Kensington," She Said, Loosening His Cummerbund

For the chance to live on a quiet street so classy it doesn't allow hotel signs, surrounded by trendy shops and colorful restaurants, call South Kensington home in London. Many locals just call it "South Ken." Shoppers will enjoy the location, a short walk from Harrods and the designer shops of King's Road and Chelsea. You'll find plenty of budget ethnic eateries around the corner on Brompton Road (each hotel has restaurant scrapbooks or wall charts). This has got to be the ultimate fairy-tale London home-away-from-home. Of course, you'll pay for it. But these places are a fine value. A splendid splurge. Sumner Place is 200 yards from the South Kensington tube station (on the Circle Line, direct connection to Heathrow, two stops from Victoria Station—top of tube stairs, exit left, cross the doubled street, go right 2 blocks down Old Brompton Road, left onto Sumner Place).

Five Sumner Place Hotel is informal but professional, "highly commended" and recently voted "the best small hotel in London." You'll talk softly but not feel like you have to dress up as you wander, with your free daily newspaper, under the chandeliers out to the Victorian-style conservatory, a greenhouse dressed in blue, for breakfast. Each room is tastefully decorated with traditional period furnishings in a 150-year-old building (Sb-£88, Db-£129, Tb-£155, elevator, easy CC reservations, non-smoking, CC:VMA, 5 Sumner Place, South Kensington, SW7 3EE, tel. 0171/584-7586, fax 0171/823-9962, e-mail: no.5@dial.pipex.com).

Aster House Hotel has classy rooms, each with a TV, telephone, and fridge. Enjoy breakfast in the whisper-elegant Orangerie, a Victorian greenhouse and lounge in the tidy backgarden (S-£60, Sb-£80, third floor Db-£110, Db-£120, deluxe four-poster Db with both bath and shower-£135, entirely non-smoking, CC:VM, 3 Sumner Place, SW7 3EE, tel. 0171/581-5888, fax 0171/584-4925, e-mail: asterhouse@ binternet.com, run by manager Simon Tan). Note: credit-card deposits are non-refundable if you cancel with less than two weeks' notice. A couple of blocks away, the big, stately **Kensington Juries Hotel** offers fine rooms for classier travelers (Db-£99–145 depending upon "availability," Queen's Gate, South Kensington, SW7 5LR, tel. 0171/589-6300, fax 0171/581-1492). If you happen to be visiting during a slow period (which could be any month) and can score a £99 room, this is an excellent value.

The Claverly, just a couple of blocks from Harrods, is on a quiet street insulated from the downtown chaos. The rooms are small but warmly furnished with elegant drapery and all the comforts (S-£70, Sb-£75–115, Db-£110–190, Tb-£160–215, some balconies, CC:VMA, 13-14 Beaufort Gardens, SW3 1PS, tube: Knightsbridge, tel. 0171/589-8541, fax 0171/584-3410, from the U.S.A., tel. 800/747-0398).

Sleeping in Notting Hill Gate Neighborhood

Residential Notting Hill Gate is the perfect traveler's neighborhood. It has quick and easy bus or tube access to downtown, it's on the A2 Airbus line from Heathrow (second stop from airport, after Kensington Hilton), is relatively safe (except during the dangerous, riot-plagued Notting Hill Carnival, the last weekend of August), and, for London, is very "homely." Notting Hill Gate has a self-serve launderette, an artsy theater, a late-hours supermarket, and lots of fun budget eateries (see below). All recommended accommodations are near the Holland Park or Notting Hill Gate tube stations. (Notting Hill Gate is in the central zone and on the Circle Line, handier and 40p cheaper from anywhere in the center than the Holland Park station.)

Vicarage Private Hotel is understandably popular. Family-run and elegantly British in a quiet, classy neighborhood, it has 19 rooms furnished with taste and quality, lots of stairs, a TV lounge, and facilities on each floor. Martin, Mandy, and Jim maintain a homey and caring atmosphere. Reserve long in advance with a one-night deposit. You won't find a better room for the price (S-£40, D-£62, T-£77, Q-£86, a six-minute walk from the Notting Hill Gate and High Street Kensington tube stations, near Kensington Palace at 10 Vicarage Gate, Kensington, W8 4AG, tel. 0171/229-4030, fax 0171/792-5989, web site:

London, Notting Hill Gate Neighborhood

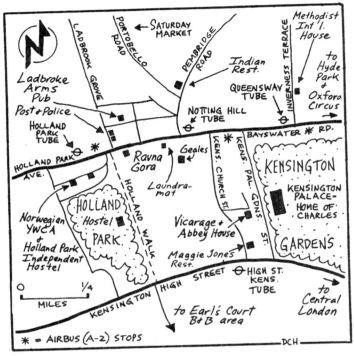

www.londonvicaragehotel.com). **Abbey House Hotel**, next door, is similar but has no lounge and is a bit less cozy (S-£38, D-£60, T-£74, Q-£86, Quint-£96, 11 Vicarage Gate, Kensington, W8 4AG, tel. 0171/727-2594).

    The Ravna Gora Hotel was formerly the mansion of 18th-century architect Henry Holland. Now it's a large Slavic-run B&B—eccentric and well-worn, but handy for the price. Manda and Rijko offer a royal TV room and a good English breakfast. It has plain, tired rooms, bags of laundry in the halls, a creaky spiral staircase, easy parking, and a Balkan ambience (S-£30, D-£50, Db-£60, T-£60, Tb-£72, Q-£76, Qb-£88, CC:VM, 50 yards from Holland Park tube station, facing but set back from a busy road, 29 Holland Park Avenue, W11 3RW, tel. 0171/727-7725, fax 0171/221-4282).

    Westland Hotel is comfortable, convenient, and hotelesque. The spacious rooms come with a phone, hair dryer, and coffee-maker (Sb-£80, Db-£95, Tb-£120, Qb-£135, elevator, free garage, CC:VMA, reserve with a credit card, 154 Bayswater Road, W2 4HP, tel. 0171/229-9191, fax 0171/727-1054). A block away, their **Westland Annex** offers bigger, plainer, quieter, cheaper rooms (Sb-£66, Db-£81, family deals also, same front desk and breakfast room as hotel).

Methodist International Center is a Christian residence filled mostly with Asian and African students. It's a great worldwide dorm experience at a price that will bolster your faith. The smoke-free rooms are studious, with a desk and reading lamp. The atmosphere is friendly, safe, clean, and controlled, with a TV lounge and laundry facilities (S-£25, D-£44, T-£60, includes breakfast and a cafeteria dinner; near Bayswater tube and a block from Queensway tube on a quiet street, 2 Inverness Terrace, W2 3HY, tel. 0171/229-5101, fax 0171/229-3170). The Center will move in April near the Euston train station (tube: Euston Steet, call directory assistance at 192 for new phone number).

Norwegian YWCA (Norsk K.F.U.K.) is for women under 30 only (and men with Norwegian passports). It's an incredible value. Located on a quiet, stately street, it offers smoke-free rooms, a study, TV room, piano lounge, and Norwegian atmosphere. All rooms (except singles) have private showers. They have mostly quads, so those willing to share with strangers are most likely to get a place (July–August: Ss-£27, bed in shared double-£25, shared triple-£21, shared quad-£18, with breakfast. September–June: same prices but with dinner included. 52 Holland Park, W11 3R5, tel. & fax 0171/727-9897). With each visit I wonder which is easier—getting a sex change or a Norwegian passport?

Sleeping in Other Neighborhoods
Bloomsbury District (near the British Museum): Cambria House, a fine value, is run by the Salvation Army (a plus when it comes to cheap big-city hotels). This smoke-free old building with a narrow maze of halls is newly painted and super clean, if institutional. The rooms are large and perfectly good. There are ample showers and toilets on each floor, and a TV lounge (S-£25.50, D-£40, Db-£50, T-£60, CC:VM, north of Russell Square at 37 Hunter Street, WC1N 1BJ, tel. 0171/837-1654, fax 0171/837-1229).

Near St. Paul's: The **City of London Youth Hostel** is clean, modern, friendly, and well-run. You'll pay about £22 for a bed in two- to five-bed rooms (CC:VM, cheap meals, 36 Carter Lane, EC4V 5AD, tube: St. Paul's, tel. 0171/236-4965, fax 0171/236-7681).

South of town: Hotel Oakley is like a B&B in a fine neighborhood (S-£29, D-£39, Db-£49, CC:VMA, 73 Oakley Street, just off King's Road, bus to Sloane Square and then walk, tel. 0171/352-5599). **Mary Ward's Guest House** is sleepable but very simple. On a quiet street in a well-worn neighborhood south of Victoria near Clapham Common, this beats the hostel. Friendly Mary Ward (Edith Bunker's English aunt) has been renting her five super-cheap rooms to budget travelers for 25 years (S-£12.5, D-£25 with English breakfast, 98 Hambalt Road, Clapham Common, SW4 9EJ London, tel. 0181/673-1077). It's 15 minutes by tube to Clapham Common, then a short bus ride or a 12-minute walk—exit left down Clapham South Road, left on Elms, right on Abbeville Road, left on Hambalt.

Near Gatwick: The peaceful **Crutchfield Inn B&B** offers three comfortable rooms in a 500-year-old renovated farmhouse. Friendly Mrs. Blok includes a ride to and from the airport (Db-£60, 2 miles from Gatwick Airport, 30 minutes by train from London, at Hookwood, Surrey, RH6 OHT, tel. 01293/863-110, fax 01293/863-233). **Barn Cottage**, a converted 17th-century barn in a large garden, has quiet rooms ten minutes from Gatwick (S-£25, D-£44, Leigh/Reigate/Surrey RH2 8RF, tel. 01306/611-347, run by friendly Pat and Mike Comer). **Lynwood Guest House** is ten minutes by train from Gatwick Airport (and 30 minutes by train from London). It offers a cozy, friendly alternative to big-city lodging in Redhill, a normal workaday English town. It's just a five-minute walk from the train station, but the gracious owner Shanta may pick you up if she's got the car. Ask for a quiet room off the street (Ss-£24–28, Ds-£38–42, Db-£40–45, Tb-£54–58, Qb-£55–65, cheaper off-season, 50 London Road, Redhill, Surrey RH1 1LN, tel. 01737/766-894).

Eating in London

If you want to dine (as opposed to eat), check out the extensive listings in *What's On* (or the train schedule for Paris). The thought of a £25 meal in Britain generally ruins my appetite, so my London dining is limited mostly to unremarkable but inexpensive alternatives. I've listed places by neighborhood—handy to your sightseeing or hotel.

Your £5 budget choices are pub grub, a café, fish and chips, pizza, ethnic, or picnic. Pub grub is the most atmospheric budget option. Many of London's 7,000 pubs serve fresh, tasty buffets under ancient timbers, with hearty lunches and dinners priced around £5. Ethnic restaurants from all over the world more than make up for England's lackluster cuisine. Eating Indian or Chinese is "going local" in London. It's also going cheap (cheaper if you take out). Pizza places all over town offer £3.50 all-you-can-stomach buffets. Most large museums (and many churches) have reasonable and handy cafeterias. Of course, picnicking is the fastest and cheapest way to go. Good grocery stores and sandwich shops, fine park benches, and polite pigeons abound in Britain's most expensive city.

Eating near Trafalgar Square

For a tasty meal on a monk's budget in an ancient crypt sitting on somebody's tomb, climb down into the **St. Martin-in-the-Fields Café in the Crypt** (Monday–Saturday 10:00–19:30, Sunday 12:00–18:00, £5–7 cafeteria plates, cheaper sandwich bar, profits go to the church; underneath St. Martin-in-the-Fields on Trafalgar Square, tel. 0171/839-4342). Down Whitehall (toward Big Ben), a block from Trafalgar Square, you'll find the touristy but atmospheric **Clarence Pub** (decent grub) and several cheaper cafeterias and pizza joints. For a classy lunch, treat your palate to the pricier **Brasserie** (open daily, on first floor of Sainsbury Wing of the National Gallery).

Eating near Piccadilly

Hungry in the theater district? Head for Panton Street (just off Haymarket, about 2 blocks southeast of Picadilly Circus) where you'll find a line of decent eateries. **Stockpot** is a mushy peas kind of place and rightly popular for its edible, cheap meals (Monday–Saturday 8:00–23:00, Sunday 8:00–22:00, 40 Panton Street). I prefer the **West End Kitchen** (across the street at #5, same hours and menu, fine seating downstairs).

The palatial **Criterion Brasserie**, serving a two-course lunch menu for £15 under gilded tiles and chandeliers, is right on Piccadilly Circus but a world away from the punk junk (opens daily at noon for lunch—a better value—and again at 18:00 for dinner at splurge prices, tel. 0171/930-0488). The

Carvery serves a £15, all-you-can-eat meaty buffet with plenty of vegetables and a salad bar, Yorkshire and bread pudding, dessert, and coffee included—a carnivore's delight with concessions to vegetarians. Puffy-hatted carvers help you slice (daily 17:15–21:00, save £2 by arriving before 19:00, Regent Palace Hotel on Glasshouse Street, a few steps northwest of Piccadilly Circus, may close in 1998, call first at 0171/734-7000). The **Wren Café** at St. James Church is exclusively vegetarian, wonderfully green, and in a pleasant garden next to one of Wren's best churches—peek in (Monday–Saturday 9:00–17:00, Sunday 10:00–16:00, two minutes southwest of Piccadilly at 35 Jermyn Street, tel. 0171/437-9419).

Eating near Recommended Victoria Station Neighborhood Accommodations

A cluster of places a couple of blocks southeast of Victoria Station offers good values. **Jenny Lo's Tea House** is a simple, for-the-joy-of-good-food kind of place serving up £5 Cantonese meals to locals in the know (Monday–Saturday 12:00–15:00 and 18:00–20:00, 14 Eccleston Street, tel. 0171/259-0399). Her father runs a classy Chinese place around the corner. For pub grub with good local atmosphere, go down the street to the **Plumbers Arms** (serves filling £5 hot meals and cheaper sandwiches, closed Saturday and Sunday nights, indoor/outdoor seating, 14 Lower Belgrave Street, tel. 0171/730-4067; ask about the murdered nanny and the distraught wife who ran into the plumber's arms). Next door, the small but classy **La Campagnola** is Belgravia's favorite budget Italian restaurant (£10 meals, closed Sunday, reservations smart on Thursday and Friday, 10 Lower Belgrave Street, tel. 0171/730-2057). Across the street, the **Maestro Bar** is the closest thing to an English tapas bar I've seen with salads, sandwiches, and ten bar stools (very cheap).

Farther down Ebury Street, the **Ebury Wine Bar** offers a French, smoky ambience with the slight splurge (£10 meals, daily 12:00–14:30 and 18:00–22:30, 139 Ebury Street, at intersection with Elizabeth Street, near the coach station, tel. 0171/730-5447). Several cheap places are around the corner on Elizabeth Street (#23 for take-out or eat-in fish and chips).

The **Duke of Wellington** pub is good, if smoky, for dinner (£5 meals, 12:00–15:00 and 18:00–21:30, closed Sunday evening, 63 Eaton Terrace). **Peter's Restaurant** is the cabbie's hangout—cheap food, smoke, and chatter (end of

Ebury, at intersection with Pimlico). Nearby, the **Flamenco** has decent, if pricey, Spanish tapas (54 Pimlico).

For picnics, the nearest supermarket is **J. Sainsbury,** a five-minute walk from Victoria Station (Monday–Saturday 7:30–20:00, Sunday 10:00–16:00, on Victoria Street just after the intersection with Palace Street). The late-hours **Whistle Stop** grocery at the station has decent sandwiches and a fine salad bar. The **Marche** is an easy cafeteria a couple of blocks north of Victoria Station at Bressenden Place.

Halfway between Victoria and the Halls of Parliament, the venerable **Albert Pub** serves a traditional three-course carvery buffet in rare cut-glass Victorian splendor (£15 appetizer, lunch or dinner, all the meat and vegetables you want, dessert, and tea or coffee, 52 Victoria Street, tel. 0171/222-5577).

Eating near Recommended Notting Hill Gate B&Bs

Costas has Greek food and eat-in or take-out fish and chips (£5 meals, Tuesday–Saturday 12:00–14:30 and 17:30–10:30, near the Coronet Theatre at 18 Hillgate Street). Next door, the **Hillgate Pub** has good food and famous hot saltbeef sandwiches (daily 11:00–23:00, indoor/outdoor seating, tel. 0171/727-8543). The **Modhubon** Indian restaurant is not too spicy and has cheap lunch specials (Sunday–Friday 12:00–15:00 and 18:00–24:00, Saturday 12:00–24:00, 29 Pembridge Road, tel. 0171/727-3399). Next door is a cheap Chinese take-out (daily 17:30–24:00, 19 Pembridge Road) and the tiny **Prost Restaurant and Schnapps Bar** which busily keeps yuppie vegetarians as well as carnivores happy (£10 meals, Monday–Friday 17:30–23:00, weekends 10:30–23:00, 35 Pembridge Road, tel. 0171/727-9620).

The small and woodsy **Arc** at 122 Palace Gardens Terrace is popular and worth the moderate splurge (£10–15 meals, Monday–Saturday 19:00–23:15, indoor/outdoor seating, call ahead, tel. 0171/229-4024). The **Churchill Arms** pub is a local hangout with good beer and old English ambience in front and hearty £5 Thai plates on an enclosed patio in the back (Monday–Saturday 11:00–23:00, Sunday from noon on, 119 Kensington Church Street, tel. 0171/727-4242). **Pizza & Pasta** does basic Italian at 145 Notting Hill Gate. The **Ladbroke Arms Pub** serves country-style meals that are one step above pub grub in quality and price (daily 12:00–14:30 and 19:00–22:00, great indoor/outdoor ambience, 54 Ladbroke Road, behind Holland Park tube station, tel. 0171/727-6648).

The almost-too-popular **Geale's** has long been considered one of London's best fish-and-chips joints (£8 meals, Tuesday–Saturday 12:00–15:00 and 18:00–23:00, 2 Farmer Street, just off Notting Hill Gate behind the Gate Cinema, tel. 0171/727-7969). Get there early for a place to sit and the best selection of fish.

The very English **Maggie Jones** serves my favorite £20 London dinner. You'll get solid English cuisine with huge plates of vegetables by candlelight (daily 18:30–23:00, CC:VMA, 6 Old Court Place, just east of Kensington Church Street, near the High Street Kensington tube stop; reservations smart, tel. 0171/937-6462). If you're going to eat well in London, eat here.

For a picnic dinner, shop at the **Europe Superstore** (Monday–Saturday 8:30–23:00, Sunday 12:00–18:00, 50 yards west of Notting Hill tube station on Notting Hill Gate).

Transportation Connections—London

Flying into London's Heathrow Airport

Heathrow Airport is user-friendly. Read signs, ask questions. Most flights land at Terminal 3, but British Air lands at Terminal 4 (same services as Terminal 3, but no Tourist Information office). In Terminal 3 you'll find exchange bureaus (24 hours daily, okay rates, £3 fees), an airport terminal information desk (pick up a map and ask questions, but for the official TI, see below), car rental agencies (if you're renting a car, stop to confirm your plans), a £3-a-day baggage check desk, and a TI. The American Express desk, with better rates than the banks, is in the underground at Terminal 4.

Heathrow's TI gives you all the help that London's Victoria Station does, with none of the crowds (daily 8:30–18:00, a five-minute walk from Terminal 3, TI next to tube station, follow signs to the "underground"). If you're riding the Airbus into London, have your partner stay with the bags at the terminal. At the TI get a free map and brochures and buy a subway pass if you're riding the tube into London.

Buses from Heathrow: The National Express Central Bus Station offers direct bus connections to **Cambridge** (hrly, 3.5 hrs, £16), **Cheltenham** (6/day, 2 hrs, £19), **York** (3/day, 6 hrs, £32), **Gatwick** (2/hr, 1 hr), and **Bath** (9/day, starting at 8:35, 10:35, and so on; direct 2.5 hrs, £19, tel.

Heathrow and the Four Terminals

LEAVING HEATHROW:

HEATHROW PERIMETER RD

to London M·4

EXIT #

M·4

(15) (4) (3)

← to West   A·4

A·4 →

* NOT TO SCALE!

M·25 → (RING ROAD)

(14)

3

(airplane)

Tube to London (45 min)

to Southwest

(13)

2   4

M·3

(12)

DCH

0990-808-080). Or try the slick 2.5-hour Heathrow–Bath bus/train connection via Reading. Buy the £26 ticket at the desk in the terminal (credit cards accepted), then catch the twice-hourly shuttle bus to Reading (RED-ding) to hop on the express train to Bath.

Transportation to London from Heathrow Airport
By Tube: For £3.20 ("free" with £3.20 all-day-after-9:30 tube pass), the tube takes you 14 miles to Victoria Station in 45 minutes (6/hr, one change).

By Airbus: All my recommended hotel neighborhoods are on one of the two airbus lines (serving each terminal, £6, 2/hr, 5:00–20:00, buy ticket on bus, tel. 0181/400-6655). If you take A1, South Kensington is the third stop and Victoria Station is the last stop. On A2, the second and third stops cover Notting Hill Gate. The tube works fine, but with baggage I prefer the airbus—no connections underground and a lovely view from the top of the double-decker bus. Ask the driver to remind you when to get off.

By Taxi: Taxis from the airport cost about £30. For four traveling together this can be a deal.

Flying into London's Gatwick Airport
More and more flights, especially charters, land at Gatwick Airport, halfway between London and the southern coast. Trains shuttle conveniently between Gatwick and London's Victoria Station (4/hr, 30 min, £9).

Trains and Buses

For train schedules and fares for any journey in Britain, call 0345/484-950 from anywhere in Britain (from the States, tel. 011/44/345-484-950). Ask for the cheapest fare for your journey; if you want to book with a credit card, you'll be referred to the appropriate rail company's phone number. You'll save money on point-to-point train tickets if you purchase in advance: To get Apex fares buy seven days ahead (available for moderate-length or longer journeys); for Super Apex fares, buy 14 days in advance (for long journeys only). For more information, see Transportation in the Introduction. This is worth the savings and trouble only if you're willing to pin down dates for your longer trips.

London, a major transportation hub in Britain, has a different train station for each region. The train station you arrive at (or leave from) depends on where you came from (or where you're going). King's Cross covers northeast England and Scotland (tel. 0171/278-2477). Paddington covers west and southwest England and South Wales (tel. 0171/262-6767). For the others, call 0171/928-5100.

National Express buses are considerably cheaper than trains. (For a busy signal, call 0990-808080, or visit the bus station a block south of Victoria train station.)

To Bath: Trains leave London's Paddington Station every hour (at a quarter after) for the £28.50, 75-minute ride to Bath. Consider taking a guided bus tour from London to Stonehenge and Bath, and simply leaving the tour in Bath. Both Evan Evans (tel. 0181/332-2222) and Greenline (tel. 0181/668-7261) offer Stonehenge/Bath day trips from London.

To points north: Trains run hourly from London's King's Cross Station stopping in York (2 hrs), Durham (3 hrs), and Edinburgh (5 hrs). For Cambridge connections, see below.

To Dublin, Ireland: The boat/rail journey takes ten hours, all day or all night (£40–60). Consider a British Midland flight (Heathrow–Dublin, 10/day, 70 min, £95, cheaper Monday–Thursday, tel. 0345/554-554; or in the U.S.A., 800/788-0555).

Crossing the English Channel

By Eurostar Train: The fastest and most convenient way to get from Big Ben to the Eiffel Tower is by rail. Eurostar is the speedy passenger train which zips you (and up to 800 others in 18 sleek, TGV-type cars) from downtown London to downtown Paris (9/day, 3 hrs) or Brussels (5/day, 3 hrs) faster and easier than flying. The train goes 100 mph in England and 160 mph on the Continent. The actual tunnel crossing is a 20-minute black, silent, 100 mph non-event. Your ears won't even pop. Change at Lille to catch a TGV directly to Paris' De Gaulle Airport or Disneyland Paris. Yes!

Channel fares (essentially the same to Paris or Brussels) are good. The following prices are from 1997—for the latest fares, call 1-800-EUROSTAR. The "Leisure" ticket is cheap ($99), but you're out of luck if you miss the train (50 percent refundable up to two days before departure). The pricier "Full-fare" tickets are fully refundable up to 120 days after the purchase date. "Full-fare" first class costs $199 including a meal (a dinner departure nets you more grub than breakfast); second class (or "standard") costs $139.

While basic round-trip tickets cost double, round-trips over a Saturday cost $178 (50 percent refundable up to two days before departure). Discounts are available for travelers holding railpasses that include France, Belgium, or Britain (about $50 off), youths under 26 ($60 off), and children under 12 (half fare). Cheaper seats can sell out. You can book your ticket from the U.S.A. When you're ready to commit to a date and time, book an "instant reservation" through your travel agent. Prices do not include FedEx delivery.

In Europe, get your Eurostar ticket at any major train station (in any country) or at any travel agency that handles train tickets (expect a booking fee). In Britain, you can order your tickets over the phone with a credit card by calling 0345/303-030; pick up your tickets at London's Waterloo station an hour before the Eurostar departure.

By Train, Bus, and Boat: The old-fashioned way of crossing the Channel is very competitive and cheaper than Eurostar; it's also twice as romantic, twice as complicated, and twice as time-consuming. You'll get better prices arranging your trip in London than you would in the U.S.A. Taking the bus is cheapest, and round-trips are a bargain. By bus: £33 one-way, £49 round-trip, ten hours, day or overnight, on Eurolines (tel. 0990/143-219) or CitySprint (tel. 0990/240-241). By train and ship: £42 one-way overnight, £59 by day, seven hours.

By Plane: Typical fares are £90 regular, £40 student stand-by. Call in London for the latest fares.

NEAR LONDON: CAMBRIDGE

Cambridge, 60 miles north of London, is world-famous for its prestigious university. Wordsworth, Isaac Newton, Tennyson, Darwin, and Prince Charles are a few of its illustrious alumni. This historic town of 100,000 people is more pleasant than its rival, Oxford. Cambridge is the epitome of a university town with busy bikers, stately residence halls, plenty of bookshops, and proud locals who can point out where electrons and DNA were discovered and where the first atom was split.

In medieval Europe, higher education was the domain of the Church and was limited to ecclesiastical schools. Scholars lived in "halls" on campus. This scholarly community of residential halls, chapels, and lecture halls connected by peaceful garden courtyards survives today in the colleges that make the universities at Cambridge and Oxford. By 1350 Cambridge had eight colleges (Oxford is roughly 100 years older), each with a monastic-type courtyard and lodgings. Today Cambridge has 31 colleges. While a student's life revolves around his or her independent college, the university organizes lectures, presents degrees, and promotes research.

The university dominates—and owns—most of Cambridge. The approximate term schedule is January 15 through March 15, April 15 through June 8, and October 8 through December 8. The colleges are closed to visitors during exams, from mid-April until late June. But the town is never sleepy.

Planning Your Time

Cambridge is worth most of a day, but not an overnight. While Cambridge can be visited on your way from London to York, the cheap day-return train plan makes Cambridge easiest and economical as a side trip from London (from London's King's Cross Station, £12.30, 2/hr, 1 hr, fast trains depart at 15 and 45 minutes past the hour each way; the budget ticket requires a departure after 9:30 except Saturday and Sunday). You can arrive in time for the 11:30 walking tour (an essential part of any visit) and spend the afternoon touring King's College and the Fitzwilliam Museum, and simply enjoying the ambience of this stately old college town. Accommodations are frustrating.

Orientation (tel. code: 01223)

Cambridge is small but congested. There are two main streets separated from the river by the most interesting colleges. The town center has a TI, a colorful marketplace, and several parking lots. Everything is within a pleasant walk.

Tourist Information: The TI is on the town square (Monday–Friday 9:00–18:00 or 19:00, Saturday 9:00–17:00, summer Sundays 10:30–15:30, closed winter Sundays, tel. 01223/322-640).

Arrival in Cambridge: To get to downtown Cambridge from the station, take a 20-minute walk, a £3 taxi ride, or the easy, "City Rail Link" shuttle bus (80p, every eight minutes). Drivers use the huge, central Short Stay Parking Lot.

Sights—Cambridge

▲▲**Walking Tour of the Colleges**—A walking tour is the best way to understand Cambridge's mix of "town and gown." Walks give a good rundown on the historic and scenic highlights of the university, as well as some fun local gossip. (Walks are run by and leave from the tourist office. July and August tours start at 10:30, 11:30, 13:30, and 14:30; the rest of the year they generally start at 11:30 and 13:30.) Tours cost £5 and include admission to King's College Chapel. Drop by the TI early to reserve a spot. (If coming from London, try calling to leave your name or at least confirm that a tour is scheduled and not full.) Private guides are also available. Guide Friday hop-on and hop-off bus tours (£6.50, departing every 15 minutes) are informative and cover the outskirts, whereas walking tours go where buses can't: right into the center.

▲▲**King's College Chapel**—Built from 1446 to 1515 by Henrys VI through VIII, England's best example of Perpendicular Gothic is the single most impressive building in town. Stand inside, look up, and marvel, as Christopher Wren did, at what was the largest single span of vaulted roof anywhere—2,000 tons of incredible fan vaulting. Wander through the Old Testament via the 25 16th-century stained-glass windows (the most Renaissance stained glass anywhere in one spot—it was taken out for safety during WWII, then painstakingly replaced). Walk to the altar and admire Rubens' masterful *Adoration of the Magi* (£3, erratic hours depending on school and events, but generally 9:30–16:30). During term you're welcome to enjoy an evensong service (Tuesday–Saturday at 17:30, Sunday at 15:30).

▲▲**Trinity College**—Half of Cambridge's 63 Nobel Prize winners came from this richest and biggest of the town's colleges, founded in 1546 by Henry VIII. Don't miss the Wren-designed library with its wonderful carving and fascinating original manuscripts (free, Monday–Friday 12:00–14:00). Just outside the library entrance, Sir Isaac Newton, who spent 30 years at Trinity, clapped his hands and timed the echo to measure the speed of sound as it raced down the side of the cloister and back. In the library you can read Newton's handwritten account of this experiment, alongside the original, handwritten *Winnie-the-Pooh*.

▲▲**Fitzwilliam Museum**—Britain's best museum of antiquities and art outside of London is the Fitzwilliam. Enjoy its wonderful painting collection (Old Masters; an impressive English section featuring Gainsborough, Reynolds, Hogarth, and others; works by all the famous Impressionists), old manuscripts, and Greek, Egyptian, and Mesopotamian collections (free, antiquities open Tuesday–Friday 10:00–14:00, paintings 14:00–17:00; everything on Saturday 10:00–17:00 and Sunday 14:15–17:00; closed Monday; tel. 01223/332-900).

Museum of Classical Archeology—This museum offers a unique chance to see accurate copies (from 19th-century casts of the originals) of virtually every famous ancient Greek and Roman statue (over 600 statues, free, Monday–Friday 9:00–17:00, Sidgwick Avenue, tel. 01223/315-153).

▲**Punting on the Cam**—For a little levity and probably more exercise than you really want, try hiring one of the traditional (and inexpensive) flat-bottom punts from stalls near either bridge and pole yourself up and down (around and around, more likely) the lazy Cam. Once you get the hang of it, it's a fine way to enjoy the scenic side of Cambridge. After 17:00 it's less crowded and less embarrassing.

Transportation Connections—Cambridge

By train to: London's King's Cross or Liverpool Station (departures at 15 and 45 minutes past the hour, 60 min), **York** (hrly, 2.5 hrs, transfer in Petersborough), **Birmingham** (6/day, 3 hrs), **Liverpool** (5/day, 5 hrs), **Heathrow** (hrly buses, 3.5 hrs). Train info tel. 0345/484-950.

Route Tips for Drivers

By car, it's 60 high-speed miles (with no gas stations) on the
M11 motorway to London. From Cambridge, any major road
going west or south will direct you to the M11 motorway leading to the London ring road. Catch the poorly marked M25
outer ring road (you'll see Heathrow and Gatwick signs) and
circle around to the best position to start your central attack.
(You can buy a good London map at the Cambridge TI for
£1.) It's a four-hour drive to York (take the more interesting
A1 instead of the more tempting M1 motorway).

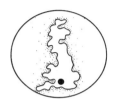

BATH

Any tour of Britain that skips Bath stinks. Two hundred years ago this city of 80,000 was the trend-setting Hollywood of Britain. If ever a city enjoyed looking in the mirror, Bath's the one. It has more "government-listed" or protected historic buildings per capita than any other town in England. The entire city, built of the creamy warm-tone limestone called "Bath stone," beams in its cover-girl complexion. An architectural chorus line, it's a triumph of the Georgian style. Proud locals remind visitors that the town is routinely banned from the "Britain in Bloom" contest to give other towns a chance to win. Bath's narcissism is justified. Even with its mobs of tourists, it's a joy to visit.

Long before the Romans arrived in the first century, Bath was known for its hot springs. What became the Roman spa town of Aquae Sulis has always been fueled by the healing allure of its 116-degree mineral hot springs. The town's importance carried through Saxon times when it had a huge church on the site of the present-day Abbey and was considered the religious capital of Britain. Things peaked in 973 when England's first king, Edgar, was crowned in the Abbey. Bath prospered as a wool town.

Bath then declined until the mid-1600s, when it was just a huddle of huts around the Abbey and a hot springs with 3,000 residents oblivious to the Roman ruins 18 feet below their dirt floors. Then, in 1687, Queen Mary, fighting infertility, bathed here. Within ten months she gave birth to a son . . . and a new age of popularity for Bath.

The town boomed as a spa resort. Ninety percent of the buildings you'll see today are from the 18th century. Local architect John Wood was inspired by the Italian architect Palladio to build a "new Rome." The town bloomed in the neoclassical style and streets were lined not with scrawny sidewalks but with wide "parades," upon which the women in their stylishly wide dresses could spread their fashionable tails.

Beau Nash (1673–1762) was Bath's "master of ceremonies." He organized both the daily regimen of the aristocratic visitors and the city—lighting and improving security on the streets, banning swords, and opening the Pump Room. Under his fashionable baton, Bath became a city of balls, gaming, concerts, and the place to see and be seen in England. This most civilized place became even more so with the great neoclassical building spree that followed.

Planning Your Time

Bath needs two nights even on a quick trip. There's plenty to do and it's a joy to do it. On a three-week British trip, spend three nights in Bath with one day for the city and one for a side trip to Wells, Glastonbury, and Avebury. Bath could easily fill another day. Ideally, you would use Bath as your jet-lag recovery pillow and do London at the end of your trip.

Consider starting a three-week British vacation this way:
Day 1: Land at Heathrow. Catch the National Express bus to Bath (departs nearly every hour, 2.5-hr trip). While you don't need or want a car in Bath, and most rental companies have an office there, those who pick up their cars at the airport can do Stonehenge (and maybe Salisbury) on their way to Bath on this day.

Day 2: 9:00, Tour the Roman Baths; 10:30, Catch the free city walking tour; 12:30, Picnic on the open deck of a Guide Friday bus tour; 14:30, Free time in the shopping center of old Bath; 16:00, Tour the Costume Museum.

Day 3: Pick up your rental car and tour Avebury, Glastonbury (Abbey and Tower), and Wells (17:15 evensong at the cathedral). Without a car, consider a one-day Avebury/Stonehenge/cute towns "Mad Max" minibus tour from Bath.

Day 4: 9:00, Leave Bath for South Wales; 10:30, Tour Welsh Folk Museum; 15:00, Stop at Tintern Abbey: then drive to Cotswolds; 18:00, Set up in your Cotswold home base (Stow or Chipping).

Orientation (tel. code: 01225)

Bath's town square, 3 blocks in front of the bus and train station, is a bouquet of tourist landmarks including the Abbey, Roman and medieval baths, and royal Pump Room.

Tourist Information: The TI is in the Abbey churchyard (walk 2 blocks up Manvers Street from the bus or train station and turn left, Monday–Saturday 9:30–19:00, Sunday 10:00–18:00, shorter hours off-season, tel. 01225/477-101). Pick up the 25p Bath map/mini-guide and the free, packed-with-info *This Month in Bath*, and browse through scads of flyers. There's an American Express outlet in the TI (decent rates, no commission on any checks, open seven days a week).

Arrival in Bath: The Bath train station is a pleasure (small-town charm, an international tickets desk, and a Guide Friday office masquerading as a tourist information service). The bus station is immediately in front of the train station. My recommended B&Bs are all within a ten- or 15-minute walk or a £3 taxi ride. For Brock House and the B&Bs on Marlborough Lane, consider using the Guide Friday city bus tour (described below) as transportation (5/hr, from Lane 1 of the bus station). Start the tour, jump out, check into your B&B, and hop back on to finish the circle. If you're driving, streets with no lines allow free unlimited parking.

Car Rental: Avis (behind the station and over the river at Unit 4B Riverside Business Park, Lower Bristol Road, tel. 01225/446-680), Budget (Brassmill Lane, tel. 01225/482-211), and Hertz (at the train station, tel. 01225/442-911) are all trying harder (consider hotel delivery, usually £8). Take the train or bus from London to Bath and rent a car as you leave Bath rather than in London.

Tours of Bath

▲▲**City Bus Tours**—The Guide Friday green-and-cream, open-top tour bus makes a 70-minute figure-eight circuit of Bath's main sights with an exhaustingly informative running commentary. For one £7 ticket, tourists can stop and go at will for a whole day. The buses cover the city center and the surrounding hills (14 signposted pick-up points, 5/hr in summer, hrly in winter, about 9:25–17:00, tel. 01225/464-446). This is great in sunny weather and a feast for photographers. You can munch a sandwich, work on a tan, and sightsee at the same time. The competing red Citytour buses (£5, family of five for

£12, tel. 01225/424-157) do basically the same tour but in 45 minutes and without the swing through the countryside, and pose the hard-to-answer question, "Why pay more?" Environmentalists ask an equally hard-to-answer question, "Why patronize these noisy hordes of street-clogging buses?"

▲▲▲**Walking Tours**—These two-hour tours, offered free by trained local volunteers who want to share their love of Bath with its many visitors, are a chatty, historical gossip-filled joy, essential for your understanding of this town's amazing Georgian social scene. How else will you learn that the old "chair ho" call for your sedan chair evolved into today's "cheerio" greeting? Tours leave from in front of the Pump Room daily at 10:30 (often at 14:00 and 19:00, May–October). For Ghost Walks and Bizarre Bath Comedy Walks, see Evening Entertainment, below.

Sights—Bath
▲▲▲**Roman and Medieval Baths**—Back in ancient Roman times, high society enjoyed the mineral springs at Bath. From Londinium, Romans traveled so often to Aquae Sulis, as the city was called, to "take a bath" that finally it became known simply as Bath. Today a fine Roman museum surrounds the ancient bath. The museum, with its well-documented displays, is a one-way system leading you past Roman artifacts, mosaics, a temple pediment, and the actual mouth of the spring piled high with Roman pennies. Enjoy some quality time looking into the eyes of Minerva, goddess of the hot springs. The included self-guided tour audio-wand makes the visit easy and plenty informative. Indepth 40-minute tours leave from the end of the museum at the edge of the actual bath for those with a big appetite for Roman history (included, on the hour, a poolside clock is set for the next departure time). You can revisit the museum after the tour. (£6, £8 "combo" ticket includes Costume Museum, a family combo costs £20, daily 9:00–18:00; in August also 20:00–22:00; slightly shorter hours off-season, tel. 01225/477-000.)

▲**Pump Room**—After a centuries-long cold spell, Bath was reheated when the previously barren Queen Mary bathed here and in due course bore a male heir to the throne (1687). Once Bath was back on the aristocratic map, high society soon turned the place into one big pleasure palace. The Pump Room, an elegant Georgian hall just above the Roman baths,

Bath

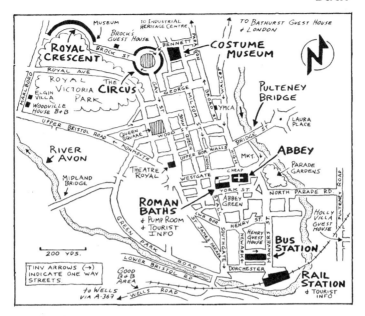

offers the visitor's best chance to raise a pinky in this Chippendale elegance. Drop by to sip coffee or tea to the rhythm of a string trio (tea/coffee and pastry for £3, live music all year 10:30–13:00, summers until 17:00). Above the newspaper table and sedan chairs a statue of Beau Nash himself sniffles down at you. Now's your chance to have a famous (but forgettable) "Bath bun" and split (and spit) a 45p drink of the awfully curative water. The Pump Room's toilets are open to the discreet public.

A quarter of a million gallons of mineral water still bubble through the spa daily. And in 2001 a new spa facility will be opened for the public to once again bathe in Bath.

▲ **Abbey**—Bath town wasn't much in the Middle Ages. But an important church has stood on this spot since Anglo-Saxon times. In 973, Edgar, the first king of England, was crowned here. Dominating the town center, the present church—the last great medieval church of England—is 500 years old and a fine example of Late Perpendicular Gothic, with breezy fan vaulting and enough stained glass to earn it the nickname "Lantern of the West" (Monday–Saturday 9:00–18:00, shorter hours on Sunday, concert and evensong schedule posted on the door, worth the £1.50 donation, handy flier narrates a 19-stop tour). **The Heritage Vaults**, within the abbey, is a small but interesting exhibit telling the story of Christianity in Bath since Roman times (£2, Monday–Saturday 10:00–16:00, closed Sunday). From the Abbey Green square, take a moment to really appreciate the Abbey's architecture.

Pulteney Bridge and Boats—Bath is inclined to compare its shop-lined bridge to Florence's Ponte Vecchio. That's pushing it. But to best enjoy a sunny Bath kind of day, pay £1 to go into the Parade Gardens below the bridge (free after 20:00). Across the bridge at Pulteney Weir, tour boats run cruises from under the bridge (£3.50, 50 minutes to Bathampton and back, one boat stops there if you'd like to walk back, the other company has a sundeck ideal for picnics).

▲▲**Royal Crescent and The Circus**—If Bath is an architectural cancan, these are the kickers. These first elegant Georgian (that's British for "neoclassical," from the 1770s) "condos" by John Wood (the Elder and the Younger) are well-explained in the city walking tours. The museum at #1 Royal Crescent offers your best look into a period house. It's worth the £3.50 admission to get behind one of those classy exteriors (Tuesday–Sunday 10:30–17:00, closed Monday, "no stiletto heels, please," tel. 01225/428-126). Stroll the Crescent after dark. Pretend you're rich. Pretend you're poor. Poke into the unmarked Royal Crescent Hotel (center door, big-name paintings in lounges near entry) consider a splurge in its elegant Old World restaurant. Study the cute little rooms below each entry walk. Notice the "ha ha fence," a drop in the front yard offering an invisible (from the windows) barrier to sheep and peasants.

▲▲▲**Costume Museum**—One of Europe's great museums, displaying 400 years of fashion—from Anne Boleyn to Twiigy—one frilly decade at a time, is housed in Bath's elegant Assembly Rooms. Follow the included and excellent radio phone "wand" self-guided tour. Learn why Yankee Doodle "stuck a feather in his cap and called it macaroni," and much more (£3.70, cheaper on combo ticket with Roman Baths, Monday–Saturday 10:00–17:00, Sunday 11:00–17:00, last admission at 16:30, tel. 01225/477-789).

▲▲**Industrial Heritage Centre**—This is the grand title for Mr. Bowler's Business, a turn-of-the-century engineer's shop, brass foundry, and fizzy-drink factory with a Dickensian office. It's just a pile of meaningless old gadgets until a volunteer guide lovingly resurrects Mr. Bowler's creative genius. Fascinating hour-long tours go regularly; you can join one in session. (£3.50, plus a few pence for a glass of genuine Victorian lemonade, daily 10:00–17:00, weekends only in winter, 2 blocks up Russel Street from the Assembly Rooms, call to be sure a volunteer is available to give a tour, tel. 01225/318-348.) There's a Bath stone exhibit downstairs and a café/shop upstairs.

Small Special-Interest Museums—The **Building of Bath Museum** offers a fascinating look behind the scenes at how the Georgian city was actually built. This is just one large room of exhibits but those interested in construction will find it worth the £3 (Tuesday–Sunday 10:30–17:00, closed Monday, near the Circus on a street called "the Paragon," tel. 01225/333-895). **Royal Photographic Society**, a hit with shutterbugs, exhibits the earliest cameras and photos and their development, along with temporary contemporary exhibits (£3, daily 9:30–17:30, tel. 01225/462-841).

▲**American Museum**—I know, you need this in Bath like you need a Big Mac. But this museum offers a fascinating look at colonial and early-American lifestyles. Each of 18 completely furnished rooms (from the 1600s to the 1800s) is hosted by an eager guide waiting to fill you in on the candles, maps, bedpans, and various religious sects that make domestic Yankee history surprisingly interesting. One room is a quilter's nirvana (£5, Tuesday–Sunday 14:00–17:00, closed Monday and November–March, at Claverton Manor, tel. 01225/460-503). The museum is outside of town and a headache to reach if you don't have a car (15-minute walk from the Guide Friday stop or a ten-minute walk from bus #18).

Walking, Biking, and Swimming—The TI has a brochure describing options. Consider the idyllic walk up the canal path to Bathampton (from downtown, walk over Pulteney Bridge, through Sydney Gardens, turn left on canal, and in 30 minutes you'll hit Bathampton with its much-loved old George pub). The Bath skyline walk is a 6-mile wander around the hills surrounding Bath (75p leaflet available at TI). Consider taking the river cruise up to Bathampton and walking back (see Pulteney Bridge and Boats, above). From Bathampton it's another two hours along the canal to the fine old town of Bradford-on-Avon, from which a train can zip you back to Bath. You could rent a bike from behind the Bath train station (£9/half day, £14/all day, tel. 01225/442-442) and bike this route. The scenic 12-mile bridle/biking/walking path along the old Bath–Bristol train tracks is also popular. The Bath Sports and Leisure Centre has a swimming pool and more (£2, just across the North Parade Bridge, 8:00–22:00, call for free swim times, tel. 01225/462-563).

Shopping—There's great browsing between the Abbey and the Assembly Rooms. Shops close at 17:30, later on Thursday. Interested in antiques? You'll find the most stalls open on Wednesday. For the best deal, pick up the local paper (usually out on Friday) and shop with the dealers at estate sales and auctions listed in the "What's On" section.

Evening Entertainment

This Month in Bath (available at the TI and many B&Bs) lists events and evening entertainment.

Plays: The Theatre Royal, newly restored and one of England's loveliest, offers a busy schedule of London West End–type plays, including many "pre-London" dress rehearsal runs (£7–14, cheap stand-by tickets, tel. 01225/448-844). You can often get late cancellation seats for sold-out performances (drop by around 18:00).

Bizarre Bath and other walks: For a walking comedy act—street theater at its best "with absolutely no history or culture"—follow JJ or Noel Britten on their very creative and entertaining Bizarre Bath walk. Their 90-minute "tour," which plays off local passersby as well as tour members, is a kick (£3.50, 20:00 nightly; heavy on magic, careful to insult all kinds of minorities and sensitivities, just racy enough but still good family fun; from the Huntsman pub near the Abbey, confirm time and starting place at TI or call 01225/335-124). Ghost Walks are another way to pass the after-dark hours (£3, 20:00, 2 hrs, unreliably Monday–Friday, tel. 01225/463-618). And for the scholarly types, there are almost nightly historical walks (19:00, 2 hrs, ask at TI).

Drinks: For a good spit-and-sawdust pub, drink real ale at the Star Pub (top of Paragon Street, Bass sold by the jug if you don't want to mess with pints). Or, for maximum entertainment, look up two particularly musical local residents, Van Morrison and Peter Gabriel.

Sleeping in Bath
(£1 = about $1.60, tel. code: 01225)
Sleep Code: **S**=Single, **D**=Double/Twin, **T**=Triple, **Q**=Quad, **b**=bathroom, **t**=toilet only, **s**=shower only, **CC**=Credit Card (**V**isa, **M**asterCard, **A**mex).

Bath is one of England's busiest tourist towns. To get a good B&B, make a telephone reservation in advance. Competition is stiff, and it's worth asking any of these places for a non-weekend, three nights-in-a-row, or off-season deal. Friday and Saturday nights are tightest (especially if you're staying only one night, since B&Bs favor those staying longer). There's a laundrette around the corner from Brock's Guest House on the cute pedestrian lane called Margaret's Buildings.

Sleeping near the Royal Crescent
Brock's Guest House will put bubbles in your Bath experience. Marion Dodd and her husband Geoffrey have redone their Georgian townhouse (built by John Wood in 1765) in a way that would make the famous architect proud. This charming house couldn't be in a better location, between the prestigious Royal Crescent and the elegant Circus (Db-£55–65, Tb-£75–80, family deals in a quad, reserve with a credit-card number far in advance, 32 Brock Street, BA1 2LN, tel. 01225/338-374, fax 01225/334-245). If you can't find a sedan chair, Brock's is a 15-minute uphill walk, £3 taxi, or short bus ride (to Assembly Rooms and short walk) from the station. Guide Friday buses stop on Brock Street. If you're in a transportation jam, Marion can occasionally arrange a reasonable private car hire.

At the **Woodville House**, Anne and Tom Toalster offer Bath's best cheap beds. This grandmotherly little house has three charming rooms, one shared shower, and a TV lounge. Breakfast is a help-yourself buffet around a big, family-style table (D-£33, minimum two nights, anyone who smokes at all is not welcome, closed January–mid-February below the Royal Crescent at 4 Marlborough Lane, BA1 2NQ, tel. 01225/319-335).

Elgin Villa, run by Richard and Christina Robinson, is also a fine value (Ds-£36, Db-£40, minimum two nights, kids £10 extra, four rooms, parking, non-smoking, 6 Marlborough

Lane, BA1 2NQ Bath, tel. 01225/424-557, fax 01225/425-
633). They serve a big continental breakfast in your bedroom.
  Other recommended B&Bs on Marlborough Lane:
Athelney Guest House (D-£36, three rooms, continental
breakfast, non-smoking, parking, 5 Marlborough Lane, tel. &
fax 01225/312-031, Sue and Colin Davies). **Parkside Guest
House** rents five classy Edwardian rooms (Db-£58, non-
smoking, 11 Marlborough Lane, tel. & fax 01225/429-444,
Erica and Inga Lynam). The **Marlborough House** is a Victorian place renting five rooms (tel. 01225/318-175, fax
01225/466-127).

Sleeping near the Train Station
Holly Villa Guest House, with a cheery garden and a cozy
TV lounge, an eight-minute walk from the station and center,
is enthusiastically and thoughtfully run by Jill McGarrigle
(D-£35, Ds-£40, Db-£46, T-£48, Tb-£60, Q-family deals,
seven rooms, strictly non-smoking, easy parking, cheap rooms
get the famous "loo with a view," 14 Pulteney Gardens, BA2
4HG, tel. 01225/310-331, fax 01225/339-334). From the city
center, walk over North Parade Bridge, take the first right,
then the second left. It's 1 block from a Guide Friday bus stop.
Ashley House B&B, two doors down, rents eight basic,
smoke-free rooms (small D-£32, D-£40, Db-£45, 8 Pulteney
Gardens, tel. 01225/425-027, Vanessa and Ron Pharo).

Sleeping in the Town Center
Henry Guest House is a clean, cheery, and vertical little eight-
room, family-run place 2 blocks in front of the train station on a
quiet side street (S-£17, D-£34, T-£51, TVs in rooms, lots of
narrow stairs, one shower and one bath for all, 6 Henry Street,
BA1 1JT, tel. 01225/424-052, Mrs. Cox). This kind of decency
at this price, centrally located, is found nowhere else in Bath.
Harington's of Bath Hotel, with 13 newly renovated rooms on
a quiet street in the town center, is run by Susan Pow (Db-
£65–85, family room deal, Sunday discounts, non-smoking, lots
of stairs, CC:VMA, extremely central at 10 Queen Street, tel.
01225/461-728, fax 01225/444-804). **Parade Park Hotel**, with
clean rooms and helpful owners, is centrally located (S-£30, Sb-
£45–50, Db-£55–65, family deals, non-smoking rooms available,
10 North Parade, BA2 4AL, tel. 01225/463-384, fax 01225/442-
322, Nita and David Derrick).

Sleeping near Pulteney Bridge

Kennard Hotel is a comfortable hotel with 14 charming Georgian rooms. Richard Ambler runs this place warmly, with careful attention to detail (S-£45, Db-£74–84, non-smoking, CC:VMA, just over Pulteney Bridge at 11 Henrietta Street, BA2 6LL, tel. 01225/310-472, fax 01225/460-054, e-mail: kennard@dircon. co.uk). **Laura Place Hotel** is another elegant Georgian place (eight rooms, two on the ground floor, Db-£60–90 from small and high up to huge and palatial, 10 percent discount with cash and this book, family suite, non-smoking, easy parking, CC:VMA, 3 Laura Place, Great Pulteney Street, just over Pulteney Bridge, tel. 01225/463-815, fax 01225/310-222, Patricia Bull). **Henrietta Hotel** is a very plain place in the same elegant neighborhood but with nearly no character (Db-£42–55, 32 Henrietta Street, tel. 01225/447-779, fax 01225/466-916).

Cheap Dorm Beds

The **YMCA**, institutional but friendly, and wonderfully central on a leafy square down a tiny alley off Broad Street, has industrial strength rooms and scuff-proof halls (S-£14.50, D-£26, T-£39, beds in huge dorms-£10, includes breakfast, discounts for two nights, families offered a day nursery for kids over five, cheap dinners, CC:VM, tel. 01225/460-471, fax 01225/462-065). **Bath Backpackers Hostel**, billing itself as a totally fun-packed mad place to stay, is an Aussie-run hostel 3 blocks up from the station renting bunk beds in six- to ten-bed co-ed rooms (£11 per bed with continental breakfast, non-smoking, no lockers, 13 Pierrepont Street, tel. 01225/446-787, fax 01225/446-305). The **Youth Hostel** is in a grand old building outside of town (£10 per bed without breakfast in two- to 14-bed rooms, bus #18 from the station, tel. 01225/465-674).

Eating in Bath

While not a great pub grub town, Bath is bursting with quaint eateries. There's something for every appetite and budget—just stroll around the center of town. A picnic dinner of take-out fish and chips in the Royal Crescent Park is ideal for aristocratic hoboes.

Eating between the Abbey and the Station

Evans Self-Service Fish Restaurant is the best eat-in or take-out fish-and-chips deal in town (Monday–Wednesday

11:30–18:30, Thursday–Saturday 11:30–20:30, closed Sunday, student discounts, 7 Abbeygate, tel. 01225/463-981). **Crystal Palace Pub**, with hearty meals under rustic timbers or in the sunny courtyard, is a handy standby (meals under £5, daily from 12:00–14:30 and 18:00–20:30, closed Sunday; children welcome on the patio, not indoors; 11 Abbey Green, tel. 01225/423-944). **Sally Lunn's House** is a cutesy, quasi-historic place for expensive doily meals, tea, pink pillows, and lots of lace (4 North Parade Passage). **Demuth's Vegetarian Restaurant** (next door, nightly, tel. 01225/446-059) serves good, three-course, £10 meals. **Eastern Eye** has tasty Indian food (daily 12:00–14:30 and 18:00–23:30, 8a Quiet Street, tel. 01225/422-323). **The Huntsman**, which was greasy before there were spoons, offers good, filling meals in a handy if tired setting (next to Sally Lunn's buns, tel. 01225/460-100). For very cheap meals, try **Spike's Fish and Chips** (open very late) and the neighboring café just behind the bus station.

Eating between the Abbey and the Circus

George Street is lined with cheery eateries (Thai, Italian, wine bars, and so on). **Guildhall Market**, across from Pulteney Bridge, is fun for browsing and picnic shopping, with a very cheap cafeteria if you'd like to sip tea surrounded by stacks of used books, bananas on the push list, and honest-to-goodness old-time locals. **Lovejoy's Café** serves light and veggie lunches (closed Sunday, upstairs in the Bartlett Street Antiques Centre). The **Green Tree Pub** is a rare pub with good grub and a non-smoking room, on Green Street (lunch only). **Pasta Galore** puts more energy into its fine Italian food than its ambience (daily 18:00–22:30, 31 Barton Street, good homemade pasta, call to reserve a table—avoid the basement, tel. 01225/463-861). Next door is a cheap and fast Mexican joint. **Devon Savouries** serves greasy, delicious take-out pasties, sausage rolls, and vegetable pies (on the main walkway between New Bond Street and Upper Borough Walls). The **Waitrose** supermarket, at the Podium shopping center, is great for groceries (open until 19:00 or 20:00, across from the post office on High Street). For a classy, intimate setting and "new English" cuisine worth the splurge, dine at **No. 5 Bistro** (main courses with vegetables £12–15, Monday and Tuesday are "bring your own bottle of wine" nights—no corkage charge, Monday–Saturday 18:30–22:00, closed Sunday, just over Pulteney Bridge at 5 Argyle

Street, tel. 01225/444-499). The **Bathtub Restaurant**, just around the corner on Grove Street, is cheaper (£8 meals) and funkier, serving international vegetarian cuisine (Monday–Friday 18:00–23:00).

Eating near the Circus and Brock's Guest House

Circus Restaurant is intimate and a good value with Mozartian ambience and candlelit prices: £15 for a three-course dinner special including great vegetables and a selection of fine desserts (daily, 34 Brock Street, tel. 01225/318-918, Felix Rosenow). **Woods Restaurant** serves modern English cuisine to well-dressed locals in a sprawling candlelit brasserie (£6 lunches, £16 three-course dinners, closed Sunday, 9-13 Alfred Street near Assembly Rooms, tel. 01225/314-812). If you want to dress up to eat, the **Royal Crescent Hotel Restaurant** is the classiest address in town (£15 lunch, £35 dinner, center of Royal Crescent, tel. 01225/739-955). On the opposite end of the decency spectrum, the **Chequers Inn** (2 blocks up the hill, 50 Rivers Street) is a smoky dive of a pub with cheap, finger-sticking, disgusting grub and darts.

Transportation Connections—Bath

To: London's Paddington station by train (hrly, 75 min, £28.50 one-way or round-trip) or cheaper by National Express bus (hrly, 3 hrs, £19 round-trip, £18 one-way, ask about £8 day returns). To get from London to Bath, consider using an all-day Stonehenge and Bath organized bus tour from London. For about the same cost as the train ticket, you can see Stonehenge, tour Bath, and leave the tour before it returns to London (they'll let you stow your bag underneath). Evan Evans (£29.50, tel. 0181/332-2222) and Greenline (£24, tel. 0181/668-7261) offer Stonehenge/Bath day trips from London. Train info tel. 0345/484-950.

London's airports: By National Express bus to **Heathrow Airport** (9/day, at 10:35, 12:35, 13:35, 14:35, 16:35, and so on, 2.5 hrs, £10, tel. 0990/808-080), and **Gatwick** (8/day, 4.5 hrs, change at Heathrow). Trains are faster but more expensive (hrly, 2.5 hrs, £22.50, see London Connections section for details). You can also take the tube from the airport to London's Paddington station, then catch the Exeter train to Bath.

The Cotswolds: By train to **Moreton-in-Marsh** (2.5 hrs, transfers in Didcot Parkway and Oxford). By National Express bus (tel. 0990/808-080) to **Cheltenham** (4/day, 2 hrs), **Stratford** (2/day, 3 hrs), and **Oxford** (3/day, 2 hrs).

Birmingham, points north: By train to **Birmingham** (hrly, 2.5 hrs, transfer in Bristol). From Birmingham, a major transportation hub, trains depart for **Blackpool, York, Durham,** and **Scotland**, or use a train/bus combination to reach **Ironbridge Gorge, North Wales,** and the **Lake District.**

NEAR BATH: GLASTONBURY, WELLS, AVE-BURY, STONEHENGE, AND SOUTH WALES

Oooo, mystery, history. Glastonbury is the ancient home of Avalon, King Arthur, and the Holy Grail. Nearby, medieval Wells gathers around its grand cathedral, where you can enjoy an evensong service. Then get neolithic at every Druid's favorite stone circles, Avebury and Stonehenge.

An hour east of Bath, at the Welsh Folk Museum, you'll find South Wales' traditional story vividly told in a park full of restored houses. Relish the romantic ruins and poetic wax of Tintern Abbey, the lush Wye River Valley, and the quirky Forest of Dean.

Planning Your Time

Avebury, Glastonbury, and Wells make a wonderful day out from Bath. Splicing in Stonehenge is possible but stretching it. Everybody needs to see Stonehenge. But I'll tell you now, it looks just like it looks. You'll know what I mean when you pay to get in and rub up against the barbed wire that keeps us at a distance. Avebury is the connoisseur's circle: more subtle and welcoming. Wells is simply a cute town, much smaller and more medieval than Bath, with a bombshell of a cathedral that's best experienced at the 17:15 evensong service. Glastonbury is normally done surgically, in two hours: See the abbey, climb the tower, ponder your hippie past (and your Gingrich future), and scram.

Think of the South Wales sights as a different grouping. Ideally, they fill the day you leave Bath for the Cotswolds. Anyone interested in Welsh culture can spend four hours in the Welsh Folk Museum. Castle-lovers and romantics will want to consider the Caerphilly Castle, Tintern Abbey, and Forest of Dean (each a worthwhile quick stop). See beginning of this chapter for a day-by-day schedule.

Bath Area

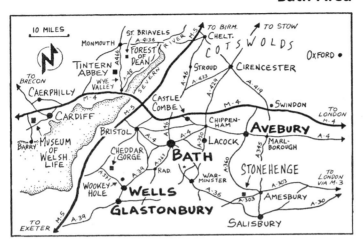

Getting Around near Bath

Wells and Glastonbury are easily accessible by bus from Bath; the Badgerline offers a "Day Rambler" ticket (£5, £10 per family, tel. 01225/464-446) and several day tours from Bath. You can get to South Wales by train via Bristol, connecting by bus from the Welsh train station to the various sights.

Avebury and Stonehenge are trickier. The most convenient and quickest way to see Avebury and Stonehenge if you don't have a car is to take an all-day bus tour. Of those tours leaving from Bath, "Mad Max" offers the cheapest and liveliest. Another way to get from Bath to Stonehenge is to take the train to Salisbury (£10 round-trip), then catch the Guide Friday bus (£7.50) from the Salisbury train station to Stonehenge.

Maddy Brookes runs all-day **"Mad Max" minibus tours** (£14, six–14 people). Her thoughtfully organized, informative, and inexpensive tours last from 8:45 to 16:40 and cover 110 miles with stops in Avebury, Stonehenge, and two cute villages—Lacock and Castle Combe. Castle Combe, the southernmost Cotswold village, is as cute as they come. Tours pick up passengers at 8:45 at the statue on Cheap Street (behind Bath Abbey). Maddy, an authority on the region's rich history and mystery, has taught her driver/guides well. To reserve a seat, call the Bath youth hostel (tel. 01225/465-674). Drivers can do a day loop from Bath to Avebury (25 miles) to Glastonbury (56 miles) to Wells (6 miles) and back to Bath (20 miles). A loop trip from Bath to South Wales is 100 miles, mostly on the 80-mph motorway. Each of the sights is just off the motorway.

GLASTONBURY

Marked by its hill, or "tor," and located on England's most powerful line of prehistoric sights (called a "ley" line), the town of Glastonbury gurgles with history and mystery.

In A.D. 37, Joseph of Arimathea carried vessels containing the blood and sweat of Jesus to Glastonbury; and with them, Christianity came to England. While this is "proven" by fourth-century writings and accepted by the Church, the Holy Grail legend which sprang from this in the Middle Ages isn't. Many think the Grail trail ends at the bottom of the Chalice Well, a natural spring at the base of the Glastonbury Tor.

In the 12th century, England needed a morale-boosting folk hero for inspiration during a war with France. The fifth-century Celtic fort at Glastonbury was considered proof enough of the greatness of the fifth-century warlord Arthur. His supposed remains (along with those of Queen Guinevere) were dug up from the abbey floor, and Glastonbury became woven into the Arthurian legends. Reburied in the abbey choir, their grave site is a shrine today.

The Glastonbury Abbey was England's most powerful in the tenth century. In the 16th century, Henry VIII, recognizing Glastonbury as a bastion of the church he fought, destroyed the abbey. For emphasis, he hung and quartered the abbot, sending the parts of his body to four different towns.

But Glastonbury rebounded. In an 18th-century tourism campaign, thousands signed affidavits stating that water from the Chalice Well healed them, and once again Glastonbury was on the tourist map. Today Glastonbury and its tor are a center for searchers, too creepy for the mainstream church but just right for those looking for a place to recharge their crystals.

Orientation (tel. code: 01458)

The tourist information office (daily 10:00–17:00, less in winter, tel. 01458/ 832-954) is on High Street (as are many of the dreadlocked folks who walk it). The Lake Village museum (in the TI) is nothing special. Tuesday is market day—a combo crafts, flea, and produce gathering behind the TI.

Glastonbury, quickly becoming "the windy city," has no

shortage of healthy eateries. The vegetarian **Rainbow's End** (next to TI, 17 High Street, tel. 01458/833-896) is a fine café for beans, salads, and New Age people-watching. If you're looking for a midwife or a male-bonding tribal meeting, check the notice board. If this all causes you to wonder if you need spiritual guidance or just an odd rune read, wander through the **Glastonbury Experience**, a New-Age mall at the bottom of High Street.

The Tor Bus shuttles visitors from the town center and abbey to the base of the tor, stopping at the Rural Life Museum and the Chalice Well (50p, 6/hr, 9:30–17:00 throughout the summer). Their brochure outlines a good tor-to-town walk.

Sights—Glastonbury

▲▲**Glastonbury Abbey**—The evocative ruins of the first Christian sanctuary in the British Isles stand mysteriously alive in a lush, 36-acre park. Start your visit in the museum where a model shows the abbey in its pre–Henry VIII splendor and exhibits tell the story of a place "grandly constructed to entice even the dullest minds to prayer." Today the abbey attracts people who find God within. Tie-dyed starry-eyed pilgrims seem to float through the grounds naturally high. Others lie on the grave of King Arthur, whose burial site is marked off in the center of the abbey ruins. The only surviving building is the conical Abbot's Kitchen (£2.50, daily 9:00–18:00, from 9:30 to dusk off-season, tel. 01458/832-267).

Somerset Rural Life Museum—The Abbey Farmhouse is now a collection of domestic and work mementos that illustrate the life of farmer John Hodges "from the cradle to the grave." Exhibits include peat digging, cider making, and cheese making. The fine 14th-century barn, with its beautifully preserved wooden ceiling, is filled with Victorian farm tools (£2, Tuesday–Friday 10:00–17:00, weekends 14:00–18:00, closed Monday, open Easter–October, free car park, tel. 01458/831-197).

Chalice Well—The well is surrounded by a peaceful garden. According to tradition, Joseph of Arimathea brought the chalice of the Lord's Supper to Glastonbury in A.D. 37. Even if the chalice is not in the bottom of the well and the water is red from rust and not Jesus' blood, the tranquil setting is one where nature's harmony is a joy to ponder. Have a drink. (£1, daily 10:00–18:00, in winter 13:00–16:00, free car park.)

Glastonbury Tor—Seen by many as a Mother Goddess symbol, the tor, a natural plug of sandstone on clay, has an undeniable geological charisma. The tower is the remains of a 14th-century church of St. Michael. A fine Somerset view rewards those who hike to its 520-foot summit.

Transportation Connections—Glastonbury
By bus to: Wells (2/hr, 30 min, tel. 01934/621-201) and **Bath** (hrly, 90 min). The nearest train station is in Bath.

WELLS
This wonderfully preserved little town has a cathedral, so it can be called a city. It's England's smallest cathedral city, with one of its most interesting cathedrals and more medieval buildings still doing what they were originally built to do than in any town you'll visit. Market day fills the town square on Wednesday and Saturday.

Tourist Information: The TI is on the main square (daily 9:30–17:30, in winter 10:00–16:00, tel. 01749/672-552).

Sights—Wells
▲▲**Wells Cathedral**—England's first completely Gothic cathedral (dating from about 1200) is the highlight of the city. The newly restored west front displays nearly 300 original 13th-century carvings (the Last Judgment and lots of kings).

Inside you're immediately struck by the general lightness and the unique "scissors" or hourglass-shaped double arch (added in 1338 to transfer weight from the west, where the foundations were sinking under the tower's weight, to the east, where they were firm). You'll be warmly greeted, reminded how expensive it is to maintain the cathedral, and given a map of its highlights.

Don't miss the fine 14th-century stained glass (the "Golden Window" on the east wall). The medieval clock does a silly but much-loved joust on the quarter-hour (north transept). The embroidery work in the choir (the central zone where the daily services are sung) is worth a close look. Walk the well-worn steps up to the grand fan-vaulted chapter house where the chaps (hence "chapter"?) of the church meet. The cathedral library (50p), with a few old manuscripts, offers a peek into a real 15th-century library. (The requested £3 donation for the cathedral is not intended to keep you out, daily

7:30–19:00 or dusk, 45-minute-long tours at 10:15, 11:15, 12:15, 14:15, and 15:15, good shop and a handy cafeteria, tel. 01749/674-483).

Lined with perfectly pickled 14th-century houses, the oldest complete street in Europe is **Vicar's Close** (just a block north of the cathedral). It was built to house the cathedral choir, and it still does. The mediocre city museum is next door to the cathedral. For a fine cathedral-and-town view from your own leafy hilltop bench, hike ten minutes up Tor Hill.

▲▲**Cathedral Evensong Service**—Weekdays at 17:15 and Sunday at 15:00, the cathedral choir takes full advantage of heavenly acoustics with a 45-minute entirely sung evensong service (boys' and men's voices, great pipe organ, you'll sit right in the old "quire;" note: generally not sung when school is out in July and August unless a visiting choir is performing, call 01749/674-483 to check). At 17:05 the verger ushers visitors to their seats. There's generally plenty of room. Unfortunately, the last bus to Bath is at 17:40 (and you can't leave the service early), so on weekdays those without a car or a bed in Wells can't enjoy this experience.

Bishop's Palace—Next to the cathedral stands the moated Bishop's Palace. While the grounds are nice and contain the idyllic spring that gave the city its name, for many the palace is not worth the time or money to tour (£3, daily in August 10:00–18:00; April–October Tuesday–Friday 11:00–18:00 and Sunday 14:00–18:00; closed in winter, tel. 01749/678-691).

Cheddar Cheese—If you're in the mood for a picnic, drop by an aromatic cheese shop for a great selection of tasty Somerset cheeses. Real farmhouse cheddar puts "American" cheddar to shame. The Laurelbank Dairy Company is a traditional cheese shop with all the local edibles (Monday–Saturday 9:00–17:30, closed Sunday, 14 Queen Street, tel. 01749/679-803). Ask for a pound's worth of the most interesting mix. The Cheddar Gorge (and the Cheddar Gorge Cheese Company which welcomes and educates guests) is just down the road.

Sleeping and Eating in Wells
(£1 = about $1.60, tel. code: 01749)
Wells is a pleasant overnight stop. The first two guest houses and the Fountain Inn are all within a block of each other behind the cathedral where the Bath road (A3139) meets the Shepton Mallet road (Tor Street, A371).

The **Tor Guest House**, with eight rooms in a 17th-century building facing the east end of the cathedral, is a good value (D-£40–45, Db-£45–54, cozy lounge stocked with great regional coffee-table books, breakfast room, quiet, non-smoking, car park, CC:VM, 20 Tor Street, BA5 2US, tel. & fax 01749/672-322, warmly run by Letitia Corray).

If that's too expensive, try Mrs. Woods' **Old Poor House**, a frumpy alternative in a 14th-century cottage next to the Fountain Inn (S-£18, D-£36, park in the triangle across the street from the Fountain Inn, 7A St. Andrew Street, BA5 2UW, tel. 01749/675-052).

Fountain Inn is great for pub grub (£6–10 meals, creative vegetarian meals, real ales, and draft cider, CC:V, behind the cathedral on St. Thomas Street, tel. 01749/672317). Their award-winning cheese plate lets you sample cheddar and its local cousins. For a good, traditional local dish, try Founders Beef Pie. The **City Arms Pub**, in the town center, is fun if you fancy grub in a former medieval jail (69 High Street, tel. 01749/673-916). **The Good Earth**, just off High Street, serves good healthy meals.

Transportation Connections—Wells
By bus to: Bath (hrly, 75 min, Badgerline Buses, tel. 01749/673-084), **Glastonbury** (2/hr, 20 min), **London** (£12, London Flyer departs daily except Sunday from Wells at 7:00 and from London at 18:00, 3 hrs, tel. 01934/616-000).

Sights—Near Wells
▲**Wookey Hole**—This lowbrow commercial venture, possibly worthwhile as family entertainment, is a real hodgepodge. It starts with a wookey-guided tour of some big but mediocre caves complete with history, geology lessons, and witch stories. Then you're free to wander through a traditional rag paper-making mill with a demonstration, and into a 19th-century circus room—a riot of color, funny mirrors, and old penny-arcade machines that visitors can actually play for as long as their pennies (on sale there) last. They even have old girlie shows. (£6.50, daily May–September 9:30–19:00, last ticket 90 minutes before closing, October–April 10:30–18:00, 2 miles east of Wells, tel. 01749/672-243.)

Scrumpy Farms—Scrumpy is the wonderfully dangerous local hard cider brewed in this part of England. You don't find it served in many pubs because of the unruly crowd it attracts. (The Beehive pub in Bath still serves its Scrumpy and seems to enjoy the consequences.) Scrumpy, 8 percent alcohol, will rot your socks. "Scrumpy Jack," carbonated mass-produced cider, is not real Scrumpy. The real stuff is "rough farmhouse cider." TIs list local cider farms open to the public, such as Mr. Wilkins Land's End Cider Farm—a great "back door" travel experience (Monday–Saturday 10:00–20:00, Sunday 10:00–13:00, in Mudgeley near Wells, 2 miles from Wedmore on the B3151 Glastonbury Road, tel. 01934/712-385). Glastonbury's Somerset Rural Life Museum has a cider exhibit. Apples are pressed from September through December. Hard cider, while not quite Scrumpy, is still West-country typical but more fashionable, decent, and accessible. You can have a pint drawn for you at nearly any pub.

AVEBURY

The stone circle at Avebury is bigger (16 times the size), less touristy, and I think more interesting than Stonehenge. You're free to wander among 100 stones, ditches, mounds, and curious patterns from the past, as well as the village of Avebury, which grew up in the middle of this fascinating, 1,400-foot-wide neolithic circle.

In the 14th century, in a kind of frenzy of religious paranoia, Avebury villagers buried many of these mysterious pagan stones. Their 18th-century descendants broke up the remaining stones and used them for building material. Today, the buried stones have been resurrected and concrete markers show where the broken-down stones once stood.

Take the mile walk around the circle. Visit the archaeology museum. Notice the pyramid-shaped Silbury Hill, a 130-foot-high, yet-to-be-explained mound of chalk just outside of Avebury. Nearly 5,000 years old, this mound is the largest manmade object in prehistoric Europe and a reminder that you've just scratched the surface of Britain's mysterious ancient and religious landscape.

The pleasant **Stones Café** serves healthy vegetarian meals and unhealthy cream teas (closed in winter, check out their mouth-watering £18 cookbook, next to the National Trust store, tel. 01672/539-514). The **Red Lion Pub** has good, inexpensive pub grub (also a B&B with three rooms, D-£35, Db-£40, CC:VM, tel. 01672/539-266).

For transportation connections, see Getting Around near Bath, above.

STONEHENGE

England's most famous stone circle, with parts older than the oldest pyramid, was built between 3100 and 1100 B.C. Many of these huge stones were brought all the way from Wales to form a remarkably accurate celestial calendar. Even today, every summer solstice (around June 21), the sun sets in just the right slot and Druids boogie. The monument is roped off, so even if you pay the £3.50 entry fee (which includes a worthwhile tape-recorded description) you're kept at a distance. Cheapskates see it free from the road. Stonehenge is open daily from 10:00 to 18:00.

For transportation connections, see Getting Around near Bath, above.

SOUTH WALES

▲**Cardiff**—The Welsh capital (pop. 300,000) has a pleasant modern center across from its castle. A castle visit is interesting only if you catch one of the entertaining tours (every half-hour). The interior is a Victorian fantasy.

▲▲**St. Fagans' Welsh Folk Museum**—This best look at traditional Welsh folk life displays more than 30 carefully reconstructed old houses from all corners of this little country in a 100-acre park under a castle. Each is fully furnished and comes equipped with a local expert warming herself by the toasty fire and happy to tell you anything you want to know about life in this old cottage. Ask questions!

A highlight is the Rhyd-y-Car 1805 rowhouse, which displays ironworker cottages as they might have looked in 1805, 1855, 1895, 1925, 1955, and 1985, offering a fascinating zip through Welsh domestic life. You'll see traditional crafts in action and a great gallery displaying crude washing machines, the earliest matches, elaborately carved "love spoons," an impressive costume exhibit, and even a case of memorabilia from the local man who pioneered cremation. Everything is well explained, although the £1.80 museum guidebook is a good investment.

The museum has three sections: houses, museum, and castle/garden. If the sky's dry, see the scattering of houses first. Spend an hour in the large building's fascinating museum. The castle interior is royal enough and surrounded by a fine garden,

but if you're tired it's not worth the hike. While the cafeteria
near the entrance (Vale Restaurant) is handy, you'll eat light
lunches better, cheaper, and with more atmosphere in the park
at the Gwalia Tea Room. The Plymouth Arms pub just outside
the museum serves the best food (£5.25, daily 10:00–18:00,
until 17:00 off-season, tel. 01222/573-500). City buses run frequently between Cardiff's central train station and the Welsh
Folk Museum (which is in the village of St. Fagans). Drivers
leaving the museum jog left on the freeway, take the first exit,
and circle back, following signs to the M4.

▲**Caerphilly Castle**—This impressive but gutted old castle is
the second-largest in Europe (after Windsor). With two concentric walls, it was considered to be a brilliant arrangement of
defensive walls and moats. Notice how Cromwell's demolition
crew tried to destroy it, creating the leaning tower of Caerphilly (£2.20, daily 9:30–18:30, shorter hours in winter, 9 miles
north of Cardiff, 30 minutes from the Welsh Folk Museum,
take train from Cardiff to Caerphilly—2/hr, 20 min—and walk
five minutes, tel. 01222/883-143).

▲▲**Tintern Abbey**—Inspiring monks to prayer, Wordsworth
to poetry, Turner to a famous painting, and rushed tourists to
a thoughtful moment, this poem-worthy ruined-castle-of-an-
abbey is worth a 5-mile detour off the motorway. Rent headphones (£1) for a tour that brings this richest abbey in Wales
to life. Founded in 1131 on a site chosen by Norman monks
for its tranquility, it functioned as an austere Cistercian abbey
from 1131 until its dissolution in 1536. (£2.20, daily
9:30–18:30, until 16:00 in winter, tel. 01291/689-251, five
buses/day from Chepstow, easy 15-min walk up to St. Mary's
church for a view of England just over the River Wye.) Visit
late to miss crowds.

The abbey's helpful TI (tel. 01291/689-566) and its shop
sell the useful Wye-Cotswolds map, the Welsh Tourist Board's
A Tourist Guide to North Wales, fine Celtic jewelry, and other
gifts. If seduced into spending the night, sleep in the 400-year-
old **Wye Barn B&B** (S-£20, Db-£42; no pets, smoking, or children, but still friendly; 200 yards from the abbey on the River
Wye bank; tel. 01291/689-456). Judith Russill, the village historian, has made this former abbey tannery quiet and comfy. She
serves a fine evening meal (£12.50, order in advance).

▲**Wye River Valley and Forest of Dean**—This land is lush,
mellow, and historic. Local tourist brochures explain the

Forest of Dean's special dialect, its strange political autonomy, and its oaken ties to Trafalgar and Admiral Nelson.

For a medieval night, check into the **St. Briavels' Castle Youth Hostel** (£9 beds in eight- to 12-bed dorms, members only, tel. 01594/530-272). An 800-year-old Norman castle used by King John in 1215 (the year he signed the Magna Carta), it's comfortable (as castles go), friendly, and in the center of the quiet village of St. Briavels just north of Tintern Abbey. For dinner, eat at the hostel or walk "just down the path and up the snyket" to the **Crown Pub** (decent food and local pub atmosphere).

Transportation Connections—Cardiff
By train to: Caerphilly (2/hr, 20 min), **Bath** (hrly, 90 min, transfer in Bristol), **Birmingham** (8/day, 2 hrs), **London** (hrly, 2 hrs), **Chepstow** (hrly, 30 min, 6 miles to Tintern by bus). Train info tel. 0345/484-950.

Route Tips for Drivers
Bath to South Wales: Leave Bath following signs for A4, then M4, then Stroud. It's 10 miles north (on A46 past a village called Pennsylvania) to the M4 super-freeway. Zip westward, crossing a huge suspension bridge into Wales (£3.70 toll westbound only). Stay on the M4 (not M48) past Cardiff, take exit 33, and follow the brown signs south to the Welsh Folk Museum. Tintern Abbey is 6 miles (up A466) off the M4 at exit 22, right where the big bridge hits Wales.

Cardiff to Cotswolds via Forest of Dean: On the Welsh side of the big suspension bridge, take the Chepstow exit and follow signs up A466 to Tintern Abbey and the Wye River Valley. Carry on to Monmouth and, if you're running late, follow the A40 and the M50 to the Tewksebury exit, where small roads will take you into the Cotswolds.

THE COTSWOLDS

The Cotswold Hills, a 25-by-50-mile chunk of Gloucestershire, are dotted with villages and graced with England's greatest countryside palace, Blenheim.

As with many fairy-tale regions of Europe, the present-day beauty of the Cotswolds was the result of an economic disaster. Wool was a huge industry in medieval England, and the Cotswold sheep grew the best wool. The region prospered. Wool money built towns and houses. Local "wool" churches are called "cathedrals" for their scale and wealth. Stained-glass slogans say things like "I thank my God and ever shall, it is the sheep hath paid for all."

With the rise of cotton and the industrial revolution, the woolen industry collapsed. Ba-a-a-ad news. The wealthy Cotswold towns fell into a depressed time warp, so poor that nobody even bothered to knock them down. Today, visitors enjoy a harmonious blend of man and nature—the most pristine of English countrysides decorated with time-passed villages, rich wool churches, tell-me-a-story stone fences, kissing gates you wouldn't want to experience alone, and the gracefully dilapidated homes of an impoverished nobility. Appreciated by hordes of 20th-century romantics, the Cotswolds are enjoying new prosperity.

Planning Your Time
The Cotswolds are an absolute joy by car (and a royal headache without one). With a car, on a three-week British

trip, I'd spend two nights and a day in the Cotswolds (sleeping in Stow or Chipping Campden). The Cotswolds' charm has a softening effect on many tight itineraries. You could spend days of enjoyable walking from a home base here.

One-day driver's 100-mile Cotswold blitz (including Blenheim; use a good map; reshuffle to fit your home base): 9:00, Browse through Stow; 10:00, Joyride through Bourton, the Slaughters, Guiting Power, Stanton, Stanway, and Snowshill; 13:00, Lunch and explore Chipping Campden; 15:00, Drive 30 miles to Blenheim Palace, take the hour-long tour (last tour departs at 16:45); 18:00, Drive home for pub dinner in home village.

Orientation

The north Cotswolds are best. Work-a-day Moreton-in-Marsh is the public transportation gateway to the region. Two of the region's coziest towns, Stow-on-the-Wold and Chipping Campden, are 4 and 8 miles, respectively, from Moreton. Any of these three towns makes a fine home base for your exploration of the thatch-happiest of Cotswold villages and walks.

Cotswold Appreciation 101

Much history can be read into the names of the area. "Cotswold" could come from the Saxon phrase meaning "hills of sheeps' coats." Or it could mean shelter ("cot" like "cottage") on the open upland ("wold").

In the Cotswolds, a town's main street (called High Street) needed to be wide to accommodate the sheep and cattle being marched to market (and today, to park tour buses). Some of the most picturesque cottages were once humble rowhouses of weavers' cottages, usually along a stream for their water wheels (Bibury, Castle Combe). The towns run on slow clocks and yellowed calendars. An entire village might not have a phone booth that accepts a telephone card.

Fields of yellow (rape seed) and pale blue (linseed) separate pastures dotted with black and white sheep. In just about any B&B, when you open your window in the morning you'll hear sheep baa-ing. The decorative "toadstool" stones that litter front yards throughout the region are medieval staddle stones. Buildings were set upon these to keep the rodents out.

Cotswold walls and roofs are made of limestone. The limestone roof tiles hang by pegs. To make the weight more

Cotswold Villages and Surroundings

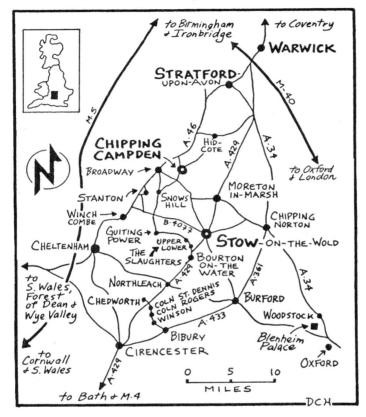

bearable, smaller, lighter tiles are higher up. An extremely strict building code keeps towns looking what many locals call "overly quaint."

The area is provincial and gossipy. People are ever so polite but commonly catch themselves saying, "It's all very . . . ummm . . . yyya." Rich people open their gardens to support their favorite charities, while the less couth enjoy "badger baiting" (a gambling cousin of cockfighting in which a badger, with his teeth and claws taken out, is mangled by right-wing dogs).

This is walking country. The English love their walks and vigorously defend their age-old right to free passage. Once a year the Rambling Society organizes a "Mass Trespass," when each of the country's 50,000 miles of public footpaths is walked. By assuring each path is used at least once a year, they stop landlords from putting up fences. Any paths found blocked are unceremoniously unblocked.

Questions to ask locals: Does badger-baiting survive? Who are the Morris men? What's a kissing gate? What's the latest on the 12th Duke of Marlborough?

Getting Around the Cotswolds

By Bus: Moreton-in-Marsh is the train traveler's gateway and a bus hub. Except for two main lines, buses within the Cotswolds are miserable (e.g., two per week). There's a good Moreton–Chipping Campden bus (5/day, 30 min) and a Moreton–Stow–Slaughter–Bourton–Cheltenham bus (10/day, 70 min). Moreton buses are generally timed to coincide with train arrivals.

By Bike: In Moreton-in-Marsh, Country Lanes Cycle Centre rents 21-speed bikes for £12 a day and offers bike tours (Easter–September Tuesday–Sunday 9:00–17:00, reserve ahead, tel. 01608/650-065).

By Foot: Walking guidebooks abound, giving you a world of choices for each of my recommended stops. Villages are generally no more than 3 miles apart and most have pubs that would love to feed and water you.

By Car: Several nearby car rental companies offer one-day £22 rentals (including all insurance and everything but gas, figure £5 for a taxi or delivery, tel. 0608/661-681, 0386/700-814, or 045/5303).

Car hiking is great. Distances are minuscule. I've covered the postcard-perfect (but discovered) villages. With a car and the local Ordnance Survey map you can easily ramble about and find your own gems. The problem with having a car is that you are less likely to hike. Try to taxi or bus somewhere so you can hike back to your car and enjoy the scenery.

By Taxi: Two or three taxi trips can make more sense than renting a car. While taking a cab cross-country seems extravagant at £1.20 per mile, the distances are short (Stow–Moreton is 4 miles, Stow–Chipping Campden is 10) and one-way walks are lovely.

By Tour: From Bath, take a Mad Max tour to Castle Combe, the charming southernmost Cotswold town. From Stratford, catch the Guide Friday tour (£15, 13:30–17:00, drive through 15 villages and stop in two, six-person minimum, departs from Civic Hall, buy tickets at Civic Hall or on bus, tel. 01789/294-466).

Sights—Central Cotswolds

▲▲**Stow-on-the-Wold**—Eight roads converge on Stow-on-the-Wold, but none interrupts the peacefulness of its main square. Stow-on-the-Wold (which means "meeting place on the uplands") has become a crowded tourist town; most, however, are day-trippers, so even summer nights are peaceful. Stow has no real sights other than itself, some good pubs, cutesy shops, and art galleries draped seductively around a big town square. At the TI on the main square (Monday–Saturday 9:30–17:30, less Sunday and off-season, tel. 01451/831-082), get the handy little 25p walking tour brochure called "Town Trail" (also sold at the hostel). A visit to Stow is not complete until you've locked your partner in the stocks on the green. For accommodations, see Sleeping, below. You can generally find a parking spot on the main square (free for two hours).

▲**Moreton-in-Marsh**—This town makes a fine home base for those without a car. It's Chipping Campden without the touristic sugar. Rather than gift and antique shops you'll find streets lined with real shops: ironmongers selling cottage nameplates and carpet shops strewn with the remarkable patterns that decorate B&B floors. A traditional market with 260 stalls filling High Street gets the town shinkicking each Tuesday. There is an economy outside of tourism in the Cotswolds and you'll feel it here. Moreton's tiny, sleepy station is 2 blocks from High Street, an unusually proficient—for the Cotswolds—tourist information office (Monday–Friday 9:00–17:00, offers luggage check, tel. 01608/650-881), and two fine B&Bs. For accommodations, see Sleeping, below.

Bourton-on-the-Water—I can't figure out if they call this the "Venice of the Cotswolds" because of its quaint canals or its miserable crowds. If you can avoid the midday and weekend crowds it's worth a drive-through, a few cynical comments, and maybe a short stop. It's easiest to enjoy after dark. The **Motor Museum,** whose owner, Mike Cavanagh, proudly greets you at the turnstile, shows off a lifetime's accumulation of vintage cars, old lacquered signs, a village life exhibit, threadbare toys, and pre-war memorabilia (£1.75, daily 10:00–18:00, in the Old Mill facing the town center, tel. 01451/821-255). Bourton is 4 miles south of Stow and a mile from the Slaughters.

Upper and Lower Slaughter—Lower Slaughter is a classic village with ducks, a working water mill, and usually an artist busy at her easel somewhere. Just behind the skip-able Old Mill Museum, two kissing gates lead to the path that goes to nearby Upper Slaughter. In Upper Slaughter walk between the yew trees (sacred in pagan days) down a lane between the raised graveyard (a buildup of centuries of graves) to the peaceful church. In the back of the fine graveyard, a wistful woman looks over the tomb of an 18th-century rector (sculpted by his son). By the way, "Slaughter" has nothing to do with lamb chops. It comes from "sloe" tree (the one used to make "sloe gin"). From Bourton, Guide Friday buses do a handy loop through Upper and Lower Slaughter (£3.50, 2/hr, handy for hikers who'd like to hop off here and on there). These towns are an easy one-hour round-trip walk from Bourton. You could also walk from Bourton through the Slaughters to Stow.

Sights—North Cotswolds

▲▲**Chipping Campden**—Ten miles north of Stow and less touristy, Chipping Campden is a working market town, home of some incredibly beautiful thatched roofs and the richest Cotswold wool merchants. Both the great British historian Trevelyan and I call Chipping Campden's High Street the finest in England.

Walk the full length of High Street (its width is characteristic of market towns) and around the block on both ends. On one end you'll find impressively thatched homes (out ugly Sheep Street, past the gas station, and right on Westington Street). Walking north on High Street you'll pass the Market Hall (built in 1627), the wavy roof of the first great wool mansion (the house of William Grevel, from 1380, on left), a fine and free memorial garden (on right), and, finally, the town's famous 15th-century Perpendicular "wool" church, down Church Street.

Chipping Campden's tourist office is opposite the town hall on High Street (tel. 01386/841-206, 10p town maps). Stop by the Guild of Handicrafts Museum on Sheep Street for an endearing look at Cotswold crafts from the late 1800s (downstairs) to today (upstairs). For accommodations, see Sleeping, below.

Stanway, Stanton, and Snowshill—Located between Stow and Broadway, these are my nominations for the cutest

North Cotswolds

Cotswold villages. Like marshmallows in hot chocolate, they nestle side by side, awaiting your arrival.

▲▲**Stanway House**—While not much of a village, Stanway is notable for its manor house. Lord Neidpath, whose family tree charts relatives back to 1270, opens his melancholy home to visitors on Tuesday and Thursday from 14:00 to 17:00 June through September, and maybe other times by appointment (£3.50, tel. 01386/584-469).

You'll buy your ticket at the 14th-century Tithe Barn (which pre-dates the manor and was originally where monks—in the days before money—would accept one-tenth of whatever the peasants produced). Peek inside—this is a great hall for village hoedowns.

While the Tithe Barn is no longer used to greet motley peasants with their feudal "rents," the lord still collects rents from his vast land holdings. But the place feels musty and poor, even though the lord has recently remarried.

Ask the ticket-taker (inside) to demonstrate the spinning rent collection table. In the great hall marvel at the one-piece oak shuffleboard table and the 1780 Chippendale excercise chair (half an hour of bouncing on this was considered good for the liver).

Guests wander through his office strewn with bills (you're welcome to play the piano) and rummage through centuries of oil-on-canvas, black-and-white, and Kodak moments. The manor dogs have their own cutely painted "family tree," but Lord Neidpath admits that his current dog, "CJ," is "all character and no breeding."

The place has a story to tell. And so do the docents stationed in each room—modern-day peasants who, even without family trees, probably have relatives going back just as far in this village. Really. Talk to these people. Probe. (Ask about the new wife. Ask what CJ stands for.) That's what they're there for. Learn what you can about this side of England. Like you do at a new friend's house, psychoanalyze his lordship by his books. You'll find titles such as: *The Last Tsar, The Medici of Florence, The Courtships of Catherine the Great,* and *The Enigmatic Edwardian.*

To get to Stanway, leave the B4077 at a statue of (Christian) George slaying the dragon (of pagan superstition); you'll round the corner and see the manor's fine Jacobean (17th-century) gate house.

Stanway and Stanton are separated by a great oak forest and grazing land with parallel waves echoing the furrows plowed by medieval farmers. Let someone else drive so you can sit on the roof under a canopy of oaks as you pass stone walls and sheep. The first building outside Stanway (on the left) is a thatched cricket pavilion overlooking the village cricket green. Dating only from 1930, it's raised up on rodent-resistant staddle stones, like in the Middle Ages. Stanton's just ahead.

▲▲**Stanton**—Pristine Cotswold charm cheers visitors down this village's main street. The church betrays a pagan past. Stanton is at the intersection of two lines of prehistoric sights (ley lines, you got me on my knees, ley lines). Churches like Stanton's, built upon a pagan holy ground, are dedicated to St. Michael. You'll see his well-worn figure above the door as you enter. Inside, above the capitals in the nave, find the pagan symbols for the sun and the moon. While the church probably goes back to the ninth century, today's building is mostly 15th century with 13th-century transepts. On the north transept, medieval frescoes weakly show through the 17th-century whitewash. Imagine the church interior colorfully decorated throughout. There's original medieval glass behind the altar. The list of rectors goes back to 1269. Finger the grooves in the back pews, worn away by sheepdog leashes. A man's sheepdog accompanied him everywhere. The popular Mount Pub is just up the hill (easy parking, indoor/outdoor seating, decent lunches, real ale).

▲**Snowshill Manor**—Another nearly edible little bundle of cuteness, Snowshill has a photogenic triangular square with a fine pub at its base. The Snowshill Manor is a dark and mysterious old palace filled with the lifetime collection of Charles Paget Wade (who looks eerily like the tragic young Lord Neidpath of Stanway House). It's one big, musty celebration of craftsmanship, from finely carved spinning wheels to frightening Samurai armor to tiny elaborate figurines carved by prisoners from the bones of meat served at dinner. Taking seriously his family motto, "Let Nothing Perish," Wade dedicated his life and fortune to preserving things finely crafted. The house (whose management made me promise not to promote as an eccentric collector's pile of curiosities) really shows off Mr. Wade's ability to recognize and acquire fine examples of craftsmanship. It's all very . . . ummm . . . yyya. The manor overlooks the town square but, ridiculously—or more likely, calculated to stoke business for the overpriced manor eatery—there's no direct town access (£5.40, April–October Wednesday–Monday 13:00–17:00, closed Tuesday and off-season, car park and shop are a pleasant 500-yard walk from the house, tel. 01386/852-410).

Broadway—Another very crowded town, worth a drive-through but not a stop. There won't be a parking place anyway (9 miles northwest of Stow).

▲**Hidcote Manor**—If you like gardens, the grounds around this manor house are worth a look. Follow your nose through a clever series of small gardens that lead delightfully from one to the next. Among the best in England, the gardens are at their fragrant peak in May, June, and July (£5.40, Saturday–Thursday 11:00–19:00, no entry after 18:00, closed Friday and off-season Tuesday, 4 miles northeast of Chipping Campden, tel. 01386/438-333).

Chastleton House—One of England's finest and most complete Jacobean houses has just opened its doors to the public. It's no longer lived in but lushly furnished to recreate the flavor of the day (£4.50, Wednesday–Saturday 13:00–17:00, 6 miles from Stow-on-the-Wold; to control crowds they require all visitors call between 9:30 and 12:30 for a visit time; tel. 01608/674-284).

Sights—South Cotswolds

▲**Cirencester**—Nearly 2,000 years ago, this was the ancient Roman city of Corinium. It's 20 miles from Stow down A429, which was called Foss Way in Roman times. In Cirencester (towns ending in "cester" were Roman camps), stop by the Corinium Museum to find out why they say, "If you scratch Gloucestershire, you'll find Rome" (£1.80, Monday–Saturday 10:00–17:00, Sunday 14:00–17:00; shorter hours and closed Monday off-season). The cutesy crafts center and workshops entertain visitors with traditional weaving, baking, potting in action, an interesting gallery, and a good coffee shop. Monday and Friday are general market days and Tuesday is cattle market day (TI tel. 01285/654-180).

▲**Bibury**—Six miles northeast of Cirencester, this is an entertaining but money-grubbing and not-very-friendly village with a trout farm, a Cotswolds museum, a stream teeming with fat trout and proud ducks, a row of very old weavers' cottages, and a church surrounded by rosebushes, each tended by a volunteer of the parish. Don't miss the scenic Coln Valley drive from A429 to Bibury through the enigmatic villages of Coln St. Dennis, Coln Rogers, Coln Powell, and Winson.

▲▲▲**Blenheim Palace**—Too many palaces can send you into a furniture-wax coma. Visiting one is enough … as long as it's Blenheim. The Duke of Marlborough's home, the largest in England, is still lived in. And that's wonderfully obvious as you prowl through it. (Note: Americans who pronounce the place "blen-HEIM" are the butt of jokes. It's "BLEN-em.")

John Churchill, first duke of Marlborough, beat the French at the Battle of Blenheim in 1704. So the king built him this nice home, perhaps the finest Baroque building in England. Ten dukes of Marlborough later, it's as impressive as ever. The 2,000-acre yard, well-designed by "Capability" Brown, is as impressive to some as the palace itself. The view just past the outer gate as you enter is a classic.

The well-organized palace tour begins with a fine Churchill exhibit centered around the bed in which Sir Winston was born in 1874 (prematurely...while his mother was at a Blenheim Palace party). Take your time in the Churchill exhibit. Then catch the guided tours (6/hr, 1 hr, included with ticket, £8, mid-March–October 10:30–17:30, last tour at 16:45, tel. 01993/811-325).

Kids enjoy the pleasure garden (a tiny train takes you from the palace parking lot to the garden, but if you're driving it's more efficient to simply drive there). A lush and humid greenhouse flutters with butterflies. A kid zone (£1) includes a few second-rate games and the "world's largest symbolic hedge maze." The maze is worth a look if you haven't seen one and could use some exercise.

Churchill fans can visit his tomb, a short walk away, in the Bladon town churchyard. The train station nearest Blenheim Palace is 4 miles away in Hanborough, on the Worcester–Oxford train line.

Blenheim Palace sits at the edge of the cute cobbled town of Woodstock. The grandmotherly **Wishaw House B&B** rents two big and comfortable rooms in a humble old house a five-minute walk from the palace (Db-£38, Browns Lane, tel. 01993/811-343).

Sleeping and Eating in the Cotswolds
(£1 = about $1.60)
Sleep Code: **S**=Single, **D**=Double/Twin, **T**=Triple, **Q**=Quad, **b**=bathroom, **t**=toilet only, **s**=shower only, **CC**=Credit Card (**V**isa, **M**asterCard, **A**mex).

Sleeping in Stow-on-the-Wold
(tel. code: 01451)
My first four listings are actually in Old Stow. The next three are across the highway, 300 yards from the square. The last two are quietest but a short drive away.

The Pound is the comfy, quaint, restored, 500-year-old, low-ceilinged, heavy-beamed home of Patricia Whitehead. She offers two bright spacious rooms with good twin beds and a classic old fireplace lounge (D-£34, non-smoking, right downtown on Sheep Street, GL54 1AU, tel. 01451/830-229).

Top of the Wold B&B has three spacious and well-appointed rooms on the third floor of a furniture shop overlooking Stow's market square (Db-£45, non-smoking, CC:VM, on the square just beyond the green, across from Queen's Head pub, tel. 01451/870-364, run by Mr. Whittock).

Stow Lodge Hotel, on the town square in its own sprawling and peaceful garden next to the church, is the best classy old-hotel value. Large, thoughtfully appointed rooms in the main building are quieter and have a bit more character than those in the annex (Sb-£55, Db-£80, Tb-£94, more expensive on Saturday, ground floor rooms in annex, non-smoking, CC:VM, GL54 1AB, tel. 01451/830-485, fax 01451/831-671). As in most Cotswold hotels, the prices are soft in case there's an opportunity for gouging.

The **Stow-on-the-Wold Youth Hostel**, on Stow's main square in a historic old building, has a friendly atmosphere, good hot meals, and a do-it-yourself members' kitchen. It's popular in summer so call ahead (£8 per bed with sheets, non-members £1.50 extra, eight–18 beds/room, closed 10:00–17:00, no lockers, CC:VM, tel. 01451/830-497).

West Deyne B&B, with a garden overlooking the countryside, has a grandmotherly charm (D-£34, evening tea and biscuits, Lower Swell Road, GL54 1LD, tel. 01451/831-011, Joan Cave).

The Limes B&B, is a comfy, modern home 2 blocks out of town on the Tewkesbury Road (D-£34, Db-£39, tel. 01451/830-034, Helen and Graham). The **Croyde B&B** is another fine option (D-£34, non-smoking, on Evesham Road, Stow-on-the-Wold, Cheltenham, GL54 1EJ, tel. 01451/831-711).

Tall Trees B&B, on the Oddington Road at the edge of Stow, is also good (D-£40, Db-£50, tel. 01451/831-296, Jennifer). **Holmleigh B&B**, in a farmhouse in the nearby hamlet of Donnington, rents the cheapest rooms around (D-£25, tel. 01451/830-792, Mrs. Garbett).

Fairview Farmhouse B&B feels more like a countryside mansion than a farmhouse. It's regally situated a mile outside Stow and comes with all the thoughtful touches (Db-40, non-smoking, just down the Bledington Road from Stow, tel. 01451/830-279, Susan and Andrew Davis).

Guiting Guest House, 6 miles west of Stow in the tiny village of Guiting Power, is my favorite sleepy-village alternative. Mrs. Sylvester rents modern, delightful doily rooms in her 400-year-old house (Sb-£28, Db-£48, CC:VM, Post Office Lane, Guiting Power, Cheltenham, GL54 5TZ, tel.

01451/850-470, fax 01451/850-034). If you're tired of pub grub, Yvonne serves a fine home-cooked dinner with the works for £15. Her husband, Bernie, is the local tourist board's B&B quality control man, so this place is either right on . . . or gets away with murder. Guiting Power is a great base for walking excursions.

Eating in Stow-on-the-Wold
Popular Stow is sprinkled with twee eateries. I've only listed basic pubs here. The formal but friendly bar in the **Stow Lodge** serves fine £5.50 lunches and £8 dinners (daily noon–14:00, 19:00–21:00). Next door, the more pub-esque **Queen's Head** serves an inexpensive decent meal and the local Cotswold brew, Donnington Ale (closed Monday).

Those with a car are likely to eat well at any of these pubs (all near Stow): **The Plow Pub** in Ford, **The Horse and Groom** in Upper Oddington (trendier than most pubs), **The King's Head** (in Bledington, moderate, closed Sunday), **The Plough** (in Cold Aston, a ten-minute drive from Stow), or **The Fox** (2 miles away in Oddington).

Sleeping in Chipping Campden
(tel. code: 01386)
These five places are small and right on High Street:

Campden Country Pine B&B, run by Frank and Jane Kennedy, offers four comfortable rooms decorated with antiques (Db-from £45, open Easter–December, non-smoking, near old church, High Street, Luysbourne, GL55 6HN, tel. 01386/840-315, fax 01386/841-740, e-mail: The Kettle@aol.com).

Sandalwood House B&B is a big, comfy, modern home with a royal lounge and a sprawling backyard, a five-minute walk from the center in a quiet woodsy/pastoral setting. Its two cheery pastel rooms are bright and spacious (D-£40–44, family deals, evening tea and biscuits included, non-smoking, GL55 6AU, tel. & fax 01386/840-091, well-run by Diana Bendall). Head south on High Street; at the church and Volunteer Inn turn right and right again; look for the sign in the hedge on your left, then head up the long driveway.

Dragon House B&B has two tight and tidy rooms run by a potter right on the center of High Street with parking and a fine garden (Db-£42, near market hall, tel. & fax 01386/840-734). **Sparlings B&B**, grandfather-clock tidy, (perhaps similarly musty) and run by the very proper Mr. Black and Mr. Douglass, is a not-quite-cramped 17th-century townhouse (D-£46.50, Db-£48.50, non-smoking, High Street, GL55 6HL, tel. 01386/840-505). **Badgers Hall Tea Room B&B** has two cozy medieval attic rooms ideal for very short people but over-priced (Db-£50 with breakfast and afternoon tea and cakes, non-smoking, center of High Street, tel. 01386/840-839). The cheap **Lygon Arms Hotel** is musty and dumpy but likely to have space when all else fails (D-£40, Db-£50, CC:VMA, High Street, tel. 01386/840-318).

Eating in Chipping Campden

Badgers Bistro serves good food for around £10 (non-smoking, in town center, on High Street). **Lygon Pub** serves old English..."cuisine" (not quite the right word). **Volunteer Pub** is good for cheap and smoky pub grub. In the Cotswolds House Hotel, the **Forbes Brasserie** (skip the formal Restaurant) has good food, quick service, and vintage Cotswolds photos on its walls (12:00–20:00). Vegetarians and carnivores alike love the **Baker's Arms** for dinner (can be smoky and crowded, slow service daily 18:00–21:30, live folk music every third Tuesday, indoor/outdoor seating, in Broad Campden, a mile out of Chipping Campden, tel. 01386/840-515). Since things change constantly, take your B&B host's pub-grub advice seriously. The one regional constant: Donnington is the best local real ale.

Sleeping in Broad Campden
(tel. code: 01386)

A tiny village locally famous for its Baker's Arms Pub, Broad Campden has several very well-run B&Bs (1 mile from Chipping Campden—addresses unnecessary, you'll see the signs, zip code: GL55 6UR).

Caroline Ashmore's **The Orchard Hill House** is a tastefully restored 17th-century farm with huge public rooms and a fun-loving atmosphere (D-£45, Db-£48, detached hayloft family suite-£57, children extra, non-smoking, from Chipping Campden drive past the pub and around the corner, tel. 01386/841-473). Janet Rawling's **Marnic House B&B** is also delightful with a cozy living room and prize-winning garden (Db-£42, non-smoking, tel. 01386/840-014, fax 01386/840-441). June Wadey's **Wyldlands** is a comfortable modern house with a breezy, relaxing mini-Hidcote of a garden (Db-£40, non-smoking, tel. 01386/840-478).

Sleeping in Moreton-in-Marsh
(tel. code: 01608)
There's a handy self-serve laundrette a block in front of the train station on New Road (Monday–Friday 7:30–20:00).

The Cottage is a 1620 cottage with low ceilings, an inglenooky lounge, and lots of character with no loss of comfort (S-£30, D-£36; charming, pastel, open-beamed "annex cottage" in the garden: Db-£45; non-smoking, 2 blocks from the station on Oxford Street, GL56 0LA, tel. & fax 01608/651-740, Lorraine and Richard Carter). The twin is quieter and more spacious than the front double. I'd pay extra to sleep with Peter Rabbit in the garden.

Acacia B&B, with four tight but clean and cheery rooms on the third floor, is friendly and very handy (S-£20, D-£36, Db-£40, less for longer stays and off-season, bunky family deals, non-smoking, on a quiet lane a block from the train station and a block from High Street, at New Road, GL56 0AS, tel. 01608/650-130, Dot and Mick Ellwood).

Townend Cottage and Coach House is a fun and funky place enthusiastically run by Chris and Jenny Gant (four small, cozy rooms, D or Db-£42, less off-season, non-smoking, fine garden, easy parking, end of High Street next to police station, GL56 0AD, tel. 01608/650-846).

Moreton House Guest House offers 11 basic rooms above an Old World lounge on the Stow end of High Street (S-£22, D-£42, Db-£48, CC:VM, High Street, GL56 0LQ, tel. 01608/650-747, fax 01608/652-747, run by the Dempster family).

The smoky **Redesdale Arms**, with dark and heavy carpets, is part of the Premier Lodge chain that has managed to give a classy old coaching inn the quality of a rundown American motel (Db-£43 without breakfast, CC:VMA, High Street, GL56 0AW, tel. 01608/650-308, fax 01608/651-843).

Eating in Moreton-in-Marsh
A stoll up and down High Street lets you survey your small-town options. Consider the **Marshmallow** (fun and basic) or the **Marsh Goose** (fine cusine but dressy and designed for big shots on expense accounts). The friendly Indian restaurant

(actually Bangladeshi), with tasty food, is a fine value, good for sit down or take-out (tel. 01608/650-798).

Transportation Connections—Cotswolds

Moreton by train to: London's Paddington Station (£19, £20 round-trip after 8:00, 10/day, 90 min), **Heathrow** (10/day, 2.5 hrs, train to Reading, shuttle bus to airport), **Bath** (10/day, 2.5 hrs, transfers at Oxford and Didcot Parkway), **Oxford** (10/day, 40 min). Train info tel. 0345/484-950.

Moreton by bus to: Chipping Campden (Castleways bus company conveniently connects with arriving trains and comes with chatty drivers, 5/day, 20 min, June–September, tel. 01242/603-715), **Stow** and **Bourton** (Pulhams, 5/day, 2 on Sunday, departs from a pub near city hall and from the station, tel. 01451/820-369), **Stratford-upon-Avon** (Barry's, round-trip 4 mornings a week, giving you 2 hours in Stratford).

Chipping Campden by bus to: Stratford (6/day, 1 hr).

Cheltenham by train to: Bath (hrly, 1 hr, easy change in Bristol), **Birmingham** (hrly, 45 min). Birmingham, a major transportation hub, is your jumping-off point for Ironbridge Gorge, North Wales, northern England, and Scotland. Bus info tel. 01452/425-543. Train info tel. 0345/484-950.

Drivers' Tips: Distances are wonderfully short (but only if you invest in the Ordnance Survey map of the Cotswolds— sold locally everywhere): Moreton to Broadway (10 miles), Chipping Campden (8 miles), Stratford (17 miles), Warwick (23 miles), Stow (4 miles).

NEAR THE COTSWOLDS: STRATFORD, WARWICK, AND COVENTRY

Shakespeare's hometown, Stratford . . . to see or not to see? A walking tour with a play's the thing to bring the bard to life in this touristy town. Explore Warwick, England's finest medieval castle, and stop by Coventry, a workaday town with a spirit that Nazi bombs couldn't destroy.

Planning Your Time

Stratford, Warwick, and Coventry are a made-to-order day for drivers connecting the Cotswolds with Ironbridge Gorge (IBG) or North Wales. While connections from the Cotswolds to IBG are tough, Stratford, Warwick, and Coventry are well served by public transportation.

Stratford is a classic tourist trap. But since you're passing through, it's worth a morning. (Don't spend the night.) Warwick is England's single most spectacular castle. It's very touristy but fun for three hours. Lunch in Warwick town. Coventry, the least important stop on a quick trip, is most interesting as a chance to see a real, struggling, north-English industrial city (with some decent sightseeing).

The area is worth only a one-day drive-through. If you're speedy, hit all three sights. If you're more relaxed, do Stratford and Warwick and get to your Ironbridge Gorge B&B in time to enjoy the evening ambience of that more interesting stop.

STRATFORD-UPON-AVON

Stratford is the most overrated tourist magnet in England, but nobody back home would understand if you skipped Shakespeare's house. The old town is compact with the TI and theater along the riverbank and Shakespeare's birthplace a few blocks off the river; you can walk easily to everything except Anne Hathaway's and Mary Arden's places. The river has an idyllic yet playful feel, with a park along the opposite bank, paddleboats, and an old, one-man, crank-powered ferry just beyond the theater.

Tourist Information: The TI has an American Express office and a town map that welcomes you in seven languages (Monday–Saturday 9:00–18:00, Sunday 11:00–17:00; off-season 9:00–17:00 and closed Sunday, tel. 01789/293-127).

Sights—Stratford-upon-Avon

▲Shakespeare's Birthplace—This half-timbered Elizabethan building is furnished as it was when young William grew up, and is filled with bits about his life and work. The attached Shakespeare Centre features costumes from the BBC's Shakespeare series. While William Shakespeare (1564–1616) was born in this house, he spent most of his career in London, where he taught his play-going public about human nature with plots that entertained the highest and the lowest minds at the same time. His tool was an unrivaled mastery of the English language. He retired—rich and famous—back in Stratford, spending his last five years at "New Place."

Little is known about Shakespeare the man. The scope of his brilliant work, his humble beginnings, and the fact that no original Shakespeare manuscripts survive raise a few scholarly eyebrows. But while some wonder who penned all these plays, most scholars accept his authorship (£3.60, Monday–Saturday 9:00–18:00, Sunday 10:00–18:00, closes at 16:00 in winter, in the town center—address unnecessary—follow the crowds).

▲**Four Other Shakespeare Properties**—Shakespeare's hometown is blanketed with opportunities for "Bardolatry." There are four other "Shakespearian properties," all run by the Shakespeare Birthplace Trust, in and near Stratford. Each comes with a garden and helpful docents who love to tell a story. **Anne Hathaway's Cottage**, a mile out of town in Shottery, is a picturesque thatched 12-room farmhouse where the bard's wife grew up. It has little to do with Shakespeare but offers an intimate peek at lifestyles in Shakespeare's day. Guides in each room do their best to lecture to the stampeding hordes. **Mary Arden's House**, the girlhood home of William's mom, is in Wilmcote, about 3 miles from town. This 16th-century farmhouse sees far fewer tourists, so the guides in each room have a chance to do a little better guiding. A 19th-century farming exhibit and a falconry demonstration are on the grounds. **Hall's Croft**, the home of Shakespeare's daughter, who married a doctor, is in the town. This fine old Tudor house, the richest house of the group, is interesting only if you're into 16th-century medicine. **Nash's House**, where the bard lived in retirement, is the least impressive of the properties. (Nash was the first husband of Shakespeare's granddaughter.) While Shakespeare's retirement home (**New Place**) is long gone, Nash's house has survived. It has the town's only general history exhibit—fascinating if you like chips of Roman pottery. All properties charge £2 to £3 each (pilgrims save money with a combo-ticket) and keep about the same hours (daily 9:00 or 9:30 to 17:00 or 17:30; off-season 10:00–16:00). Shakespeare's grave is in the riverside Holy Trinity Church (a ten-minute walk past the theater).

▲▲**Guide Friday Bus Tours**—These open-top buses constantly make the rounds, allowing visitors to hop on and hop off at every sight in town. The full circuit takes about an hour and comes with a steady and informative live commentary (£7.50, buses leave from the TI every 15 minutes from 9:30, less frequent off-season, tel. 01789/294-466). Guide Friday offers longer tours of the Cotswolds (£15, 13:30–17:00, drive through 15 villages with stops in two, six-person minimum, departs from Civic Hall, buy tickets at Hall or on bus, tel. 01789/294-466).

▲▲**Walking Tour**—A guided walk makes this historic but oversold town endearing. Mrs. Pat Bouverat gives a great walk for £20 (tel. 01789/269-890).

The World of Shakespeare—This is a gimmicky but fun look at Elizabethan and Renaissance England (£4, daily 9:30–17:00, later in July and August, 25-minute shows on the half-hour, between the big theater and bridge/TI next to McDonald's, tel. 01789/269-190).

▲▲**Royal Shakespeare Company**—The RSC, undoubtedly the best Shakespeare company on earth, splits its season between London and Stratford. If you're a Shakespeare fan, see if the RSC schedule fits into your itinerary either here or in London. Tickets range from £7 to £36 (Monday–Saturday at 19:30, Thursday and Saturday matinees at 13:30). You'll probably need to buy your tickets in advance, although 50 restricted-view and standing-room places are saved to be sold each morning, and returned tickets can often be picked up the evening of an otherwise sold-out show (box office tel. 01789/295-623, 24-hour ticket availability information tel. 01789/269-191). If you have a car, Stow and Chipping Campden are only 30 minutes from Stratford and an evening of classy entertainment.

Theater tours are given most days (£4, 13:30 and 17:30, not on matinee days). A huge collection of historical theatrical paintings is on display (Monday–Saturday 9:15–20:00, Sunday 12:00–17:00). Perhaps the most entertaining free thing to do in Stratford is to play in a bin of props left in the lobby of the Swan Theater.

Transportation Connections— Stratford-upon-Avon

To: London (£15, £18 round-trip, 4 trains/day, 2.5 hrs, direct from Paddington Station, maybe 9:18–11:27 or 11:18–13:24), **Chipping Campden** (3 buses/day, 1 hr, tel. 01788/535-555), **Warwick** (hrly, 15 min, by bus or train), **Coventry** (hrly buses, 1 hr, tel. 01788/535-555). There is a Stratford–Warwick–Cambridge bus service (£12, 3/day, 2.5 hrs, tel. 01223/423-900). Train info tel. 0345/484-950.

Driving is easy: Stow to Stratford (20 miles), Warwick (8 miles), Coventry (10 miles).

WARWICK AND COVENTRY

▲▲**Warwick Castle**—England's finest medieval castle is almost too groomed and organized, giving its hordes of visitors a decent value for the steep £9 entry fee. This cash-poor but enterprising lord hired the folks at Madame Tussaud's to wring maximum tourist dollars out of the castle. The latest marketing strategy is to build up the "kingmaker" reputation of the Earl of Warwick (WAR-ick).

With a lush, green, grassy moat and fairy-tale fornications, Warwick will entertain you from dungeon to lookout. Standing inside the castle gate, you can see the mound where the original Norman castle of 1068 stood. Under this "motte," the wooden stockade, or "bailey," defined the courtyard as the castle walls do today. Today the castle is a 14th- and 15th-century fortified shell holding an 18th- and 19th-century royal residence surrounded by another dandy "Capability" Brown landscape job.

There's something for every taste—a fine and educational armory, a terrible torture chamber, a knight in shining armor on a horse that rotates with a merry band of musical jesters, a Madame Tussaud re-creation of a royal weekend party with an 1898 game of statue-maker, a grand garden, and a peacock-patrolled, picnic-perfect park. The new "King Maker" exhibit (it's 1471 and the town's folk are getting ready for battle . . .) is highly promoted but not quite as good as a Disney ride. Be warned: The tower is a one-way, no-return, 250-step climb offering a view not worth a heart attack. The 80-minute cassette tape tour for £2.50 is informative but slow-moving. If you tour without its help, you'll find plenty of earnest and talkative docents (daily 10:00–18:00, sandwiches on sale in park, tel. 01926/406-600, 24-hour recorded message).

The Stables self-serve restaurant upstairs is much nicer than the cafeteria near the turnstiles. From the castle there's a lane that leads to the old town center, a block away, where you'll find the TI (tel. 01926/492-212) and several pubs serving better lunches.

▲**Coventry's Cathedral**—The Germans bombed Coventry to smithereens in 1940. From that point on, the German word for "to really blast the heck out of a place" was "to coventrate." But Coventry rose from smithereens, and its message to our world is one of forgiveness and reconciliation. The symbol of Coventry is the bombed-out hulk of its old cathedral with the huge new one adjoining it. The inspirational complex welcomes visitors. Climb the tower (180 steps). If you're touring the church, first see the 18-minute movie, *The Spirit of Coventry*, downstairs (£1.25 for the movie, plus a requested donation at the church door, Monday–Saturday 10:00–16:00, closed Sunday, tel. 01203/227-597).

Coventry's most famous hometown girl, Lady Godiva, rode bareback through the town in the 11th century to help lower taxes. You'll see her bronze statue a block from the cathedral (near Broadgate). Just beyond that is the Museum of British Road Transport—the first, fastest, and most famous cars and motorcycles came from this British "Detroit" (£3.30, daily 10:00–17:00). Browse through Coventry, the closest thing to normal workaday urban England you'll see. (TI tel. 01203/832-303.)

Route Tips for Drivers

Stratford to Ironbridge Gorge via Warwick and Coventry: Entering Stratford from the Cotswolds, you cross a bridge. Veer right (following "through traffic," "P," and "Wark" signs), go around the block turning right and right and right over the speed humps, then enter the multi-story garage (50p/hr, you'll find nothing easier or cheaper). The TI and Guide Friday bus stop are a block away. Leaving the garage, circle to the right around the same block but stay on the "Wark" (Warwick, A439) road. Warwick is 8 miles away. The castle is just south of town on the right. If the free castle lot is full you'll be directed to a city lot. You might lurk across the street until someone leaves. After touring the castle, carry on through the center of Warwick, following signs to Coventry (still A439, then A46). If stopping in Coventry, follow signs painted on the road into the "city centre" and then to cathedral parking. Grab a place in the highrise car park. Leaving Coventry, follow signs to Nuneaton and M6 North through lots of sprawl and you're on your way. If skirting Coventry, M69 (Leicester) leads to M6. The M6 threads through giant Birmingham. Try to avoid the 16:00–19:00 rush hour. From M6 (northwest), take M54 to the Telford/Ironbridge exit. Following the Ironbridge signs, you do-si-do through a long series of roundabouts until you're there.

IRONBRIDGE GORGE

The Industrial Revolution was born in the Severn River Valley. In its glory days, this valley (blessed with abundant deposits of iron ore and coal and a river for transport) gave the world its first iron wheels, steam-powered locomotive, and cast-iron bridge. The museums in Ironbridge Gorge (IBG) take you back into those days when Britain was racing into the modern age and pulling the rest of the West with her.

Planning Your Time

Without a car, IBG isn't worth the headache. Drivers can slip it in between Cotswolds/Stratford/Warwick and North Wales. For a short, reasonable visit, arrive in the early evening to browse the town and spend the morning and early afternoon touring the sights before driving on to North Wales (10:00, visitors centre; 11:00, Blists Hill Museum for lunch and sightseeing; 15:30, Drive to Wales).

Speed demons zip in for a midday tour of Blists Hill, look at the bridge, and speed out. With a month in Britain, I'd spend two nights and a leisurely day: 9:30, Iron Bridge and the town; 10:30, visitors centre; 11:30, Coalbrookdale Museum of Iron, lunch at Coalbrookdale Inn or Blists Hill Museum pub; 14:30, Blists Hill Museum.

Orientation (tel. code: 01952)

The town is just a few blocks gathered around the Iron Bridge, which spans the Severn River. While the smoke-belching bustle is long gone, knowing that this sleepy river valley was the Silicon Valley of the 19th century makes wandering its brick streets almost a pilgrimage. The actual museum sites are scattered over 3 miles. While the modern cooling towers that loom ominously over these red brick remnants (for coal, not nuclear energy) seem strangely appropriate, they're slated for destruction in 1999. Questions to ask a local: What's a tontine? What's a coracle?

Tourist Information: The TI is a block from the Iron Bridge (Monday–Friday 8:45–18:00, weekends from 10:00, off-season closing at 17:00, tel. 01952/432-166). In July and August an old-time shuttle bus connects all the sights. Otherwise, those without wheels are in for a walk.

Sights—Ironbridge Gorge

▲▲**Iron Bridge**—This first iron bridge was built in 1779, while England was at war with her American colonies, to show off a wonderful new building material. Lacking experience with iron, the builders erred on the side of sturdiness and constructed it as if it was made out of wood. The valley's centerpiece is free, open all the time, and thought-provoking. Walk along the tow path downstream.

▲▲▲**Ironbridge Gorge Industrial Revolution Museums**—Blists Hill admission is £6.50. Other sights are £3 or £4. The £9 combo ticket gets you into the seven sights, all of which have the same hours: daily 10:00–17:00, maybe until 18:00 in summer (tel. 01952/433-522 on weekdays, 01952/432-166 on weekends). Even though several of the sights may not be worth your time, seeing Blists Hill, the Visitors Centre, and the Museum of Iron costs £12.50 without the passport.

Start your visit at the **Iron Bridge Visitors Centre,** the orientation center in the Severn Warehouse (500 yards upstream, £2, 10:00–17:00, 18:00 in summer). See the ten-minute introductory movie, check out the exhibit and the model of the gorge in its heyday, and buy your guidebook and combination ticket. From the Visitors Centre parking lot, a tiny tour boat does a 45-minute, round-trip Severn River tour (£3.50, departs at the top of each hour; slow-moving taped commentary, peaceful photo opportunity for bridge, and lazy fisherman along riverbanks; tel. 01952/418-844). Farther upstream is the fine riverside Dale End park with picnic areas and a playground.

Save most of your time and energy for the **Blists Hill**

Ironbridge Gorge

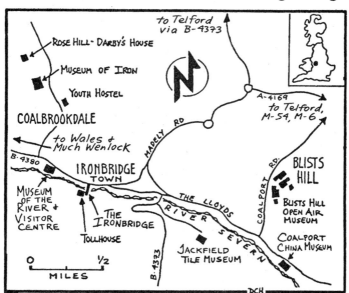

Open-Air Museum: 50 acres of Victorian industry, factories, and a re-created community from the 1890s, complete with Victorian chemists, an ancient dentist's chair, candlemakers, a working pub, a fascinating squatter's cottage, and a snorty, slip-slidey pigsty. Don't miss the explanation of the winding machine at the Blists Hill Mine. Walk along the canal to the "inclined plane" and have a picnic, or lunch in the Victorian Pub or the cafeteria near the squatter's cottage and old-time children's rides. The board by the entry lists which exhibits are staffed and lively. The £2 Blists Hill guidebook gives a good step-by-step rundown (admission is £6.50).

The **Coalbrookdale Museum of Iron** does a fine job of explaining the original iron-smelting process (£4). Across the way, Abraham Darby's blast furnace sits like a shrine inside a big glass pyramid (free), surrounded by the evocative Industrial Age ruins. This is where, in 1709, Darby first smelted iron using coke as fuel. If you're like me, "coke" is a drink and "smelt" is the past tense of smell, but this event kicked off the modern Industrial Age and this museum explains how. **Rosehill House**, just up the hill, is the 18th-century Darby mansion furnished as it was.

The **Coalport China Museum** and **Jackfield Tile Museum**, housed in their original factories, showcase the region's porcelain and decorated tile industries. These industries were developed to pick up the slack when the iron industry shifted away from Severn Valley. The museums feature finely decorated pieces and low energy workshops.

Skiing, Swimming, and Fishing—There's a small, brush-covered ski slope with two poma lifts in Madeley, 2 miles from Ironbridge Gorge; you'll see signs as you drive into IBG (£6.50/hr including gear, less for kids, open daily until 20:00 or 22:00, Telford Ski Centre, tel. 01952/586-862). There's a public swimming pool next door. The Woodlands Farm, on Beech Road, runs a private fishing business where only barb-less hooks are used and locals toss their catch back to hook again (kind of a fish Hell).

Sleeping in Ironbridge Gorge
(£1 = about $1.60, tel. code: 01952)
Sleep Code: **S**=Single, **D**=Double/Twin, **T**=Triple, **Q**=Quad, **b**=bathroom, **t**=toilet only, **s**=shower only, **CC**=Credit Card (**V**isa, **M**asterCard, **A**mex).

Hill View Farm is a peaceful, clean, friendly farmhouse B&B run by Rosemarie Hawkins while her husband John raises a "beef suckler herd." If you're looking for calm and country—Auntie Em-style—this is it, in a great rural setting overlooking the ruins of a 12th-century abbey (S-£16, D-£32; non-smoking, Buildwas, Ironbridge, Shropshire, TF8 7BP, tel. 01952/432-228). It's just outside of Ironbridge on the Much Wenlock road (A4169); pass the huge modern power plants, take a left over the bridge, and go about a quarter mile (sign on right).

If you like the country and Hill View Farm is full, try **Grove Farm House B&B** (S-£20, D-£34, Db-£38, less for two nights, non-smoking, 3 miles from IBG on road to Shrewsbury in Buildwas, tel. & fax 01952/433-572, Pat and Clive Pygott).

The Library House is "better-homes-and-gardens" elegant. In the town center, right across from the bridge, it's classy but friendly and a fine value. Chris and George Maddocks run a smoke-free place and their breakfast won a "healthy heartbeat" award (Sb-£40, Db-£50, Tb-£65, family price-£65, 11 Severn Bank, 1B, Shropshire TF8 7AN, tel. 01952/432-299, fax 01952/433-967, e-mail: libhouse@enta.net).

Severn Lodge offers three rooms in an 1832 captain-of-industry mansion with a garden and views of the lush hills (but not of the river where the sweatshops used to groan). This spacious place has all the hotel extras and easy parking. Playing by the tourist board rules, Nita and Alan Reed won the coveted "Deluxe" (top 1 percent) category—so rare, people don't even know it's a category (three rooms, Db-£52; from the Wharfage Cottage go 1 block up the skinny and steep New Road, Ironbridge, Shropshire, TF8 FAX, tel. & fax 01952/432-148).

Two places right in the town center overlooking the bridge, but with less character, are **Eley's Bridge View B&B** (five rooms, Db-£40, CC:VM, tel. & fax 01952/432-541, Jayne) and the big, musty, Industrial-Age **Tontine Hotel** (D-£38, Db-£52, CC:VMA, tel. 01952/432-127, fax 01952/432-094).

Hostels

Coalport Youth Hostel is a plush new hostel filling an old factory at the China Museum in Coalport (most beds are in quads but they have plenty of Ds for £20). On the other end of the Iron Bridge area, the **Ironbridge Gorge Youth Hostel**, built in 1859 as the grand Coalbrookdale Institute, is another fine hostel (a 20-minute walk from the Iron Bridge down A4169 toward Wellington, four- to six-bed rooms). Each hostel charges £9.60 per bed with sheets, serves meals, is closed from 10:00–17:00, welcomes travelers without memberships, and uses the same telephone number: tel. 01952/588-755.

Wilderhope Manor Youth Hostel, a beautifully remote and haunted 500-year-old manor house, is one of Europe's best hostels. One day a week, tourists actually pay to see what we hostelers sleep in for £9 (closed Sunday night, dinner served at 19:00, tel. 01694/771-363). It's 6 miles from Much Wenlock down B4371 toward Church Stretton.

Eating in Ironbridge Gorge

The best values and most local crowds are found outside of the IBG town. To simply eat well, go to the **Meadow Inn**, a local favorite with prize-winning pub grub (a pleasant 15-minute walk along the riverside park from the town center, dinners nightly 18:00–21:45, tel. 01952/433-193). For a local crowd, fine spit-and-sawdust ambience, excellent ales, and surprisingly good food, try the **Coalbrookdale Inn** (dinner served 18:00–20:00 except Sunday, occasional folk music, across the street from the

Museum of Iron a mile from IBG, tel. 01952/433-953). This former "best pub in Britain" has a tradition of offering free samples from a line-up of featured beers. Each are listed on a blackboard with their price and alcohol content. Ask a local to explain . . . or ask if he's ever tried a brew called The Prior's Piddle.

For a break from pub grub, you have three "European cuisine" choices serving £10 meals next to the Iron Bridge: **Coracle Restaurant** (Tuesday–Saturday 19:00–21:30, closed Sunday and Monday, reservations smart, tel. 01952/433-913), **Oliver's** (a smoke-free vegetarian place, reservations always necessary, tel. 01952/433-086), and **Old Vaults Wine Bar** (a hipper, younger place, plenty of indoor/outdoor seating, healthy food, real ale, tel. 01952/432-716).

For a pleasant evening, drive down Wenlock Edge on B4371. At the Wenlock Edge Inn, park and walk to the cliff for a marvelous view of Shropshire at sunset (made nearly famous by the poet A. E. Housman). Then drive farther to Much Wenlock and eat at the cozy and entertaining **George and Dragon Pub**—it draws a fun local crowd.

Transportation Connections— Ironbridge Gorge

Public transportation is miserable. Buses (every two hours) and cabs run the 7 miles between Ironbridge and the nearest train station at Telford. Adding insult to injury, the Telford bus and train stations are a 15-minute walk apart.

Telford by train to: Birmingham (hrly, 45 min), **Blackpool** (hrly, 4.5 hrs, with four transfers: Birmingham–Shrewsbury, hrly, 1 hr; Shrewsbury–Crewe, hrly, 40 min; Crewe–Preston, 2/hr, 45 min; Preston–Blackpool, 2/hr, 20 min), **Lake District** (allow up to 6.5 hrs total; follow directions toward Blackpool, above; transfer at Preston for Penrith, 2/hr, 75 min, and bus into Keswick, 6/day, 40 min), **Edinburgh** (8 hrs, with several transfers). Train info tel. 0345/484-950.

By Car: Driving in from the Cotswolds and Stratford, take M6 through Birmingham then M54 to the Telford/Ironbridge exit. Follow the brown Ironbridge signs through lots of roundabouts to Ironbridge Gorge. The traffic north through Birmingham is miserable from 14:00 to 20:00 on Fridays. Consider the Kidderminster/Bridgnorth alternative route. Driving from IBG to Ruthin in North Wales is an easy two hours.

NORTH WALES

Wales' top historical, cultural, and natural wonders are found in the north. From towering Mount Snowdon to lush forests to desolate moor country, North Wales is a poem written in landscape. For sightseeing thrills and diversity, North Wales is far and away the most interesting slice of Britain's Celtic crescent. But be careful not to be waylaid by the many gimmicky sights and bogus "best of" lists. The region's economy is poor, and they're wringing every possible pound out of the tourist trade. Sort carefully through your options.

Welsh

Language: The Welsh language, Cymru, has been a written language since about A.D. 600 and was spoken 300 years before French or German. It remains alive and well. Although English imperialism tried to kill it, today Welsh and those who speak it are protected by law. In Northwest Wales well over half the population is fluent in Welsh. It's either the first or the required second language in the public schools. Tourists hardly notice that the locals chatter away in Welsh and, as they turn to you, switch seamlessly to English.

Welsh is a Celtic language (like Irish) and most closely related to the Breton language in western France. The common "ll" is pronounced as if you were ready to make an "l" sound and then blew it out. The language is phonetic but comes with a few tricks: the Welsh "dd" sounds like the English "th", f = v, ff = f, w = oo, and y = i. In a pub, impress your friends (or make some)

North Wales

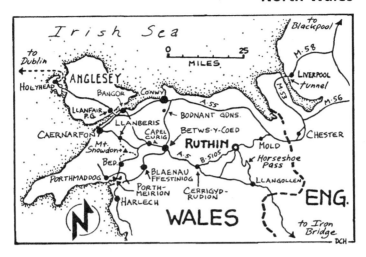

by toasting the guy who just bought your drink. Say "*Yeach-hid dah*" ("Good health to you") and "*Dee olch*" ("Thank you") or "*Dee olch un vowr*" ("Thanks very much"). If the beer's bad, just make something up.

Choirs: Every town has a choir (men's or mixed) which practices weekly. Visitors are usually welcome to observe and very often follow the choir down to the pub afterwards for a good, old-fashioned, beer-lubricated sing-song. Ask your B&B hostess for specifics. These choirs welcome visitors and practice weekly in the towns of **Ruthin** (mixed choir at the Tabernacle Church or Old Town Hall, Thursday 19:30–21:30), **Llangollen** (men's choir on Monday and Friday at 19:30 at the Hand Hotel, 21:00 pub sing-song afterwards, tel. 01978/860-303), **Denbigh** (Cormeibion men's choir on Monday at 19:00), **Pwylglas** (mixed choir on Tuesday at 20:00, 2.5 miles from Ruthin), and **Wrexham** (Rhos Orpheus men's choir on Wednesday at 19:30 in the Grango Rhos school).

Planning Your Time

Give North Wales two nights and a day (on a three-week British trip) and it'll give you a medieval banquet, a mighty castle, giant slate mines, and some of Britain's most beautiful scenery. Many visitors are charmed and find an extra day. With a car and an interest in the medieval banquet, set up in Ruthin and do this loop:

9:00	Drive over Llanberis mountain pass to Caernarfon (with possible short stops in Trefriw Mill, Betws-y-Coed, Pen-y-Gwryd Hotel, and Llanberis).
12:00	Caernarfon Castle. Catch noon tour and 13:00 movie in Eagle Tower. See Prince Charles (of Wales) exhibit. Climb to top for view. Walk through Caernarfon town, lunch, shop.
14:30	Drive the scenic road (A4085) to Blaenau Ffestiniog.
15:30	Tour Llechwedd Slate Mine.
17:30	Drive home to Ruthin.
19:00	Arrive in Ruthin.
19:45	Medieval banquet at castle (if not last night).

With a car and no interest in the banquet, skip Ruthin and shorten your drive time by spending two nights in Conwy. Without a car, skip Ruthin. From Conwy you can tour Snowdonia and Caernarfon by bus and train.

With a second day, add the train up Snowdon (or take a hike) and visit Conwy. With more time and a desire to hike, consider using the mountain village of Beddgelert as a base.

Getting Around North Wales

North Wales (except Ruthin) is well-covered by a combination of buses and trains. A main train line zips along the north coast from Chester to Holyhead via Llandudno Junction, Conwy, and Bangor (hrly). From Llandudno Junction the Conwy Valley line goes scenically south to Betws-y-Coed and Blaenau Ffestiniog (5/day, 1 hr). With these two train lines, public buses (get the *Gwynedd Public Transport Guide*), and Sherpa buses (which circle Snowdonia National Park with the needs of hikers in mind, tel. 01286/679-535), those without a car should manage fine. Day passes such as Rover (bus, all day on Sherpa buses, £2, buy ticket from driver) or Ranger (bus and train) save money if you're traveling a lot.

RUTHIN

Ruthin (rith-in) is a low-key, workaday market town, whose charm is in its ordinary Welsh-ness. The people are the sights. Admission is free if you start the conversation. The market

square, castle, TI, bus station, and in-town accommodations
are all within 5 blocks of each other. Ruthin is as Welsh as can
be, makes a handy base for drivers doing North Wales, and
serves up a great medieval banquet. The TI (daily 10:00–17:30
in summer, until 17:00 off-season, tel. 01824/703-992) is in a
busy crafts center.

Sights—Ruthin

▲▲**Ruthin Castle Welsh Medieval Banquet**—English, Scottish, Irish, and Welsh medieval banquets are all variations on the
same touristy theme. This one is fun, more culturally justifiable
(if that's necessary), and less expensive than most. You'll be
greeted with a chunk of bread dipped in salt, which the maiden
explains will "guarantee your safety." Your medieval master of
ceremonies then seats you and the candlelit evening of food,
drink, and music rolls gaily on. You'll enjoy harp music, angelic
singing, and lots of entertainment, including insults slung at the
Irish, Scots, English, and even us brash colonists. With fanfare
(and historic explanation), wenches serve mead, spiced wine, and
four hearty traditional courses. Drink from a pewter goblet, wear
a bib, and eat with your fingers and a dagger. Food and mead are
unlimited—just ask for more (£26.75, CC:VMA, starts at 19:45,
two to five nights a week depending upon demand, vegetarian
options, smoke-free, easy doorstep parking, down Castle Street
from the town square, call for reservations, tel. 01824/703-435
or, after hours, the hotel at 01824/702-664).

Walks—For a scenic and interesting one-hour walk, try the
Offa's Dyke Path to Moel Famau (the "Jubilee Tower," a 200-
year-old war memorial on a peak overlooking stark moor-
lands). The trailhead is a ten-minute drive from Ruthin. Dave
Murray is a local guide who takes visitors on walks (tel.
01824/705-032).

▲▲**Welsh Choir**—The mixed choir performs at the Tabernacle
Church or Old Town Hall on Thursday from 19:30 to 21:30.

Sleeping in Ruthin

(£1 = about $1.60, tel. code: 01824)
Sleep Code: **S**=Single, **D**=Double/Twin, **T**=Triple, **Q**=Quad,
b=bathroom, **t**=toilet only, **s**=shower only, **CC**=Credit Card
(**V**isa, **M**asterCard, **A**mex).

   Bryn Awel, a warm, traditional, charming farmhouse
B&B with a paradise garden, is run by Beryl and John Jones in

Ruthin

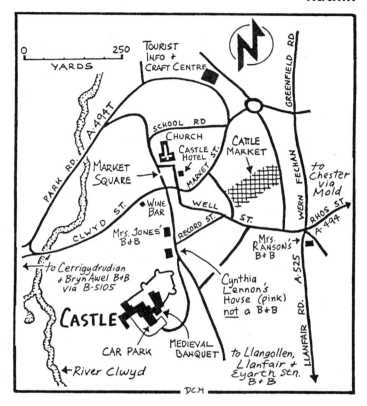

the hamlet of Bontuchel just outside of Ruthin (Db-£34, £37 for one-nighters, non-smoking, LL15 2DE Bontuchel, tel. 01824/702-481). Beryl, a prize-winning quilter, is eager to help you with touring tips, walks near her farm, booking the medieval banquet, and key Welsh words. From Ruthin, take the Bala road, #494, then the B5105 Cerrigydrudion road. Turn right after the church, at the Bontuchel/Cyffylliog sign. It's on the right, 1.8 fragrant miles down the narrow road. If you get to the Bridge Hotel, backtrack 200 yards.

Eleanor Jones' B&B, in a cozy 15th-century Tudor home between the castle and the town square, serves a royal breakfast and has a library, dog, grand piano, and three huge, frumpy, well-worn rooms (Db-£35, 8a Castle Street, tel. 01824/702-748).

Margaret Ranson's B&B is friendly, comfortable, and moderately priced (three rooms, Db-£34, entirely smoke-free, Rhianfa, Ffordd Llanrhydd, Ruthin, Clwyd, LL15 1PP, a ten-minute walk from the castle; from Anchor Pub drive 100 yards toward the hospital; it's the first big, red, brick house on right; Rhianfa sign on stone wall, tel. 01824/702-971). Margaret's husband, John, a natural tour guide, will lend you an excellent North Wales road map. Or you can just play croquet in their sprawling backyard.

Eyarth Station, a modern home in what used to be a train station, is set peacefully in the countryside near Ruthin (Db-£46, six rooms, no smoking in rooms, turn right off A525 a mile out of Ruthin, Llanfair D.C., LL15 2EE, tel. 01824/703-643). Jen Spencer, another wealth of local information, runs her place like a small hotel.

The Castle Hotel, not to be confused with the Ruthin Castle Hotel, is a friendly, well-worn, 24-room hotel on the town square (Db-£42, family suites, front rooms are larger and overlook the town square, some non-smoking rooms, reasonable evening meals, CC:VMA, St. Peter's Square, LL15 1AA, tel. 01824/702-479, fax 01824/704-924, energetically run by Fred Llewellyn-Jones).

Moelfa B&B on the Denbigh Road is modern, nondescript, and on a busy road, but comfortable and friendly (D-£30, leave town on Denbigh Road, first B&B sign on left, tel. 01824/702-468, Meg Jones).

Ruthin Castle is the ultimate in creaky Old World elegance for North Wales (Sb-£70, Db-£90, show this book for 10 percent off room rates or 10 percent off their two-night-with-a-banquet deal, CC:VMA, tel. 01824/702-664, fax 01824/705-978). Enjoy lavish public places, armor, antlers, ghosts, and your private snooker table (giant billiards, £1/hour). Explore the fascinating grounds complete with a drowning pool and 40 peacocks. You'll wake up to their cry thinking it's a loony-tune damsel in distress.

For cheap beds go to the **Llangollen Youth Hostel** (15 miles from Ruthin, tel. 01978/860-330, see below).

Eating in Ruthin

There's no reason to rush home for dinner in Ruthin if you're not going to the medieval banquet. No one place is a clear winner, but you'll eat reasonably well at the **Eagles**

Pub, the **Anchor Pub**, **Cross Keys Inn** (just west of town), the **Wynnstay Arms**, the **Castle Hotel**, and, for a little extra, the **Manor House Hotel Restaurant**. For fish 'n' chips, locals paddle over to **Finns** on Clwyd Street.

LLANGOLLEN

Worth a stop if you have a car, Llangollen is famous for its musical International Eisteddfod (six days in early July; July 7–12 in 1998), a very popular and very crowded festival of folk songs and dance. Monday and Friday nights throughout the year is men's choir practice (19:30 at the Hand Hotel, 21:00 pub sing-song afterwards, tel. 01978/860-303).

You can walk or ride a horse-drawn boat down the old canal (£3, 45-minute, 3-mile round-trip, summer only, tel. 01978/860-702) toward the lovely 13th-century Cistercian Vale Crucis Abbey (£1.70) near the even older cross called Eliseg's Pillar. (TI: tel. 01978/860-828.)

Llangollen has a handful of other amusements and attractions including scenic steamtrain trips, the world's largest permanent exhibition of model railways, and the biggest "Doctor Who" exhibition anywhere.

Gale's Hotel is a decent value (15 rooms, Db-£50, good food, CC:VMA, Bridge Street, tel. 01978/860-089, fax 01978/861-313) and the **Llangollen Youth Hostel** is cheap (£9 per bed in four- to 20-bed rooms, tel. 01978/860-330).

Llangollen is 15 miles and a 30-minute drive from Ruthin (no bus connection). Hourly buses connect Llangollen with train stations at Chirk, Ruabon, and Wrexham.

KING EDWARD'S CASTLES

In the 13th century the Welsh, under two great princes named Llywelyn, created a united and independent Wales. The English King Edward I fought hard to end this Welsh sovereignty. In 1282 Llywelyn was killed (and went to where everyone speaks Welsh). King Edward spent the next 20 years building or rebuilding 17 great castles to consolidate his English foothold in troublesome North Wales. The greatest of these were masterpieces of medieval engineering with round towers (tough to undermine by tunneling), a castle-within-a-castle defense (giving defenders a place to retreat and wreak havoc on the advancing enemy . . . or just wait for reinforcements), and sea access (safe to stock from

England). These were English islands in the middle of angry Wales. Most were built with a fortified grid-plan town attached and were filled with English settlers. (With this blatant abuse of Wales, you have to wonder, where was Greenpeace 700 years ago?)

Castle lovers will want to tour each of Edward's five greatest castles. I'd rate them in this order: **Caernarfon** is most entertaining and best presented (described below). **Conwy** is attached to the cutest medieval town and the best public transport (described below). **Harlech** is the most dramatic (£3, daily 9:30–18:30, tel. 01766/780-552). **Beaumaris** was the last, largest, and most romantic, surrounded by a swan-filled moat (daily 9:30–18:30, tel. 01248/810-361). **Criccieth**, built in 1230 by Llywelyn, is also dramatic and remote (daily 10:00–18:00, tel. 01766/522-227).

CONWY

This garrison town was built at the same time as the castle in the 1280s to give Edward I an English toehold on Wales (see above). What's left today are the best medieval walls in Britain, surrounding a humble resort and crowned by the bleak and barren hulk of an awesome-in-its-day castle. Conwy's charming High Street leads from Lancester Square (with the tiny bus and train station and a column honoring the town's founder, Welsh prince Llywelyn the Great) down to a fishy harborfront that permitted Edward to safely restock his castle.

Since the highway was tunneled under the town, a strolling ambience has returned to Conwy. Much of the wall is walkable (free). Stroll the harbor past Britain's smallest house (see below), the tour boat (£2.50, 30 min), an aquarium, the town lifeboat house, and a fresh-fish trailer selling 10p crab sticks. Near the castle the "meadery" gives samples of mead and lets kids of any age shoot a bow and arrow. Beyond the castle, the mighty Telford suspension bridge is a 19th-century slice of English imperialism, built in 1826 to better connect (and control) the route to Ireland. The newly restored bridge is open to pedestrians only.

Tourist Information: The TI is at the castle entry (daily 9:30–18:30, less off-season, tel. 01492/592-248). Don't confuse it with the tacky "Visitors Centre" near the station with its goofy little 50p TV show.

Conwy and Snowdonia National Park

LLANDUDNO

BEAU-MARIS

CONWY

TO
HOLYHEAD
(FERRY TO IRELAND)
A-5

A-55

LLANDUDNO
JUNCTION

TO
CHESTER
& RUTHIN

BANGOR

BODNANT
GARDENS

CAERNARFON

TREFIW
WOOLEN
MILLS

A-5

LLANBERIS

A-4086

BETWS-Y-COED

A-4085

A-497

CAPEL
CURIG

A-5

TO
RUTHIN &
LLANGOLLEN

MT
SNOWDON

BEDDGELERT

GLODDFA
GANOL
SLATE
MINE

LLECHWEDD
SLATE MINE

PORTH-MADOG

A-498

BLAENAU
FFESTINIOG

CRICCIETH

FFESTINIOG

PORTHMEIRION

5 MILES

HARLECH

= CASTLE

Sights—Conwy

▲**Conwy Castle**—Built dramatically on a rock overlooking the sea with eight linebacker towers, it has an interesting story to tell (£3, daily 9:30–18:30, less in winter, tel. 01492/592-358). Guides wait inside ready to take you on a 40-minute, £1 tour. If the booth is empty, look for the group and join it.

St. Mary's Parish Church—Built in 1186, it's still the core of the town and worth a look for its fine interior and wispy graveyard. Originally a Cistercian church, it is actually older than the town.

Houses—By the harbor, the tiniest house in Britain is 72" wide, 122" high, and 50p to see. Two old houses on High Street may tempt you. "Plas Mawr," billed as the oldest house in Wales, offers a frail look at domestic life in 16th-century Wales (£3,

Tuesday–Sunday 10:00–18:00, closed Monday). The Aberconwy House at the bottom of the street is even less exciting (£2).
▲**Bodnant Garden**—This sumptuous display of floral color— set in the lush green of Snowdonia—is one of Britain's best. It's famous for its magnolias, rhodies, camellias, and floral arch (£4.50, daily 10:00–17:00 in season, best spring through June, 6 miles south of Conwy, tel. 01492/650-460).

Sleeping in Conwy
(£1 = about $1.60, tel code: 01492)
Conwy has several decent budget B&Bs each located within a three-minute walk from the bus and train station. **Gwynedd Guest House**, spacious, thoughtfully decorated, and charmingly run by Margaret Salminen, is the best value (S-£15, D-£28, T-£42, family deals, 2 blocks from bus and train station, 10 Upper Gate Street, LL32 8RF, tel. & fax 01492/596-537). **Llys Llywe-lyn Hotel** is well-worn but stately with easy parking, a big lounge, and some views (Db-£34, just outside the town wall at Mount Pleasant, tel. 01492/593-257, Karen Morton).

In the old town near the train station: **Rose Hill House B&B** rents three small, tidy rooms (S-£13, D-£26, 20 Rose Hill Street, tel. 01492/593-435, Mrs. Curran). **The Town House** is a cramped little place next door (S-£17, D-£27, three Db-£33, CC:VMA, Rosehill Street, tel. 01492/596-454). The extremely cute **Pen y Bryn** rents three rooms above its tea-house (Db-£35, Lancaster Square, tel. 01492/596-445) and the big, musty old **Castle Hotel** rents 40 overpriced rooms (Db-£80, CC:VMA, High Street, tel. 01492/592-324, fax 01492/583-351).

Conwy's new **hostel** is a 15-minute walk from the castle (£9 per bed in two-, four-, and six-bed rooms, all with showers and lockers, family rooms, Larkhill, Sychnant Pass Road, tel. 01492/593-571, fax 01492/593-580).

When hungry in Conwy, stroll up High Street compar-ing the cute teahouses and smoky pubs. At the top, on Lan-caster Square, is **Alfredo's Restaurant**, a family-friendly place which serves good and reasonable Italian food nightly (tel. 01492/592-381). The **Malt Loaf** pub hosts the local folk music club each Monday from 20:30 on (across from the sta-tion). **The Wall Place** is the only vegetarian cyber café in town (Chapel Street, tel. 01492/596-326, web site: www.nol.co.uk/~wall/).

CAERNARFON

A small but lively town, Caernarfon (ka-NAR-von) bustles with shops, cafés, and people. The TI is across from the castle entrance (tel. 01286/672-232). Donna "Caernarfon is more than a castle" Goodman leads historic walks several times a week (£3, call 01286/677-059 for her schedule). The charming old town, within the walls which spread from the castle, still follows its original ancient street plan and is worth a wander.

▲▲**Caernarfon Castle**—Edward I built this impressive castle 700 years ago to establish English rule over North Wales. Modeled after the striped and angular walls of ancient Constantinople, the castle is eager to entertain. Watch the 20-minute movie (broad mix of Welsh legend and history, on the half-hour in the Eagle Tower) and climb the Eagle Tower for a great view. Take the guided tour (50-minute tours for £1 leave on the hour from the center of the courtyard in front of entry; if you're late, ask to join one in progress). See exhibits on the history of Wales (ground floor of Eagle Tower) and the investiture of the Princes of Wales—most recently, Prince Charles in 1969 (£3.80, daily 9:30–18:30; winter Tuesday–Saturday 9:30–16:00, Sunday 11:00–16:00, tel. 01286/677-617).

Sleeping in Caernarfon
(£1 = about $1.60, tel code: 01286)

Isfryn B&B is just down the street from the castle, overlooking the water (S-£18.50, D-£35, Db-£40, family deals, non-smoking, 11 Church Street, L5 51SW, tel. & fax 01286/675-628, Graham). **Totters Hostel** is a creative little hostel well-run by Bob and Henriette (30 beds in five dorm rooms, £9 per bed with bedding, continental breakfast, and lockers; couples can have their own room when available; open all day, welcoming gameroom/lounge, use of kitchen, a block from the castle at 2 High Street, tel. 01286/672-963).

SNOWDONIA NATIONAL PARK

Snowdonia National Park is Britain's second-largest national park, with Mount Snowdon—the tallest mountain in England and Wales—as its centerpiece. Each year half a million people choose one of seven different paths to the top of 3,560-foot Snowdon. Hikes take from five to seven hours. If you're reasonably fit and the weather cooperates, it's an exciting day. Trail info abounds.

Sights—Snowdonia

Betws-y-Coed—The resort center of Snowdonia National Park, Betwys-y-Coed, bursts with tour buses and souvenir shops. It has a good National Park and Tourist Information office (daily 10:00–18:00, tel. 01690/710-426). But I don't understand why everyone seems to stop here. As you drive west out of town on A5, you'll see the car park for scenic Swallow Falls, a pleasant five-minute walk from the road. A mile or so past the falls, on the right, you'll see "The Ugly House," built overnight to take advantage of a 15th-century law that let any quickie building avoid fees and taxes. A regular bus service connects Conwy and Betws-y-Coed. Trains run from the north coast through Betws-y-Coed to Blaenau (6/day).

Trefriw Woolen Mills—The mill in Trefriw, 5 miles north of Betws-y-Coed, is free and surprisingly interesting if the machines are running (Monday–Friday 9:30–13:00 and 14:00–17:30, tel. 01492/640-462). Follow the 11 stages of wool transformation: warping, weaving, carding, hanking, spanking, spinning, and so on. The handspinning house (next to the WC) has a charming spinster and a petting cupboard of all the fibers which can be spun into cloth. Then enjoy the fine woolen shop, pleasant town (more so than Betws-y-Coed), and coffee shop. The woolen mill at Penmachno (also near Betws-y-Coed) is smaller and less interesting.

Beddgelert—Beddgelert (17 miles from Betws-y-Coed) is the quintessential Snowdon village, packing a scenic mountain punch without the tourist crowds. Set on a river in the shadow of Snowdon and her sisters, with a fine variety of hikes from its doorstep and pretty good bus service, Beddgelert makes a good stop for those wanting to experience the peace of Snowdonia.

Locals can recommend walks. You can follow the lane along the river (3 miles round-trip), walk down the river and around the hill (three hours, 6 miles, 900-foot gain, via Cwm Bycham), hike along (or around) Llyn Gwynant Lake and 4 miles back to Beddgelert (ride the bus to the lake), or try the more dramatic higher ridge walks on Moel Hebog (Hawk Hill).

Sleeping in Beddgelert: Plas Tan Y Graig Guest House and Hostel, at the village bridge, is the best deal in town (D-£32 with breakfast, beds in a six-bed dorm £9 with bedding but no breakfast, family room, hostelers may end up alone enjoying a single or double at dorm prices, LL55 4LT, tel. 01766/890-329). The owners Brian and Gwen Maddison are a wealth of hiking information and run their classy old house with a caring touch. There's a fine lounge and loaner hiking maps. Don't let the "hostel" business scare you. This comfy place is a winner. **Plas Colwyn Guest House** is not quite as inviting (D-£32, Db-£39, non-smoking but still a bit musty, CC:VM, tel. 01766/890-458). **The Royal Goat Hotel** offers well-worn, chandeliered, woody elegance in a grand hotel built for the rugged 19th-century aristocrat (Db-£70, some non-smoking rooms, CC:VMA, tel. 01766/890-224, fax 01766/890-422).

Mountaineers note that this area was used by Sir Edmund Hillary and his men as they practiced for the first ascent of Mount Everest. The **Pen-y-Gwryd Hotel Pub** (at the top of the pass north of Beddgelert) is strewn with fascinating Hillary and Mount Everest memorabilia (D-£40, Db-£50, saggy beds; smoky, old-time-elegant public rooms; those in D rooms get to use museum-piece Victorian tubs, tel. 01286/870-211). Situated in the peaceful middle of nowhere, with a crampon ambience, this is ideal for well-bred hikers.

Llanberis—Llanberis, a town of 2,000 people and as many tourists on a sunny day, is a popular base for Snowdon activities. Along with the station for the Snowdon train, there is a good information center, a few touristy museums, pony trekking, and good bus connections.

▲▲Mount Snowdon and the Mountain Railway—The easiest and most popular ascent of Mount Snowdon is by the Snowdon Mountain Railway, a rack-and-pinion railway from 1896 which climbs 3,000 feet over 4.5 miles from Llanberis to the summit of Snowdon (£14.50 round-trip, 2.5 hours including a 30-minute stop at the summit, CC:VM, tel. 01286/870-223). First departure is usually at 9:00. While the schedule flexes with weather and demand, they try to run at least a 9:30, 11:30, and 13:30 daily mid-March through October (two departures per hour in peak season). Off-season trains often stop short of the summit. On sunny summer days trains fill up (waits are longer in the afternoon, arrive early and get a departure appointment time—usually a wait of an hour or two). While they "don't really do this," you might telephone and see if you can get your name on the list.

BLAENAU FFESTINIOG

This quintessential Welsh slate-mining town is notable for its slate-mine tour and its old steam train. The town—a dark,

poor place—seems to struggle on, oblivious to the tourists who
nip in and out. Take a walk. The shops are right out of the
1950s. There are some buses from the town to the slate mines;
the road isn't pedestrian-friendly. (TI: tel. 01766/830-360.)

Sights—Blaenau Ffestiniog

▲▲**Llechwedd Slate-Mine Tour**—Slate mining played a
blockbuster role in Welsh heritage, and this mine on the
northern edge of the bleak town of Blaenau Ffestiniog does a
fine job of explaining the mining culture of Victorian Wales.
The Welsh mined and split most of the slate roofs of Europe.
And for every ton of usable slate found, 10 tons were mined.
Two 30-minute tours are offered: The "deep mine" tour features a tape-recorded dramatization of social life, a serious
descent, and a half-mile of walking. The "tramway" tour is a
level train ride with two stops, no walking, and a live guide,
focusing on working life and traditional mining techniques.
Both are different and, considering the cheap combo-ticket,
worthwhile. Don't miss the slate-splitting demonstration, open
to all, at the end of the tramway tour (£6.25 for one tour or
£9.50 for both, daily 10:00–18:00, closes at 17:00 in winter, tel.
01766/830-306). Dress warmly—I mean it. You'll freeze
underground without a sweater.

▲**Gloddfa Ganol Slate Mine**—The world's largest slate
mine, across the street from the Llechwedd Mine, offers a less
commercial visit for a serious look at today's mining opera-
tions. After an A-V presentation, hard-hatted visitors are basically free to roam the 150-year-old main tunnel and gaze into
the open pit (£5.50, Monday–Friday 10:00–17:30, closed winter, tel. 01766/830-664).

▲**Ffestiniog Railway**—This 13-mile, narrow-gauge train line
was built in 1836 for small horse-drawn wagons to transport
the slate from the Ffestiniog mines to the port of Porthmadog.
In the 1860s horses gave way to steam trains. Today hikers and
tourists enjoy these tiny titans (£13 round-trip, hrly, 2.5 hrs
round-trip; diesel trains are £2 cheaper, first-class observation
cars are £5 extra, tel. 01766/512-340). This is a novel steamtrain experience, but the full-size Llandudno–Blaenau Ffestiniog train is more scenic and works better for hikers.

Portmeirion—Ten miles southwest of Blaenau Ffestiniog, this
"Italian Village" was the lifework of a rich local architect, who
began building it in 1925. Set idyllically on the coast just

beyond the poverty of the slate-mine towns, the extravagance of this flower-filled fantasy is particularly striking. Surrounded by lush Welsh greenery and a windswept mudflat at low tide, the village is an artistic glob of palazzo arches, fountains, gardens, and promenades filled with cafés, tacky shops, a hotel, and local tourists who always wanted to go to Italy (or who are fans of the cultish British 1960s TV series *The Prisoner*). The architect explains his purpose in a videotaped slide presentation. Not worth the £3.50 (daily 9:30–17:30, 2 miles from Porthmadog, tel. 01766/770-228).

Transportation Connections—North Wales

Conwy to: Llandudno Junction (to catch the Conwy Valley train; 2 buses/hr, 5 min, or walk), **Trefriw–Betws-y-Coed–Penygwryd–Llanberis** (bus 19, every 2 hrs, 90 min).

Llandudno Junction by train to: Chester (2/hr, 1 hr), **Birmingham** (2/hr, 2.5 hrs), **London**'s Euston Station (hrly, 3.5 hrs). Train info tel. 0345/484-950.

Caernarfon to: Conwy (direct hourly bus, 75 min, buy ticket on bus; or train then bus, 2/hr, 75 min; or by bus with transfer in Bangor), **Llanberis** (2 buses/hr, 30 min), **Beddgelert** (hrly buses, 30 min, summer only), **Blaenau–Ffestiniog** (hrly buses, 80 min), **Beddgelert–Penygwryd–Llanberis** (bus 95, every 2 hrs, 90 min).

Llanberis to: Beddgelert (buses hrly, 45 min, £11.50).

Ruthin to: Llangollen (15 miles; connections are doable, but discouraging), **Betsw-y-Coed** (30 miles; doable but time-consuming with transfers), **Chester** (6 buses/day, 30 min, or a £15 taxi).

Chester by train to: London (hrly, 3 hrs), **Liverpool** (2/hr, 50 min), **Birmingham** (2/hr, 2 hrs), points in **North Wales** (2/hr).

Ferry Connections—North Wales and Ireland

Holyhead and Dun Laoghaire: Stena Line sails between Holyhead (North Wales) and Dun Laoghaire near Dublin (5/day, 100 min, £25–35 one-way walk-on fare, £20 round-trip in a day if you have no baggage, plus £5 tax if buying ticket in Ireland, reserve by phone as soon as you can—they book up long in advance on summer weekends, Dublin tel. 01/204-7777, recorded info 01/204-7799, Holyhead tel. 01407/762-304).

Holyhead and Dublin: Irish Ferries sails between Holyhead (North Wales) and Dublin (2/day, 3 hrs, £20–25 one-way walk-on fare, Dublin tel. 01/661-0511, recorded info 01/661-0715, Holyhead tel. 0990-329-129, web site: www.iol.ie/irish-ferries, e-mail info@irish-ferries.ie). Car fares vary from £100 to £400 (with passengers, depending on season).

Sleeping near Holyhead dock: The fine **Monravon B&B** has seven smoke-free rooms (Db-£32, Porth-Y-Felin Road, five-minute walk from dock, tel. & fax 01407/762-944).

Route Tips for Drivers

Ironbridge Gorge to Ruthin: Drive for an hour to Wales via A5 through Shrewsbury, crossing into Wales at the pretty castle town of Chirk. There, take A5 to Llangollen. Cross the bridge in Llangollen, turn left, and follow A542 and A525 past the romantic Valle Crucis abbey, over the scenic Horseshoe Pass, and into Ruthin. Driving to Conwy is faster via Wrexham and then the A55.

Ruthin to Caernarfon (56 miles) to Blaenau (34 miles) to Ruthin (35 miles): This route connects the top sights with the most scenic routes. From Ruthin, take B5105 (steepest road off main square) and follow signs to Cerrigydrudion. Then follow A5 into Betws-y-Coed with a possible quick detour to the Trefriw Woolen Mill (5 miles north on B5106, well signposted). Climb west on A5 through Capel Curig, then take A4086 over the rugged Pass of Llanberis, under the summit of Mount Snowdon (to the south, behind those clouds), and on to Caernarfon. Park under the castle in the harborside car park (£2).

Leaving Caernarfon, take the lovely A4085 southeast through Beddgelert to Penrhyndeudraeth. (Make things even more beautiful by taking the little B4410 road from Garreg through Rhyd.) Then take A487 toward Maentwrog, and A496 to Blaenau Ffestiniog. Go through the dark, depressing mining town of Blaenau Ffestiniog on A470 into hills of slate and turn right into the Llechwedd Slate Mine.

After the mine, continue on A470, snapping photos north through Dolwyddelan (passing a fine old Welsh castle ruin) and back to A5. For a high and desolate detour, return to Ruthin via the windy, curvy A543 road over the stark moors to the Sportsman's Arms Pub (the highest pub in Wales, good food), through Denbigh, and home.

BLACKPOOL

This is Britain's fun puddle. It's England's most-visited attraction, the private domain of its working class, a faded and sticky mix of Coney Island, Las Vegas, and Woolworth's. Juveniles of any age love it. My kids declared it better than Disneyland.

Blackpool grew up with the Industrial Revolution. In the mid-1800s entire mill towns would close down and take a two-week break in Blackpool. They came for the fresh air—much needed after a hard year in the mills—and to drink the sea water. Back then they figured it was healthy to drink the sea water. Blackpool's heydays are past now as more and more working people can afford the cheap charter flights to sunny Spain. Still, this is an accessible and affordable fun zone for the Anne and Andy Capps of northern England. People come year after year. They stay for a week and they love it.

Most Americans don't even consider a stop in Blackpool. Many won't like it. It's an ears-pierced-while-you-wait, tipsy-toupee kind of place. Tacky, yes. Lowbrow, okay. But it's as English as can be, and that's what you're here for. An itinerary should feature as many facets of a culture as possible. Blackpool is as English as the Queen—and even more fun.

Spend the day "muckin' about" the beach promenade of fortune-tellers, fish-and-chips joints, amusement piers, warped mirrors, and Englanders wearing hats with built-in ponytails. A million greedy doors try every trick to get you inside. Huge arcade halls advertise free toilets and broadcast bingo numbers into the streets; the wind machine under a wax Marilyn

Monroe blows at a steady gale; and the smell of fries, tobacco, and sugar is everywhere. Milk comes in raspberry or banana in this land where people under incredibly bad wigs look normal. If you're bored in Blackpool, you're just too classy.

Planning Your Time

Ideally, get to Blackpool around lunchtime for a free afternoon and evening to make bubbles in this cultural mudpuddle. Blackpool is easy by car or train. Speed demons with a car can treat it as a midday break (it's just off the M6) and continue north. If you have kids, they'll want more time here (hey, it's cheaper than Disneyland). If you're into nightlife, this town is a slam dunk. If you're before or beyond kids and not into kitsch and greasy spoons, skip it. If the weather's great and you love nature, the lakes are just a few hours north. A visit to Blackpool does sharpen the wonders of Windermere.

Orientation (tel. code: 01253)

Everything clusters along the 6-mile beachfront promenade, a tacky, glittering strip-mall of fun. Each of the three amusement piers has its own personality: north—sedate, central—young fun, south—family. The piers were built for Victorian landlubbers who wanted to go to sea but were afraid of getting seasick. The Pleasure Beach rides are near the south pier. Jutting up near the north pier is Blackpool's stubby Eiffel-type tower. The most interesting shops, eateries, and theaters are inland from the north pier.

Tourist Information: There are two TIs near the tower, one on Clifton Street, one on the Promenade (Monday–Saturday 9:00–17:00, Sunday 10:00–16:00, shorter hours off-season, tel. 01253/621-623, the same number gives recorded entertainment info after hours). Get the city map (50p), pick up brochures on the amusement centers, and ask about special shows.

Arrival in Blackpool: The train station is just 3 blocks from the town center. The motorway funnels you into a giant parking zone (formerly the central station).

Getting Around Blackpool

Vintage trolley cars run 13 miles up and down the waterfront, connecting all the sights. This first electric tramway in Europe dates from 1885 (80p–£1.50, depending on the

Blackpool

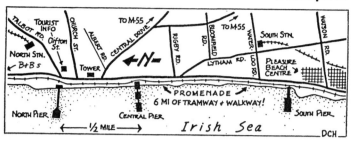

length, £4.00 for an all-day pass; they come every five minutes or so, just jump on and pay the conductor). Taxis are very easy to snare in Blackpool.

Sights—Blackpool

▲**Blackpool Tower**—This vertical fun center celebrated its 100th birthday in 1994. You pay £6 to get in; after that, the fun is free. Work your way up from the bottom through layer after layer of noisy entertainment: circus (three acts/day, usually at 12:30, 15:30, and the big show at 20:00, you can return on a ticket for £1), bug zone, space world, dinosaur land, aquarium, and wonderful old ballroom with barely live music and golden oldies dancing to golden oldies all day. Enjoy a break at the dance floor–level pub or on a balcony perch. Kids love this place. With a little marijuana, adults would too. Ride the elevator to the tip of the 500-foot-tall symbol of Blackpool for a smashing view, especially at sunset (daily 10:00–23:00, tower closed when windy).

▲**Pleasure Beach**—These 42 acres, littered with more than 80 rides (including "the best selection of white-knuckle rides in Europe"), ice-skating shows, cabarets, and amusements attract 7 million people a year. The most talked about attraction is the Pepsi Max Big One, "the world's fastest and highest" roller coaster (235 feet, 85 mph). The newest sensation is "Play Station," which rockets you straight up before letting you bungee down. Also memorable is a frightening race called "Steeple Chase" (imagine carousel horses stampeding down a roller coaster track). Admission is free, rides cost a couple of pounds each (hours vary with weather and season, tel. 01253/341-033). There are several other major amusement centers, including a popular water-park called Sand Castle (across the street from Pleasure Beach).

▲▲▲**People-Watching**—Blackpool's top sight is its people. You'll see England here as nowhere else. Grab someone's hand and a big stick of "rock" (candy), and stroll. Grown men walk around with huge teddies looking for "bowlingo" places. Ponder the thought of actually retiring here to spend your last years, day after day, surrounded by Blackpool and wearing a hat with a built-in ponytail. Blackpool puts people in a talkative mood. Ask someone to explain the difference between tea and supper.

▲▲**Variety Show**—Blackpool always has a few razzle-dazzle music, dancing-girl, racy-humor, magic, and tumbling shows. Box offices around town can give you a rundown on what's available (tickets £5–12). I enjoy the old-time music hall shows. They're corny—neither hip nor polished—but it's fascinating to be surrounded by hundreds of partying British seniors, swooning and waving their hankies to the predictable beat. Busloads of happy widows come from all corners of North England to giggle at jokes I'd never tell my grandma. Your B&B has the latest. If that's too lowbrow, Blackpool is second to London in theater. You can always watch a good play.

▲▲**Funny Girls**—The current hot bar in Blackpool seems to be Funny Girls, just a block from the North Pier. Every night from 20:30 to 23:30 they put on a "glam bam thank you ma'am" burlesque-in-drag show which delights footballers and grannies alike. Cover is only £3. Get your drinks at the bar unless the transvestites are dancing on it. The show, while racy, is not raunchy. The music is very loud. The crowd is young, old, straight, gay, very down-to-earth, and fun-loving. Go on a weeknight. Friday and Saturday are jammed.

Blackpool's clubs and discos are cheap, with live bands and an interesting crowd (22:00–1:00). The pubs of Blackpool have a unique tradition of "and your own, luv." Say that here and your barmaid will add 20p to your bill and drop it into her tip jar. (Say it anywhere else and they won't know what you mean.)

▲**Illuminations**—Blackpool was the first town in England to "go electric." Now, every September and October, Blackpool stretches its tourist season by illuminating its 6 miles of waterfront with countless lights, all blinking and twinkling. The American in me kept saying, "I've seen bigger and I've seen better," but I filled his mouth with cotton candy and just had some simple fun like everyone else on my specially decorated tram.

Sleeping in Blackpool
(£1 = about $1.60, tel. code: 01253)
Sleep Code: **S**=Single, **D**=Double/Twin, **T**=Triple, **Q**=Quad, **b**=bathroom, **t**=toilet only, **s**=shower only, **CC**=Credit Card (Visa, MasterCard, Amex).

Blackpool's 140,000 people provide 120,000 beds in 3,500 mostly dumpy, cheap, nondescript hotels and B&Bs. Remember, the town's in the business of accommodating the people who can't afford to go to Spain. Most have the same design—minimal character, maximum number of springy beds—and charge £12 to £18 per person. Empty beds abound except for September through November and summer weekends. It's only really tight on Illumination weekends. The first three listings below are on the waterfront in the quiet area they call "the posh end," a mile or two north of the Tower, with easy parking and easy access to the center by trolley. The last two are near the train station. Prices go up during the Illuminations and are soft off-season.

Robin Hood Hotel is a super place, cheery and family-run, with a big, welcoming living room and ten newly and tastefully refurbished rooms with the only sturdy beds I found (Sb-£18, Db-£36, less for two nights, family deals, CC:VM, entirely non-smoking, trolley stop: St. Stevens Avenue, 1.5 miles north of Tower across from a peaceful stretch of beach, 100 Queens Promenade, North Shore FY2 9NS, tel. 01253/351-599, Pam and Colin Webster).

Beechcliffe Private Hotel is clean, smoke-free, and family-run with more charm than average (S-L15, Dt-L33, Tt-L50, less for two nights, trolley stop: Uncle Tom's, walk a block away from the beach, 16 Shaftesbury Avenue, North Shore, FY2 9QQ, tel. 01253/353-075, David and Brenda).

Prefect Hotel is all smiles and pink-flamingo pretty. Shabby, but spacious-for-Blackpool with all the fun touches, this place is the appropriate springboard for the town (Sb-£17, Db-£34, ask for a view room, trolley to Bispham, 2 miles north of Tower at 204 Queens Promenade, FY2 9JS, tel. 01253/352-699, Bill and Pauline Acton).

Valentine Private Hotel is a bit smoky but has a smoke-free breakfast room (S-£13, D-£26, Db-£30, family deals, plenty of showers, CC:VMA, 3 blocks from the station at 35 Dickson Road, FY1 2AT, tel. 01253/622-775, Denise and Garry Hinchliffe). **Sandylands Guest House** is a plain "homely" little place 2 blocks from the station (S-£12, D-£24, smoky, 47 Banks Street, tel. 01253/294-670, Kevin Poole).

Eating in Blackpool

Your hotels may serve a cheap, early-evening meal. The following places are all between the Tower and the North Pier: For good fish and chips, go to the "world famous" **Harvey Ramsden's** near the tower (60 The Promenade, tel. 01253/294-386). Their advertising brings out the smart alec in you. The **Oyster Bar** at the corner of West Street and the Promenade is a fixture which actually predates the resort (as do some of its employees). Around the corner on West Street is the **Mitre Bar**—drop in to survey the great photos of old Blackpool. Across the street from the bar, **The Scullery** is a humble, hardworking pantry serving healthy/hearty food for great prices (10 West Street). Food in the tower is terrible, but it's not much better elsewhere.

Transportation Connections—Blackpool

If you're heading to (or from) Blackpool by train, you'll usually need to transfer at Preston (2/hr, 30 min). Train info tel. 0345/484-950.

Preston to: Keswick, the Lake District (hrly trains, 1 hr to Penrith, transfer to bus, 6 buses/day, 40 min to Keswick), **York** (hrly trains, 4.5 hrs, change at Manchester), **Edinburgh** (8/day, 3 hrs).

Points south: For **Ironbridge Gorge, Cotswolds, Bath**, and **North Wales**, you'll have several transfers but find fast and frequent trains. To **London**, change in Manchester (2/hr, 5 hrs).

Drivers leaving Blackpool: The quickest way out of town is to drive the Promenade to the Central Pier and turn inland. Under the bridge take an immediate left (take exit for M55). This gets you into the huge parking lot which leads directly to the motorway.

NEAR BLACKPOOL: LIVERPOOL

Liverpool, a gritty but surprisingly enjoyable city, is a fascinating stop for Beatles fans and those who would like to look urban England straight in its problem-plagued eyes.

The TI is with everything else—on Albert Dock (tel. 0151/708-8854). The bus and train stations are very central.

Sights—Liverpool

▲▲**Albert Dock**—Opened in 1852 by Prince Albert and enclosing 7 acres of water, the dock is surrounded by 5-story-high brick warehouses. In its day, Liverpool was England's greatest seaport. It prospered as one corner of the triangular commerce of the 18th-century slave trade. As England's economy boomed so did the port of Liverpool. From 1830 to 1930, 9 million emigrants sailed from Liverpool to find their dreams in the new world. But the port was not deep enough for the big new ships; trade declined after 1890 and by 1972 it was closed entirely. Like Liverpool itself, the docks have enjoyed a renaissance, and today they are the featured attraction of the city. The city's main attractions are lined up here out of the rain and padded by lots of shopping mall–type distractions. There's plenty of parking.

▲**Merseyside Maritime Museum**—This museum, which tells the story of this once-prosperous shipping center, gets an A for effort but feels designed for visiting school groups. The ships section is pretty dull, but the smuggling and customs, slavery, and emigration sections are interesting. The associated **Museum of Liverpool Life** offers a good look at the workaday story of the town (one £3 ticket for both, daily 10:00–17:30).

Tate Gallery Liverpool—This prestigious 20th-century gallery is next to the Maritime Museum. It won't entertain you as well as its London sister, but if you're into modern art, any Tate's great (slated to reopen in early 1998, free, Tuesday–Sunday 10:00–18:00, closed Monday, tel. 0151/709-0507).

▲**The Beatles Story**—It's kind of sad to think the Beatles are stuck in a museum (and Ringo's in reruns of *Shining Time Station*). While overpriced and not very creative, the story's a great one and even an avid fan will pick up some new information (£6 but discount coupons abound, try not to pay full fare, daily 10:00–18:00, tel. 0151/709-1963). The shop is an impressive pile of Beatles buyables. Die-hard Beatles fans may want to invest a couple of hours in one of several Beatles city bus tours (the lads' homes, Penny Lane, and so on), offered by Phil (tel. 0151/228-4565) and others.

▲**Matthew Street**—Beatles fans will want to explore Matthew Street (a 15-minute walk into the center from Albert Dock), including the site of the famous Cavern Club, the new "Cavern Club" nearby, and the Beatles Shop at #31.

Transportation Connections—Liverpool

By train to: Blackpool (hrly, 2 hrs, transfer at Preston), **York** (hrly, 2.5 hrs), **London** (hrly, 2.5 hrs), **Crewe** (18/day, 45 min). Train info tel. 0345/484-950.

Route Tips for Drivers

Ruthin to Blackpool via Liverpool: From Ruthin, get to the M53, which tunnels under the Mersey River (£1). Once in Liverpool, follow signs to City Center, Pier Head, and Albert Dock, where you'll find a huge car park next to all the sights. Leaving Liverpool, drive north along the waterfront following signs to M58 (Preston), then M6, and finally M55 into Blackpool.

Ruthin to Blackpool (100 miles): From Ruthin, take A494 through the town of Mold and follow the blue signs to the motorway. M56 zips you to M6, where you'll turn north toward Preston and Lancaster. Don't miss your turnoff: A few minutes after Preston, take the not-very-clearly-signed next exit (#32, M55) into Blackpool and drive as close as you can to the stubby Eiffel-type tower in the town center. Downtown parking is terrible. If you're not spending the day, head for one of the huge £6/day garages. If you're spending the night, drive to the waterfront and head north. My top B&Bs are north on the Promenade (easy parking).

LAKE DISTRICT

In the pristine Lake District, Wordsworth's poems still shiver in trees and ripple on ponds. This is a land where nature rules and man keeps a wide-eyed but low profile. Relax, recharge, take a cruise or a hike, maybe even write a poem. Renew your poetic license at Wordsworth's famous Dove Cottage.

The Lake District, about 30 by 30 miles, is nature's lush, green playground. Explore it by foot, bike, bus, or car. While not impressive in sheer height (Scafell Pike, the tallest peak in England, is only 3,206 feet), there's a walking-stick charm about the way nature and the local culture mix. Walking along a wind-blown ridge or climbing over a rock fence to look into the eyes of a ragamuffin sheep, even tenderfeet get a chance to feel very outdoorsy.

The sky will cloud and clear. You'll probably have rain mixed with brilliant bright spells. Handy pubs offer atmospheric shelter at every turn. And as the locals are fond of saying, "There's no such thing as bad weather, only unsuitable clothing."

While the south lakes (Windermere, Bowness, Beatrix Potter's cottage) get the promotion and tour crowds and are closer to London, the north lakes (Ullswater, Derwentwater, Buttermere) are less touristy and at least as scenic.

This chapter should actually be called the "North Lakes District." The town of Keswick, the lake called Derwentwater, and the vast time-passed Newlands Valley will be our focus. The area works great by car or train/bus. And Wordsworth and Potter fans can easily side-trip south to see their homes.

Planning Your Time

If great scenery is commonplace in your life, the Lake District can be more soothing (and rainy) than exciting. To save time, you could easily make this area a one-night stand—or even a quick drive-through. With a car and a three-week trip in Britain, I'd spend two days and two nights in the area. The quickest way in is to leave the motorway at Penrith. With more time, arrive by late morning, drive along Windermere, tour Dove Cottage, and get to Glenridding on Ullswater in time for the 14:00 boat. Hike 6 miles (14:30–18:00) from Howtown back to Glenridding. Drive to your farmhouse B&B near Keswick.

On your second day, explore Buttermere Lake, drive over Honister Pass, explore Derwentwater, and do the Cat Bells High Ridge walk. Spend the evening at the same B&B.

Those without a car will use Keswick as a springboard. Cruise the lake and hike in the Cat Bells area. If you need a vacation from your vacation, use this day to vegetate and recharge.

Getting Around the Lake District

Those based in Keswick without a car can manage fine.

By Foot: Piles of hiking information are available everywhere you turn. Skip the green "Lakeland Leisure Walks" flyer (confusing, not-to-scale) in favor of a more detailed map (such as Ordnance Survey). The best ridge walk is immediately outside of town (see Cat Bells High Ridge Hike, below).

By Boat: A circular boat service glides you easily around Derwentwater (for a sail/hike option, see Derwentwater, below).

By Bus: Buses take you quickly and easily (if not very frequently) to all nearby points of interest. Pick up the free 30-page Lakeland Explorer bus brochure for schedules, prices, and suggested bus/hike outings.

By Bus Tour: Mountain Goat Tours run an interesting variety of all-day (£22) and half-day (£12) minibus tours daily in summer from Keswick. They are rugged, informative (led by established mountain guides), and great for people who'd like to see the area without hiking. Unfortunately, you may not know if your tour will reach its minimum number of six passengers until shortly before departure (office at Keswick central car park, tel. 017687/73962).

By Car: Nothing is very far from Keswick and Derwentwater. Get a good map, get off the big roads, and leave the car, at least occasionally, for some walking. In summer, the

Keswick–Ambleside–Windermere–Bowness corridor (A591) suffers from congestion.

KESWICK

As far as touristy lake-district centers go, Keswick (kezz-ick, pop. 5,000) is far more enjoyable than Windermere, Bowness, or Ambleside. An important mining center (slate, copper, lead) through the Middle Ages, Keswick became a resort in the 19th century. Its fine Victorian buildings recall those romantic days when city slickers first learned about "communing with nature." Today the compact town is lined with tea shops, pubs, gift shops, and hiking gear shops. For up-to-date Lake District weather, call 017687/75757.

Keswick is the ideal home base: plenty of good B&Bs (see Sleeping, below), an easy bus connection to the nearest train station at Penrith, and a prime location on the best lake in the area, Derwentwater. Keswick's market square, tourist and hiking information office (daily 9:30–17:30, winter 10:00–16:00, tel. 017687/72645), recommended B&Bs, bike rental shop, municipal pitch-and-putt golf course, bus station, Mountain Goat minibus tour starting point, lakeside boat dock, and a central car park are all within a five-minute walk of each other. Saturday is market day and the town square is packed and lively.

Sights—Keswick

▲**Pencil Museum**—Graphite was first discovered centuries ago in Keswick. A hunk of the stuff proved great for marking sheep in the 15th century and the rest is history (which you can learn all about here). While you can't tour the 150-year-old factory where the famous Derwent pencils are made, the charming museum on the edge of Keswick is a good way to pass a rainy hour (£2, daily 9:30–16:00, rentable headsets are not necessary but the fine and free 20-minute film is; cheap brass-rubbing in the shop, tel. 017687/73626).

Walks—The TI organizes daily walks of varying levels of difficulty with local guides (£4, daily 10:00–17:00, tel. 017687/72645).

Plays—Locals are proud of their Century Theater which is moving into a new playhouse and offers plays nearly nightly during summer (£10, three different plays by professional actors, usually including plays by Noel Coward or Neil Simon, tel. 017687/74411).

Lake District

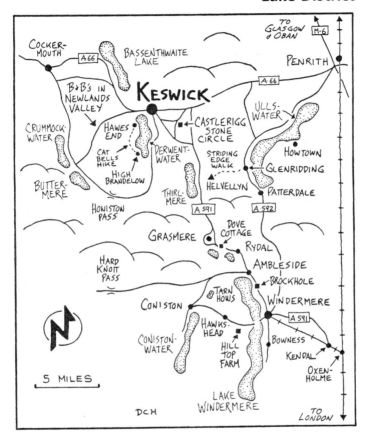

Swimming—The Leisure Center has a pool kids love, with a huge water slide (a short walk from the town center, tel. 017687/72760 for hours).

Sights—Derwentwater Area

▲▲**Derwentwater**—This is one of the region's most photographed and popular lakes. With four islands, good circular boat service, plenty of trails, and the pleasant town of Keswick at its north end, Derwentwater entertains.

The roadside views aren't much, so walk or cruise. You can walk around the lake (fine trail, but floods in heavy rains, 9 miles,

3 hrs), cruise it (50 min), or do a hike/sail mix. I suggest a hike/sail trip around the lake. Boats run from Keswick about every 30 minutes (alternating clockwise and "anti-clockwise") from 10:00 to 19:30, making seven stops on each 50-minute round-trip. The best hour-long lakeside walk is the 1.5-mile path between the docks at High Brandlehow and Hawse End. You could continue, with a tea break at Lingholm Gardens, on foot along the lake back into Keswick. The boat trip costs £5 per circle with free stopovers, or 70p per segment. Stand on the pier or the boat may not stop (tel. 017687/72263).

▲▲**Cat Bells High Ridge Hike**—For a great (and easy) "king of the mountain" feeling, sweeping views, and a close-up look at the weather blowing over the ridge, hike about two hours from Hawes End up along the ridge to Cat Bells (1,480 feet) and down to High Brandlehow. From there you can catch the boat or take the easy path along the shore of Derwentwater to your Hawes End starting point. This is probably the most dramatic family walk in the area. From Keswick, the lake, or your farmhouse B&B, you can see silhouetted stick figures hiking along this ridge. Drivers can park free at Hawes End (not particularly safe) or at the Littletown Farm on the Newlands Valley side of Cat Bells (£1).

Cat Bells is just the first of a series of peaks all connected by a fine ridge trail. Heartier hikers continue up to 9 miles along this same ridge, enjoying valley and lake views as they arc around the Newlands Valley toward (and even down to) Buttermere. After High Spy you can descend an easy path into Newlands Valley. An ultimate day plan would be to bus to Buttermere, climb Robinson, and follow the ridge around to Cat Bells and back to Keswick.

▲▲**Car Hiking from Keswick**—Distances are short, roads are narrow with turnouts, and views are rewarding. Ask your B&B host for advice. Particularly scenic drives include Latrigg (from a car park just north of Keswick, walk a few minutes to the top of the hill for a commanding view of the town and lake). Two miles south of Keswick on the lakeside B5289 Borrowdale Valley Road, take the small road left (signposted Watendlath) for a half mile to a packhorse bridge (a quintessential Lake District scene) and, a half-mile farther, to a car park and the "surprise view" of Derwentwater. Return down to B5289 and back to Keswick or farther south to the scenic Borrowdale and Buttermere.

▲▲**Buttermere**—This ideal little lake with a lovely, encircling 4-mile stroll offers non-stop, no-sweat, Lakeland beauty. If you're not a hiker but kind of wish you were, take this walk. If you're very short on time, at least stop here and get your shoes dirty. (Parking and pubs in Buttermere village.) Buttermere is connected with Borrowdale and Derwentwater by a great road over the rugged Honister Pass, strewn with glacial debris and curious shaggy Swaledale sheep (looking more like goats with their curly horns). In the other direction you can explore the cruel Newlands Valley or carry on through gentler scenery along Crummock Water and through the forested Whinlatter Pass (fine new visitor's center with a café the flying squirrels love) and back to Keswick.

▲▲**Castlerigg Stone Circle**—These 38 stones, 90 feet across and 3,000 years old, are mysteriously laid out on a line between the two tallest peaks on the horizon. For maximum goosepimples (as they say here), show up at sunrise or sunset (free, open all the time, just east of Keswick, follow brown signs, three minutes off A66, easy parking).

▲▲**More Hikes**—The area is riddled with wonderful hikes. B&Bs all have fine advice. From downtown Keswick you can walk the 7-mile Latrigg hike; include the Castlerigg Stone Circle. From the car park at Newlands Pass, at the top of Newlands Valley, an easy 1-mile walk to Knottrigg probably offers more thrills per calorie burned than any walk in the region.

Sights—Windermere Area

▲**Brockhole National Park Visitors Centre**—Check the events board as you enter. The center offers a 20-minute "Enjoying Lakeland" introduction-to-the-lakes slideshow (played upon request), an information desk, organized walks, exhibits, a bookshop, a good cafeteria, gardens, nature walks, and a large car park. It's in a stately old lakeside mansion between Ambleside and the town of Windermere on A591 (daily April–October 10:00–17:00, free entry but £3.50 to park, tel. 015394/46601). The bookshop has an excellent selection of maps and guidebooks. I enjoyed Hunter Davies' refreshingly opinionated (but now a bit dated) *Good Guide to the Lakes* (£5).

▲▲**Dove Cottage**—William Wordsworth, the poet whose appreciation of nature and back-to-basics lifestyle put this area on the map, spent his most productive years (1799–1808) in this well-preserved old cottage on the edge of Grasmere.

Today it's the obligatory sight for any Lake District visit. Even if you're not a fan, Wordsworth's "plain living and high thinking," his appreciation of nature, his romanticism, and the ways his friends unleashed their creative talents are very appealing. The 20-minute cottage tour (departures every few minutes) and adjoining museum are excellent. Even a speedy, jaded museum-goer will want at least an hour here (£4.30, daily 9:30–17:30, tel. 015394/35544).

Rydal Mount—Wordsworth's final, higher-class home with a lovely garden and view lacks the charm of Dove Cottage. Just down the road from Dove Cottage, it's worthwhile only for Wordsworth fans (£3, daily 9:30–17:00, tel. 015394/33002).

▲Beatrix Potter's Hill Top Farm and Other Sights— Many come to the lakes on a Beatrix Potter pilgrimage. Sensing that, entrepreneurial locals have dreamed up a number of BP sights. This can be confusing. Most important (and least advertised) is **Hill Top Farm**, the 17th-century cottage where Potter wrote many of her Peter Rabbit books (£3.60, April–October Saturday–Wednesday 11:00–17:00, closed Thursday and Friday, next to Sawrey, near Hawkshead, tel. 015394/36269). Small, dark, and crowded, it gives a good look at her life and work. Visitors should note that the short walk to the tiny nearby lake, Tarn Hows, is one of the most popular (and crowded) 1.5-mile strolls in the Lake District.

The **Beatrix Potter Gallery** (in the neighboring, likeable town of Hawkshead) shows off BP's original drawings and watercolor illustrations used in her children's books, and tells more about her life and work (£2.70, Sunday–Thursday 10:30–16:30, closed Friday and Saturday, on Main Street, tel. 015394/36355). The gimmicky **World of Beatrix Potter** tour—which features a five-minute video trip into the world of Mrs. Tiggywinkle and company, a series of tableaus starring the same imaginary gang, and a 15-minute video biography of BP—is a hit with children (not worth £3, daily 10:00–19:00, in Bowness near Windermere town, tel. 015394/88444).

Hard Knott Pass—Only 1,300 feet above sea level, this pass is a thriller, with a narrow, winding, steeply graded road. Just over the pass are the scant but evocative remains of the Hard Knott Roman fortress. Great views, miserable rainstorms, frustrating, and very slow when the one-lane road with turnouts is clogged by traffic (avoid in summer).

Sights—Ullswater Area

▲▲▲**Ullswater Hike and Boat Ride**—Long, narrow Ullswater offers 8 miles of diverse and grand Lake District scenery. While you can drive it or cruise it, I'd ride the boat from the south tip halfway up and hike back. Boats leave Glenridding regularly (£2.80, from 10:00–16:30, until 17:45 in July and August; get there a little early in summer; 35-minute ride, cheap and safe parking lot, pick up their 25p map/guide for the walk, tel. 017684/82229). Ride to the first stop, Howtown, halfway up the lake. Then spend four hours hiking and dawdling along the well-marked path by the lake south to Patterdale and then along the road back to Glenridding. This is a serious 7-mile walk with good views, varied terrain, and a few bridges and farms along the way. Wear good shoes and be prepared for rain. For a shorter hike, consider a circular walk from Howtown Pier. (Round-trip boat rides cost only 60p more than one-way.) There are several steamer trips daily up and down Ullswater. A good rainy-day plan is to ride the covered boat up and down the lake (2 hrs) or to Howtown and back (£3.10, 1 hr).

Helvellyn—Often considered the best high-mountain hike in the Lake District, this breathtaking, round-trip route from Glenridding includes the spectacular Striding Edge ridge walk. Be careful; do this six-hour hike only in good weather, and get advice from the Glenridding tourist office. While there are shorter routes, the Glenridding ascent is best.

Sleeping in the Lake District
(£1 = about $1.60, tel. code: 017687)

Sleeping in Keswick
Sleep Code: **S**=Single, **D**=Double/Twin, **T**=Triple, **Q**=Quad, **b**=bathroom, **t**=toilet only, **s**=shower only, **CC**=Credit Card (**V**isa, **M**asterCard, **A**mex).

The Lake District abounds with attractive B&Bs, guest houses, and youth hostels. It needs them all when summer hordes threaten the serenity of this romantic mecca. With the mobility of a car, you should have no trouble finding a room. But to get a particular place (especially on a Saturday), call ahead. Those using public transportation should stay in Keswick. With a car, drive into a remote farmhouse experience. Lakeland hostels are fine money-savers and filled with an interesting crowd. The Keswick TI can give you phone numbers of places with vacancies if you call. If you drop in they can book you a room for no fee.

In Keswick I've featured two streets, each within 3 blocks of the bus station and town square. "The Heads" is a classier street lined with proud Victorian houses, close to the lake, overlooking a golf course. Stanger Street, a bit humbler but also quiet and handy, has smaller homes. All of my listings are strictly smoke-free. The launderette is around the corner from the bus station on Main Street (7:30–18:30, self-service, change machine and coin-op flake dispenser).

Sleeping on The Heads

Berkeley Guest House, a big slate mansion enthusiastically run by Barbara Crompton, has a pleasant lounge, cramped hallways, and carefully appointed, comfortable rooms. Request a view room. The chirpy, skylight-bright double in the attic is a fine value if you don't mind the stairs (small D-£30, Db-£40–44; The Heads, Keswick, Cumbria, CA12 5ER, tel. 017687/74222).

The Parkfield is thoughtfully run and decorated by Fay and Bob Watson. This big house is bright and pastel with a fine view lounge (eight rooms, D£36, Ds-£40, Db-£46, car park, CC:VM, The Heads, CA12 5ES, tel. & fax 017687/ 72328, email: parkfield-keswick@kencomp.net.

Howe Keld Lakeland Hotel offers more of a small hotel feel with 15 rooms, a bar, and evening meals (S-£20, Sb-£25, D-£40, Db-£46–50, two ground floor rooms, CC:VM, 5-7 The Heads, CA12 5ES, tel. & fax 017687/72417, David and Valerie Fisher). **West View Guest House**, next door, is smaller, simpler, and also a decent value (tel. 017687/73638).

Sleeping on Stanger Street

Abacourt House is an old Victorian slate townhouse completely redone by Sheila and Bill Newman. Bill, who just finished climbing all the "Wainwright" peaks, is a wealth of Lakeland sightseeing information and happy to point you in the most scenic direction. All five doubles have firm beds, TVs, and shiny, modern bathrooms (Db-£42, no children, 26 Stanger Street, Keswick, CA12 5JU, tel. 017687/72967).

A few doors down the **Dunsford Guest House** is another small, cheery place, run by a young couple who get their exercise fellrunning (Db-from £39, veggie breakfast options, 16 Stanger Street, tel. 017687/75059, Pat and Peter Richards).

Fell House B&B is a charming place. Proprietor Barbara Hossack serves tea and homemade cakes each evening (six rooms, S-£16, D-£32, Db-£38, 28 Stanger Street, CA12 5JU, tel. 017687/72669). **Badgers Wood B&B** is at the top of the street (D-£32, Db-£38, 30 Stanger Street, tel. 017687/72621, Irene and David).

Two former hotels now operate as hostels with £8 dorm beds: **Keswick** (four- to 12-bed rooms, center of town just off Station Road, tel. 017687/72484) and **Derwentwater** (2 miles south of Keswick, tel. 017687/77246).

Sleeping in Newlands Valley

With a car, I'd drive ten minutes past Keswick down the majestic Newlands Valley. Hiking opportunities are wonderful. If the place had a lake, it would be packed with tourists. But it doesn't—and it isn't. The valley is studded with 500-year-old farms that have been in the same family for centuries. Shearing day is reason to rush home from school. Sons get school out of the way ASAP and follow their dads. Neighbor girls marry sons and move in. Grandparents retire to the cottage next door. With the price of wool depressed, most of the wives supplement the family income by running B&Bs. Traditionally, farmhouses lacked central heating, and while they are now heated, you can still request a hot-water bottle to warm up your bed.

Newlands Valley is just over the Cat Bells ridge from Derwentwater between Keswick and Buttermere. Leave Keswick heading west on the Cockermouth Road (A66). Take the second Newlands Valley exit through Braithwaite and follow signs through Newlands Valley (drive toward Buttermere). You'll pass Stoneycroft B&B and Ellas Crag first, then the curious purple house (and the turnoff to Low Skelgill), then Birkrigg Farm B&B, and finally Keskadale Farm (about 4 miles before Buttermere). The road is one-lane with passing turnouts. **Birkrigg Farm** is the ideal farmhouse B&B. Mrs. Margaret Beaty offers visitors a comfy lounge, evening tea (good for socializing with her other guests), a classy breakfast, territorial view, and perfect peace on this 220-acre working farm. Take your toast and last cup of tea out to the front yard bench (£16–17 per person in S, D, T, or Q, family deals, one shower and one tub for six rooms, March–November, Birkrigg Farm, Newlands Pass Road, Keswick, Cumbria, CA12 5TS, tel. 017687/78278).

Keskadale Farm B&B is another great farmhouse experience with valley views and flapjack hospitality. This is a working farm with lots of curly-horned sheep and three rooms to rent (£17 per person in D or T, March–November, non-smoking, one minute farther down Newlands Pass Road to Buttermere Road on a hairpin turn, Keskadale Farm, Newlands, Keswick CA12 5TS, tel. 017687/78544, Margaret Harryman). One of the oldest farms in the valley, it's actually made from 500-year-old ship beams.

Low Skelgill Farm, with three rooms sharing one bathroom, is immediately under Cat Bells. This is ideal for hikers since you can leave your car there for the Cat Bells ridge walk (S-£16, D-£32, take the Buttermere Road to Stair and then follow the "narrow-gated" road to Skelgill, tel. 017687/78453, Ann Grave). She also runs a rustic "camping barn" with mattresses for £3 a night (no bedding provided).

Stoneycroft B&B, an elegant old farm with a "new" 100-year-old extension, rents six spacious rooms—the most comfortable in the valley (D-£38, Db-£44, non-smoking, evening meal if ordered early, CA12 5TS, tel. 017687/78240, e-mail: stoneycroft@btinternet.com, Sue and Mike Felton). While the other farms feel more real, this place is posher, with more garden and fewer children.

Ellas Crag B&B, while in the same glorious setting, is a more comfortable stone house and not a farm. This homey place, with a good mix of modern and traditional, is enthusiastically run by Tony, Jean, and Catherine Hartley (S-£20, Ds-£40, no twin beds, only doubles; non-smoking, dinner available, Stair, Newlands Valley, CA12 5TT, tel. 017687/78217).

The Bridge Hotel, just beyond Newlands Valley at Buttermere, offers a classy, musty, Old World countryside hotel experience (£60 per person with a five-course dinner, cheaper for longer stays, B&B only upon request, smoke-free rooms, CC:VM, Buttermere, Cumbria, CA13 9UZ, tel. & fax 01768/770252). Rooms lack TVs. There are no shops within 10 miles—only peace and quiet a stone's throw from one of the region's most beautiful lakes.

Lake District Hostels

The Lake District's inexpensive hostels, usually located in great old buildings, are handy sources of information and social fun (£6–9 a bed). Local TIs have lists. The Lake District's free booking service (tel. 015394/31117) can tell you which of the area's 30 hostels have beds available and can even book a place on your credit card (no more than seven days in advance). Since most hostels don't answer their phones during the day and many are full, this is a helpful service.

The Buttermere King George VI Memorial Hostel, a quarter-mile south of Buttermere village on Honister Pass Road, has good food, family rooms, and a royal setting (tel. 017687/70245). The well-run Borrowdale Hostel is secluded in Borrowdale Valley just south of Rosthwaite (drying rooms, tel. 017687/77257).

Eating in the Lake District

Eating in Keswick
The bus station faces a fine supermarket (Monday–Saturday 10:00–19:00, Sunday 10:00–16:00) which has a smoke-free **Coffee Shop Café**, popular with locals, featuring a healthy-for-your-body-and-your-pocketbook menu and regional specialties (last hot service at 17:30). **Mayson's Whole Food Restaurant** is favored for its homecooking: curry, cajun, vegetarian options, and not a chip in sight. It feels Californian (£6 meals, family-friendly, on Lake Road, tel. 017687/74101). **La Primavera**, an excellent but pricey (£18 meals) Italian restaurant, has a pub serving £6 meals from the same kitchen (out Main Street past the bus station, across from the Pencil Museum, tel. 017687/74621). For fish and chips, Keswickians go to **The Old Keswickian** (facing the TI, take-out or a smoke-free restaurant upstairs).

Locals will tell you that Keswick restaurants have it too easy and you need to drive for a really good meal. The **Old Posting House**, a 15-minute drive west of Keswick, serves excellent meals in a non-smoky pub setting (just beyond Cockermouth at Deanscales, tel. 01900/823-278).

Eating in Newlands Valley
Since most farmhouses don't serve dinner to their guests, take the lovely ten-minute drive to Buttermere for your evening meal at the **Fish Hotel** pub (£5, nightly 18:00–21:00, family-friendly, limited menu, good fish, chips for vegetables) or the more expensive but much cozier and tastier **Bridge Hotel** pub (£6 or £7, nightly 18:00–21:30, more interesting menu and

crowd). On the Keswick side of the valley, the **Farmer's Arms** pub in Portinscale also serves good pub grub. The **Swinside Inn**, the only pub actually in the valley, while a little tatty, serves decent meals.

Transportation Connections—Lake District

Keswick by bus to: Buttermere (4/day via Whinlatter Forestry Centre and Crummock Water, 40 min), **Borrowdale** (8/day to the powerfully scenic valley south of Derwentwater, Grange, and Seatoller, 30 min), **Grasmere/Ambleside/Windermere** (hrly, 1 hr), **Penrith** (6/day between 8:00 and 18:20, fewer on Sunday, 40 min, £3, offered by X5 Lakes Link buses). Buses run from the Penrith train station to Ullswater and Glenridding (5/day, 1 hr). Bus info tel. 01946/ 63222.

Penrith by train to: Oban (hrly to Glasgow, 2 hrs; then to Oban, 3/day, 3 hrs), **Edinburgh** (8/day, 2 hrs), **Blackpool** (hrly, 2 hrs, transfer in Preston), **Liverpool** (hrly, 2.5 hrs), **Birmingham** (hrly, 3 hrs), **London**'s Euston Station (hrly, 4.5 hrs). Train information tel. 0345/484-950.

Route Tips for Drivers

North Wales or Blackpool to the Lake District: The direct, easy way to Keswick is to leave the M6 at Penrith and take the A66 highway 16 miles to Keswick. For the scenic sightseeing drive through the south lakes to Keswick, exit the super M6 on A590/A591 through the towns of Kendal and Windermere to reach Brockhole National Park Visitors Centre. From Brockhole, take the A road to Keswick or the tiny road northeast directly to Troutbeck. Then follow A592 to Glenridding and lovely Ullswater.

For the drive north to **Oban**, see the Highlands chapter.

YORK

Historical York is loaded with world-class sights. Marvel at the York Minster, the finest Gothic church in England. Ramble through the Shambles, York's wonderfully preserved medieval quarter. Enjoy a walking tour led by an old Yorker. Hop a train at Europe's greatest Railway Museum, travel to the 1800s in the York Castle Museum, and head back to Viking York at the Jorvik exhibit.

York has a rich history. In A.D. 71 it was Eboracum, a Roman provincial capital. Constantine was proclaimed emperor here in A.D. 306. In the fifth century, as Rome was toppling, a Roman emperor sent a letter telling England it was on its own, and York became Eoforwic, the capital of the Anglo-Saxon kingdom of Northumbria. A church was built here in 627, and the town was an early Christian center of learning. The Vikings later took the town and from about 860 to 950 it was a Danish trading center called Jorvik. The invading and conquering Normans destroyed, then rebuilt the city, giving it a castle and the walls you see today. Medieval York, with 9,000 inhabitants, grew rich on the wool trade and became England's second city. Henry VIII spared the city's fine minster in order to use York as his Anglican church's northern capital. The Archbishop of York is second only to the Archbishop of Canterbury in the Anglican church. In the Industrial Age, York was the railway hub of north England. When it was built, York's train station was the world's largest. Today, except for its huge chocolate factory (Kit-Kats are made here), York's leading industry is tourism.

Planning Your Time

York rivals Edinburgh as the best sightseeing city in Britain after London. On even a ten-day trip through Britain, it deserves two nights and a day. For the best 36 hours, follow this plan: Catch the 19:00 city walking tour on the evening of your arrival. The next morning be at Jorvik at 9:00 when it opens (to avoid the midday crowds). The nearby Castle Museum is worth the rest of the morning (10:00–noon, I could even spend more time here). If you're rough, have lunch in the Golden Fleece pub. If you're fancy, lunch in a teahouse. Three options for your early afternoon: shoppers browse the Shambles, train buffs tour the National Railway Museum, and scholars do the Yorkshire Museum. Tour the minster at 16:00 before catching the 17:00 evensong service. Finish your day with an early evening stroll along the wall and perhaps through the abbey gardens. This schedule assumes you're there in the summer (evening orientation walk) and that there's an evensong on. Confirm your plans with the TI first.

Orientation (tel. code: 01904)

The sightseer's York is small. Virtually everything is within a few minutes' walk: the sights, train station, tourist information, and B&Bs. The longest walk a visitor might take (from a B&B across the old town to the Castle Museum) is 15 minutes.

Bootham Bar, a gate in the medieval town wall, is the hub of your York visit. At Bootham Bar (and on Exhibition Square facing it) you'll find the TI, the starting points for most walking tours and bus tours, handy access to the medieval town wall, Gillygate (lined with good eateries), and streets leading to my recommended B&Bs. (In York, a "bar" is a gate and a "gate" is a street. Go ahead, blame the Vikings.)

Tourist Information: The TI at Bootham Bar sells a 65p map. Ask for the free *What's On* guide (July–August Monday–Saturday 9:00–19:00, Sunday 10:00–18:00; September–June Monday–Saturday 9:00–17:00, tel. 01904/621-756).

Arrival in York: Upon arrival, grab a bench at the station and enjoy the enchanting voice of the woman announcer singing the train arrivals. The station is a five-minute walk from town; turn left down Station Road and follow the crowd toward the Gothic towers of the minster. After the bridge a block before the minster, signs to the TI send you left. Buses #30, #31, and #32 go from the station to my

York

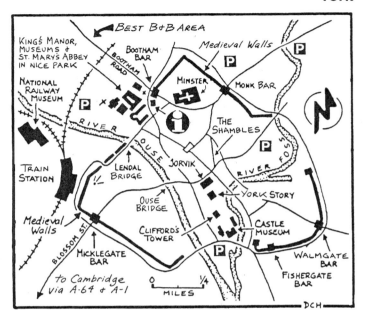

recommended B&Bs. Otherwise, they are a ten-minute walk or a £3 taxi ride.

Tours of York

▲▲▲**Walking Tours**—Charming local volunteer guides give energetic, entertaining, and free two-hour walks through York (daily, 10:15 all year and 14:15 April–October, plus 19:00 June–August, from Exhibition Square across from the TI). There are many other commercial York walking tours. York-Walk Tours have reliable guides and many themes (£2, TI has schedule). The ghost tours, offered after nightfall, are more entertaining than informative. Of the many ghost tours from which to choose, the "Original" and the "Haunted" are least gimmicky. But even their featured characters are pretty lame.

▲**Guide Friday Hop-on and Hop-off Bus Tours**—York's Guide Friday offers tour guides on speed who can talk enthusiastically to three sleeping tourists in a gale on a topless double-decker bus for an hour without stopping. Buses make the hour-long circuit, covering secondary York sights that the city walking tours skip. Tickets cost £7 on the bus, £6 from the TI (hop on and off all day, departures every ten or 15 minutes from 9:20 until around 18:00, tel. 01904/640-896). While you can hop on and off where you like, the York route is of no value from a transportation-to-the-sights point of view. I'd catch it at the TI and ride it for an orientation all the way around (1 hr) or get off at the Railway Museum, skipping the last five minutes. Many figure the information is kids' stuff after doing the free city walk. Guide Friday's competitors give you a little less for a little less.

Sights—York

▲**City Walls**—The historic walls of York provide a fine 2-mile walk. Walk from Bootham Bar (gate) to Monk Bar for outstanding cathedral views. Open until dusk (barring attacks) and free.

▲▲▲**York Minster**—The pride of York, this largest Gothic church north of the Alps (540 feet long, 200 feet tall) is a brilliant example of how the High Middle Ages were far from dark.

Your first impression might be the spaciousness and brightness of the nave (built 1280–1350). This is from the middle period of Gothic, called "Decorated Gothic," and it is one of the widest Gothic naves in Europe. Notice the Great West Window (1338) above the entry. The heart in the tracery is called "the heart of Yorkshire." The mysterious dragon's head (sticking out over the nave) was probably used as a crane to lift a font cover.

The north and south transepts are the oldest part of today's church (1220–1270). The oldest complete window in the minster, with the modern-looking "grisaille" pattern, is the Five Sisters' Window in the north transept (1260).

The fanciful choir and the east end (high altar) is from the last stage of Gothic, Perpendicular (1360–1470). The Great East Window (1405), the largest medieval glass window in existence, shows the beginning and the end of the world with scenes from Genesis and the Book of Revelation. A chart (on the right, with a tiny, more helpful chart within) highlights the core Old Testament scenes in this hard-to-read masterpiece.

The "foundations" (£2) give you a chance to climb down, archaeologically and physically, through the centuries to see the roots of the much smaller but still huge Norman church (Romanesque, 1100) which stood on this spot, and below that, to the Roman excavations. Constantine was proclaimed Roman emperor here in A.D. 306. Peek also at the modern concrete save-the-church foundations and the church treasury.

There are three more extra visits to consider: The chapter house, an elaborately decorated 13th-century Gothic dome, features playful details carved in the stonework (pointed out in the flier that comes with the 70p admission). You can step into the crypt which features 12th-century Romanesque art (70p), or scale the tower (£2, long climb, great view).

The cathedral is open daily 7:30–20:30 (tel. 01904/624-426). The chapter house, tower, and "foundations" have shorter hours, usually 10:00 to 18:00. Follow the *Welcome to the York Minster* flyer and ask about a free guided tour (they go frequently, you can join one in progress). The helpful blue-armbanded minster guides are happy to answer your questions. While a donation of £1.50 is reasonably requested, if I'm visiting the foundations or climbing the tower, I give it (and more) in the form of those admissions.

Evensong is a chance to experience the cathedral in musical and spiritual action. Evensong services are held daily at 17:00 (16:00 on Saturday and Sunday, but usually spoken on Monday and when the choir is off).

▲**The Shambles**—This is the most colorful old York street in the half-timbered, traffic-free core of town. Ye olde downtown York, while very touristy, is a window-shopping, busker-filled, people-watcher's delight. Don't miss the more frumpy Newgate Market or the old-time candy store just opposite the bottom end of the Shambles.

▲▲▲**York Castle Museum**—Truly one of Europe's top museums, this is a walk with Dickens, the closest thing to a time-tunnel experience England has to offer. It includes the Victorian Kirkgate: a fine collection of old shops well-stocked exactly as they were 150 years ago, along with costumes, armor, an eye-opening Anglo-Saxon helmet (from A.D. 750), and the entertaining "every home should have one" exhibit showing the evolution of vacuum cleaners, toilets, TVs, bicycles, stoves, and so on, from their crude beginnings to now. (£4.50, Monday–Saturday 9:30–17:30, Sunday 10:00–17:30, 1960s cafeteria, shop, car park; the £2.50 guidebook, while not necessary, makes a nice souvenir, tel. 01904/653-611.) Clifford's Tower (across from the Castle Museum) is all that's left of York's castle (13th century, site of a 1190 massacre of local Jews).

▲**Jorvik**—Sail the "Pirates of the Caribbean" north and back 800 years and you get Jorvik—more a ride than a museum. Innovative ten years ago, the commercial success of Jorvik inspired copycat ride/museums all over England. You'll ride a little Disney-type train car for 13 minutes through the re-created Viking street of Coppergate. It's the year 948 and you're in the village of Jorvik. Next your little train takes you through the actual excavation sight that inspired this. Finally you'll browse through a small gallery of Viking shoes, combs, locks, and other intimate glimpses of that redheaded culture (£4.50; daily from 9:00, last entry at 17:30; November–March last entry, at 15:30; tel. 01904/643-211). Avoid hour-long mid-day waits by going very early or very late. Some love this "ride"; others call it a gimmicky rip-off. If you're looking for a serious museum, see the Viking exhibit at the Yorkshire Museum. It's better. If you're thinking Disneyland with a splash of history, Jorvik's great. I like Jorvik, but it's not worth a long line.

▲▲**National Railway Museum**—This thunderous museum shows 150 fascinating years of British railroad history. Fanning out from a grand roundhouse are an array of historic cars and engines, including Queen Victoria's lavish royal car and the very first "stagecoaches on rails." There's much more, including exhibits on dining cars, post cars, sleeping cars, train posters, and videos. This biggest and best railroad museum anywhere is interesting even to people who think "Pullman" is Japanese for "tug-o-war" (£5, daily 10:00–18:00, tel. 01904/621-261).

▲**Yorkshire Museum**—Located in a lush and lazy park next to the stately ruins of St. Mary's Abbey, the Yorkshire Museum is the city's forgotten serious "archaeology of York" museum. While the hordes line up at Jorvik, the best Viking artifacts are here—with no crowds and in a better historical context. You have to walk through this museum, but the stroll takes you through Roman, Saxon, Viking, Norman, and Gothic York. Its prize piece is the delicately etched 15th-century pendant called the "Middleham Jewel." The video about the creation of the abbey is worth a look (£3.50, open daily 10:00–17:00).

Honorable Mention—York has a number of other sights and activities (described in TI material) which pale in comparison to the biggies. The Fairfax House is perfectly Georgian inside (£3.50, Monday–Saturday 11:00–16:30, Sunday 13:30–16:30). The York Story offers a 45-minute video on the history of

York—it's good, straight history (£2, associated with, across the street from, and pushed by the Castle Museum). The Richard III "museum" at Monk Bar is interesting only for Richard III enthusiasts (£1). The Antiques Centre is a fun browse (41 Stonegate near minster).

Sleeping in York
(£1 = about $1.60, tel. code: 01904)
Sleep Code: **S**=Single, **D**=Double/Twin, **T**=Triple, **Q**=Quad, **b**=bathroom, **t**=toilet only, **s**=shower only, **CC**=Credit Card (**V**isa, **M**asterCard, **A**mex).

I've listed peak-season book-direct prices. Don't use the TI. Outside of July and August some prices go soft. My recommendations are in the handiest B&B neighborhood, just outside the old-town wall's Bootham gate, along the road called Bootham. All are within a five-minute walk of the minster and TI and a ten-minute walk or £3 taxi ride from the station. If driving, head for the cathedral and follow the medieval wall to the gate called Bootham Bar. Bootham "street" leads away from Bootham Bar. The B&Bs are within 3 blocks on the left. These B&Bs are small and family-run. They will generally hold a room with a phone call, work hard to help their guests sightsee and eat smartly, have lots of fairly steep stairs, and are all on quiet, residential side streets. Most have permits for street parking. And most take no credit cards.

Airden House, the most central of my Bootham-area listings, has eight spacious rooms, a grandfather clock–cozy TV lounge, and brightness and warmth throughout. Susan and Keith Burrows keep their place simple, comfortable, and friendly. They are a great source of local travel tips (D-£38, Db-£46, non-smoking, 1 St. Mary's, York Y03 7DD, tel. 01904/638-915).

The Sycamore, run by Margaret and David Tyce, is a fine value with homey rooms and piles of personal touches, at the end of a dead-end opposite a fun-to-watch bowling green (D-£32, Db-£40, family deals, no lounge but TVs in the rooms, non-smoking, 19 Sycamore Place off Bootham Terrace, YO3 7DW, tel. & fax 01904/624-712).

The Hazelwood is my most hotelesque listing. Ian and Carolyn McNabb run this elegant and spacious old 14-room place in a stately, proper way, paying careful attention to details and serving a classy breakfast (Db-£50–53, Db with four-poster-£5 extra, family deals, non-smoking; a fridge, ice,

York, Our Neighborhood

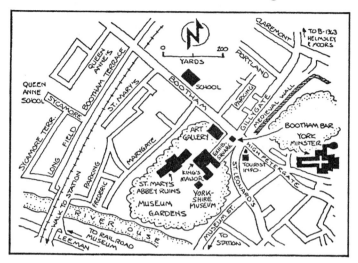

and great travel library in the basement lounge; CC:VM, 24 Portland Street, Gillygate, YO3 7EH, tel. 01904/626-548, fax 01904/628-032).

Abbeyfields Guest House has cozy, freshly decorated rooms and lots of stairs (S-£18, Sb-£26, Db-£44, 19 Boothham Terrace, YO3 7DD, tel. 01904/636-471, Richard and Gwen).

Claremont Guest House is a friendly, non-smoking house offering two rooms, thoughtful touches, and solid beds. Gill and Martyn Cornell offer laundry service and will cook an evening meal (D-£32, Db-£42, 18 Claremont Terrace off Gillygate, YO3 7EJ, tel. 01904/625-158).

White Doves is a cheery little place with four comfy rooms (Db-£40, family deals, 20 Claremont Terrace off Gillygate, YO3 7EJ, tel. 01904/625-957, Pauline and David Pearce).

23 St. Mary's is a rococo riot. Mrs. Hudson has done everything super-correctly, and offers nine rooms with strong beds, modern facilities, a classy lounge, and all the doily touches (Sb-£30–34, Db-£56–66 depending on season and size, non-smoking, 23 St. Mary's, YO3 7DD, tel. 01904/622-738).

Queen Anne's Guest House has six compact, clean, and cheery rooms (D-£30, Db-£34, family deals, non-smoking, 24 Queen Anne's Road, tel. 01904/629-389, Judy and David West).

Arrow Lodge B&B is also good (S or D-£13–16 per person, family room, non-smoking, 8 Queen Anne's Road, tel. 01904/642-344, Edith and Dave Mowbray).

The Golden Fleece, a "haunted" 400-year-old pub, offers five rooms and a funky, murky, creaky experience right in the center of the old town. The floors aren't level, the beds are four-posters, and the local crowd fills the ground-floor pub with smoke and belly laughs (pub closes at 23:00, D-£40, huge family room with a four-poster and bunks, small Jacuzzi in the shared bathroom, private car park, at the bottom end of the Shambles, 16 Pavement, York, YO1 2ND, tel. 01904/625-171, Sally and Dave Pyne).

York's Youth Hotel is well run, with lots of extras like a kitchen, Laundromat, games, and bar (D-£26, £11 in four- to six-bed dorms, sheets and breakfast extra, £1 less for multi-night stays, CC:VM, ten-minute walk from station at 11 Bishophill Senior Road, York YO1 1EF, tel. 01904/625-904 or 01904/630-613).

Eating in York

Good Meals Downtown
The old center is slathered with cute eateries. Consider one of several places along the street called Pavement. **The Golden Fleece** pub is a hopping place for lunch, serving famous Yorkshire pudding and hearty meals with the highest-priced beer in town (see Sleeping, above). **Kites,** closer to the center, on Grape Lane, serves tasty, fresh, and unusual French and English meals at good prices. **Ye Olde Starre Inn,** the oldest pub in town, has yet to learn the art of cooking.

York is famous for its elegant teahouses. Drop into one around 16:00 for tea and cakes. Ladies love **Betty's** (£4, daily 9:00–21:00, mostly non-smoking, St. Helen's Square, fine people-watching from a window seat, usually a line, wait for a main floor table), but several others can satisfy your king- or queen-for-a-day desires.

Eating near Bootham Bar and Your B&B
Walk along Gillygate and choose from a fun array of eateries including **Mama Mia's** (authentic Italian, indoor/outdoor patio, daily 11:30–14:00 and 17:30–23:00, 20 Gillygate, tel. 01904/622-020), **Miller's Yard** (extremely vegetarian take-out,

good desserts, Monday–Saturday 10:00–17:00, closed Sunday, in a courtyard opposite Mama Mia's, tel. 01904/610-676), **Cafe 8** (classy and good food), **Wagon and Horse** (basic pub grub with non-smoking section), **Rahima Indian Restaurant** (just beyond Gillygate on Clarance Street), the **Phoenix** (pricey Chinese, eat-in or take-out), and a traditional little fish-and-chips joint, **Gillygate Fisheries**, at #59 where tattooed people eat in and housebound mothers take out. For the closest you'll get to Mexico in Britain, try **Fiesta Mehicana** (17:30–19:00, sit-down or take-out, 14 Clifford Street, tel. 01904/610-243). **Cafe Concerto** has a loyal following (on Petergate, under Bootham Bar). For pub dinners, consider the **Coach House** (nightly 18:30–21:30, 20 Marygate, tel. 01904/652-780). The people who run your B&B know what's good.

Transportation Connections—York
By train to: Durham (2/hr, 40 min), **Edinburgh** (hrly, 2 hrs, £39), **London** (2/hr, 2 hrs, £44), **Bath** (via Bristol, hrly, 5 hrs), **Cambridge** (nearly hrly, 2 hrs with a change in Petersborough), **Birmingham** (8/day, 3 hrs). Train info tel. 0345/484-950.

By bus to: Keswick (1/day, 4 hrs).

By car: If you're nearing the end of your trip, consider dropping your car upon arrival in York. The money saved by turning it in early nearly pays for the train ticket that whisks you effortlessly to Edinburgh or London. Avis, Hertz, Kenning, and Budget all have car rental offices in York.

NEAR YORK: NORTH YORK MOORS
The North York Moors are a vacant lot compared with the Cumbrian Lake District. But that's unfair competition. In the lonesome North York Moors, you can wander through the stark beauty of its time-passed villages, bored sheep, and powerful landscapes.

Sights—North York Moors
▲**The Moors**—Car hike across the moors on any small road. You'll come upon tidy villages, old Roman roads, and maybe even a fox hunt. Danby Lodge, the North York Moors Visitors Centre, provides the best orientation for exploring the moors. It's a grand old lodge offering exhibits, shows, nature walks, an information desk with plenty of books and maps, brass-rubbing, a cheery cafeteria, and brochures on several

good walks that start right there (free, daily April–October
10:00–17:00, closed off-season, a half-mile from the train station, tel. 01287/660-654).

▲**North Yorkshire Moors Railway**—This 18-mile, one-hour
steam engine ride from Grosmont and Goathland to Pickering
goes through some of the best parts of the moors almost hourly.
Even with the windows small and dirty (wipe off the outside of
yours before you roll) and the track mostly in a scenic gully, it's
a good ride (£9 round-trip, tel. 01751/472-508).

Pickering, with its rural-life museum, castle, and Monday
market, is worth a stop. You could catch the York–Pickering
bus (hrly, 75 min), see Pickering, ride the train with a stop
along the way to take a moors walk, and carry on to Grosmont,
which is on a regular train line with good connections to
Whitby and points north.

▲**Hutton-le-Hole**—This postcard-pretty town is home of the
fine Ryedale Museum, which illustrates "farm life in the
moors" through reconstructed and furnished 18th-century
local buildings (£3, daily April–October 10:00–17:30, tel.
01751/417-367).

Castle Howard—Especially popular since the filming of
Brideshead Revisited, this fine palatial home is about half as
interesting as the Cotswolds' Blenheim Palace (open late
March–October, two buses a day from York, 30 minutes).

Rievaulx Abbey—A highlight of the North York Moors and
beautifully situated, but if you've seen other fine old abbeys,
this is a rerun.

▲**James Herriot Country**—Herriot fans will be more interested in the Yorkshire Dales than the neighboring moors.
Local booklets at the TI lay out the route for drivers. The easy
way to make your *All Creatures Great and Small* pilgrimage is to
take one of several all-day bus tours from York (done once a
week by various companies) that cover all the sights, with commentary, for around £14.

Staithes/Whitby—See Durham/Northeast England chapter.

DURHAM AND NORTHEAST ENGLAND

Some of England's best history is harbored in the northeast. Hadrian's Wall reminds us that Britain was an important Roman colony 2,000 years ago. After a Roman ramble, you can make a pilgrimage to Holy Island where Christianity gained its first toehold in Britain. The logical next stop is Durham, to marvel at England's greatest Norman church and enjoy an evensong service. And, for a trip into the less distant past, spend a morning in the year 1913 at the Beamish Open-Air Folk Museum.

Planning Your Time

Of the sights described in this chapter, only Durham is convenient and worth a stop on a three-week British train trip. By car you'll be driving right by Hadrian's Wall, Holy Island, Bamburgh, and the Beamish Folk Museum, so they're worth considering. Whitby and Staithes are seaside escapes worth a stop only for the seagulls and surf. Whitby is accessible by train, but if you have a car, go for Staithes.

By car, connect Edinburgh and York by this string of sights, spending a night near Hadrian's Wall and a night in Durham on a one-month trip, just a night in Durham on a two- or three-week trip.

For drivers with 36 hours between Edinburgh and York, leave Edinburgh early, tour Hadrian's Wall and the fort, take a walk and have lunch, and get to Durham in time to tour the cathedral and enjoy the 17:15 evensong service. Sleep in

Durham. Tour Beamish (15 minutes north of Durham) or drive through the North York Moors the next day, arriving by late afternoon in York.

DURHAM

Without its cathedral, it would hardly be noticed. But this magnificently situated cathedral is hard not to notice (even zooming by on the train). Durham sits, seemingly happy to go nowhere along its river, under its castle and famous cathedral. It has a workaday, medieval, cobbled atmosphere and a scraggly peasant's market just off the main square. While Durham is the home of England's third-oldest university, the town feels rough and working-class, surrounded by newly closed coal mines and filled with tattooed and stapled people in search of job security.

Orientation (tel. code: 0191)

Tidy little Durham clusters everything safely under its castle within the tight, protective bend of its river. The longest walk you'd make would be a 15-minute walk from the train station to the cathedral.

Tourist Information: On the town square, the TI organizes free 90-minute city walks Wednesday and Saturday at 14:15 in season (Monday–Saturday 9:30–18:30, Sunday 14:00–17:00, less off-season, tel. 0191/384-3720).

Sights—Durham

▲▲▲**Cathedral**—Built to house the much-venerated bones of St. Cuthbert from Lindisfarne, the cathedral is the best and purest look at Norman architecture in England (free, daily 7:15–20:00, less off-season, limited access during services; the tower, treasury, and monks' dorm are open 10:00–16:00, shorter hours Sunday).

St. Cuthbert, an inspirational leader of the early Christian church in Northern England, lived in the Lindisfarne monastery on Holy Island (100 miles north of Durham). He died in 687. Eleven years later his body was exhumed and found to be miraculously preserved. This stoked the popularity of his shrine and pilgrims came in growing numbers. When Vikings raided Lindisfarne in 875, the monks fled with his body (and the famous illuminated Lindisfarne Gospels). After years of roaming, they settled (in 995) in Durham, on

Durham

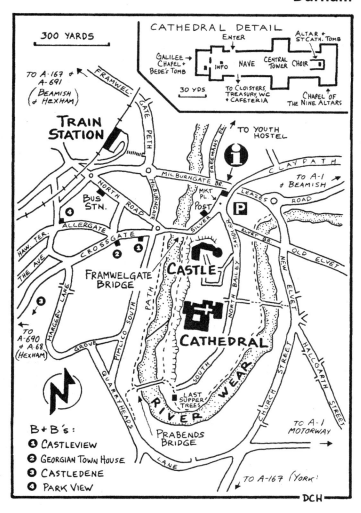

CATHEDRAL DETAIL

B+B's:
❶ CASTLEVIEW
❷ GEORGIAN TOWN HOUSE
❸ CASTLEDENE
❹ PARK VIEW

an easy-to-defend hairpin bend in the Wear River. The cathedral was built over Cuthbert's tomb.

The cathedral is particularly harmonious because it was built in a mere 40 years (1093–1133). Few additions were made and the bulk of what you see today is Norman (that's British for Romanesque). The round arches and zigzag carved decorations are textbook Norman. The church was also proto-Gothic, built by well-traveled French masons and architects who knew the latest innovations from Europe. Its stone and ribbed roof, first pointed arches, and first flying buttresses were revolutionary in England. It's not as cluttered as other churches for several reasons. Out of respect for St. Cuthbert, for centuries no one else was buried here. During the Reformation, Henry VIII destroyed anything Catholic, and subsequent fires and wars destroyed what he didn't.

A Tour Plan: From the cathedral green, notice how this fortress of God stands boldly across from the Norman keep of Durham's fortress of man. (The castle, now part of the university, is not worth touring.) At the cathedral door the big bronze lion-faced knocker (a replica of the 12th-century original, which is in the treasury) was used by criminals seeking sanctuary (read the explanation).

Immediately inside you'll see the information desk. Church attendants happily answer questions. Ideally, follow a church tour (Monday–Friday at 10:30 or other times by appointment; there's usually one in session somewhere that you're welcome to join, £2 donation). The 40p "walkabout" guide pamphlet is informative but dull.

The black marble strip on the floor was as close to the altar as women were allowed in the days when this was a Benedictine church (until 1540). Sit down (ignoring the black line) and let the fine proportions of England's best Norman (and arguably Europe's best Romanesque) nave stir you. Any frilly woodwork and stonework were added in later centuries.

Enter the Galilee Chapel in the back of the nave (late Norman, from 1175). Notice the paintings of St. Cuthbert and St. Oswald (seventh-century king of Northumbria) on the side walls of the altar niche, rare examples of Romanesque or Norman paintings. In the center is the tomb of the Venerable Bede, "the father of English learning," who died in 735 and was buried here in the 11th century.

Back in the main church, stroll down the nave to the center under the highest bell tower in Europe (218 feet). Gaze up. The ropes pull hammers that ring the bells. Continuing east (all medieval churches faced east), you enter the "choir." Monks worshiped many times a day, and the choir in the center of the church provided a cozier place to gather in this vast, dark, and cold building. This is the heart of the cathedral where Mass has been said daily for 900 years. The fancy wooden chairs are from the 17th century. The Norman choir leads to the Gothic east end of the church. Passing the lacy Neville Screen (1380), you'll find the tomb of St. Cuthbert.

Finally, step into the relatively extravagant, 13th-century Chapel of the Nine Altars—taller, lighter, and more vertical than the Norman nave.

The treasury (well worth £1) is filled with medieval bits and holy pieces. It fleshes out this otherwise stark building. The actual relics from St. Cuthbert's tomb are at the far end. The view from the tower will cost you 325 steps and £2. The "Monks' Dormitory" is now a library with an original 14th-century timber roof filled with Anglo-Saxon stones (worth 80p). The unexceptional A-V show in the unexceptional undercroft tells about St. Cuthbert (50p). The fine cafeteria (smoke-free, serving lunch 12:00–14:30), bookshop, and WCs are next to the treasury.

Evensong: For a thousand years this cradle of English Christianity has been praising God. To really experience the cathedral, go for an evensong service. Arrive early and ask to be seated in the choir. It's a spiritual Oz as 40 boys sing psalms—a red-and-white-robed pillow of praise, raised up by the powerful pipe organ. If you're lucky and the service went well, the organist runs a spiritual musical victory lap as the congregation breaks up. (September through mid-July at 17:15 almost nightly, Sunday at 15:30, normally not sung on Monday or when school term is out, which is mid-July–August; no sermon or offering plates; tel. 0191/386-2367.)

Riverside Walk—For a 20-minute woodsy escape, walk Durham's riverside path from busy Framwelgate Bridge to sleepy Prebends Bridge. Just beyond the Prebends Bridge on the old-town side of the river, you'll find *The Upper Room*, a cluster of trees carved to show the Last Supper when seen from the tree-trunk throne provided. Where are the apostles? Count the tree trunks.

Sleeping in Durham
(£1 = about $1.60, tel code: 0191)
Sleep Code: **S**=Single, **D**=Double/Twin, **T**=Triple, **Q**=Quad, **b**=bathroom, **t**=toilet only, **s**=shower only, **CC**=Credit Card (**V**isa, **M**asterCard, **A**mex).

My recommended B&Bs are along or near Crossgate (between the train station and cathedral; from the city center, cross Framwelgate Bridge, take the first left, up the hill). They are within a five- or ten-minute walk of both the town square and train station.

Castleview Guest House, 400 yards off Framwelgate Bridge, is a good bet. It's creaky, but it has been remodeled in a modern style, with eight comfortable rooms and a classy lounge (Sb-£28, Db-£48; 4 Crossgate, DH1 4PS, tel. & fax 0191/386-8852, Mike and Anne Williams). **The Georgian Town House**, next door, is also handy and comfortable (Db-£50, non-smoking, 10 Crossgate, tel. 0191/386-8070, Jane Weil).

Castledene B&B is tidy, simple, and friendly (twin-£36; continue up Crossgate to Palatine View, cross the street, go up ten steps to the pedestrian lane and walk 100 yards parallel to and above Crossgate Path to the last house, 37 Nevilledale Terrace; parking, tel. 0191/384-8386, Lorna and Brian Byrne).

Park View B&B is an unremarkable place with three rooms and a handy location (Db-£40, family deals, 1 Allergate Terrace, tel. 0191/386-7034, June Buxton). Consider the simpler **Bromme Farm Guest House** which is good but out of town (four rooms, D-£35, across from Love's Pub in Broom Park, tel. 0191/386-4755).

Durham Castle, a student residence actually on the castle grounds facing the cathedral, rents 100 singles and 30 doubles (July–September only, £20 per person, £30 with private facilities, elegant breakfast hall; parking, with luck, on the cathedral green; tel. 0191/374-3873). Request a room in the classy old main building or you may get bomb shelter–style modern dorm rooms.

Eating in Durham

Trust your host's advice, or stroll from Framwelgate Bridge through Market Place up Saddler and take what looks good. **La Trattoria**, near Market Place, is popular for Italian (arrive early or wait). And **Albert** is a good typical English pantry in the town center. **Shaheens**, in the old post office up Saddler Street, serves Indian meals with a healthy twist (nightly from 18:00). **The Stones**, on Silver Street, is a trendy 1960s burger place. Consider the **Royal County** for a £20 splurge. **The Duke of Wellington**, serving decent and big-enough-for-two meals in great pub atmosphere, is worth the drive (1.5 miles down the A1050/Darlington Road).

Transportation Connections—Durham

By train to: Edinburgh (5/day, 2 hrs), **York** (hrly, 1 hr), **London** (hrly, 3 hrs), **Newcastle** (hrly, 15 min, then trains or buses to Hadrian's Wall). Train info tel. 0345/484-950.

Parking in Durham: While there are a few parking spots right on the cathedral green, the high-rise parking garage in the town center (£1.60/day) is easier. From the garage's seventh floor, a walkway takes you right into the old town.

HADRIAN'S WALL

This is one of England's most thought-provoking sights. Around A.D. 130, during the reign of Emperor Hadrian, the Romans built this great stone wall. Its actual purpose is still debated. While Rome ruled Britain for 400 years, it never quite ruled its people. The wall may have been used to define the northern edge of the empire, protect Roman Britain from invading Scottish tribes (or at least cut down on pesky border raids), monitor the movement of people, or simply give an otherwise bored army something to do. (Nothing's more dangerous than a bored army.) Stretching 74 miles coast to coast across the narrowest stretch of northern England, it was built by and defended by nearly 20,000 troops. The wall was flanked by ditches, with castles guarding gates every mile, two turrets between each castle, and a military road on the south side. The mile castles are numbered. (Eighty of them cover the 74 miles because a Roman mile was slightly shorter than our mile.) Today, several chunks of the wall, ruined forts, and museums thrill history buffs.

Sights—Hadrian's Wall

▲▲**Housesteads Fort**—With its fine museum, national park information center, the best-preserved segment of the wall, and surrounded by powerful scenery, this is your best single stop (museum £2.50, daily 10:00–18:00, less off-season, car park, snack bar, tel. 01434/344-363).

▲▲**Hiking the Wall**—From Housesteads, hike west along the wall speaking Latin. For a good, craggy, 3-mile walk along the best-preserved segment of the wall, hike between Housesteads and Steel Rigg. You'll pass a mile castle sitting in a nick in a crag (castle #39, called Castle Nick). There's a car park near Steel Rigg (take the little road up from the Twice Brewed Pub).

▲**Vindolanda**—This larger Roman fort (which actually predates the wall by 40 years) and museum is just south of the wall and

Durham and Northeast England

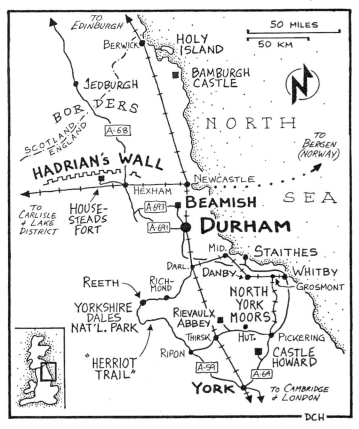

worth a visit only if you've devoured the Housesteads museum and are still hungry. From the car park you'll walk through 600 meters of grassy parkland decorated by the foundation stones of the Roman fort and a full-size replica chunk of the wall. At the far side of the site is the best Roman museum in the area. Eight forts were built on this spot. By carefully sealing the foundations from each successive fort, Roman demolition teams left 20th-century archaeologists 7 meters of remarkably well-preserved artifacts to excavate. The earliest examples of Roman writing were recently discovered here, shining a new light on life on the northern fringe of the Empire. While the actual fragments are in

London's British Museum, see the interesting, detailed video here (£3.50; £5.25 combo ticket includes Roman Army Museum, below; daily 10:00–18:00, closes earlier off-season, tel. 01434/344-277). The **Roman Army Museum** (£2.80, or buy combo ticket, above; same hours), a few miles farther west at Greenhead, is redundant if you've seen Vindolanda.

Sleeping near Hadrian's Wall
(£1 = about $1.60, tel code: 01434)
To sleep literally up against the wall, the **Sewing Shields Farm B&B** is a great value with three farm-fancy rooms and a marvelous setting (S-£16, D-£32, and a quad, family deals, evening meals if ordered ahead; just east of Housesteads Fort, Haydon Bridge, Hexham, NE47 6NW, tel. 01434/684-418, run by friendly Lyn Murray). This is worth calling ahead for. If you're without a car (to get to restaurants), request meals well in advance. The 45-minute walk from Sewing Shields along the wall to Housesteads Fort is an experience you'll never forget.

Crindledykes Farm is a classier building in an equally idyllic and peaceful setting but a mile south of the wall (small D-£30, spacious twin room with view-£32, room for a child's bed; WC down the hall, non-smoking, signposted from the B6318 at Housesteads, Bardon Mill, Hexham, NE47 7AF, tel. 01434/344-316, Judy Davidson).

The nearby **Mile Castle Pub** cooks up all sorts of exotic game and offers the best dinner around, according to hungry national park rangers. Two miles west of Housesteads, the **Twice Brewed Pub and Hotel** serves decent pub grub nightly to a local darts-and-pool crowd (S-£17, D-£34, dreary rooms, rarely full, tel. 01434/344-534). Next door to the Twice Brewed Pub is the comfortable **Once Brewed Youth Hostel** (£9 per bed, with breakfast, four to seven beds per room, tel. 01434/344-360).

Crow's Nest B&B offers six rooms in a remodeled farmhouse a quarter-mile from the Wall (D-£30, East Twice Brewed, Bardon Mill, Hexham, tel. 01434/444-348).

Cuan Dor Cottage in Hallington, 11 miles north of Hexham, is a good value (Db-£40–45, tel. 01434/672-412, Liz and Ian Veitch).

Transportation Connections—Hadrian's Wall
To reach Hadrian's Wall, catch a train from Durham to Newcastle (hrly, 15 min), then head east on the Newcastle–Carlisle

line (6/day) to Bardon Mill (45 min from Newcastle), the stop nearest Housesteads Fort; from Bardon Mill, catch a taxi to the fort or your B&B (your host can arrange this). In summer, special Hadrian's Wall buses go between the Hexham and Haltwhistle train stations connecting the various wall sights (4/day, tel. 01434/344-396). Train info tel. 0345/484-950.

If you're driving, take B6318, which parallels the wall and passes several viewpoints, minor sights, and "severe dips." (If there's a certified nerd or bozo in the car, these road signs add a lot to a photo portrait.)

Other Sights near Durham

▲▲**Beamish Open-Air Museum**—This huge museum, which re-creates the year 1913 in northeast England, takes at least three hours to explore. A vintage tram shuttles visitors around the park stopping at each of the four stations: Coal Mine Village, Home Farm, The Town, and an 1820s Manor House. This isn't wax. If you touch the exhibits, they may smack you. Attendants at each stop explain everything.

Start with the colliery village (company village around a coal mine), with school, church, miners' homes, and a fascinating—if claustrophobic—20-minute tour into a real "drift" mine. "The Town" (along with the mine tour) is the highlight. This bustling street features a 1913 candy shop, dentist's office, garage, working pub (fun for a smoky beer), and a 1990s smoke-free cafeteria. The old train station isn't much. The Pockerley Manor (first part of a new section re-creating the 1820s) is barely worth the climb. The Home Farm is the least interesting section. (£8, daily 10:00–18:00, shorter hours as the season wanes, closed in winter Monday and Friday; check events schedule as you enter, last tickets two hours before closing, tel. 01207/231-811.)

Durham–Beamish buses go hourly, stopping 700 yards from the museum. A summer-only museum shuttle bus (Durham station to museum door) leaves three times each morning and returns three times each afternoon. Drivers find the museum well signposted, located between the villages of Stanley and Chester-le-Street. From Durham, drive north on the M1 to the first exit (Chester-le-Street) and follow the signs.

▲**Whitby**—Whitby (on the coast of the North York Moors) is a fun resort town with a busy harbor and steep and salty old streets, a carousel of Coney Island–type amusements overseen by the stately ruins of its seventh-century abbey. Whitby has been an important port since the 12th century. The **Captain Cook Memorial Museum** offers an interesting look at the famous hometown sailor and his exotic voyages (£1.80, daily 9:45–17:00, in the old town, just over the bridge). Two of Captain Cook's boats (*Resolution* and *Endeavour*) were built in the Whitby shipyards. The tourist office (daily 9:30–18:00, tel. 01947/602-674) is on the harbor next to the train and bus stations.

Whitby has plenty of rooms. August is the only tight month. **The Crescent House** has six rooms with modern bathrooms, most with sea views (Db-£37, family deals, non-smoking, on the bluff just south of the harbor at 6 East Crescent, YO21 3HD, tel. 01947/600-091, Janet and Mike Paget). **The Dolphin Hotel** is in the heart of the old town at the bridge overlooking the harbor (D-£33–37, 3 blocks from the train station, tel. 01947/602-197). It's basically a pub (closes at 23:00) with a few very well-worn scruffy rooms upstairs. The **hostel** (£8 per bed, 70 beds in ten rooms, closed 10:00–17:00, tel. 01947/602-878) is next to the abbey.

Buses connect Whitby and York (5/day, 2 hrs, tel. 01653/692-556). Eight trains a day connect Durham with Middlesbrough (50 min); the Middlesbrough–Whitby train (4/day, 90 min) stops at Grosmont (where you can catch the Moors steam train) and Danby (half-mile from the Moors info center).

▲**Staithes**—A poor and not particularly pretty village where the boy who became Captain James Cook got his first taste of the sea, this is a salty tumble of cottages bunny-hopping down a ravine into a tiny harbor. Ten years ago the town supported 20 fishing boats—today, only three. But fishermen (who pronounce their town "steerths") still outnumber tourists in undiscovered Staithes. There's nothing to do but drop by the life-boat house (these are a big deal in England; page through the history book, read the not-quite-stirring accounts of every time the boats were called to duty, drop a coin in the box), walk the beach, and relax to the tune of seagulls singing its praise.

I sleep in Staithes. The town is struggling. Tourists just aren't coming. It's changed little since Captain Cook's days. There are no fancy rooms. Each of these three- or four-bedroom places is cramped with old carpets, bad wallpaper, lumpy beds, and tangled floorplans that make you feel like a stowaway. The first is on the harborfront (worth the extra money for the view but not the rooms). The last three are small homes a block or two up High Street.

Harborside Guest House provides basic beds, sea view rooms, breakfast in a fish-and-chips shop, and the sound of waves to lull you to sleep (D-£39, four rooms, tel. 01947/841-296). Also, check out **Toffee Crackle House** (two £32 twins and a family room, non-smoking, tel. 01947/841-401, Kay Lanny); **Endeavour Restaurant B&B** (S-£18, D-£38, Db-£42, tel. 01947/840-825, Lisa Chapman); and **Salmon Cottage** (a £32 twin and a family room, tel. 01947/841-193, Geoff and Isabel Elliott). Staithes' zip code is TS13 5BH.

There's good bar food at the **Royal George** on High Street (dinners daily 19:00–21:00, throw darts while you wait). The oddly-classy-for-this-town **Endeavour Restaurant** serves excellent £15 dinners (fresh seafood, vegetarian, reservations at 01947/840-825). **The Cod and Lobster Pub**, while no one's choice for dinner, overlooks the harbor with outdoor benches and a cozy living room warmed by a coal fire.

Staithes is a short drive north of Whitby and worthwhile by car. Whitby–Staithes buses run hourly (30 min).

▲**Holy Island and Bamburgh**—Twelve hundred years ago, this "Holy Island" was Christianity's toehold on England. It was the home of St. Cuthbert. We know it today for the Lindisfarne Gospels, decorated by monks in the seventh century with some of the finest art from Europe's "Dark Ages" (now in the British Museum). It's a pleasant visit, a quiet town with an evocative priory and striking castle (not worth touring), reached by a 2-mile causeway that's cut off daily by high tides. Tidal charts are posted, warning you when this holy place becomes Holy Island and you become stranded (for tide information, tel. 01289/330-733). For a peaceful overnight, a few good B&Bs cluster in the town center (**Britannia Guest House**, D-£26, Db-£32, four rooms, tel. 01289/389-218).

Holy Island is a 30-minute bus ride from Berwick (2/day except Sunday), a town 70 minutes north of Durham on the London–Edinburgh train line. A few miles farther south down the coast from Holy Island is the grand **Bamburgh Castle**, overlooking the loveliest stretch of beach in Britain. Its impressive interior is worth touring (£2.50, daily April–October 11:00–17:00, tel. 01669/621-555). Berwick TI tel. 01289/330-733.

EDINBURGH

Edinburgh, the colorful city of Robert Louis Stevenson, Walter Scott, and Robert Burns, is Scotland's showpiece and one of Europe's most entertaining cities. Historical, monumental, fun, and well-organized, it's a tourist's delight.

Take a royal hike down the Royal Mile through the Old Town. Historic buildings pack the Royal Mile between the castle (on the top) and Holyrood Palace (on the bottom). Medieval skyscrapers stand shoulder-to-shoulder, hiding peaceful courtyards connected to High Street by narrow lanes or even tunnels. This colorful jumble, in its day the most crowded city in the world, is the tourist's Edinburgh.

Edinburgh (ED'n-burah) was once two towns divided by a lake. To alleviate crowding, the lake was drained and a magnificent Georgian city, today's New Town, was laid out to the north. Georgian Edinburgh, like the city of Bath, shines with broad boulevards, straight streets, square squares, circular circuses, and elegant mansions decked out in colonnades, pediments, and sphinxes in the proud, neoclassical style of 200 years ago.

Planning Your Time

While the major sights can be seen in a day, on a three-week tour of Britain, I'd give Edinburgh two days.

Day 1: Orient yourself with a Guide Friday bus tour. Do the whole loop, getting off only to tour the Georgian House. After lunch catch a 14:00 walking tour of the Royal Mile. If you tour

Holyrood Palace, do it after your walk, at about 16:00. Evening:
Scottish show, folk pub, or haunted walk.

Day 2: Climb Sir Walter Scott Memorial for a city view, then
take the 10:30 "City, Sea, and Hills" bus tour (or tour the
National Gallery). Visit the castle and spend the rest of the
afternoon on the Royal Mile museum-going or shopping.

Orientation (tel. code: 0131)

The center of Edinburgh holds the Princes Street Gardens
park and Waverley Bridge, where you'll find the TI, Waverley
Shopping and Eating Center, train station, bus info office, the
starting point for most city bus tours, festival office, the
National Gallery, and a covered dance-and-music pavilion.
Weather blows in and out—bring your sweater.

Tourist Information: The crowded TI has become a
profit-seeking business with advice colored by who gives the
best commissions. It's central as can be atop the Waverley Market on Princes Street (Monday–Saturday 9:00–20:00, Sunday
11:00–20:00, shorter hours and closed Sunday in off-season, tel.
0131/557-1700, airport TI tel. 0131/333-2167). Ideally, skip it
and telephone if you have questions. Their misnamed *Essential
Guide to Edinburgh* (which costs 25p and shuffles a little information between lots of ads) has a cruddy little map. *The List*,
the best monthly entertainment listing, is sold for £1.50 at
newsstands. Book your room direct without the TI's help.

For real info sans the sales push, visit the **Old Town
Information Centre** at Tron Church, South Bridge at the
Royal Mile, for a great free map of the Royal Mile. A couple of
blocks down the Mile, at 5 Blackfriars Street, the Backpackers'
Centre is a good source of budget travel information.

Banking: Barclays has decent rates without the typical 2
percent service charge if you have Barclays or Visa checks
(daily 9:30–17:00, 50 meters into New Town from TI and station at 18 South Andrew Street).

Sunday Activities: Many sights close on Sunday, but
there's still a lot to do: Royal Mile walking tour, city bus tour,
Edinburgh Castle, St. Giles Cathedral, Holyrood Palace, Royal
Botanic Gardens, Arthur Seat hike, shopping, and people-
watching at Princes Street Gardens. The Georgian House and
National Gallery open Sunday afternoon.

Arrival in Edinburgh: Arriving by train puts you in the
city center, a few steps from the TI and the city bus to my

Edinburgh

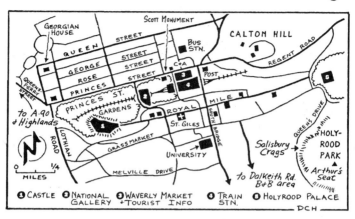

recommended B&Bs. Both National Express and Scottish Citylink buses use the bus station a block from the train station in the Georgian town on St. Andrew Square.

Edinburgh's slingshot-of-an-airport is 10 miles northwest of the center and well connected by shuttle buses (4/hr from Waverley Bridge, £3.40, flight info: tel. 0131/333-1000, British Midlands tel. 0345/554-554, British Air tel. 0345/222-111). Taxi to airport: £14.

Getting Around Edinburgh

Nearly all Edinburgh sights are within walking distance.

City buses are handy and inexpensive (average fare-60p, LRT info office, corner of Waverley Bridge and Market Street, tel. 0131/555-6363). Tell the driver where you're going, drop exact change into the box or lose the excess, grab your ticket as you board, push the stop button as you near your stop (so your stop isn't skipped), and exit from the middle door. All-day "Freedom Ticket" passes (£2.20) are sold at the LRT office on Waverley Bridge. Taxis are reasonable (easy to flag down, several handy pickup points, 90p drop charge, 60p extra after 18:00, average ride between downtown and B&B district—£3).

Bus Tours of Edinburgh

▲**Hop-on and Hop-off City Bus Tours**—Two companies, Guide Friday and LRT's "Edinburgh Classic Tour," offer buses that circle the town center—Waverley Bridge, around the castle, Royal Mile, Calton Hill, Georgian New Town, and Princes Street—in about an hour, with pick-ups about every 15 minutes and an informative narration. You can stop and go all day on one ticket. Overlapping can be interesting, since each guide has her own story to tell. On sunny days they go topless (the buses), but can suffer from traffic noise and congestion. (Guide Friday, £7, tel. 0131/556-2244; Classic Tour, £5.50, tel. 0131/555-6363.)

▲**City Bus Tours**—"City, Sea, and Hills" is the best 90-minute tour of greater Edinburgh (£3.50, daily at 10:30, information at LRT office, on Waverley Bridge, tel. 0131/555-6363). Several all-day bus tours can take you as far as Loch Ness. Tours leave from near the train station.

Sights—Along the Royal Mile

(In walking order from top to bottom.)

▲▲▲**Royal Mile**—This is one of Europe's most interesting historic walks. Each step of the way is entertaining. Start at the top and amble down to the palace. I've listed the top sights of the Royal Mile—working downhill.

The Royal Mile is actually a series of different streets in a straight line. All along, you'll find interesting shops, cafés, and *closes* (lanes leading to tiny squares), providing the thoughtful visitor a few rough edges of a town well on its way to becoming a touristic mall. See it now. In a few years, tourists will be riding down it on bagpipe skateboards.

Royal Mile Walking Tours: Follow a local guide along the Royal Mile (£4, free during Edinburgh Festival, daily usually at 10:00, 11:00, and 14:00, about 2 hrs long). Of the competitive, hardworking little companies that offer these entertaining tours, Robin's is most historic (start at TI, tel. 0131/661-0125) and Mercat is chattier (Mercat Cross on the Royal Mile, tel. 0131/661-4541). The guides, who enjoy making a short story long, ignore the big sights, taking you behind the scenes with piles of barely historic gossip, bully-pulpit Scottish pride, and fun but forgettable trivia.

▲▲**Edinburgh Castle**—The fortified birthplace of the city 1,300 years ago, this is the imposing symbol of Edinburgh. While the castle has been a royal residence since the 11th century, most of the buildings today are from its more recent use as a military garrison. Start with the free and wonderfully droll 30-minute guided introduction tour (3/hr, departs from

Royal Mile

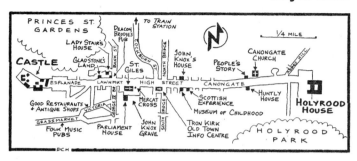

entry, see clock for the next departure). Then see the Scottish National War Memorial, Great Hall, Scottish Crown Jewels, the room full of Battle of Culloden mementos, St. Margaret's Chapel (oldest building in town), the giant cannon, and the city view from the ramparts (in that order). There's also a 20th-century military museum and a daily "one-o'clock gun." Allow two hours, including the tour. (£5.50, daily 9:30–18:00, until 17:00 in winter and on holidays, cafeteria; tel. 0131/225-9846.)

Scotch Whiskey Heritage Centre—This touristy ambush is designed to distill £4.20 out of your pocket. You get a video history, a little whiskey-keg train-car ride, and a free sample before finding yourself in the shop. People do seem to enjoy it, but that might have something to do with the sample (tel. 0131/220-0441). The Camera Obscura, across the street, is just as rewarding.

▲▲Gladstone's Land—Take a good look at this typical 16th- to 17th-century house, complete with a lived-in furnished interior and guides in each room who love to talk (£2.60, April–October Monday–Saturday 10:00–17:00, Sunday 14:00–17:00, good Royal Mile photo from the top-floor window or from the top of the entry stairway through the golden eagle).

▲Lady Stair's House/Writers' Museum—This interesting house, which dates back to 1622, is filled with manuscripts and knickknacks of Scotland's three greatest literary figures: Robert Burns, Sir Walter Scott, and Robert Louis Stevenson. Worth a few minutes for anyone, fascinating for fans (free, Monday–Saturday 10:00–18:00, till 17:00 off-season, closed Sunday).

Deacon Brodie's Tavern—A decent place for a light meal (see Eating, below); read the story of its notorious namesake on the wall facing Bank Street.

▲**St. Giles Cathedral**—Wander through Scotland's most important church. Don't miss this engaging Gothic church's ornate, neo-Gothic—from 1911—thistle chapel (£1 donation, to the right of the altar, find the angels playing bagpipes) or the Scottish crown steeple on top (daily 9:00–19:00, until 17:00 off-season, fine café downstairs). John Knox (whose statue is in the back of the church), founder of austere Scottish Presbyterianism, is buried out back, austerely, under the parking lot (spot 44).

Parliament House—Stop in to see the grand hall with its fine hammer-beamed ceiling and stained glass. For a trip into the 18th century, Tuesday through Friday around 10:00 or 10:30 is the best time to see all the wigged and robed legal beagles hard at work pacing the hall deep in discussion. Greater eminence . . . longer wig. The doorman is helpful (free, public welcome Monday–Friday 9:00–16:30, open-to-the-public trials 10:00–16:00, entry behind St. Giles Cathedral near parking spot 21).

▲**Tron Kirk**—This fine old building houses an interesting (free) Old Town history display and the genuinely helpful Old Town tourist information center. No crowds, just caring help by an outfit working to better organize and show off Edinburgh's historic Old Town.

Museum of Childhood—This is a 5-story playground of historical toys and games (free, Monday–Friday 10:00–18:00, till 17:00 off-season, closed Sunday).

▲**John Knox's House**—Fascinating for Reformation buffs, this fine 16th-century house offers a well-explained look at the life of the great reformer (£1.75, Monday–Saturday 10:00–16:30, closed on Sunday).

Scottish Experience—This touristy little side trip (free but commercial) is where you can reserve a spot for a Scottish Folk Evening (see below). The video and historic kilt room are free before the show.

People's Story—This interesting exhibition traces the lot of the working class through the 18th, 19th, and 20th centuries (free, Monday–Saturday 10:00–18:00, till 17:00 off-season, closed Sunday).

▲**Huntly House**—Another old house full of old stuff, worth a look for its early Edinburgh history and handy ground-floor

WC. Don't miss the copy of the National Covenant written on an animal skin or the sketches of pre-Georgian Edinburgh with its lake still wet (free, Monday–Saturday 10:00–18:00, closed Sunday). Just a toot farther downhill is Bagpipes Galore.

▲**Holyrood Palace**—At the bottom end of the Royal Mile, this is where the queen stays when she's in town. The building is rich in history and decor, but without information or a guided tour ("there's none of either," snickered the guy who sells the £3.50 museum guidebooks) you're just another peasant in the dark. Docents in each room are happy to give you the answer if you know the question. After wandering through the elegantly furnished rooms and a few dark older rooms filled with glass cases of historic bits and Scottish pieces that must be fascinating, you're free to wander through the ruined abbey and the queen's gardens (£5.30, Monday–Saturday 9:30–18:00, Sunday 10:30–16:30, closed when the queen's home, tel. 0131/556-7371).

More Bonnie Wee Sights

▲**Walter Scott Monument**—Built in 1840, this elaborate, neo-Gothic monument honors the great author, one of Edinburgh's many illustrious sons. The 200-foot monument shelters a marble statue of Scott. He is surrounded by busts of 16 great Scottish poets and 64 characters from his books. Climb 287 steps for a fine view of the city (£1, Monday–Saturday 9:00–18:00, until 17:00 off-season, closed Sunday).

▲▲**Georgian House**—This refurbished Georgian house, set on Edinburgh's finest Georgian square, is a trip back to 1796. A volunteer guide in each room is trained in the force-feeding of stories and trivia. Start your visit with the interesting video (£4, Monday–Saturday 10:00–17:00, Sunday 14:00–17:00, 7 Charlotte Square, tel. 0131/225-2160). From this museum, walk through Georgian Edinburgh. The grand George Street, connecting St. Andrew and Charlotte Squares, was the centerpiece of the elegantly planned New Town.

Princes Street Gardens—This grassy park, a former lake-bed, separates Edinburgh's New and Old Towns and offers a wonderful escape from the city. There are plenty of free concerts and country dances in the summer, and the oldest floral clock in the world. Join the local office workers for a picnic-lunch break.

National Gallery—An elegant neoclassical building with a small but impressive collection of European masterpieces and the best look you'll get at Scottish paintings (free, Monday–Saturday 10:00–17:00, Sunday 14:00–17:00, tel. 0131/556-8921).

Royal Botanic Garden—Britain's second-oldest botanical garden (established in 1670 for medicinal herbs) is now one of Europe's best (free, daily 10:00–20:00 in season, £2 "rainforest to desert" tours daily at 11:00 and 14:00, 1 mile north of the center at Inverleith, tel. 0131/552-7171).

▲▲**Arthur's Seat Hike**—A 30-minute hike up the 822-foot volcanic mountain (surrounded by a fine park overlooking Edinburgh), starting from the Holyrood Palace, Commonwealth Pool, or your B&B, gives you a rewarding view. It's the easiest "I climbed a mountain" feeling I've ever had. You can drive up most of the way from behind (follow the one-way street from the palace, park by the little lake) or run up like they did in *Chariots of Fire*. Ask a local for the best way up.

Brush Skiing—If you'd rather be skiing, the Hillend Ski Centre is an open-all-year hill covered with brush, with a chairlift, T-bar, and rentable skis, boots, and poles, on the edge of town (£6/hr with gear, daily 9:30–21:00, less on weekends, probably canceled if it snows, tel. 0131/445-4433).

Royal Commonwealth Games Swimming Pool—The biggest pool I've ever seen is open to the public, with Café Aqua (overlooking the pool), weights, saunas, and plenty of water rides, including Europe's biggest "flume," or water slide (£2, Monday–Friday 9:00–21:00, Saturday and Sunday 8:00–19:00, tel. 0131/667-7211).

Greyhound Races—This is a pretty lowbrow scene. But if you've never seen dog racing, this is a memorable night out combining great dog- and people-watching with a chance to lose some money gambling. Races are held about two nights a week at Powderhall Stadium.

Edinburgh Crystal—Blowing, molding, cutting, polishing, and engraving, the Edinburgh Crystal Company glassworks tour smashes anything you'll see in Venice. The 35-minute tours start at regular intervals between 9:15 and 15:30, Monday through Friday and summer weekends (£2, children under age 8 and large dogs are not allowed in for safety reasons). There is a shop full of "bargain" second-quality pieces, a video show, and a cafeteria. A free red minibus shuttle service from Waverley Bridge departs hourly (10:00–15:00) in summer, or drive 10 miles south of town on A701 to Penicuik. You can schedule a more expensive super tour where you actually blow and cut glass (tel. 01968/675-128).

Shopping—The best shopping is along Princes Street (don't miss elegant old Jenner's Department Store), Victoria Street (antiques galore), and the Royal Mile (touristy but competitively priced, shops usually open 9:00–17:30, later on Thursday).

Edinburgh Festival

One of Europe's great cultural events, Edinburgh's annual festival turns the city into a carnival of culture. There are enough music, dance, art, drama, and multicultural events to make even the most jaded traveler drool with excitement. Every day is jammed with formal and spontaneous fun. The official and fringe festivals rage through much of August (August 16–September 5 in 1998), with the Military Tattoo starting a week earlier. Many city sights run on extended hours and those that normally close on Sunday, don't. It's a glorious time to be in Edinburgh.

The official festival is more formal and serious, with entertainment by festival invitation only. Major events sell out well in advance (show office at 21 Market Street, £4–45, CC:VMA, booking from April on, tel. 0131/225-5756).

The less-formal **Fringe Festival** features "on the edge" comedy/theater (ticket/info office just below St. Giles Cathedral on the Royal Mile, tel. 0131/226-5259, bookings tel. 0131/226-5138). Its many events have, it seems, more performers than viewers. Tickets are usually available at the door (or strewn on the streets).

The **Military Tattoo** is a massing of the bands, drums, and bagpipes with groups from all over what was the British Empire. Displaying military finesse with a stirring lone-piper finale, this grand spectacle fills the castle esplanade nightly except Sunday, normally from a week before the festival starts until a week before it finishes: August 7 to 29 in 1998 (£8–16, CC:VMA, booking starts in January, tel. 0131/225-1188, Friday and Saturday shows sell out, Monday–Thursday shows rarely do). If nothing else, it is a really big show. The BBC airs the Tattoo in a grand TV spectacle throughout Britain once each season (worth watching).

If you do manage to hit Edinburgh during the festival, extend your stay by a day or two and book a room far in advance. While Fringe tickets and most Tattoo tickets are available the day of the show, you may want to book an official event or two in advance. Do it directly by telephone, leaving your credit-card number. You can pick up your ticket at the office the day of the show or at the door just before curtain time. Several publications list and evaluate festival events, including the festival's official schedule, the *Festival Times*, *The List*, *Fringe Program*, and the *Daily Diary*.

Entertainment in Edinburgh

▲▲**Evening Walking Tours**—These walks, more than a pile of ghost stories, are an entertaining and cheap night out (offered nightly, usually 19:00 and 21:00). The creatively staged Witchery Tours are the most established of the ghost tours (£5, 90 minutes, tel. 0131/225-6745). The new Literary Pub Tour leaves from the Beehive Pub on Grassmarket (£6, 2 hours, daily at 18:00 and 20:30 in season, tel. 0131/554-0777).

▲**Scottish Folk Evenings**—These £35 to £40 dinner shows, generally for tour groups, are held in huge halls of expensive hotels. (Prices are bloated to include 20 percent commissions, without which the show don't go on.) Your "traditional" meal is followed by a full slate of swirling kilts, blaring bagpipes, and Scottish folk-dancing with an "old-time music hall"–type emcee.

Prince Charlie's Extravaganza at the Edinburgh Old Town Weaving Company on the Royal Mile, is a fun show (just below the castle, near the Esplanade). You'll get a tasty four-course meal (Scotch broth, haggis with neeps and tatties, and a beef pastry with vegetables, wine, ice cream and coffee; salmon or vegetarian alternatives available). The dancing and music—piping, accordion, singing—are good, and if you book directly and show this book you get a 20 percent discount off the £36 price. The boss, Gavin Cruickshank, promised this discount for 1998. Shows are usually offered nightly. Come between 18:00 and 19:00 to see the "sheep to shop" display; try the tartan loom. You'll normally be seated with a wee band o' me bonnie readers. Dinner's at 19:00 and you sing "Auld Lang Syne" by 22:15 (180 seats, smoke-free, CC:VMA, tel. 0131/226-1555). During the day, you can rent a kilt at their shop.

Carlton Highland Hotel offers a Scottish folk evening without dinner (£12, at intersection of High Street and North Bridge).

▲▲ **Folk Music in Pubs**—Edinburgh is a good place for

folk music. There's always a pub or two with a folk evening on. *The Gig* (a 50p monthly) lists all the live music action. Just off the Royal Mile on South Bridge, the **Tron Tavern and Ceilidh House** is home of the Tron Folk Club. They have nightly ad-lib traditional music from about 21:00 and a £3 folk concert on Saturday nights (tel. 0131/220-1550). **Whistle Binky** offers live folk music several nights a week (also near High Street) and **Finnigan's Wake** specializes in Irish folk music (a block off High Street on Victoria Street, tel. 0131/226-3816). On Grassmarket (below the castle), you'll find the **Fiddlers Arms** (fiddlers on Monday, tel. 0131/229-2665), **White Hart Inn**, and **Black Bull**, among others, all regularly featuring live folk music.

Theater—Even outside of festival time, Edinburgh is a fine place for lively and affordable theater. Pick up *The List* for a complete rundown of what's on.

Sleeping in Edinburgh
(£1 = about $1.60, tel. code: 0131)

Sleep Code: **S**=Single, **D**=Double/Twin, **T**=Triple, **Q**=Quad, **b**=bathroom, **t**=toilet only, **s**=shower only, **CC**=Credit Card (**V**isa, **M**asterCard, **A**mex).

The annual festival fills the city each August. Conventions, school holidays, and other surprises can make room-finding tough at almost any time. Call in advance or pay 30 percent extra for a relative dump. Downtown hotels are overpriced (minimum £70 doubles). For the best prices, book direct (rather than through the greedy TI) and, again, call in advance! "Standard" rooms, with toilets and showers a tissue-toss away, save you £8 a night.

My recommendations are south of town near the Royal Commonwealth Pool, just off Dalkeith Road. This comfortably safe neighborhood is a 20-minute walk or short bus ride from the Royal Mile. All listings are on quiet streets, a two-minute walk from a bus stop, and well-served by city buses. Near the B&Bs, you'll find plenty of eateries (see Eating, below), easy free parking, and a handy laundromat (Monday–Saturday 9:00–17:00, £5 for a self-serve load; £1 extra for B&B pick-up and drop-off service, 208 Dalkeith Road, tel. 0131/667-0825).

To reach the hotel neighborhood from the train station, TI, or Scott Monument, cross Princes Street and wait under

Edinburgh, Our Neighborhood

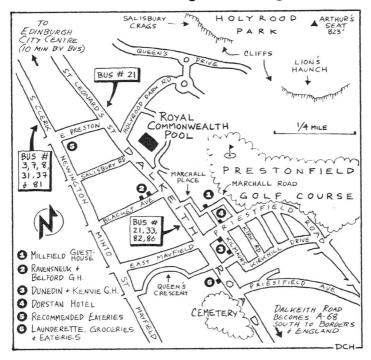

TO EDINBURGH CITY CENTRE (10 MIN BY BUS)

SALISBURY CRAGS

HOLYROOD PARK

ARTHUR'S SEAT 823'

QUEEN'S DRIVE

CLIFFS

LION'S HAUNCH

BUS # 21

ST LEONARD'S ST

HOLYROOD PARK RD

ROYAL COMMONWEALTH POOL

1/4 MILE

E PRESTON ST

ST CLERK

BUS # 3, 7, 8, 31, 37 & 81

NEWINGTON

SALISBURY RD

DALKEITH

MARCHALL PLACE

MARCHALL ROAD

PRESTONFIELD

GOLF COURSE

BLACKET AVE

BUS # 21, 33, 82, 86

MINTO

PRIESTFIELD

PRIESTFIELD ROAD

KIRK RD

KIRKHILL DRIVE

EAST MAYFIELD

KILMANS

QUEEN'S CRESCENT

MAYFIELD ST

CEMETERY

PRIESTFIELD AVE

DALKEITH ROAD BECOMES A-68 SOUTH TO BORDERS & ENGLAND

❶ MILLFIELD GUEST HOUSE
❷ RAVENSNEUK & BELFORD G.H.
❸ DUNEDIN & KENVIE G.H.
❹ DORSTAN HOTEL
❺ RECOMMENDED EATERIES
❻ LAUNDERETTE, GROCERIES & EATERIES

DCH

the C&A sign (60p, buses #21, #33, #82, or #86, 60p, red bus: exact change or pay more, green bus: makes change, ride ten minutes to first stop 100 yards after the Pool, push the button, exit middle door). These buses also stop at the corner of North Bridge and High Street on the Royal Mile. Room prices are for peak-season 1998 (but not festival time when they can go sky high). Off-season prices go soft.

Millfield Guest House, run by Liz and Ed Broomfield, is thoughtfully furnished with antique class, a rare sit-and-chat ambience, and a comfy TV lounge. Since the showers are down the hall, you'll get spacious rooms and great prices (S-£21, D-£35–36, T-£48–52 for direct bookings only, good beds, absolutely non-smoking, quiet but friendly, CC:VM, easy reservation with CC which lets you arrive late, 12 Marchhall Road, EH16 5HR, tel. 0131/667-4428). Decipher the breakfast prayer by Robert Burns. Then try the "Taste of

Scotland" breakfast option. See how many stone (14 lb) you weigh in the elegant throne room. This place is worth calling well in advance.

Kenvie Guest House offers lots of personal touches (one small twin-£35, D-£38, Db-£46 with this book in 1998, family deals, non-smoking, 16 Kilmaurs Road, EH16 5DA, tel. 0131/668-1964, Dorothy Vidler).

Belford House is a tidy, simple, cheery place offering a warm welcome and a fine value (D-£34, T-£51, kid-friendly with family deals, CC:VM, a bit smoky, 13 Blacket Avenue, tel. 0131/667-2422, Isa and Tom Borthwick). They're adding baths to some rooms; ask the price.

Dunedin Guest House is bright and Scottish, non-smoking, and a good value for those who need a private bathroom (seven rooms, S-£22–27, Db-£44–54, family deals, handicapped-accessible, solid beds, strong showers, NASA lighting, TVs with satellite channels in rooms, Scotland and Edinburgh videos in lounge, 8 Priestfield Road, EH16 5HH, tel. 0131/668-1949, fax 0131/668-2181, Annette and Max Preston). The Prestons also offer mini-bus tours of Edinburgh.

Turret Guest House is teddy-on-the-beddie cozy with a great bay-windowed family room and a vast breakfast menu that includes haggis and vegetarian options (S-£18–24, D-£36–54 with this book through 1998, less off-season, 8 Kilmaurs Terrace, tel. 0131/667-6704, Mrs. Jackie Cameron).

Ravensneuk Guest House is also good—quiet, comfortable, and very Victorian (D-£40–50, Db-£50–60, prices vary with season and room size, family deals, great lounge, solid beds, all non-smoking rooms, 11 Blacket Avenue, EH9 1RR, tel. & fax 0131/667-5347, Chris and Toni Henry).

Dorstan Private Hotel is small and personable, but professional and hotelesque with all the comforts. Several of its 14 prim rooms are on the ground floor (Ds-£58, Db-£66, family rooms, CC:VM, 7 Priestfield Road, EH16 5HJ, tel. 0131/667-6721, fax 0131/668-4644, Mairae Campbell).

Priestville B&B is a big old place with charming rough edges and a friendly welcome (D-£36, Db-£44 with this book through 1998, family deals, non-smoking, 10 Priestfield Road, tel. 0131/667-2435, Audrey and Jim Christie).

Highland Park House is simple and bright (S-£20, D-£38 with this book, family deals, 16 Kilmaurs Terrace, tel. 0131/667-9204, Brian Love).

Hostels

Although Edinburgh's youth hostels are well run, open to all, and provide £9 bunk beds (an £8 savings over B&Bs), they don't include breakfast and are comparatively scruffy.

High Street Independent Hostel is well-run, perfectly located, bursting with user-friendly services, and a grapevine for shoestring, nose-ring travelers. Little old ladies have reportedly enjoyed a stay here. My mom wouldn't sleep a wink but my little sister would dig it. Everyone's welcome (eight- to 16-bed rooms, no membership needed, videos, CC:VM, 50 yards off the Royal Mile, 8 Blackfriars Street, tel. 0131/557-3984). This young, hip hostel runs another place up the street.

For more regulations and less color, try the IYH hostels: **Bruntsfield Hostel** (on a park, 7 Bruntsfield Crescent, buses #11, #15, and #16 to and from Princes Street, tel. 0131/447-2994) and **Edinburgh Hostel** (four to 22 beds per room, 18 Eglinton Crescent, tel. 0131/337-1120).

Eating in Edinburgh

Eating Along the Royal Mile

Historic pubs and doily cafés with reasonable, unremarkable meals abound. **Deacon Brodie's Pub** serves soup, sandwiches, and snacks on the ground floor and good £6 meals upstairs (daily 12:00–22:00). Or munch prayerfully in the **Lower Aisle** restaurant under St. Giles Cathedral (Monday–Friday 10:00–16:30). At **The Brambles Tea Room** (next to Huntley House at 158 Cannongate), Shona serves light lunches and Starbucks coffee. **Food Plantation** has great, inexpensive fresh sandwiches to eat-in or take-out (274 Cannongate). **Clarinda's Tea Room**, near the bottom of the Royal Mile, is also good (daily 8:30–16:45). **Bann's Vegetarian Café** serves carnivore-pleasing veggie cuisine that goes way beyond tofu and granola (daily 10:00–23:00, just off South Bridge at 5 Hunter Square, tel. 0131/226-1112). **Dubh Prais Restaurant** offers decent Scottish food in a small, stone-walled basement (£15 and up, Tuesday–Saturday lunch and 18:30–22:30, closed Sunday and Monday, below St. Giles Cathedral at 123b High Street, reserve in advance, tel. 0131/557-5732, chef/owner James McWilliams). On Victoria Street, consider the very French **Pierre Victoire** (£5 lunch deals, closed Sunday, 9 Victoria Street, tel. 0131/225-1721) or the upstairs café in the Byzantium antique mall, across the street from Pierre Victoire. Gordon's Trattoria offers Italian cuisine, great service, and cheap prices (231 High Street). **Rafters,** upstairs from the Beehive Pub, serves fine three-course dinners for £11 (Grassmarket Street).

Eating in the New Town
Waverley Center Food Court, below the TI and above the station, is a food circus of flashy, trendy, fast-food joints (including The Scot's Pantry for quick traditional edibles) littered with paper plates and shoppers. Local office workers pile into **Lanterna** for good Italian food (family-run, fresh and friendly, 83 Hanover Street, 2 blocks off Princes Street, tel. 0131/226-3090). For a generation, New Town vegetarians have munched salads at **Henderson's Salad Table and Wine Bar** (Monday–Saturday 8:00–22:45, closed Sunday, non-smoking section, strictly vegetarian, between Queen and George Streets at 94 Hanover Street, tel. 0131/225-2131). The bohemian but elegantly Georgian **Café 1812** must be holding a fine French cook prisoner (£6 lunch, £11 dinner deals, 29 Waterloo Place on Calton Hill, tel. 0131/556-5766). Rose Street has tons of pubs.

Eating in Dalkeith Road Area, near Your B&B
Within a block of the corner of Newington and Preston Streets are all kinds of eateries. For a fun local atmosphere that makes up for the food, the **Wine Glass Pub** serves filling "basket meals" (£4, Sunday–Thursday 18:00–20:30). **Chinatown,** next to the Wine Glass, is moderate and good. **Chatterbox** is fine for a light meal with tea (8:30–20:00, down East Preston from the pool). **Jade Palace** has tasty Chinese food (take-out only, closed Tuesday, 212 Dalkeith Road). **Jaipur Mansion** serves meals worth the £15 splurge in a maharajah's setting (across from the Wine Glass Pub at 10 Newington Road). **Brattisanis** is your basic chippie (lousy milkshakes, cheap haggis, 87 Newington Road). The huge **Commonwealth Pool** has a noisy cafeteria for hungry swimmers and budget travelers (pass the entry without paying, sit with a poolside view).

Transportation Connections—Edinburgh
By train to: Inverness (7/day, 4 hrs), **Oban** (3/day, change in Glasgow, 4.5 hrs), **York** (hrly, 2.5 hrs), **London** (hrly, 5 hrs),

Durham (hrly, 2 hrs), **Lake District** (south past Carlisle to Penrith, catch bus to Keswick; 6/day, 40 min), **Birmingham** (6/day, 4.5 hrs), **Crewe** (6/day, 3.5 hrs). Train info tel. 0345/484-950.

By bus to: Oban (3/day, 5 hrs) and **Fort William** (3/day, 5 hrs). For bus info, call National Express (tel. 0131/452-8777) or Scottish Citylink (tel. 0990/505-050).

Route Tips for Drivers

Arriving in Edinburgh from the north: Signs to "city centre" lead to the black, towering neo-Gothic Scott Memorial (near the castle). From there, drive down Princes Street, turn right over the North Bridge, and follow the A68/Jedburgh signs to my recommended B&Bs, all just beyond the big, flat, white Royal Commonwealth Pool building on Dalkeith Road. (For most, take the first left off Dalkeith Road after the pool.)

Arriving from the south: Coming into town on A68 from the south, take the "A7 city centre" exit off the roundabout. A7 becomes Dalkeith Road. When you see the huge swimming pool, you've gone a couple of blocks too far.

Edinburgh to Hadrian's Wall (100 miles) and Durham (150 miles): From Edinburgh, Dalkeith Road leads south, becoming A68 (handy Cameron Toll supermarket with cheapest gas in Edinburgh is on left as you leave Dalkeith Town, ten minutes south of Edinburgh, gas and parking behind store). A68 takes you to Hadrian's Wall in two hours. You'll pass Jedburgh and its abbey after one hour. (For one last shot of shop-Scotland, there's a coach tour's delight just before Jedburgh, with kilt-makers, woolens, and a sheepskin shop.) Across from Jedburgh's lovely abbey is a free parking lot, a good visitor's center, and public toilets. The England/Scotland border is a fun, quick stop (great view, Mr. Softy ice cream and tea caravan). Before Hexham, roller-coaster 2 miles down A6079 to B6318, following the Roman wall westward. (See Hadrian's Wall in Durham chapter for more driving instructions.)

OBAN AND THE HIGHLANDS

Filled with more natural and historical mystique than people, the Highlands are where you find extreme Scotland; legends of Bonnie Prince Charlie swirl around rotten castles as pipers and kilts swirl around tourists. The harbor of Oban is a fruit crate of Scottish traditions, and the wind-bitten Hebrides are just an island hop, skip, and jump away.

The Highlands are cut in two by the impressive Caledonian Canal, with Oban at one end and Inverness at the other. The major sights cluster along the scenic 120-mile stretch between these two towns. Oban is a fine home base for western Scotland, and Inverness makes a good overnight stop on your way through eastern Scotland.

Planning Your Time
While Ireland has more charm and Wales has better sights, this area provides your best look at rural Scottish culture. There are a lot of miles, but they're scenic and the roads are good. In two days you can get a feel for the area with the car hike described below. To do the islands, you'll need more time. Iona is worthwhile, but adds a day to your trip. Generally, the region is hungry for the tourist dollar and everything overtly Scottish is that way to woo the tourist. You'll need more than a quick visit to get away from that.

With a car and two days to connect the Lake District and Edinburgh, consider this plan:

Day 1: 9:00, Leave Lake District after a stop at Castlerigg
Stone Circle; 13:00, Lunch on Loch Lomond, then joyride on,
stopping briefly at Inveraray; 16:00, Arrive in Oban, tour
whiskey distillery, drop by the TI; 20:30, Have dinner with
music at McTavish's Kitchen or dinner at The Studio.
Day 2: 9:00, Leave Oban; 10:00, Explore the valley of Glencoe; 11:00, Drive to Fort Augustus; 12:00, Follow Caledonian Canal, stopping at Loch Ness to take care of any monster
business; 15:00, Visit the evocative Culloden Battlefield near
Inverness; 16:00, Drive south; 19:00, Set up in Edinburgh.

With more time, spend a second night in Oban and tour
Iona, get to know Arthur Smith at Glencoe, or sleep in Inverness or Pitlochry, both fun towns.

OBAN

Oban, called the "gateway to the isles," is a busy little ferry-and-
train terminal with no important "sights," but a charming shiver-
and-bustle vitality that gives you a feel for small-town Scotland.
Wind, boats, gulls, several layers of islands, and the promise of a
wide-open Atlantic beyond give it a rugged and salty charm.

Orientation (tel. code: 01631)

Oban's business action, just a couple of streets deep, stretches
along the harbor and its promenade. The sights are close
together and the town seems eager to please its many visitors.
There's live, touristy music nightly in several bars and restaurants, shops sell woolen and tweed with cash registers cocked
(open until 20:00 and on Sunday), and posters announce a variety of enticing day tours to Scotland's wild and rabbit-strewn
western islands. The unfinished "colosseum" on the hill overlooking the town (McCaig's Tower, 1897) was an "employ the
workers and build me a fine memorial" project undertaken by
an early Oban tycoon.

Tourist Information: The TI has brochures on everything
from saunas to launderettes to horseback riding to rainy-day
activities, and a fine bookshop (Monday–Saturday 9:00–21:00,
Sunday 9:00–19:00, less off-season, just off the harbor in the center a block from the train station, tel. 01631/563-122).

Sights—Oban

▲**West Highland Malt Scotch Whiskey Distillery
Tours**—The 200-year old Oban whiskey distillery produces

Oban

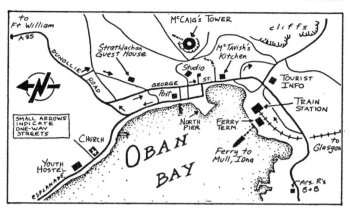

14,000 liters a week. They offer serious and fragrant 40-minute, £2 tours explaining the process from start to finish, with a free, smooth sample in the middle and a discount coupon for the shop at the end. The free exhibition preceding the tour gives a quick, whiskey-centric history of Scotland. This is the handiest whiskey tour you'll see, just a block off the harbor (Monday–Friday and in-season Saturday, 9:30–17:00, last tour at 16:15; to avoid a wait, call to reserve a place, tel. 01631/564-262).

▲**Tour Iona and Mull**—For the best one-day look at the dramatic and historic Hebrides island scenery around Oban, take one of several Iona/Mull tours offered in Oban. The Isle of Mull, the third largest in Scotland, has 300 scenic miles of coastline, a castle, and a 3,169-foot-high mountain. The stark, historic, and car-free island of Iona is connected to the western tip of Mull by a tiny ferry. St. Columba brought Christianity to Scotland via the Iona Abbey in A.D. 560. Near the abbey is a 13th-century Benedictine nunnery, a burial place of ancient kings, an ecumenical community, a museum, and a few shops, pubs, and B&Bs.

The island tours include the Oban–Mull ferry (40 min), an entertaining and informative bus ride across the Isle of Mull (90 min), the small ferry connection to Iona (10 min), time to roam on Iona (2 hrs), and a return to Oban via the ferry (£16 on Bowman's; allow from 10:00–17:40 for the whole tour;

great in fair weather, pretty bleak otherwise, tel. 01631/563-221). Some companies offer flexible schedules if you want more time in Mull or an extension to the wildly scenic Isle of Staffa with Fingal's Cave. Guides are hardworking local boys who know how to spin a yarn, making historical trivia fascinating, or at least fun. There are several tours and companies you can choose from. Taking your car onto the ferry is very expensive (at least £20 each way).

Kerrera—This stark but very green island, opposite Oban, offers a quick, easy opportunity to get that romantic island experience (£2 round-trip, upon request, at Gallanach's dock, 2 miles south of Oban).

Isle of Seil—Enjoy a walk, solitude, and the sea. Drive 15 miles south of Oban to the Isle of Seil, connected to the mainland by a bridge (for more info, see Eating, below).

Sleeping in Oban
(£1 = about $1.60, tel. code: 01631)
Sleep Code: **S**=Single, **D**=Double/Twin, **T**=Triple, **Q**=Quad, **b**=bathroom, **t**=toilet only, **s**=shower only, **CC**=Credit Card (**V**isa, **M**asterCard, **A**mex).

Strathlachlan Guest House is a winner. Mrs. Rena Anderson's place is stocking-feet cozy, crackerjack friendly, and chocolate-box tidy. It's a spacious, uncluttered place with six rooms, solid beds, a great TV lounge, easy parking, and a good central location 2 blocks off the water, a five-minute walk from the train station (S-£16, D-£32, family deals, some smoke-free rooms, 2 Breadalbane Street, Oban, Argyll, tel. 01631/563-861).

Tanglin B&B, next door, is another fine value. Liz and Jim Montgomery offer a bright, non-smoking, and brand-new-feeling place with springy beds, TVs in the rooms, and an easygoing atmosphere (S-£15, D-£29, Db-£36, off-season rates and family deals, 3 Strathaven Terrace, Breadalbane Street, tel. 01631/563-247).

Glenara B&B has been recently remodeled, adding private bathrooms (Sb-£22, Db-£42–54, non-smoking, friendly, 3 blocks off the waterfront on Rockfield Road, tel. 01631/563-172, Dorothy and Duncan Bingham). Ask Duncan about haggis.

Raniven Guest House (D-£32, Db-£38, some non-smoking rooms, two nights minimum, Strathlachlan Terrace, tel. 01631/562713) and **MacColl's B&B** (S-£17, D-£34, firm beds, noisy street, around the corner on Dunollie Road, tel. 01631/565-361) are sleepable.

Barriemore Hotel is the last place (and only good value) on Oban's grand waterfront esplanade. It has a classy, dark, woody, equestrian feel with 15 spacious and comfortable non-smoking rooms furnished like living rooms (Db-£50–56, firm beds, grand views, some easy-access ground-floor rooms; CC:VM, the esplanade, PA34 5AQ, tel. 01631/566-356, Evelyn and Jim McLean).

The **hostel**, on the esplanade alongside the finest hotels in town, is in a grand building with a smashing harbor/island view (£9.15 per bed with sheets, non-members of any age welcome for £1.50 extra, four- to 16-bed rooms, great facilities and public rooms, closed winter, tel. 01631/562-025).

The **Jeremy Inglis B&B**, just a block from the TI and train station, is normally filled with backpackers in summer (£7 per bed in basic, shared rooms with a continental breakfast, 21 Airds Crescent, tel. 01631/565-065 or 01631/563-064).

Just south of town, **Mrs. Robertson's B&B** is a mini-estate in a lush garden with a commanding view of the bay and islands. She rents a twin and a double (Db-£38, Dungrianach, Pulpit Hill, Oban, Argyll, PA34 4LX, tel. 01631/562-840). From the TI, head up Albany Street, take the second right up Pulpit Hill, and, when it levels out, turn right at the "Dungrianach" sign a half-block before the phone booth.

Eating in Oban

To mix a folk show inexpensively with dinner, eat at **McTavish's Kitchen**. This huge eating hall is an Oban institution featuring live, but tired, folk music and dancing nightly (May–September). Like anything so Scottishly cliché, this is your basic tourist trap filled with English vacationers. The food is inexpensive and edible (£5 basic plate, £13 super Scottish multi-course menu). The piping, dancing, and singing happen nightly from 20:30 to 22:30 (the three-person band plays the hour-long cycle twice, so you'll cover all the cultural bases in an hour). The show costs £3 without a meal, £1.50 with dinner, or free with dinner with a coupon from your B&B. No reservations required. Non-smokers get the best harbor views.

Gallery Restaurant has a £5 two-course high tea (before 18:30) and a three-course dinner for £11 (daily 10:00–16:00,

17:00–22:00; a half-block from TI near Argyll Square, tel. 01631/564-641). **Kitchen Garden,** a good place for a £4 lunch, serves up salads, soups, and sandwiches (daily 9:00–17:00, above the kitchen shop at 14 George Street).

Everyone's favorite nice dinner out is at **The Studio,** a small, candlelit restaurant featuring serious, first-class Scottish cooking (£11 for a full Scottish meal, nightly 17:00–22:00, reservations smart, tel. 01631/562-030). It has great trout, salmon, and a prawn-and-clam chowder that hits the spot on a stormy day. The restaurant at the **Manor House** hotel is pricier and worthwhile.

For an interesting drive and dinner, head south from Oban on A816 to B844. Just over the bridge on the Isle of Seil is a pub called **Tigh-an-Truish** ("house of trousers"). After a 1745 English law forbade the wearing of kilts on the mainland, Highlanders used this pub to change from kilts to trousers before crossing the bridge. The pub serves great meals to those in kilts or pants (daily 12:00–14:15, 18:00–20:30, darts anytime, good seafood dish, crispy vegetables, tel. 01852/300-242). Five miles across the island, on a tiny second island, is Easdale, a historic, touristy, windy, little slate-mining town facing the open Atlantic (shuttle ferry goes the 300 yards, slate-town museum, incredibly tacky egomaniac's "Highland Arts" shop).

Transportation Connections—Oban
Oban to: Inverness (6 buses/day, 4 hrs), **Glasgow** (3 trains/day, 3 hrs). Ferries fan out from Oban to the **southern Hebrides.** Train info tel. 0345/484-950. Bus info tel. 01631/562-856. Caledonian MacBrayne Ferry info tel. 01631/562-285.

Transportation Connections—Glasgow
Glasgow is a major transportation hub in the region.

Glasgow to: Edinburgh (2 trains/hr, 1 hr), **Inverness** (hrly buses, 4.5 hrs), **Penrith** (9 trains/day, 2 hrs; 6 buses/day from Pensith to Keswick, Lake District), **London** (8 trains/day, 6 hrs). Train info tel. 0345/484-950.

THE HIGHLANDS: FROM OBAN TO INVERNESS
Discover Glencoe's dark secrets in the Weeping Glen where Britain's highest peak, Ben Nevis, keeps its head in the clouds. Explore the locks and lochs of the Caledonian canal while the

Loch Ness monster plays hide-and-seek. Hear the music of the Highlands in Inverness and the echo of muskets in Culloden, where the English defeated Bonnie Prince Charlie and his Scottish hopes.

Getting Around the Highlands

The trains are scenic but if schedules frustrate, take the bus. Six buses a day connect the towns from Oban to Inverness (4 hrs). Ask at the station to see how schedules work for sight-hopping.

Sights—Scottish Highlands

▲▲**Glencoe**—This valley is the essence of the wild, powerful, and stark beauty of the Highlands (and, I think, excuses the hurried tourist from needing to go north of Inverness). Along with its scenery, Glencoe offers a good dose of bloody clan history. The visitor's center in the village of Glencoe has a fine exhibit with a 14-minute video about the 1692 massacre when the Redcoats killed the sleeping MacDonalds and the valley got its nickname, "The Weeping Glen" (50p, daily 9:30–17:30, shorter hours or closed off-season, just east of town on A82, tel. 01855/811-307).

Walks: For a steep 1-mile hike, climb the Devil's Staircase (trail leaves from A82, 8 miles east of Glencoe). For a three-hour hike, ask at the visitor's center about walking to the Lost Valley of the MacDonalds (trail leaves from A82, 3 miles east of Glencoe).

Many find Glencoe more interesting than Oban for an overnight stop. In Glencoe village, Arthur Smith runs the **Cala Sona B&B**, aptly named "haven of happiness" in Gaelic. He entertains his guests with a peat fire, ghost stories, and tales of the Glencoe massacre (S-£15, D-£30, less if necessary, on the main street, tel. 01855/811-314). The nearest TI is in Ballachulish (tel. 01855/811-296). If Arthur's place is full, try **Greenhill B&B** (Ds-£28, just before Cala Sona B&B, tel. 01855/811-391, Ann Blake).

Ben Nevis—From Fort William, take a peek at Britain's highest peak, Ben Nevis (over 4,400 feet). Thousands of visitors walk to its summit each year. On a clear day you can admire it from a distance. Britain's only mountain cable cars can take you to the not-very-lofty, 2,150-foot level of a nearby peak (£6, daily 10:00–17:00, 12-minute ride, signposted on A82, tel. 01397/705-825).

Oban and the Highlands

▲**Caledonian Canal**—Three lochs and a series of canals cut Scotland in two. Oich, Lochy, and Ness were connected in the early 1800s by the great British engineer Thomas Telford. For a good look at the locks, see "Neptune's Staircase," where you'll find a park built along a series of ten locks (2 miles north of Fort William, detour 1 mile on A830). Fort Augustus is another good lock stop. Traveling between Fort William and Inverness (60 miles), you'll follow Telford's work—20 miles of canals and locks between 40 miles of lakes, raising ships from sea level to 51 feet (Ness) to 93 feet (Lochy) to 106 feet (Oich).

Loch Ness—I'll admit it. I had my zoom lens out and my eyes on the water. The local tourist industry thrives on the legend of the Loch Ness monster. It's a thrilling thought, and there have been several seemingly reliable "sightings" (monks, policemen, and now sonar images). The loch, 24 miles long, less than a mile wide, and the third-deepest in Europe, is deepest near the Urquhart Castle. Most monster sightings are in this area.

The Nessie commercialization is so tacky that there are two "official" Loch Ness Exhibition Centres within 100 yards of each other. Each has a tour-bus parking lot and more square footage devoted to their shop than to the exhibit. The exhibits are fascinating, but way overpriced. The exhibition in the big stone mansion (closest to Inverness) is the better one, with a 40-minute series of video bits on the geological and historical environment that bred the monster story and the various searches (£4, daily 9:00–20:30). The other (closest to Oban) is a high school–quality photo report followed by the 30-minute "We believe in the Loch Ness monster" movie, featuring credible-sounding locals explaining what they saw and a review of modern Nessie searches (£4, daily 9:00–19:30). The nearby Urquhart Castle ruins (£3, daily 9:30–18:30) are gloriously situated with a view of virtually the entire lake. It's an empty shell of a castle with crowds and parking problems.

▲**Culloden Battlefield**—Scottish troops under Bonnie Prince Charlie were defeated here by the English in 1746. This last land battle fought on British soil spelled the end of Jacobite resistance and the fall of the clans. Wandering the battlefield, you feel that something terrible happened here. Locals still bring flowers and speak of "46" as if it were this century.

The excellent visitor's center shows a stirring 16-minute audiovisual every 20 minutes. Wander through a furnished old cottage and around the memorial battlegrounds (£2, daily 9:00–18:00, shorter hours off-season, good tea room, tel. 01463/790-607).

Inverness—The only sizable town in the north of Scotland, with 42,000 people, Inverness is pleasantly located on a river at the base of a castle (not worth a look) with a free little museum (worth a look, cheap café). Its Highland Music Museum traces local music from heroic warrior songs to Gaelic rock (£2 to scan six hours of music, daily 10:00–17:00, Balnain House, tel. 01463/715-757). Check out the bustling pedestrian downtown and central TI (tel. 01463/234-353). Ask about the inexpensive and very informative "Gordon's" minibus tours to Culloden and Loch Ness (most days 10:30–16:30). Trains link Inverness, Pitlochry, and Edinburgh (9/day, 3.5 hrs, tel. 01463/238-924), and buses run betwen Oban and Inverness (6/day, 4 hrs, tel. 01463/233-371).

Sleeping in Inverness (tel. code: 01463): These rooms are all a short walk from the train station and town center. The first two are on a quiet street just up the steps from the pedestrian High Street. **Ardconnel House** is tasteful, bright, spacious, classy, and less than friendly (S-from £18, D-£36, family deals, non-smoking, TVs in rooms, 21 Ardconnel Street, IV2 3EU, tel. 01463/240-455, Mrs. MacKenzie). **The Hollies** is much simpler, but still a fine value, with only three rooms and sturdy beds (S-£15, D-£30, T-£45, family deals, disappointing breakfast, 24 Ardconnel Street, tel. 01463/231-291, run by friendly, helpful Mrs. Proudfoot). Cheap and central places include the **hostel** (£9 including sheets, six- to 20-bed rooms, up the street from the castle at 1 Old Edinburgh Road, tel. 01463/231-771) and the much more laid-back **Inverness Student Hotel** (£9 per bed with sheets, ten six-bed rooms, across the street from the hostel at 8 Culduthel Road, tel. 01463/236-556).

Pitlochry—This pleasant tourist town, famous for its whiskey, makes an enjoyable overnight stop. Its Edradour Scotch distillery offers a free one-hour guided tour, ten-minute audiovisual show, and, of course, tasting (3/hr, Monday–Saturday 9:30–17:00, summer Sundays 12:00–16:15, 2 miles east of town, tel. 01796/472-095). The Blair Athol Distillery gives £3 hour-long tours with a sample at the end (2/hr, Monday–Saturday 9:30–16:15, Sunday 12:00–16:15, half-mile from town, tel. 01796/472-234). Pitlochry also has plenty of forest walks and a salmon ladder (jumping May and June, free viewing area, ten-minute walk from town). The town theater offers a different play every night. (TI, daily 9:00–20:00, tel. 01796/472-215.)

Sleeping in Pitlochry (tel. code: 01796): Try **Craigroyston House**, a big Victorian country house with eight Laura Ashley–style rooms, just up the steps from the TI and run by charming Gretta Maxwell (Db-£40–52, flexing with demand, next to the church at 2 Lower Oakfield, PH16 5HQ, tel. 01796/472-053). Mrs. Maxwell can find you another B&B if her place is full. Pitlochry's fine **hostel** is on Knockard Road above the main street (£7 bunks, tel. 01796/472-308).

Route Tips for Drivers

Lake District to Oban (220 miles): From Keswick, take A66 18 miles to M6 and speed nonstop north (via Penrith and Carlisle), crossing Hadrian's Wall into Scotland. The

Scottish Words

aye	yes	**inch, innis**	island
ben	mountain	**inver**	river, mouth
bonnie	beautiful	**kyle**	strait
carn	heap of stones	**loch**	lake
creag	rock, cliff	**neeps**	turnips
tattie	potato		

haggis   rich assortment of oats and sheep organs stuffed into a chunk of sheep intestine, liberally seasoned, boiled, and eaten mostly by tourists. Usually served with "neeps and tatties." Tastier than it sounds.

road stays great, becoming the M74 south of Glasgow. To slip quickly through Glasgow, leave M74 at Junction 4 onto M73, following signs to M8/Glasgow. Leave M73 at Junction 2, exiting onto M8. Stay on M8 west through Glasgow, exit on Junction 30, cross the Erskine Bridge (60p), and turn left on A82, following signs to Crianlarich. (For a scenic drive through Glasgow, take exit 17 off M8 and stay on A82 toward Dumbarton.) You'll soon be driving along scenic Loch Lomond. The first picnic turnout has the best lake views, lots of benches, a grassy park, and a kids' playground. Halfway up the loch, at Tarbet, take the "tourist route" left on to A83, drive along saltwater Loch Long toward Inveraray via Rest-and-Be-Thankful Pass. (This colorful name comes from the 1880s, when second- and third-class coach passengers got out and pushed the coach-and first-class passengers up the hill.) Stop in Inveraray, a lovely castle-town on Loch Fyne. Park near the pier. The town jail, now museum, is a "19th-century living prison" (£4, daily 9:30–18:00, last admission 17:00, tel. 01499/302-381). Leaving Inveraray, drive through a gate (at the Woolen Mill) to A819, through Glen Aray, and along scenic Loch Awe. A85 takes you into Oban.

    Oban to Glencoe (45 miles) to Loch Ness (75 miles) to Inverness (20 miles) to Edinburgh (150 miles): Barring traffic, you'll make great time on good, mostly two-lane roads. Americans are generally timid about passing. Study the British. Be careful, but if you don't pass diesel fumes and large trucks might be your memory of this drive. From Oban, follow the

coastal A828 toward Fort William. At Loch Leven and Ballachulish village, leave A828, taking A82 into Glencoe. Drive
through the village into the valley for ten minutes for a grand
view of the vast Rannoch Moor. Then make a U-turn and
return through the valley. Continue north on A82, over the
bridge, past Fort William toward Loch Ness. Follow the Caledonian Canal on A82 for 60 miles, stopping at Loch Ness, then
continuing on A82 to Inverness.

Leaving Inverness, follow signs to A9 (south toward
Perth). Just as you leave Inverness, detour 4 miles east off A9
on B9006 to visit the Culloden Battlefield Visitors Centre.
Back on A9, it's a wonderfully speedy and very scenic highway
(A9, M90, A90) all the way to Edinburgh. If traffic is light and
your foot is heavy, you can drive from Inverness to Edinburgh
in three hours.

For a scenic shortcut, head north only as far as Glencoe
(Loch Ness is not much to see) then cut over to Edinburgh via
Rannoch Moor and Tyndrum.

DUBLIN

With reminders of its stirring history and rich culture on every corner, Ireland's capital and largest city is a sightseer's delight. Dublin's fair city will have you humming "Alive, alive-O."

Founded as a Viking trading settlement in the ninth century, Dublin grew to be a center of wealth and commerce second only to London in the United Kingdom. Dublin, the seat of English rule in Ireland for 700 years, was the heart of a "civilized" Anglo-Irish area (eastern Ireland) known as "the Pale." Anything "beyond the Pale" was considered uncultured and almost barbaric . . . purely Irish.

The Golden Age of English Dublin was the 18th century. Britain was on a roll and Dublin was Britain's second city. Largely rebuilt during this Georgian era, Dublin became an elegant and cultured capital. Everything was okay until nationalism and human rights got in the way. The ideas of the French Revolution inspired Irish intellectuals to buck British rule and, after the revolt of 1798, life in Dublin was never quite the same. But the 18th century left a lasting imprint on the city. Georgian (that's British for neoclassical) squares and boulevards gave the city a grand elegance. The National Museum, National Gallery, and many government buildings are in the Georgian section of town. Few buildings (notably St. Patrick's Cathedral and Christchurch Cathedral) pre-date this Georgian period.

In the 19th century, with the closing of the Irish Parliament, the famine, and the beginnings of the struggle for independence, Dublin was treated and felt more like a colony than a partner. The tension culminated in the Rising of 1916 and the battle that followed. While many of Dublin's grand streets were left in ruins, the city emerged as the capital of the only former colony in Europe.

While bullet-pocked buildings and dramatic statues keep memories of Ireland's recent struggle for independence alive, the city is looking to a bright future. Visitors enjoy a big-town cultural scene wrapped in a small-town smile.

Planning Your Time

On a two-week trip through Ireland, Dublin deserves three nights and two days. Consider this sightseeing plan:

Day 1: 9:30, Dublin Experience; 10:30, Trinity College walk; 11:00, Book of Kells and Old Library; 12:00, Browse Grafton Street, lunch there or picnic on St. Stephen's Green; 13:30, National Museum; 15:00, Historical town walk; 17:00, Return to hotel, rest, dinner; 19:30, Evening walk (literary or musical); 22:00, Irish music in Temple Bar area.

Day 2: 10:00, Kilmainham Jail; 12:00, Guinness Brewery tour; 13:30, Lunch (with a faint buzz); 15:00, Tour Dublin Castle; catch a play or concert in the evening.

Orientation (tel. code: 01)

Greater Dublin sprawls with about 1 million people—nearly a third of the country's population. But the center of touristic interest is a tight triangle between O'Connell Bridge, St. Stephen's Green, and Christchurch Cathedral. Within this triangle you'll find Trinity College (Book of Kells), Grafton Street (top pedestrian shopping zone), Temple Bar (trendy nightlife center), Dublin Castle, and the hub of most city tours and buses.

The River Liffey cuts the town in two. Focus on the southern half (where nearly all your sightseeing will take place). Dublin's main drag, O'Connell Street (near the Abbey Theater and outdoor produce market) stretches from the very central O'Connell Bridge north of the river. Over the river, this main city axis continues—mostly as Grafton Street—to St. Stephen's Green. Only the Kilmainham Jail and the Guinness Brewery (both west of the center) are outside your home triangle.

Tourist Information

The TI fills an old church on Suffolk Street (a block off Grafton Street). While packed with tourists, promotional brochures, an

American Express office, a café, and traditional knickknacks, it's
short on hard info. Less crowded but equally helpful TI branches
are on Baggot Street and at the airport (daily 8:00–22:30). To
talk to the TI on the phone you'll pay 60p per minute (1-550-
112-233)—welcome to Dublin. The TI gives a free newspaper
with a lousy map, lots of advertisements, and the fliers that fill
racks all over town. The best extensive publication they offer is
Dublin's Top Visitor Attractions (which you can buy for £2.50 at
the TI bookshop without any wait). This has a map and the latest on all the town's sights (many more than I list here). For a
schedule of happenings in town, buy the excellent *In Dublin* at
any newsstand (fortnightly, £1.50).

Arrival in Dublin

By Train: Trains arrive at Heuston Station (serving the west
and southwest) on the west end of town. Dublin's second train
station, Connolly Station (serving the north, northwest, and
Rosslare), is closer to the center—a ten-minute walk from
O'Connell Bridge. Each station has a luggage-check facility.
    Bus 90 connects both train stations and the bus station and
the city center (60p flat fee, 6/hr, runs along river).
    By Bus: Bus Eireann, Ireland's national bus company, uses
the Busaras Central Bus Station next to Connolly Station
(catch bus 90 to the city center).
    By Ferry: Irish Ferries dock at the mouth of the River
Liffey (near the town center) while the Stena Line docks at
Dun Laoghaire (easy DART train connections into Dublin, at
least 3/hr, 15 min).
    By Plane: From the airport, milk-run buses 41 and 41C
go to O'Connell Bridge (£1.10, 3/hr). The faster Airlink direct
bus connects the airport with the Heuston train station and
Busaras bus station near Connolly Station (£3, 4/hr, 30 min).
Taxis from the airport into Dublin cost about £10.

Getting Around Dublin

You'll do most of Dublin on foot. Big green buses are cheap
and cover the city thoroughly. Most lines start at the four
Quays nearest O'Connell Bridge. Tell the driver where you're
going and he'll ask for 60p (one to five stops) or 80p (five to
ten stops). The bus office at 59 Upper O'Connell Street has
free "route network" maps and sells bus passes (one-day pass
£3.30 adults, £5.50 per family, four-day adult pass-£10.00, bus

information tel. 01/873-4222). DART trains connect Dublin with Dun Laoghaire (ferry terminal and recommended B&Bs, at least 3/hr, 15 min, £1.10). Taxis seem honest, and they are plentiful, friendly, and good sources of information (£3 for most downtown rides).

Tours of Dublin

While the physical treasures of Dublin are mediocre by European standards, the city has a fine story to tell and people with a natural knack for telling it. It's a good town for walking tours—and the competition is fierce for your business. You'll find pamphlets touting creative walks all over town. There are medieval walks, literary walks, Georgian Dublin walks, and more. The two evening walks are great ways to meet other travelers.

Historical Walking Tour of Dublin—This is your best introductory walk. A group of hardworking history graduates (many who claim to have done more than just kiss the Blarney Stone) fill Dublin's basic historic strip—Trinity College-Old Parliament House-Dublin Castle-Christchurch Cathedral—with the story of their city from its Viking origin to the present. You stand in front of buildings that aren't much to see but are lots to talk about and listen to your guide's story. Guides talk at length about "the Troubles" and the roots of Ireland's struggle with Britain (£5, two hours, depart from gate of Trinity College, Monday–Saturday 11:00, 12:00, 15:00; Sunday 11:00, 12:00, 14:00, 15:00; winter schedule: Saturday and Sunday 12:00, tel. 01/845-0241).

Jameson Literary Pub Crawl—Two actors take 30 or so tourists on a walk stopping at four pubs. Half the time is spent enjoying their entertaining banter which introduces the novice to the high *craic* (conversation) of Joyce, O'Casey, and Yeats. The 2.5-hour tour is punctuated with 20-minute pub breaks (free time). It can be great fun socially, but the content suffers. Meet any night at 19:30 (or Sunday at noon) in the Duke Pub off Grafton on Duke Street (£6, runs three nights a week in winter, tel. 01/454-0228).

Traditional Irish-Music Pub Crawl—This is like the Literary pub crawl but features music. You meet at 19:30 at Gogarty's Pub (in the Temple Bar area) and spend 20 minutes in the upstairs rooms of four pubs listening to two musicians talk about, play, and sing traditional Irish music. While having only two musicians makes the music a bit thin and

Irish music aficionados will tell you you're better off just finding a good session, the evening—while touristy—is not gimmicky. The musicians demonstrate four instruments and really enjoy introducing rookies to their art (£6 plus beer, nightly May–October except Friday, weekends only in winter, allow 2.5 hours, tel. 01/478-0191).

Hop On/Hop Off Bus Tours—Several companies offer the basic center-of-Dublin orientation. Dublin City Tour (£5, tel. 01/873-4222) and Guide Friday (£7, tel. 01/676-5377) do identical 90-minute circuits of the town allowing you to hop on and hop off at your choice of ten stops (two topless buses per hour with running commentaries; they go to Guinness Brewery but not to Kilmainham Jail). Just hop on and pay the driver. Your ticket's good for the entire day. Tours, which go from about 9:45 to 18:00, are especially enjoyable for photographers on sunny days. I see no reason to pay more for the Guide Friday tours.

Sights—Dublin's Trinity College

▲**Trinity College**—Started in 1592 by Queen Elizabeth I to establish a Protestant way of thinking about God, Trinity has long been Ireland's most prestigious college. Originally the student body was limited to rich, Protestant males. Women were admitted in 1903 and Catholics, while allowed entrance by the school much earlier, were given permission to study at Trinity in the 1970s. Today half of Trinity's 11,000 students are women and 70 percent are culturally Catholic (although only about 20 percent of Irish youth are churchgoing).

▲**Trinity College Tour**—Inside the gate of Trinity, students organize and lead 30-minute tours of their campus. You'll get a rundown on the mostly Georgian architecture, a peek at student life, both in the early days and today, and mostly enjoy a chance to hang out with a witty Irish college kid as he talks about his school (daily 10:15–15:30, the £4.50 tour fee includes the £3.50 fee to see the Book of Kells where the tour leaves you).

▲▲▲**Book of Kells/Trinity Old Library**—The 65-meter-long main chamber of the Old Library (from 1732) is home to an original copy of the 1916 Proclamation of the Irish Republic, the oldest Irish harp (from the 15th century), and stacked to its towering ceiling, 200,000 of the library's oldest books. The artistic prize of the library—and all Ireland—is the magnificent Book

Dublin

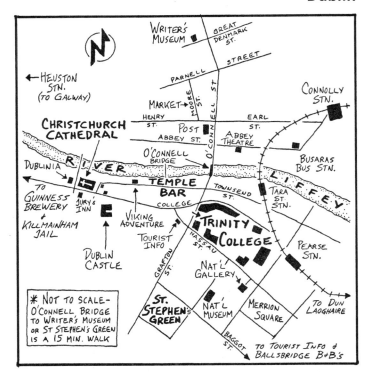

N

WRITER'S MUSEUM

GREAT DENMARK ST.

STREET

PARNELL

←HEUSTON STN. (TO GALWAY)

CONNOLLY STN.

MARKET→ MOORE ST. O'CONNELL ST.

HENRY ST.

EARL ST.

POST

CHRISTCHURCH CATHEDRAL

ABBEY ST.

ABBEY THEATRE

O'CONNELL BRIDGE

BUSARAS BUS STN.

DUBLINIA

R I V E R

L I F F E Y

TO GUINNESS BREWERY + KILLMAINHAM JAIL

JURY'S INN

TEMPLE BAR

TOWNSEND ST.

TARA ST. STN.

COLLEGE

VIKING ADVENTURE

TRINITY COLLEGE

TOURIST INFO

PEARSE STN.

DUBLIN CASTLE

NASSAU ST.

GRAFTON ST.

NAT'L GALLERY

TO DUN LAOGHAIRE

✳ NOT TO SCALE— O'CONNELL BRIDGE TO WRITER'S MUSEUM OR ST STEPHEN'S GREEN IS A 15 MIN. WALK

ST. STEPHEN'S GREEN

NAT'L MUSEUM

MERRION SQUARE

BAGGOT ST.

TO TOURIST INFO & BALLSBRIDGE B&B's

of Kells stored in the library's treasury. A first-class exhibit puts the 680-page illuminated manuscript in its historical and cultural context and prepares you for the original book and other precious manuscripts in the collection. Written on vellum (baby sheepskin) in the ninth century—probably by Irish monks in Iona (Scotland)—and taken to the Irish monastery at Kells in 806 after a series of Viking raids, this enthusiastically decorated copy of the four gospels is arguably the finest piece of art from what is generally called the Dark Ages. It shows how monastic life in this far fringe of Europe was far from dark. The book has been bound into four separate volumes. At any given time, two of the gospels are on display. You'll see four richly decorated 1,200-year-old pages—two text and two decorated cover pages—under glass (£3.50, Monday–Saturday 9:30–17:00, Sunday 9:30–16:30, shorter hours off-season, tel. 01/608-1171). The

library also displays the Book of Armagh (A.D. 807) and the Book of Durrow (A.D. 680), neither of which can be checked out.
▲**The Dublin Experience**—Shown in a modern building next to the Trinity Old Library, this 40-minute video giving a historic introduction to Dublin is one more tourist movie with the sound turned up. It's good but pricey and riding on the coattails of the Book of Kells (£3, save a little with a combo Kells/video ticket, Trinity College Library, Monday–Saturday 9:30–17:00, Sunday 12:00–16:30).

More Sights—Dublin

▲▲**Dublin Castle**—Built on the spot of the first Viking fortress, this castle was the seat of British rule in Ireland for 700 years (until 1922). Located where the Poddle and Liffey Rivers came together making a black pool ("dubh linn" in Irish), Dublin Castle was the official residence of the Viceroy who implemented the will of the British royalty. Today it's used for fancy state and charity functions. The 45-minute tours offer a room-by-room walk through the lavish state apartments of this most English of Irish palaces (£2.50, about 4/hour, Monday–Friday 10:00–17:00, weekends 14:00–17:00, tel. 01/677-7129). The tour finishes with a look at the foundations of the Norman tower and the best remaining chunk of the 13th-century town wall.

▲**Dublin's Viking Adventure**—This really is an adventure. You start in a box of seats that transforms into a Viking ship. Your chieftain joins you and suddenly you're in a storm, waves splash, smoke rolls, and you land in a kind of Viking summer camp where you spend 30 minutes being shuttled from one friendly original Dubliner to the next (a trader, a sassy maiden, a monk building a church, and so on). A short film about the Vikings follows with a look at artifacts recently uncovered in the adjacent excavation sight. It feels hokey, but the cast is certainly hardworking and you leave feeling if not having visited a Viking town, at least having visited the set for a B-grade Viking movie. This is on Essex Street a block off the riverside Essex Quay in Temple Bar—exactly where the Vikings established their first Dublin settlement in 841 (£4.75, Monday–Saturday 10:00–16:30, Sunday 11:30–17:30, tel. 01/679-6040).

Dublinia—This tries and fails to be a "bridge to Dublin's medieval past." The amateurish look at the medieval town starts with a goofy 12-minute Walkman tour followed by a few rooms of medieval exhibits and finishes with a hard-to-follow movie dramatizing medieval political wrangling. Possibly entertaining for a school field-trip, it just isn't worth the £4 or time (daily 10:00–17:00). The ticket does get you a tower-top city view and into Christchurch Cathedral (£1 otherwise).

Christchurch Cathedral—The oldest building in Dublin, the cathedral marks the spot where the Vikings established their town on the river. The first church here was built of wood in 1038 by King Sitric. The present structure dates from a mix of periods: Norman, Gothic, and mostly Victorian neo-Gothic (1870s restoration work). Because of its British past, neither of Dublin's two top churches are Catholic. Christchurch Cathedral and the nearby St. Patrick's Cathedral are both from the Church of Ireland. In Catholic Ireland they feel hollow and are more famous than visit-worthy.

▲▲▲National Museum—Showing off the treasures of Ireland from the Stone Age to the 20th century, this museum is wonderfully digestible under one dome. Ireland's Bronze Age gold fills the center. The prehistoric Ireland exhibit rings the gold, and in a corner you'll find the treasury with the most famous pieces (brooches, chalices, and other examples of Celtic metalwork) and an 18-minute video giving an overview of Irish art through the 13th century. Jumping way ahead, a special corridor features "The Road to Independence" with guns, letters, and death masks recalling the fitful birth of the "Terrible Beauty" (1900–1921 with a focus on the Easter Rising of 1916). The best Viking artifacts in town are upstairs (free, Tuesday–Saturday 10:00–17:00, Sunday 14:00–17:00, closed Monday, between Trinity College and St. Stephen's Green on Kildare Street, tel. 01/677-7444). Greatest-hits tours are given several times a day (£2, 45 minutes, call for schedule).

National Gallery—Along with a hall featuring the work of top Irish painters, this has Ireland's best collection of paintings by the European masters. It's impressive—unless you've been to London or Paris (free, Monday–Saturday 10:00–17:30, Thursday until 20:30, Sunday 14:00–17:00, tel. 01/661-5133).

Streets, Squares, and Parks—Dublin

▲Grafton Street—Once filled with noisy traffic, today Grafton Street is Dublin's liveliest pedestrian shopping mall. You'll find colorful pubs, fancy shops, singing buskers, and lots of browsers.

The Powerscourt Townhouse Shopping Centre (nearby on William Street South) is a hit with shoppers. Grafton Street connects Trinity College with St. Stephen's Green.

▲**St. Stephen's Green**—This city park, originally a medieval commons, was enclosed in 1664 and gradually surrounded with fine Georgian buildings. Today it provides 22 acres of grassy refuge for Dubliners.

Merrion Square—This square offers an insider's look at Georgian Dublin. Tour the carefully restored house at **Number 29 Lower Fitzwilliam Street** for a walk through a Dublin home in 1790 (£2.50, Tuesday–Saturday 10:00–17:00, Sunday 14:00–17:00, closed Monday). Notice the fine doors around the square—a Dublin trademark—and the elegant Georgian knobs and knockers.

▲**O'Connell Street and surroundings**—Dublin's grandest street leads from O'Connell Bridge through the heart of north Dublin. Since the 1740s it's been a 45-meter-wide promenade. Ever since the first O'Connell Bridge connected it to the Trinity side of town in 1794, it's been Dublin's main drag. The street, while lined with fast-food and souvenir shops, echoes with history. Much of the fighting during the 1916 Easter Rising and the Civil War a few years later took place here. The imposing **General Post Office** is where Patrick Pearse read the Proclamation of Irish Independence. The GPO building itself—a kind of Irish Alamo—was the rebel headquarters and scene of a five-day bloody siege during the Rising. While there's little to see, its facade remains pockmarked with bullet holes.

The statues lining the street celebrate great figures in Ireland's fight for independence. One monument which didn't—a tall column crowned by a statue of the British hero of Trafalgar, Admiral Nelson—was blown up in 1966 as locals celebrated the 50th anniversary of the Rising.

Make a point to get away from tourists' Dublin. A good way to do that is to stroll the smaller streets north of the Liffey. Just a block west of O'Connell Street, the **Moore Street Market** is a colorful commotion of produce and hawkers. For workaday Dublin, the long pedestrian mall of Mary Street, Henry Street, and Talbot Street is a people-watchers' delight.

Explore. The prestigious **Abbey Theatre**, now a modern, ugly building, is still the much-loved home of the Irish National Theater (a block off the river on Abbey Street). **St.**

Mary's Pro-Cathedral is the leading Catholic church in town, but curiously not a cathedral since Christchurch was made one in the 12th century (the pope chose to ignore the fact that it hasn't been Catholic for centuries). Georgian **Parnell Square** has a Garden of Remembrance honoring the victims of the 1916 Rising.

The **Dublin Writers' Museum** is a must for anyone interested in Irish literature, featuring the lives and works of Dublin's greats (£2.90, Monday–Saturday 10:00–17:00, Sunday 11:30–18:00, 18 Parnell Square North, tel. 01/872-2077). With hometown wits such as Swift, Yeats, Joyce, and Shaw, literary fans will have a checklist of residences and memorials to see.

▲▲**Temple Bar**—For many visitors the heart of Dublin is its hot and much-promoted nightlife center, the Temple Bar district. While promoted as Dublin's "Left Bank," it's actually on the right bank (as central as can be and just south of the river). It's a pedestrians-only hive of creative energy day and night. The central Meeting House Square (just off Essex Street) hosts free street theater and is surrounded by interesting cultural centers. For a listing of events, visit the Temple Bar Information Centre (Eustace Street, tel. 01/671-5717). Trendy shops, cafés, theaters, galleries, pubs with live music, and restaurants (Italian, American, and even Irish) vie for your attention. Rather than follow particular recommendations, simply wander the main drag and venture down a few side lanes to see what looks good. Gallagher's Boxty House is a good bet for traditional Irish food (call to reserve at 01/677-2762). You'd eat their boxty (a stuffed dinner pancake) or Irish stew in anticipation of a famine. The Bad Ass Café remains as popular as can be (students-in-a-warehouse ambience, vegetarian and Italian). Pub grub abounds. (To get some folk music away from the tourist crowds, walk five minutes up the river to Merchants Quay where, on Lower Bridge Street, you'll find the Merchants Pub and the Brazen Head.) The pedestrian-only Ha' Penny Bridge, named for the half-pence toll originally levied from those who walked it, leads over the Liffey to Temple Bar. ("Bar" means a walkway along the river.)

Sights—Outer Dublin
The Jail and the Guinness Brewery are the only sights outside of the old center. Combine these in one visit.

▲▲▲**Kilmainham Gaol (Jail)**—Built in 1789 as a debtors' prison and considered a model in its day, it was used for most of its life as a political prison by the British. Many of those who fought for Irish independence were held or executed here, including leaders of the rebellions of 1798, 1803, 1848, 1867, and 1916 (most notably Robert Emmett and Charles Stewart Parnell). The last prisoner to be held here was Eamon de Valera (later president of Ireland). He was released on July 16, 1924, the day Kilmainham was finally shut down. The buildings, virtually in ruins, were restored in the 1960s. Today it's a shrine to the Nathan Hales of Ireland.

Your visit starts with an excellent exhibit on Ireland's fight for independence, followed by a 30-minute video. Then a guide shows you around for 30 minutes. Touring the cells and places of execution while hearing tales of terrible colonialism and heroic patriotism—alongside Irish schoolkids who know these names well—is moving. Finally the museum explains Victorian prison life and the battle for independence. Don't miss the dimly lit hall off the second floor displaying the stirring last letters patriots sent to loved ones hours before facing the firing squad (£2, daily 9:30–18:00, last tour at 16:45; off-season Sunday–Friday 10:00–17:00, closed Saturday; £4 taxi, bus 51 or 79 from Aston Quay, tel. 01/453-5984).

▲**Guinness Brewery**—A visit to the Guinness Hop Store is almost a pilgrimage for many. The home of Ireland's national beer welcomes visitors (for £3) with a museum, video, and drink. Arthur Guinness began brewing the famous stout here in 1759. By 1868 it was the biggest brewery in the world. Today the sprawling brewery fills several city blocks. Around the world Guinness brews over 10 million glasses a day. You can learn as much or as little about the brewing process as you like. Highlights are the cooperage (with old film clips showing the master wood-kegmakers plying their now extinct trade) and a display of the brewery's clever ads. The video is a well-done ad for the brew that makes you feel almost patriotic as you run down to the sample bar to turn in your coupon for a half pint of the real thing (£3, Monday–Saturday 9:30–17:00, Sunday 10:30–16:30, enter on Crane Street off Thomas Street, bus 68A or 78A from Aston Quay near O'Connell Bridge, tel. 01/453-6700 ext. 5155). Hop on/hop off bus tours stop here. (Why is there no museum of Irish alcoholism, which is a serious but rarely discussed problem in this land where the social world seems to float in a sea of beer?)

Entertainment and Theater in Dublin

Ireland produced some of the finest writers in both English and Gaelic, and Dublin houses some of Europe's finest theaters. While Handel's *Messiah* was first performed in Dublin (1742), these days Dublin is famous for its rock bands (U2, Thin Lizzie, and Sinead O'Conner all got started here).

You have much to choose from: Abbey Theatre is Ireland's National Theatre. Gate Theatre does foreign plays as well as Irish classics. Point Theatre, once a railway terminus, is now the country's top live music venue. At the National Concert Hall, the National Symphony Orchestra performs most Friday evenings. Street theater takes the stage in Temple Bar on summer evenings. Folk music rings in the pubs and street entertainers are everywhere. For the latest, pick up a copy of the twice-monthly *In Dublin* (£1.50, any newsstand).

Irish Music in nearby Dun Laoghaire

For an evening of pure Irish music, song, and dance, check out the **Comhaltas Ceoltoiri Eireann**, an association working to preserve this traditional slice of Irish culture. It got started when Elvis and company threatened to steal the musical heart of the new generation. Judging by the pop status of traditional Irish music these days, Comhaltas accomplished its mission. Their "Fonntrai" evening is a costumed stage show mixing traditional music, song, and dance (£5, mid-June–August Monday–Thursday at 21:00). These are followed by an informal music session at 22:30. Fridays all year long they have a Cailidh where everyone dances (£5, 21:30–00:30). Saturday nights feature an informal session by the fireside. Performances are held in the Cuturlann na Eireann, near the Seapoint DART stop or a 20-minute walk from Dun Laoghaire, at 32 Belgrave Square, Monkstown (tel. 01/280-0295). Their bar is free, and often filled with music.

Sleeping in Dublin
(£1 = about $1.60, tel. code: 01)

Sleep Code: **S**=Single, **D**=Double/Twin, **T**=Triple, **Q**=Quad, **b**=bathroom, **t**=toilet only, **s**=shower only, **CC**=Credit Card (**V**isa, **M**asterCard, **A**mex).

Dublin is popular and rooms can be tight. Big and practical places (both cheap and moderate) are most central at Christchurch on the edge of Temple Bar. For classy, older Dublin accommodations you'll pay more and stay a bit farther out in the direction of Ballsbridge (embassy row). For a smalltown escape with the best budget values, side-trip by the convenient DART train (at least 3/hr, 15 min) from nearby Dun Laoghaire (see below).

Sleeping in Christchurch

These places each face Christchurch Cathedral, a great locale five minutes' walk from the best evening scene at Temple Bar and eight minutes from the sightseeing center (Trinity College). Buses 50, 54, 65, and 77 stop here. For an easy meal near your hotel, try Leo Burdocks Fish & Chips, popular with locals (2 Werburgh Street, off Christchurch).

Jurys Christchurch Inn, like its sister in Galway, is well-located offering business-class comfort in all its identical rooms. This no-nonsense, modern, American-style hotel has a winning keep-it-simple-and-affordable formula. If old is getting old (and you don't mind big bus-tour groups), you won't find a better value in town. All 190 rooms cost the same: £60 for one, two, or three adults, or two adults and two kids, breakfast not included. Each room has a modern bathroom, direct-dial telephone, and TV. Two floors are strictly non-smoking. Request a room far from the noisy elevator (CC:VMA Christchurch Place, Dublin 8, tel. 01/454-0000, fax 01/454-0012, in U.S.A. 800/843-3311). A 234-room **Jurys Custom House Inn** (£60, tel. 01/607-5000) has just opened on Custom House Quay in Dublin.

Kinlay House, across the square from Jurys, is its backpackers' equivalent—definitely the place to go for cheap beds with a good location, privacy, and an all-ages-welcome atmosphere. This huge, red-brick, 19th-century Victorian building has 120 metal, prison-style beds in spartan, smoke-free rooms: singles, doubles, and four- to six-bed dorms (generally co-ed). It fills up most days. Call well in advance especially for summer weekends (S-£18, D-£26, Db-£30, dorm beds-£12–13, includes continental breakfast, self-catering kitchen, launderette, left luggage, and so on, Christchurch, 2-12 Lord Edward Street, Dublin 2, tel. 01/679-6644, fax 01/679-7437). If Kinlay is full, a similar place is the well-located **Avalon House** (D-£24–28, dorm beds-£7.50–10.50, just south of Temple Bar at 55 Aungier Street, tel. 01/475-0001, fax 01/475-0303, e-mail: tkennedy@avalon.iol.ie).

Harding Hotel is a hardwood, 20th-century, Viking-style place with 53 hotelesque rooms. The hotel is as comfortable as Jurys but on a more intimate scale and without the tour-group scene (Sb-£45, Db or Tb-£55–60, breakfast extra, CC:VM, Copper Alley across the street from Christchurch, tel. 01/679-6500, fax 01/679-6504, web site: www.iol.ie/usitaccm/hotel.htm, e-mail: harding@usit.ie).

Sleeping East of St. Stephen's Green

The Fitzwilliam rents 12 hotel-ish rooms in a classy guest-house (Sb-£45, Db-£80, CC:VMA, 41 Upper Fitzwilliam Street, Dublin 2, tel. 01/662-5155, fax 01/676-7488).

Mespil Hotel is a huge, modern, business-class hotel renting 153 identical three-star rooms, each with all the comforts and at a very good price. Half the rooms overlook a canal greenbelt (Sb, Db, or Tb-£72, continental breakfast-£4, Irish breakfast-£7, elevator, one non-smoking floor, CC:VMA, Mespil Road, Dublin 4, tel. 01/667-1222, fax 01/667-1244, e-mail: mespil@leehotels.ie).

Albany House is Georgian style throughout and completely smoke-free. Each of the 29 rooms are tastefully designed with old elegance and modern comfort. Request the huge "superior" rooms which are the same price (Sb-£70, Db-£100, £70 in slow times, back rooms are generally bigger and quieter, the included breakfast is a healthy first-class continental buffet, CC:VMA, 1 block south of St. Stephen's Green at 84 Harcourt Street, Dublin 2, tel. 01/475-1092, fax 01/475-1093).

The next three listings are on Northumberland Road. While Trinity College is only a 15-minute walk away, buses 7, 7A, and 8 (to O'Connell Street) lumber down Northumberland Road to the city center every ten minutes.

Northumberland Lodge is a quiet, elegant mansion. Bridget and Tony Brady run a tight, comfortable, and friendly ship (Sb-from £55, Db-from £85, CC:VM, 68 Northumberland Road, Ballsbridge, Dublin 4, tel. 01/660-5270, fax 01/668-8679).

Bush House is small and homey with a pleasant lounge and six rooms mostly on the ground floor (Sb-£40, Db-£70, £60 for two nights or more, CC:VMA, 33 Northumberland Road, tel. & fax 01/668-3927, Diane Armstrong).

Glenveagh Town House, next door, has 13 classy rooms but is unreliable about reservations (Sb-£42, Db-£72, less in slow times, CC:VM, 31 Northumberland Road, tel. 01/668-4612, fax 01/668-4559).

Sleeping in nearby Dun Laoghaire
(tel. code: 01, mail: County Dublin)

The first three listings are a three-minute walk to the Sandy-cove DART station and a seven-minute walk to the Dun Laoghaire DART station/ferry landing. The rest are closest to the Dun Laoghaire DART station. Except for the first place, all are a bit tattered around the edges. While buses go into Dublin, the DART is much faster (6/hour in peak times, at least 3/hr otherwise, 15 min, £1.10; for a longer stay consider the four-day Rambler ticket covering DART and Dublin buses). The **Dun Laoghaire TI** is in the ferry terminal (daily 10:00–21:00 year-round). The Society of the Preservation of Irish Folk Music has a lively branch in Dun Laoghaire (see above).

Mrs. Kane's B&B is a modern house with three big, cheery rooms and a welcoming guests' lounge. While a few blocks farther out than the others, it's worth the walk for its great, bright, friendly feeling (Db-£45, completely smoke-free, past Rosmeen Gardens to 2 Granite Hall, tel. 01/280-9105).

Ferry House B&B is a stately old place facing a quiet square with a tennis court. It's warmly run by Mr. and Mrs. Field with seven huge rooms and a cozy lounge (S-£21, D-£36, Db-£40, CC:VM, 15 Clarinda Park North, tel. 01/280-8301, fax 01/284-6530).

Sandycove House, a comfortable old place overlooking a park and the harbor, is run in a no-nonsense kind of way. Its 12 rooms are generally large and fluffy (Sb-£29, Db-£45, Db overlooking the sea-£50, CC:VM, a £2 taxi or five-minute walk from the ferry landing and 2 blocks from the Sandycove DART station, Marine Parade, Sandycove, tel. 01/284-1600).

Lynden B&B, with a classy 150-year-old interior hiding behind a somber front, offers four big rooms run by the charming and energetic Maria Gavin (S-£23, D-£35, Db-£39, past Mulgrave Street to 2 Mulgrave Terrace, tel. 280-6404). Next door, the similar **Belmont B&B** rents three rooms (D-£33, Db-£37, tel. 01/280-1422).

Dun Laoghaire

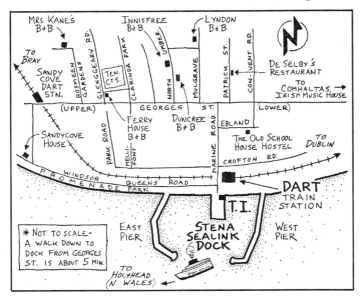

Innisfree B&B is a well-worn place with a fine lounge and six big, bright rooms (D-£32, Db-£37, CC:VM, from George Street follow the "Yellow Fever Vaccination Centre" sign to 31 Northumberland Avenue, tel. 01/280-5598, Brendan and Mary Smith). **Duncree B&B** is similar with four mostly large rooms on a quiet street (S-£19.50, D-£35, Db-£39, 16 Northumberland Avenue, tel. 01/280-6118, Mrs. O'Sullivan).

The Old School House Hostel is a shoestring traveler's dream-come-true. It's just 2 blocks from the DART station and ferry landing with incredibly cheap beds in two- to six-bed rooms and a hardworking and creative staff. The only problem is that it's a hostel: old carpets, bare walls, and a general scruffiness. Having said that, it's clean with good beds and plenty of privacy and feels secure and safe (£9 bunks in six-bed dorms, £10 in a quad, £24 doubles, showers down the hall, or for 50p extra, in your room, breakfast not included, some non-smoking rooms, self-catering kitchen, restaurant, £3 laundry service, and 24-hour staff; CC:VMA, from ferry, go up Marine Road, take first left onto Eblana Avenue; tel. 01/280-8777, fax 01/284-2266, e-mail: osh@iol.ie).

Eating in Dun Laoghaire

George Street, the town's main drag and three blocks inland, has plenty of eateries and pubs, often with live music. Probably the best bet for a good mid-range meal is **De Selby's Restaurant**, serving traditional Irish food, stew, and seafood (£12 meals, nightly 17:30–23:00, a block off George Street at 17 Patrick Street, tel. 01/284-1761). The **Purty Kitchen Pub/Restaurant** has good seafood.

Transportation Connections—Dublin

By bus to: Belfast (7/day, 3 hrs), **Ennis** (7/day, 4.5 hrs), **Galway** (8/day, 4 hrs), **Limerick** (6/day, 3.5 hrs), **Tralee** (5/day, 6 hrs). Bus info tel. 01/836-6111.

By train to: Rosslare (3/day, 3 hrs), **Tralee** (5/day, 4 hrs), **Galway** (4/day, 3 hrs, talking timetable tel. 01/855-4422), **Ennis** (4/day, 4 hrs), **Portrush** (5/day, 4 hrs, £19 one-way, £25 round-trip; stops in Belfast on the way south), **Belfast** (12/day, 1.5 hrs, talking timetable tel. 01/855-4477). The new Dublin–Belfast train will connect the two Irish capitals in 90 minutes at 90 mph on one continuous welded rail (£15 one-way, £23 round-trip, round-trip the same day Monday–Friday only £15, from the border to Belfast one-way £8.50, £10.50 round-trip). Train info tel. 01/836-6222.

The **Dublin Airport**, 12 miles from the city center, is well-connected to the center (see Arrival in Dublin). British Air flies to London's Gatwick Airport (4/day, £99, toll-free tel. 800/626747 in Ireland and 800/247-9297 in the U.S.A.), as do Aer Lingus (tel. 01/705-6705) and British Midland (tel. 01/283-8833 in Ireland and 800/788-0555 in the U.S.A.). Dublin airport info tel. 01/844-4900.

Transportation Connections— Ireland and Britain

Dublin and London: The boat/rail journey takes ten hours, all day or all night (£40–60). Dublin train info tel. 01/836-6222.

Dublin and Holyhead: Irish Ferries sails between Dublin and Holyhead in North Wales (5/day, 2.5 hrs, £20–29 one-way walk-on fare, Dublin tel. 01/661-0511, Holyhead tel. 01407/760-222).

Dun Laoghaire and Holyhead: Stena Line sails between Dun Laoghaire (near Dublin) and Holyhead in North Wales (5/day, 2.5 hrs, £22–30 one-way walk-on fare,

£10 round-trip in a day if you have no baggage, plus £5 port tax, reserve by phone early—they book up long in advance on summer weekends, Dublin tel. 01/204-7777, recorded information 01/204-7799).

Ferry Connections—Ireland and France

Irish Ferries connect Ireland (Rosslare and Cork) with France (Le Havre, Cherbourg, and Roscoff) daily from June through mid-September and three times weekly the rest of the year. While Le Havre has the quickest connection to Paris, your overall time between Ireland and Paris is about the same regardless of which port is used on the day you sail. One-way fares vary from £60 to £90 (round-trips are much cheaper). Except for a £4 port tax, Eurailers go free and get beds or cabins for half price (depending on availability). In both directions departures are generally between 15:00 and 17:00 and arrivals are around midday of the following day. While passengers can nearly always get on, reservations are wise on weekends in July and August. If you anticipate a crowded departure you can reserve a seat for £5. Beds in a quad start at £8. A double (or single) costs £44. The easiest way to get a bed (except during summer weekends) is from the information desk upon boarding. The cafeteria serves bad food at reasonable prices. Upon arrival in France, buses and taxis connect you to your Paris-bound train (Irish Ferries: Dublin tel. 01/661-0511, recorded info tel. 01/661-0715, Paris tel. 01 44 94 20 40, web site: www.iol.ie/irishferries, e-mail: info@irish-ferries.ie).

NEAR DUBLIN: WICKLOW MOUNTAINS AND GLENDALOUGH

While only 10 miles south of Dublin, the Wicklow Mountains feel remote—remote enough to have provided a handy refuge for opponents to English rule. Rebels who took part in the 1798 Irish uprising hid out here for years. When the frustrated British built a military road in 1800 to help flush out the rebels of '98, the area became more accessible. Now known as the R115, this same road takes you through the Wicklow area to Glendalough at its south end. While the darling of the Dublin day trip tour organizers, the valley itself doesn't live up to its hype. But two blockbuster sights make a visit worth considering.

Getting Around the Wicklow Mountains

By car or tour, it's easy. If you lack wheels, it's not worth the trouble.

By Tour: Several tour companies run day trips through the Wicklow Mountains from Dublin (Dublin Bus is cheapest). Mary Gibbon's Tours visit both the monastery and the gardens in a four-hour trip (£16, be careful—they spend an hour picking up tourists at Dublin hotels before leaving, tel. 01/283-9973).

By Car: It's a joy. You might consider detouring through the Wicklow area as you drive between Dublin and the west coast. Take the freeway south to Enniskerry, your gateway to the Wicklow Mountains. Signs direct you to the gardens. From Glendalough you can leave the valley (and pick up the highway to the west) over the famous, but dull, mountain pass called the Wicklow Gap.

Sights—Wicklow Mountains

▲▲Gardens of Powerscourt—While the mansion around which they were built was gutted by a fire in 1974, these meticulously kept aristocratic gardens are the most beautiful in Ireland. Commissioned in the 1730s by Richard Wingfield, first viscount of Powerscourt, the gardens are called "the grand finale of Europe's formal gardening tradition . . . probably the last garden of its size and quality ever to be created." I'll buy that.

Upon entry you'll get a flyer laying out 40-minute and 60-minute walks. Do the "hour walk" (which takes 30 minutes at a slow amble). With the impressive summit of the Great Sugar Loaf Mountain as a backdrop and a fine Japanese garden, Italian garden, and a goofy pet cemetery along the way, this garden provides the scenic greenery I hoped to find in the rest of the Wicklow area. The lush movie *Barry Lyndon* was filmed in this well-watered aristocratic fantasy.

The gardens, a mile above the village of Enniskerry, cover several thousand acres within the 16,000 acre estate. The driveway alone is a mile long. It's an easy stop by car, but probably not worthwhile if relying on public transport (£3, daily March–October 9:30–17:30, tel. 01/286-7676). Skip the associated waterfall (£1.50, 3 miles away).

▲▲Glendalough—The steep wooded slopes of Glendalough ("glen-da-lock", which means "valley of the two lakes"), at the south end of Wicklow's military road, hides one of Ireland's most impressive monastic settlements. Founded by St. Kevin in the sixth century, the monastery flourished (despite repeated Viking raids) throughout the "Age of Saints and Scholars" until the English destroyed it in 1398. While it was finally abandoned during the Dissolution of the Monasteries in 1539, pilgrims kept coming, especially on St. Kevin's Day, June 3. (This might have something to do with the fact that a pope said seven visits to Glendalough had the same indulgence value as one visit to Rome.) While much restoration was done in the 1870s, most of the buildings date from the eighth through the 12th centuries.

The valley sights are split between the two lakes. The lower lake has the visitor's center and the best buildings. The upper lake, with scant ruins, feels like a state park with a grassy lakeside picnic area, school groups, and fine walks.

General Glendalough plan: Park free at the visitor's center (£2, daily 9:00–18:30, closes earlier off-season, tel. 0404/45325). For a complete visit, begin with the video and history exhibit in the center, wander the ruins around the Round Tower, walk the traffic-free Green Road 1 mile to the upper lake, and then walk back to your car. (You can drive to the upper lake but it's £1.50 to park). If you're rushed, skip the upper lake. The tour bus crowds seem to be bad only from 11:00 to 14:00.

Glendalough Visitors Centre: Start your visit here. The 20-minute video provides a good thumbnail background on the monastic society in medieval Ireland. While the video is more general than specific to Glendalough, the adjacent museum room features this particular monastic settlement. The model in the center of the room recreates the fortified village in the year 1050 (although there were no black-and-white Frisian cows in Ireland back then—they would have been red cows). A browse here shows the contribution these monks made to intellectual life in Dark-Age Europe (such as Irish minuscule, a more compact alphabet developed in the seventh century, and illuminated manuscripts such as the Book of Kells from the ninth century). From the center, a short walk along the Green Road takes you scenically to the Round Tower.

The Monastic Village: Easily the best ruins of Glendalough gather around its famous 110-foot-tall Round Tower. Towers like this (60–110 feet tall, standard features in such settlements), functioned as beacons for pilgrims, bell towers, storage lofts, and places of final refuge during Viking raids. They had a high door with a pull-up ladder. Several ruined churches (eighth–12th centuries) and a sea of grave markers complete this evocative scene. Markers give short descriptions of the ruined buildings.

In an Ireland without cities, these monastic communities were mainstays of the Irish civilization. They were remote outposts where ascetics (with a taste for scenic settings) gathered to commune with God. In the 12th century, with the arrival of grander monastic orders such as the Franciscans and the Dominicans, and with the growth of cities, these monastic communities were eclipsed. Today Ireland is dotted with the reminders of this age—illuminated manuscripts, simple churches, carved crosses, and about 100 round towers.

Upper Lake: The Green Road continues peacefully 1 mile farther up the valley to the upper lake (where the marriage scene from the movie *Braveheart* was filmed). The oldest ruins—scant and hard to find—lie near this lake. If you're looking for a scenic Wicklow walk, this is the place to start.

DINGLE PENINSULA

Dingle Peninsula, the westernmost tip of Ireland, offers just the right mix of far and away beauty, ancient archeological wonders, and desolate walks or bike rides all within convenient reach of its main town. Dingle Town is just big enough to have all the necessary tourist services and a steady nocturnal beat of Irish folk music.

While the big tour buses clog the neighboring Ring of Kerry before heading east to slobber all over the Blarney Stone, Dingle—while crowded in the summer—still feels like the fish and the farm matter. Fifty fishing boats sail from Dingle, and a faint whiff of peat still fills its nighttime streets.

For 15 years my Irish dreams have been set here on this sparse but lush peninsula where locals are fond of saying "The next parish is Boston." There's a closeness to the land on Dingle. When I asked a local if he was born here, he thought for a second and said, "No, it was about 6 miles down the road." When I told him where I was from, a far-away smile filled his eyes, he looked out to sea and sighed, "Ah, the shores of Americay."

Dingle feels so traditionally Irish because it's a Gaeltacht, a region where the government subsidizes the survival of the Irish language and culture. While English is always there, the signs, menus, and songs come in Gaelic. Even the local preschool brags "ALL Gaelic."

Of the peninsula's 10,000 residents, 1,300 live in Dingle Town. Its few streets, lined with ramshackle but gaily painted shops and pubs, run up from a rain-stung harbor always busy with fishing boats and yachts. During the day kids—already working on ruddy beer-glow cheeks—roll kegs up the streets and into the pubs in preparation for another night of music and *craic* (conversation).

Dingle History

The wet sod of Dingle is soaked with medieval history. In the darkest depths of the Dark Ages, peace-loving, bookwormish monks fled the chaos of the Continent and its barbarian raids. They sailed to the drizzly fringe of the known world—places like Dingle. These monks kept literacy alive in Europe. Charlemagne, who ruled much of Europe in the year 800, imported Irish monks to be his scribes.

It was from this peninsula that the semi-mythical explorer monk, St. Brandon, is said to have set sail in the sixth century in search of a legendary western paradise. Some think he beat Columbus to North America by nearly a thousand years.

Dingle (An Daingean in Gaelic) was a busy seaport in the late Middle Ages. Along with Tralee, it was the only walled town in Kerry and a gateway to Northern Spain—a three-day sail due south. Many 14th- and 15th-century pilgrimages left from Dingle for Santiago di Compostela in Spain.

When its position as a medieval trading center ended, Dingle faded in importance. In the last century it was a linen-weaving center. Until 1970 fishing dominated. The only visitors were scholars and students of old Irish ways. In 1970, the movie *Ryan's Daughter* introduced the world to Dingle. The trickle of Dingle fans has grown to a flood in the 1990s as word of its musical, historical, gastronomical, and scenic charms—not to mention its friendly dolphin—has spread.

Planning Your Time

For the shortest visit, give Dingle two nights and a day. It takes about six hours to get there from Dublin, Galway, or the boat dock in Rosslare. I like two nights because you feel more like a local on your second evening in the pubs. You'll need the better part of a day to explore the 30-mile loop around the peninsula by bike, car, or tour bus (see Circular Tour, below). To do any serious walking or relaxing you'll need two or three days. It's not uncommon to find Americans slowing way, *way* down in Dingle.

Orientation (tel. code: 066)

Dingle is extremely comfortable on foot. The town hangs on a medieval grid of streets between the harborfront (where the Tralee bus stops) and Main Street (3 blocks inland). Nothing in town is more than a five-minute walk away. Dingle is so small that street numbers are used only when more than one place is run by a family of the same name. Most locals know most locals, and people on the street are fine sources of information. Remember, tourism is what puts soda bread on the table here and the locals offer a warm and sincere welcome.

Tourist Information: The Bord Failte (TI) is at the bottom of Main Street, 3 blocks off the water (April–October Monday–Saturday 9:30–18:00, Sunday in summer, tel. 066/51188). In the summer the TI organizes town walks. For more creative help, drop by the Mountain Man shop (on Strand Street, see below).

Helpful Hints

Crowds: Dingle gets so crowded during summer holiday weekends that the police actually close down the road access. July 15 to August 30 is bad (you might consider the less-discovered Beara Peninsula, south of the Ring of Kerry). The absolute craziest is St. Brandon's festival (three days in mid-July), Dingle Races (second weekend in August), and Dingle Regatta (third weekend in August). Dingle's dead before May 1: no music, activities, tours, or tourists.

Banking: There are two banks in town, both uphill from the TI on Main Street (Monday–Friday 10:00–12:30, 13:30–16:00). The Bank of Ireland has a cash machine.

Supermarket: The Super Valu supermarket/department store is at the base of town (Monday–Saturday 8:00–19:00, Sunday 8:00–13:00).

Launderette: At this full-service shop, you can drop off a load and pick it up three hours later (small-£3.50, large-£5.50, Monday–Saturday 9:15–17:15, on Green Street behind El Toro restaurant).

Bike Rental: Bike rental shops abound in Dingle. You can get good mountain bikes at Paddy's Bike Hire (daily 9:00–7:00, £5/day, £6 for a 24-hour period, on Dykegate), Sciuird Tours, the Mountain Man, and the Ballintaggert Hostel. Plan on leaving a credit card, driver's license, or passport as security.

Dingle Peninsula

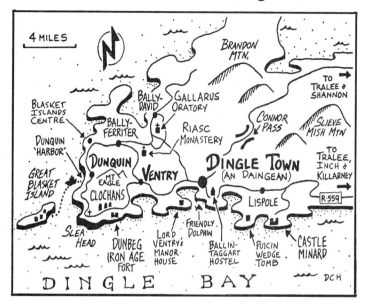

Dingle Activities: The **Mountain Man**, a hiking shop run by two local guides, Con and Mike, is a clearinghouse for information, local tours, and excursions (located just off the harbor at Strand Street, tel. 066/51868, fax 066/51980). Pick up the free *Kerry Gems* booklet. For bike rentals and ideas on biking, hiking, horse riding, climbing, peninsula tours (which they offer), and trips to the Blaskets, stop by here. They are the Dingle Town contact for the Dunquin–Blasket Islands boats (see Blaskets, below).

Sights—Dingle Town

▲▲▲**Folk Music in Dingle Pubs**—Even if you're not into pubs, take a nap then give these a whirl. Dingle is renowned among traditional musicians as a place to get work ("£30 a day, tax-free, plus drink"). The town has 50 pubs. There's music every night (and never a cover charge). The scene is a decent mix of locals, Americans, and Germans. Music normally starts around 21:30 and the last call for drinks is "half eleven" (23:30). For a seat near the music, arrive early. If the place is

Dingle Town

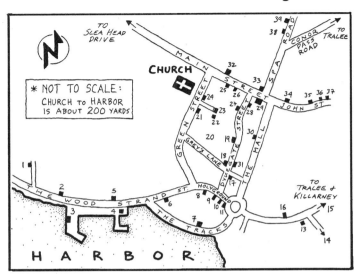

1 Smeara Dubha	16 Alpine House Guest House	29 Tourist information
2 Oceanworld	17 Sciuird Tours/Kirrary B&B	30 Captain's House B&B
3 Dingle Sailing Club		31 Cinema
4 Cruiseboat offices	18 Corner House B&B	32 Adam's Bar and Restaurant
5 Maire De Barra Restaurant	19 Connors B&B	33 Small Bridge Bar
6 Mountain Man	20 City park	34 Doyle's and Half Door Restaurants
7 Bus Station	21 Dick Mack	
8 Greany's Restaurant	22 Café Ceo	35 Sraid Eoin B&B
9 Super Value	23 Laundry	36 Kellihers Ballyegan House
10 Tig Lise	24 El Toro	37 Greenmount House
11 O'Flahertys	25 Grapevine Hostel	
13 Bambury's B&B	26 Bank	38 Hillgrove Hotel
14 Trail to lighthouse	27 Bike rental	39 Ard Na Greine House B&B
	28 An Cafe Litearta	
15 Ballintaggert Hostel		

chock-a-block, power in and find breathing room in the back. By midnight the door is closed and the chairs are stacked. While two pubs, the Small Bridge Bar and O'Flahertys, are the most famous for their good beer and folk music, make a point to wander the town and follow your ear. Smaller pubs may feel a bit foreboding to a tourist, but people—locals as well as travelers—are out for the *craic* (pronounced "crack," slang for the good time and fun conversation). Pubs are smoky and hot (leave your coat home). The more offbeat pubs are more likely to erupt into leprechaun karaoke.

The best pub crawl is along the Strand to O'Flaherty's (rough-and-tumble Murphy's is liveliest, offering rock as well as traditional music). Then head up Green Street. Dick Mack is a tiny leather shop by day/pub by night with two snugs (private booths), reliably good beer, and a strangely fascinating ambience; notice the Hollywood-type stars on the sidewalk recalling famous visitors. Wander up and down Main Street (Small Bridge Bar at the bottom is best) and then up Spa Road a few doors (often less crowded but with good music). During the day, music lovers will enjoy dropping by Danlann Gallery, a music shop on Dykegate Street (Monday–Saturday 10:00–18:00, Sunday 11:00–14:00).

More Evening Fun—Somewhere almost every night, a pub hosts "Set Dancing" with live music (Garvey's Bar does it on Monday after 21:30). The Hillgrove Hotel (up Spa Road a few hundred meters) is a mod hotel with traditional dances every Thursday (and pop dancing other nights in summer). Locals say the Hillgrove "is a good time if you're pissed." Dingle has a great little theater (The Phoenix on Dykegate). The film club (50 or 60 locals) meets for coffee, cookies, and a film every Tuesday at 20:30.

▲Oceanworld—The only place charging admission in Dingle is worth considering. This new aquarium offers a little peninsula history, 160 different local fish and other sea creatures in thoughtfully described tanks (including a unique chance to walk under the fish in the "ocean tank"), and the easiest way to see Fungi the dolphin—on video (£4, £10 for families, daily 10:00–20:00 in summer, until 18:00 or earlier in off-season, just past the harbor on the west edge of town, tel. 066/52111).

Fungi—In 1983 a dolphin moved into Dingle Harbor and became a local celebrity. Fungi is now the darling of the town's tourist trade and one reason you'll find so many tour buses parked along the harbor. With a close look at Fungi as bait, tour boats are thriving. (While she's too cute to kill, I'll happily give a free copy of the next edition of this book to anyone who can make Fungi leave.)

▲**Short Harbor Walk from Dingle**—For an easy stroll along the harbor out of town (and a chance to see the dolphin) head east from the roundabout on R561. Just after Bambury's B&B, take a right following signs to Skelligs Hotel. At the beach, climb the steps over the wall and follow the seashore path to the mouth of Dingle harbor (marked by a tower—some 19th-century fat-cat's folly). Ten minutes beyond that is a lighthouse. This is Fungi's neighborhood. If you see tourist boats out, you're likely to see her. If you continue walking you'll get to a dramatic cliff.

The Harbor—The harbor is on land reclaimed (with imported Dutch expertise) five years ago. The roundabout is new to let traffic skirt the town center. The string of old stone shops facing the harbor was the loading station for the narrow-gauge railway which hauled the fish from Dingle to Tralee (1891–1953). The Esk Tower on the distant hill is a marker built in 1847 during the famine as a make-work project. In pre-radar days, it helped ships locate Dingle's hidden harbor. The fancy mansion across the harbor is Lord Ventry's 17th-century Manor house.

Cruises—The SS *Merlin* takes £30 day-long cruises with commentary to the Skelligs (with a visit to early Christian ruins) and to the Blaskets (with a stop on the big island). Their harborside office has specifics (tel. 088/533-858 or 066/59876). The Dingle Sailing Club rents one-man sailboats (£15 per three hours) and larger boats. The *currachs* (Ireland's traditional lightweight fishing boats, easy to haul, easy to make: cover a wooden frame with canvas and paint with tar) stacked near the Sailing Club are owned by the Dingle rowing club and go out most evenings. The beaches nearby are popular in the summer.

Sleeping in Dingle Town

(£1 = about $1.60, tel. code: 066, mail: Dingle, Co. Kerry)
Sleep Code: **S**=Single, **D**=Double/Twin, **T**=Triple, **Q**=Quad, **b**=bathroom, **t**=toilet only, **s**=shower only, **CC**=Credit Card (**V**isa, **M**asterCard, **A**mex).

Sraid Eoin B&B, on the quiet end of town with four spacious pastel rooms and giant bathrooms, is warmly run by Kathleen and Maurice O'Connor (Sb-£25, Db-£32, family deals, CC:VM, John Street, tel. 066/51409, fax 066/52156). Maurice runs Galvin's Travel Agency on the ground floor (same phone number).

Kellihers Ballyegan House is a big, plain building with six comfortable rooms on the edge of town, run by friendly Mrs. Hannah Kelliher (£17.50, no CC, Upper John Street, tel. 066/51702).

Greenmount House sits among palm trees at the top of town, in the countryside with a commanding view of the bay and mountains, but just three minutes' walk from the town center. John and Mary Curran run one of Ireland's classiest B&Bs with six fine rooms (Db-£40) and six sprawling suites (Db-£60) in a modern building with lavish public areas and breakfast in a solarium (no singles or children under 8, lower prices off-season, CC:VM, up John Street to Gortonora, reserve in advance, tel. 066/51414, fax 066/51974).

Corner House B&B is my long-time Dingle home. It's a simple, traditional place with five rooms run with a twinkle and a smile by Kathleen Farrell (S-£16, D-£30, T-£42, plenty of plumbing but it's down the hall, no CC, reserve with a phone call and reconfirm a day or two ahead or risk losing your bed, central as can be on Dykegate Street, tel. 066/51516).

Captain's House B&B is a salty-feeling place in the town center with eight classy rooms (Sb-£30, Db-£44, CC:VMA, the Mall, tel. 066/51531, fax 066/51079, Jim and Mary Milhench).

Connors B&B, well-located and likely to have a room available, has 15 big, basic, uninspiring rooms (£18 per person in July and August, £14 other months, CC:VMA, in the center on Dykegate Street, tel. 066/51598, Mrs. Connor).

Ard Na Greine House B&B is a charming, windblown, modern house on the edge of town. Mrs Mary Houlihan rents four well-equipped, comfortable rooms to non-smokers (Sb-£22, Db-£36, Tb-£48, CC:VM, on the edge of town a ten-minute walk up Spa Road, three doors beyond the Hillgrove Hotel, tel. 066/51113, fax 066/51898).

Ballintaggert Hostel, a backpacker's complex, is housed in a stylish old manor house used by Protestants during the famine as a soup kitchen (for those hungry enough to renounce their Catholicism). It comes complete with horse riding, bike rental, laundry service, kitchen, café, classy study, family room with a fireplace, a shuttle into town, and a resident ghost (166 beds, £7 in eight- to 12-bed dorms, £10 in quads, £13 in singles and doubles, breakfast extra, 1 mile east of town on Tralee Road, tel. 066/51454, fax 066/52207, e-mail: btaggert@iol.ie).

Grapevine Hostel is a clean and friendly establishment with a cozy fireplace lounge and a fine members' kitchen. Each four- to eight-bed dorm has its own bathroom. Dorms are co-ed but there's usually a girls' room established. No curfew or lockout (32 beds, £6.50 each, Dykegate Street, tel. 066/51434).

Alpine House Guest House (tel. 066/51250) and Bambury's B&B (tel. 066/51244), each big, modern buildings on the main Tralee Road a block or so from the roundabout, might have a reasonable bed when the others are full.

Eating in Dingle Town

For a rustic little village, Dingle is swimming in high and fun cuisine. Many of the best values close after 18:00. Most pubs also stop serving food early (to make room for maximum beer). The town's grocery stores stay open until about 21:00.

Adam's Bar and Restaurant serves traditional food at great prices. Try their corned beef and cabbage (last meal at 18:00, Upper Main Street).

Tig Lise offers a good, simple menu with a tasty lasagna-and-salad meal and good vegetarian selections (meals are £5, closed at 18:00, near the roundabout at Holyground).

An Cafe Litearta, a popular and friendly eatery hiding behind an inviting bookstore, has good sandwiches, salads, and hot food (10:00–17:30, Dykegate Street).

Greany's Restaurant, just off the roundabout, is a local hit serving good, basic food at decent prices in a cheery, modern atmosphere (12:30–21:00, Holyground).

El Toro offers a candlelit splash of Italy with good seafood, salads, and pizzas (12:30–15:00 and 17:30–20:30, Green Street, tel. 066/51820). Maire De Barra has simple traditional food and seafood (£5, the Pier).

Smeara Dubha is a small vegetarian restaurant down by the harbor (evenings only, 18:00–21:00, The Wood, Dingle). The funky Café Ceo is vegetarian-friendly (11:00–14:00 and 18:30 on, in the courtyard opposite the church).

Dingle's long-established top-notch restaurants are Doyle's Seafood Bar (more famous, John Street, tel. 066/51174) and the Half Door (heartier portions, John Street, tel. 066/51600). Both offer three-course early-dinner specials for £15 between 18:00 and 18:30 and more expensive dining after that. Reservations are necessary in both places.

Transportation Connections—Dingle Town

The nearest train station is in Tralee. Buses connect Dingle and Tralee nine times a day in summer, less off-season and on Sunday (75 min, £6). Dingle has no bus station and only one stop, on the waterfront behind the Super Valu supermarket (bus info tel. 066/23566). See Tralee Transportation Connections, below, for more information.

Drivers choose two roads into town, the easy southern route or, much more dramatically, the treacherous Conor Pass (see Tralee Transportation Connections, below). It's 30 miles from Tralee either way.

Dingle Peninsula: Circular Tour by Bike or Car

A ▲▲▲ sight, this loop trip is about 30 miles long (five hours by bike, three hours by car, including stops; do only in clockwise direction). While you can take a guided tour of the peninsula (below), it's not necessary with the route described in this section. A fancy map is also unnecessary with my instructions. I've keyed in mileage to help locate points of interest. If you're driving, as you leave Dingle reset your odometer at the Oceanworld. Even if you get off track or are biking, derive distances between points from these numbers. To get the most out of your circle, read through this entire section before departing. Then go step by step (staying on R559 and following the "The Slea Head Drive" signs). Note: Roads are very congested in August.

The Dingle Peninsula is 10 miles wide and runs 40 miles from Tralee to Slea Head. The top of its mountainous spine is Mount Brandon—at 3,300 feet, the second-tallest mountain in Ireland. While only tiny villages lie west of Dingle Town, the peninsula is home to 500,000 sheep.

Leave Dingle Town west along the waterfront (0.0 miles at Oceanworld). There's an 8-foot tide here. The seaweed was used to nourish reclaimed land. Across the water the fancy Milltown House B&B was Robert Mitchum's home for a year during the filming of *Ryan's Daughter*.

0.4 miles: Turn left over the bridge. The building on the right was a corn-grinding mill in the 18th century.

0.8 miles: The Milestone B&B is named for the **pillar stone** ("Gallaun" in Gaelic) in its front yard. This may have been a prehistoric grave marker or a boundary marker

Dingle Peninsula Tour

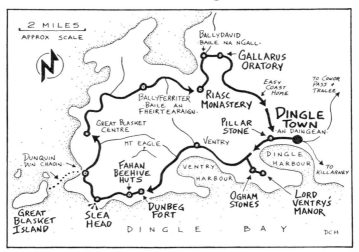

between two tribes. The stone goes down as far as it sticks up. Another pillar stone stands in the field across the street in the direction of the yellow manor house of Lord Ventry. The peninsula, literally an open-air museum, is dotted with more than 2,000 monuments dating from the Bronze Age through early Christian times.

2.1 miles: Pass through a rare grove of trees and turn left ("Leather Workshop" sign). After 100 yards, enter the **Lord Ventry Manor** taking the first left (unmarked, through white gate) and going up the long one-lane drive past small 18th-century estate houses and the palms, magnolias, fuschias, and exotic flora introduced to Dingle by Lord Ventry. Because of the mild climate (cradled by the gulf stream), fuschias line the roads all over the peninsula and fill the countryside with red from June to September. At the fork in the road, turn right. Fifty yards before the yellow mansion, stop at the six stones.

The **Ogham Stones** (third–seventh century, named for the Celtic goddess of writing) decorating the drive are rare examples of early Celtic writing. With variations on five straight lines, they could make 20 letters—the original bar code. Of the 300 known Ogham Stones, 100 are in Dingle. Lord Ventry, whose family came to Dingle as landlords in 1666, built this mansion in about 1750. Today it houses an all-Gaelic boarding school for 140 high school-age girls. Return to the main road and turn left (3.1 miles).

4.1 miles: Stay off the "soft margin" as you enjoy views of Ventry Bay and its 4-mile-long beach. Mt. Eagle (1,660 feet), the end of Ireland, is beyond. In the little town of Ventry, Gaelic is the first language.

6.0 miles: The rushes on either side of the road are the kind used to make the local thatched roofs. Thatching, which nearly died out because of the fire danger, is more popular now that anti-flame treatments are available. Magpies fly.

6.6 miles: The Irish football star Paidi O Se (Paddy O'Shea) is a household name in Ireland. He now trains the Kerry team and runs the pub on the left.

6.9 miles: The blue house hiding in the trees on the left (view through the white gate) was kept cozy by Tom Cruise and Nicole Kidman during the filming of *Far and Away*.

7.9 miles: "Taisteal go Mall" means "go slowly"; there's a yellow schoolhouse on the right.

8.2 miles: The circular mound on the right is a late–Stone Age ring fort. In 500 B.C. it was a petty Celtic chieftain's head-quarters, a stone-and-earth stockade filled with little stone houses. These survived untouched through the centuries because of superstitious beliefs that they were "fairy forts." While this is unexcavated, recent digging has shown that people have lived on this peninsula since 4000 B.C.

8.6 miles: The Hungarian red deer on the right are the work of the European community (easier on the land, but higher fences are needed). Grass-fed deer (venison) is in the Euro cards, not more sheep.

9.0 miles: **Dunbeg Fort**, a series of defensive ramparts and ditches around a central clochan, while ready to fall into the sea, is open to tourists. While there are no carvings to be seen, the small (beg) fort (dun) is dramatic (£1, daily 9:00–20:00, descriptive handout). Forts like this are the most important relics left from Ireland's Iron Age (500 B.C. to A.D. 500). Since erosion will someday take this fort, it has been excavated.

9.6 miles: The Fahan group of **beehive huts**, or clochans, is a short walk uphill. These mysterious stone igloos cluster together within a circular wall (£1; this is a better sight than the Fahan beehive huts a mile down the road). Farther on, you'll ford a stream. There has never been a bridge here; the road was designed as a ford.

10.6 miles: Pull off to the left at this second group of beehive huts. Look downhill at the scant remains of the scant home which was burned as the movie equivalent of Lord Ventry evicted the tenants in *Far and Away*. Even without Hollywood, this is bleak, godforsaken land. Look above at the patches of land slowly reclaimed by the inhabitants of this westernmost piece of Europe. Rocks were moved and piled into fences. Sand and seaweed were laid on the clay and in time it was good for grass. The created land was generally not tillable. Much has fallen out of use now.

11.4 miles: At **Slea Head**, marked by a crucifix, a pullout, and great views of the Blasket Islands (described below), you turn the corner on this tour.

11.9 miles: Pull out here to view the Blaskets and Dunmore Head (the westernmost point in Europe) and to review the roadside map (which traces your route) in the parking lot. The scattered village of Dunquin has many ruined rock homes—abandoned during the famine. They were built with small windows to minimize taxation. Some have been fixed up as this is a popular place these days for summer homes. (The lead singer of the Irish rock band The Cranberries just built a huge home a mile or so down the road.) You can see more good examples of land reclamation, patch by patch, climbing up the hillside.

13.4 miles: The Blasket Islanders had no church or cemetery on the island. This was their cemetery. The famous Blasket storyteller Peig Sayers (1873–1958) is buried in the center. Just past a washed-out bit of road, a lane leads left (100 yards) to a marker remembering the 1588 shipwreck of the *Santa Maria de la Rosa* of the Spanish Armada. Below that is the often tempestuous Dunquin Harbor from where the Blasket ferry departs.

13.5 miles: Back on the main road, follow signs to the Great Blasket Centre.

15 miles: Leave the Slea Head Road left for the modern Blasket Centre (described below).

15.7 miles: Back at the turnoff, head left (sign to Louis Mulcahy Pottery).

16.4 miles: Passing land which was never reclaimed, think of the work it took to pick out the stones, pile them into fences, and bring up sand and seaweed to nourish the clay and make soil for growing potatoes. On the left is a shadow of the main street of the fake poor village built to film *Far and Away*.

Beyond that is the "Sleeping Giant" island—with hand resting happily on his beer belly.

16.8 miles: The view is spectacular, especially when the waves are "racing in like white horses." Ahead on the right study the top fields, untouched since the planting of 1845 when the potatoes rotted in the ground. The vertical ridges of the potato beds can still be seen—a reminder of the famine. Before the famine, 60,000 people lived on this peninsula.

20.2 miles: **Ballyferriter** (Baile an Fheirtearaigh), established by a Norman family in the 12th century, is the largest town on this end of the peninsula. The pubs serve grub and the schoolhouse is a museum (£1.50, daily in summer 10:00–17:30, off-season Monday–Friday 10:00–12:00, 14:00–16:00). The early Christian cross looks real. Tap it . . . it's a fiberglass prop from *Ryan's Daughter.*

21.0 miles: At the T-junction, signs direct you to Dingle (An Daingean 11 km) either way. Go left, via Gallarus. Take a right over the bridge, still following signs to Gallarus.

21.4 miles: Just beyond the bridge and a few yards before the sign to Mainistir Riaise (Riasc Monastic enclosure), detour right up the lane. After .2 miles (the unsigned turnout on your right) you find the scant remains of the walled **Riasc Monastery** (fifth–12th centuries). Step over the rocks and inside. The inner wall divided the community into work and religious sections. The layer of black felt marks where the original rocks stop and the excavators' reconstruction begins. The pillar stone is Celtic (from 1000 B.C.). When the Christians arrived in the fifth century they didn't throw out the Celtic society. Instead, they carved a Maltese-type cross over the Celtic scrollwork. The square building was an oratory (church). The round buildings would have been dwellings. The monasteries had cottage industries. Just outside the wall (opposite the oratory) find a stone hole with a passage facing the southwest wind. This was a kiln. Locals would bring their grain to be dried and ground. The monks would keep a "tithe." With the arrival of the Normans in the 12th century, these small religious communities were replaced by relatively big-time state and church governments.

21.9 miles: Back on the main road, continue to the right.

23.0 miles: At the big pink restaurant, turn left.

23.7 miles: At another restaurant, go right up an unmarked one-lane road.

24.0 miles: The **Gallarus Oratory** (£1), built about 1,200 years ago, is one of Ireland's best-preserved early-Christian churches. Its shape is reminiscent of an upturned boat, and the dry-stone walls are so perfectly fitted together that they are still waterproof. Notice the holes for some covering at the door and the fine alternating stonework on the corners. Continue up the rugged one-lane road.

24.6 miles: Turn left on the two-lane road, then right (to An Daingean, 7 km) where you'll crest and enjoy a 3-mile coast back into Dingle Town in the direction of the Esk Tower.

27.6 miles: At the intersection, just look for the happy dolphin. Head that way, over the bridge and back into Dingle Town (28.4 miles). Well done.

Dingle Peninsula Tours

Sciuird archaeology tours are offered by the Sciuirds, a family that has Dingle history—and a knack for sharing it—in its blood. Tim Coilean (a retired Dingle policeman), his son Tim Jr., and daughter Maura give serious 2.5-hour, £6.50 minibus tours one, twice, or three times a day depending upon demand. Drop by the Kirrary B&B (at intersection of Dykegate and Grey's Lane in Dingle Town) or call 066/51937 to put your name on the list. Call early. Tours fill quickly in summer. Off-season, you may have to call back to see if the necessary four people signed up to make a bus go. While skipping the folk legends and the famous sights (such as Slea Head), your guide will drive down tiny farm roads (the Gaelic word for road is "cow path"), leading your group over hedges and up ridges to hidden Celtic forts, mysterious stone tombs, and forgotten castles with sweeping seaside views. The running commentary gives an intimate peek into the history of Dingle. Sit as close to the driver as possible to get all the information. They do two completely different tours: west (Gallarus Oratory) and east (Minard castle and a wedge tomb). I enjoyed both. In summer they also offer a 75-minute historic town walk (£2.50). Dress for the weather. In a literal gale with horizontal winds, my guide kept saying "you'll survive it."

Moran's Tour does three-hour guided minibus trips around the peninsula with a more touristic slant (£6, normally at 10:30 and 14:00 from the Esso station near the roundabout in Dingle Town, tel. 066/51155). The **Mountain Man** also offers three-hour minibus tours of the peninsula (tel 066/51868).

Blasket Islands

This rugged group of six islands off the tip of Dingle Peninsula seems particularly close to the soul of Ireland. The population of Great Blasket Island, home to as many as 160 people, dwindled until the last handful of residents were moved by the government to the mainland in 1953. These people were the most traditional Irish community of the 20th century—the symbol of antique Gaelic culture. Their special closeness to their island—combined with their knack for vivid storytelling—is inspirational. From this poor, primitive but proud fishing/farming community came three writers of international repute whose Gaelic work—basically tales of life on Great Blasket—is translated into many languages. You'll find *Peig* (by Peig Sayers), *Twenty Years a-Growing* (Maurice O'Sullivan), and *The Islander* (Thomas O'Crohan) in shops all over the peninsula.

In the summer there may be a café, shop, and hostel on the island, but it's little more than a ghost town overrun with rabbits on a peaceful, grassy, 3-mile-long poem. The ferry schedule is dictated by demand and weather. In 1997, there should be two or three buses a day from Dingle Town to Dunquin (usually around 9:00, 14:00, and 16:00, returning about 10:00, 14:30, and 18:00) coordinated with ferry departures; check at the Mountain Man shop in Dingle Town (£3 each way by bus, £16 round-trip with boat trip to Blasket, Dunquin ferry tel. 066/56455).

▲▲**Blasket Islands Centre**—This state-of-the-art Blasket and Gaelic heritage center creatively gives visitors the best look possible at the language, literature, and way of life of the Blasket Islanders. See the fine video (shows on the half-hour), hear the sounds, read the poems, browse through old photos, and then gaze out the big windows at those rugged islands and imagine. Even if you never got past limericks, the poetry of these people—so pure and close to each other and nature—will have you dipping your pen into the cry of the birds (£2.50, daily Easter–September 10:00–18:00, until 19:00 in July and August, on the mainland facing the islands, well signposted, tel. 066/56444) Visit this center before visiting the islands.

Sights—East of Dingle Town

▲**Minard Castle**—Three miles southwest of Annascaul is Minard Castle, the largest fortress on the peninsula. Built by the Norman Knights of Kerry in about 1450, it was destroyed by Cromwell in about 1650.

Wander around the castle. With its corners undermined by Cromwellian explosives, it looks ready to split. Look up the garbage/toilet chute. As you enter the ruins, find the faint scallop in the doorway—the symbol of St. James. The castle had a connection to Santiago de Compostela in Spain. Medieval pilgrims would leave from here on a seafaring pilgrimage to northern Spain. Inside, after admiring the wall flowers, recreate the floorplan: ground floor for animals and storage, main floor with fireplace, thin living quarters floor, and, on top, the defensive level.

The setting is dramatic with the Ring of Kerry across the way and Storm Beach below. Storm Beach is notable for its sandstone boulders which fell from the nearby cliffs. Grinding against each other because of the wave and tidal action, the boulders eroded into cigar-shaped rocks. Some of these rocks, inscribed by prehistoric people, became the Ogham Stones (see Circular Tour, above).

▲**Puicin Wedge Tomb**—While pretty obscure, this is worth the trouble for its evocative setting. Above the hamlet of Lispole in Doonties you'll park your car and hike ten minutes up a ridge. At the summit is a pile of rocks made into a little room with one of the finest views on the peninsula. Beyond the Ring of Kerry you may just make out the jagged Skellig Rock, noted for its ninth-century monastery.

Inch Strand—This 4-mile sandy beach, shaped like a half-moon, was made famous by *Ryan's Daughter*.

TRALEE

While Killarney is the tour bus capital of county Kerry, Tralee is its true leading city. Except for the tourist complex around the tourist office and during a few festivals, the town feels like a bustling Irish city.

Tralee's famous Rose of Tralee International Festival (a week in late August), while a celebration of arts and music, climaxes with the election of the "Rose of Tralee"—the most beautiful woman at the festival. While the rose garden in the Castle Gardens surrounding the tourist office is in bloom from summer through October, Tralee's finest roses are going about their lives in the busy streets of this workaday town.

Orientation (tel. code: 066)

For the tourist, the heart of Tralee is the Ashe Memorial Hall, housing the TI and Kerry the Kingdom museum, located near the rose garden, and surrounded by the city park. Beyond the park is the Aqua Dome and steam railway which, if you were here 50 years ago, would chug chug you to Dingle. Today it goes only to the touristy windmill.

Tourist Information: The TI is in Ashe Memorial Hall (Monday–Saturday 10:00–18:00, closed Sunday, shorter hours off-season, tel. 066/21288).

Arrival in Tralee: From the train and bus station (located in the same building), the TI is a ten-minute walk through the center of town. From the station, head down Edward Street then turn right on Castle Street and left on Denny. At the end of Denny is the TI. Drivers will knock around the town center until they find a sign to the TI. Parking on the street requires a disc (40p, sold at TI and newsstands, have them date it for you).

Sights—Tralee

▲▲**Kerry the Kingdom**—This is the place to learn about life in Kerry. The museum has three parts: Kerry slide show, museum, and medieval town train ride. Get in the mood by relaxing for 20 minutes through the Enya-style slideshow of Kerry's spectacular scenery (continuous), then wander through 7,000 years of Kerry history. The Irish say that when a particularly stupid guy moved from Cork to Kerry he raised the IQ in both counties—but this is pretty well done. The museum starts with good background on the archaeological sights of Dingle and goes right up to a video showing highlights of the Kerry football team (a fun look at Irish football). The attempted finale is a 15-minute four-person train ride down Tralee's Main Street in 1450 (£3.50, daily 10:00–18:00, until 19:00 in August, less in winter, tel. 066/27777, 40p disk at TI for two hours parking). Before leaving, garden enthusiasts will want to ramble through the rose garden in the adjacent park.

Blennerville Windmill—On the edge of Tralee, just off the Dingle road, spins a restored mill originally built in 1800. Its ten-minute video tells of the famine (£1.50, daily April–October 10:00–18:00, tel. 066/21064). A restored narrow-gauge steam railway runs hourly from Tralee's Ballyard Station to the wind-mill (tel. 066/28888 for services). In the 19th century, Blennerville was a major port for America-bound immigrants. **Siamsa Tire Theatre**—The National Folk Theater of Ireland stages two-hour dance and theater performances based on Gaelic folk traditions. They're in Irish, but work as mime (£9, 20:30 most evenings May–mid-October, next to TI in park, tel. 066/23055).

Music and other distractions—Tralee has a fine pub scene with several pubs within a few blocks of each other offering live traditional music most evenings. There's greyhound racing (Tuesday and Friday at 20:00, ten-minute walk from the station or town center, tel. 066/24033). It costs a few pounds plus what you lose gambling. At just about any time of day you can drop into a betting office to see the local gambling scene. The **Aqua Dome** is a modern swim center—the largest indoor water world in Ireland—under a dome at the Dingle end of town. Families enjoy the huge slide, wave pool, and other wet amusements (£6, £4 for kids, daily April–September 10:00–22:00, tel. 066/29150).

Sleeping in Tralee
(£1 = about $1.60, tel. code 066, mail: Tralee, County Kerry)
O'Shea's B&B, a simple, tidy, modern house, rents four comfy rooms (Sb-£20, Db-£32, Tb-£45, no CC, leaving the station, walk five minutes up Oakpark Drive to #2 Oakpark, tel. & fax 066/80123, Mairead O'Shea).

Collis-Sandes House, a mile or so north of the station and town center, is a neo-Gothic mansion in a peaceful forest with 100 cheap beds (£7 beds in four- to eight-bed rooms, D-£16, Db-from £18, sheets included, breakfast not included, CC:VMA, from the station head up Oakpark Drive, after about 8 blocks you'll see the sign on the left, tel. & fax 066/28658). They have a free shuttle service when the minibus is working.

Two good and central hostels with £7 dorm beds and £18 doubles without breakfast are **Finnegan's Hostel** (a block in front of the TI in the town center at 17 Denny Street, tel. 066/27610) and **Lisnagree Hostel** (two quads and five dou-bles, from the center, follow Boherboy to Ballinorig Road, tel. 066/27133). **Atlas House Budget Accommodation** also offers cheap dorms and tidy doubles (D-£24, Db-£27, £9 beds in four- to eight-bed rooms, with continental breakfast, no CC, 2 blocks from the train station on Castle Street, tel. 066/20722, fax 066/20747).

Transportation Connections—Tralee

By train to: Dublin (5/day, 3/day on Sunday, 4 hrs), **Rosslare** (2/day, 5 hrs). Train info: 066/23522.

By bus to: Dingle (9/day, less off-season and on Sunday, 75 min, £6), **Galway** (5/day), **Limerick** (5/day, 2 hrs), **Doolin/Cliffs of Moher** (daily at 9:30 and 15:30), **Ennis** (5/day), **Rosslare** (daily at 9:50 and 12:00, £16), **Shannon** (5/day). Tralee's bus station is at the train station. Bus info: 066/23566.

Car Rental: Duggan's Garage Practical Car Hire rents Fiat Unos (£40 for 24 hours, £70 for 48 hours, CC:VM, 3 blocks from the station on Ashe Street, tel. 066/21124, fax 066/27527).

Kerry Airport, a 45-minute drive from Dingle Town, now offers direct flights to Dublin, London (daily, £99), and even points on the Continent (tel. 066/64644).

Route Tips for Drivers

Between Tralee and Dingle: Drivers choose between the narrow, but very exciting, Conor Pass road or the faster, easier, but still narrow, N86 through Lougher and Anascaul. On a clear day Conor Pass comes with incredible views over Tralee Bay and Brandon Bay, the Blasket Islands, and the open Atlantic. Pull over at the summit viewpoint to look down on Dingle Town and the harbor. While in Kerry, listen to Radio Kerry FM 97. To practice your Gaelic tune into FM 94.4.

Between Tralee and Galway/Burren/Doolin: The Killimer–Tarbert ferry connection allows those heading for the Cliffs of Moher to avoid the 80-mile detour around the Shannon River. If you're going to Galway, the Limerick route is faster but the ferry route is more scenic (hrly trips, 15 min ride, £8 per carload, leaves on the half-hour going north and top of the hour going south in peak times, tel. 065/53124).

 **GALWAY, ARAN ISLANDS, AND COUNTY CLARE**

GALWAY

Galway feels like a boom town—rare in western Ireland. With 52,000 people, it's the area's main city—a lively university town and the county's industrial/administrative center. Amid the traditional regions of Connemara, James Joyce country, and the Aran Islands, it's also a Gaelic cultural center.

For the tourist, Galway is well-connected to Dublin, a traditional music capital, and the convenient jumping-off point for a visit to the Aran Islands.

While Galway has a long and interesting history, its British overloards (who ruled here until 1922) had little use for anything important to the Irish heritage and, consequently, precious little from old Galway survives. What does survive has the interesting disadvantage of being built by the local limestone which, even if medieval, looks like modern stone construction. A spirit of preservation came with the city's quincentennial celebration in 1984.

What Galway lacks in turnstile sights, it makes up for in ambience. Just to wander its medieval streets with their delightfully ramshackle mix of colorful facades, labyrinthine pubs, weather-resistant buskers, and steamy eateries, is an entertaining way to while away an afternoon.

Galway gets even better after dark with fine theaters and a pub scene Dubliners travel for. Visitors mix with old-timers and students as the traditional music goes round and round.

Galway, Aran Islands, and County Clare

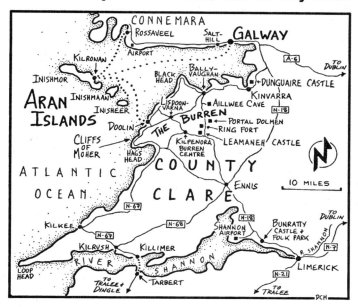

If you hear a strange language on the streets and wonder where those people are from . . . it's Irish and so are they.

Galway History

The medieval fishing village of Galway went big-time when the Normans captured the territory from the O'Flaherty family in 1234. Making the town a base, they invited in their Anglo friends, built a wall (1270), and kicked out the Irish. Galway's Celtic name (Gaillimh) comes from an old Irish word, *gall*, which means foreigner. Except for a small section in the Eyre Square Shopping Center and a chunk at the Spanish Arch, that Norman wall is gone.

In the 14th century, 14 merchant families, or "tribes" as they were known, controlled Galway's commercial traffic, including the lucrative wine trade with Spain and France. These English families were constantly clashing with the local Irish. While the wall was built to "keep out the Os and the Macs," it didn't always work. A favorite prayer at the time was "From the fury of the O'Flaherty's, good Lord deliver us."

Galway's support of the English king helped it prosper. But with the rise of Oliver Cromwell, Galway paid a price. After sieges in 1651 by Cromwell, and in 1691 by the Protestant King William, Galway declined. It wasn't until the last half of this century that it regained some of its importance and wealth.

Galway Legends

Because of the dearth of physical old stuff, the town milks its legends. Here are a few you'll encounter repeatedly:

In the 15th century, the mayor, one of the Lynch tribe, condemned his son to death for the murder of a Spaniard. When no one in town could be found to hang the popular boy, the dad—who loved justice more than his son—did it himself.

Columbus is said to have stopped in Galway in 1477. He may have been inspired by tales of the voyage of St. Brandon, the Irish monk, who is thought by some (mostly Irish) to have beaten Columbus to the New World by nearly a thousand years.

On the main drag you'll find a pub called the King's Head, originally given to the man who chopped the head off of King Charles I in 1649. For his own safety he was given this building and settled in Galway, about as far from London as an Englishman could go back then.

Every sight in town finds a way to tell you the story about the Claddagh ring—so I won't.

Planning Your Time

Galway's sights are little more than pins to hang the old town on. The joy of Galway is its street scene. You could see its "sights" in three hours but without an evening in town, you would miss the best. Many spend three nights here with two days: one for the town and another for a side trip to Connemara, the Burren, or the Aran Islands.

Orientation (tel. code: 091)

The center of Galway is Eyre Square. Within 2 blocks of the square you'll find the TI, Aran boat offices, bike rental shop, tour pickup point, best place for cheap central beds, and train station. The train and bus station butt up against the Great Southern Hotel, a huge grey railroad hotel which overlooks and dominates Eyre Square. The lively old town lies between Eyre Square and the river. From Eyre Square, Williamsgate Street leads right through the old town (changing names several times) to Wolfe Tone Bridge. Nearly everything you'll see and do is within a few minutes' walk of this spine.

Tourist Information: The TI, just off the lower side of Eyre Square at the corner of Victoria Place and Merchants Road, is a big, busy center with a bookshop and many booking services (daily 8:30–17:45, summer until 19:30, tel. 091/563-081).

Helpful Hints: Expect huge crowds during the Galway Arts Festival (ten days in mid-July) and the Galway Races (late July/early August, three days in mid-September, and three days in late October). Pick up the TI's *Jr. Chamber of Commerce Galway Tourist Guide* (free, includes fine walking tour). Chieftain Cycles is the handiest bike rental place (daily 8:30 to 18:30, £7/day, next to TI on Victoria Place, tel. 091/567454). Greyhounds race on Tuesday and Friday evenings from 8:30 to 22:00 (£2.50, ten-minute walk from Eyre Square to the stadium).

Sights—Galway's Medieval "Latin Quarter"

From the top of Eyre Square, Williamsgate Street (named for the old main gate of the Norman town wall which once stood here) is the spine of medieval Galway, leading downhill straight to the Corrib River. While the road changes names several times (William, Shop, High, and Quay Streets), it leads generally downhill and straight past these sights:

Lynch's Castle (now a bank), Galway's best surviving 16th-century fortified townhouse, was the home of the Lynch family—the most powerful of the town's 14 tribes. Over 60 Lynch mayors ruled Galway in the 16th and 17th centuries.

St. Nicholas' Church (half a block off the main street, on the right) is the finest surviving medieval building in town (1320), dedicated to St. Nicholas of Myra, the patron saint of sailors. Columbus is said to have worshiped here (1477) while undoubtedly contemplating a scary voyage. Its interior is littered with obscure town history (£1 donation for admission). On Saturday morning a wonderful market surrounds the church.

Quais Pub and Restaurant, once owned by "Humanity Dick," an 18th-century member of parliament who was the original animal-rights activist, is worth a peek inside for its lively interior. The lane just before it leads to the 100-seat Druid Theatre. Drop by to see if anything's playing tonight (£8 tickets for top-notch contemporary Irish theater).

Spanish Arch/City Museum, overlooking the Corrib River (on the left), is the best-surviving chunk of the old city wall. The Spanish Arch (1584), the place where Spanish ships would unload their cargo, is a reminder of the trading importance Galway once enjoyed. The tiny museum is really pretty weak—but if you're looking for fragments of old Galway, this is where they're kept (£1, daily May–October 10:00–13:00, 14:15–17:15, less off-season, tel. 567641).

At the **Corrib River**, you'll find a riverside park perfect for a picnic (although the town's best chippie, McDonagh's, is across the street). Over the river (southeast of the bridge) is the modern housing project which, in the 1930s, replaced the original **Claddagh**. The Claddagh was a picturesque fishing village with a strong tradition of independence—and open sewers. This gaggle of thatched cottages actually functioned as an independent community with its own "king" until early in this century. Nothing survives today except for the tradition of the popular Claddagh ring—two hands holding a heart—which comes with a fascinating story.

Notice the monument (just before the bridge) given Galway by the people of Genoa celebrating Columbus' visit here in 1477. (That acknowledgment, from a town known in Italy for its stinginess, helps to substantiate the murky visit.) Look up the river from the bridge. The green copper dome marks the new city cathedral. Down the river is a tiny harbor with a few of Galway's famous square-rigged "hooker" fishing ships tied up and on display. Beyond that, a huge park of reclaimed land is popular with the local kids for Irish football and hurling. From there the promenade leads to the resort town of Salthill.

Sights—Galway

▲▲▲**Walking Tour**—Kay Davis enjoys taking small groups on intimate walks through old Galway. Starting at the TI, she covers Eyre Square, the cathedral, and the old town, finishing up at the Spanish Arch. Her 90-minute walks leave daily except Sunday at 11:30 (£3.50, June–August, tickets at TI, Kay does private walks for £12, tel. 091/794435). Western Heritage does a similar walk at 14:30 (same price and starting point, specifics at TI). While several bus companies do one-hour £5 Galway tours, Galway is better seen on foot.

▲**Eyre Square**—In the Middle Ages, this was a green just outside the town wall. The square is named for the mayor who, in

Galway

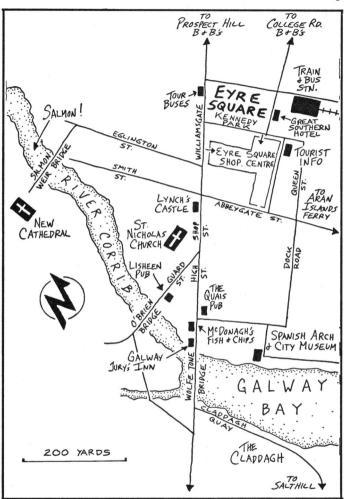

1710, gave the land to the city. While still called Eyre Square, it's filled with John F. Kennedy Park—established in memory of the Irish president's visit in 1963 a few months before he was assassinated. On a sunny day it's a popular grassy hangout. Walk to the rust-colored *Quincentennial Fountain* (built in 1984 to celebrate the 500th anniversary of something). The sails represent Galway's "hooker" fishing ships and the trading vessels which made the town a trading center so long ago. The Browne Doorway, from a 1627 fortified townhouse, is a reminder of the 14 family "tribes" which once ruled the town. Each had a town castle—much like the towers that characterize the towns of Tuscany with their feuding noble families. So little survives of medieval Galway that the town makes a huge deal of any surviving window or crest. The cannons are from the Crimean War (1854). The statue is of Patrick O'Connor, Galway's favorite Gaelic poet, who'd sit on a limestone wall, as sculpted, recording the local life.

The Eyre Square Shopping Center (arcaded entry from the square) leads to a surviving piece of the old-town wall including two reconstructed towers. Today it's a modern, people-filled shopping mall.

▲▲**Cathedral** (of our Lady Assumed into Heaven and Saint Nicholas)—Opened by Cardinal Cushing of the U.S.A. in 1965, this is one of the last great stone churches built in Europe. The interior is a treat: mahogany pews set on green Connemara marble floors under a Canadian cedar ceiling. The acoustically correct cedar is good for the church's fine pipe organ. Two thousand worshipers sit in the round facing the central altar. A Dublin woman carved 14 larger-than-life stations of the cross. The carving above the chapel (left of entry) is from the old St. Nicholas Church. Explore the modern stained glass. Find the Irish holy family—with Mary knitting and Jesus offering Joseph a cup of tea. The window depicting the Last Supper is particularly creative—find the 12 apostles. Church bulletins in the pews tell of upcoming Masses and concerts.

Salmon Weir Bridge—This bridge was the local bridge of sighs. It led from the courthouse (opposite the church) to the prison (torn down to build the church). Today the bridge provides a fun view of the fishing action. Salmon run up this river most of the summer. Fishermen in hip boots, with walking sticks to withstand the strong current, book long in advance to get half-day appointments for a spot from which to cast. Canals multiplied in this city (sometimes called the Venice of Ireland) to power more water mills.

▲**Galway Irish Crystal Heritage Center**—This is a grand-sounding name in a grand new building for a sight made-to-order for big bus groups. Still, this cheap and handy (for drivers) tour is the place to see Irish crystal made. Tours go every half-hour. After a ten-minute video subliminally sells you crystal while wowing you with Galway sights, you follow a rushed guided tour past craftsmen cutting crystal and through a small museum. The museum, actually more interesting then Galway's City Museum, gives you a good rundown on the Claddagh Village and a chance to see a large "hooker" named *Fiona* (£1, daily 9:00–20:00, less on weekends and off-season, good cafeteria, five minutes out of Galway on the Dublin Road N6 or take any bus—runs every 20 minutes—from Eyre Square to Merlin Park, tel. 091/757311).

▲**Salthill**—This small resort packs pubs, discos, amusement centers, and a fairground up against a fine mile-long beach promenade. For sunny time on the beach, a relaxing sunset stroll, or late-night traditional music or later-night disco action, Salthill hops (bus 1 or 2 from Eyre Square).

▲▲▲**Traditional Irish Music in Pubs**—Galway (like Dingle and Doolin) is a mecca for good Irish music. Unlike Dingle and Doolin, this is a university town and the pubs are often overrun with noisy students. Still, the chances of landing a seat close to a churning band surrounded by new Irish friends are pretty good any evening of the year. There is live pub music around Eyre Square and in Salthill, but the most popular are in the old town (nightly 21:30–23:30). Pop into the **Cellar Bar**—there's music up and downstairs—if there's a cover for an Irish group, pay it and be thankful for the smaller, more serious audience (Eglinton Street a block below Eyre Square). Other pubs known for Irish music include **Taaffe's** (nightly music, Thursday, Friday, and Saturday at 17:00, Shop Street, across from St. Nicholas Church) and **The Quays** (very young scene, Quay Street). For me, the best was **The Lisheen**. There's generally no cover and beer is £2 a pint. Enjoy the painting on the wall of the firelit "crossroads dance"—which still happens (5 Bridge Street, tel. 091/563804).

Sleeping in Galway
(£1 = about $1.60, tel. code: 091)
Sleep Code: **S**=Single, **D**=Double/Twin, **T**=Triple, **Q**=Quad, **b**=bathroom, **t**=toilet only, **s**=shower only, **CC**=Credit Card (**V**isa, **M**asterCard, **A**mex).

There are three price tiers for most beds in Galway: high season (Easter–October), off-season, and charge-what-you-like festival times (e.g., race weekends). I've listed high-season rates. B&Bs simply play the market. If you're on a tight budget, call a few and see what the prices do. All B&Bs include a full fried breakfast in their price.

Kinlay House is the no-nonsense place for budget train travelers to sleep. Just 100 yards from the train station, it's incredibly well run with 150 beds (one–eight per room) in bare, clean, and simple rooms. Prices range from £8 for a bed in an eight-bed room to £30 for a double with bath (includes continental breakfast, elevator, self-service kitchen, laundrette, luggage storage, budget USIT travel agency downstairs, CC:VM, across the street from the TI on Merchants Road, tel. 091/565-244, fax 091/565-245). Easygoing people of any age will feel comfortable here. **Great Western House,** even closer to the station, is similar but bigger, scruffier, and a bit more expensive (Frenchville Lane, tel. 091/561-150).

Expensive B&Bs on College Road

Drivers, following center city signs into Galway, drive right by a string of B&Bs just after the Greyhound racing stadium. These are a five-minute walk from Eyre Square. The first two listed are the best values. Most are clever and scheming in the battle for the tourist punt. **Petra House,** a peaceful brick building which rents seven rooms including one family room, is the best I have found on the street (Sb-£30, Db-£45, CC:VM, second door from stadium on the right at 29 College Road, tel. & fax 091/566580, run by Joan and Frank Maher). **College Crest Guest House,** a more formal affair with ten rooms, feels like a small hotel (Sb-£30, Db-£50, Tb-£60, almost smoke-free, CC:VM, closest to town at 5 College Road, tel. & fax 091/564744, Marion Fitzgerald). **Balcony House B&B** rents nine rooms, all with private bathrooms (£22.50, CC:VM, 27 College Road, tel. 091/563438, Michael and Teresa Coyne). **The Graduate B&B** is an industrious place with ten rooms; some are wonderful and the ones on the garden out back are pretty small and cramped for the price (Db-£45, CC:VM, 26A College Road, tel. 091/569534). **Copper Beech House B&B** rents five rooms for a bit less money than its neighbors but with an absentee owner (Db-£36–45, CC:VM, 26 College Road, tel. 091/569544).

Cheap B&Bs on Prospect Hill

Prospect Hill Road is lined with small rowhouses, many of which do B&B. These are very central, just 2 blocks off Eyre Square (from Richardson's Bar). **Mrs. Bridie Flanagan's B&B** is a humble, friendly old home with a welcoming living room and four rooms—two big and two cramped (fine Db-£30, tiny D-£28, 85 Prospect Hill, tel. 091/561515). Feisty **Mrs. Joan O'Sullivan's B&B** has five rooms proudly old-fashioned with only a sink (S-£14, D-£26–28, showers down the hall, 46 Prospect Hill, tel. 091/566324).

Jurys Galway Inn offers all the American comforts in a 128-room modern hotel ideally located where the old town hits the river. Big, bright rooms have two double beds and huge modern bathrooms (£60 for all rooms whether filled by a single, couple, three adults, or a family of four, £48 in the off-season, breakfast is extra, noisy elevators, lots of tour groups, parking-£5, CC:VMA, Quay Street, tel. 091/566444, fax 091/568415, reservation line in U.S.A. tel. 800/843-3311).

Out of Town in Salthill

Carraig Beag B&B, the classiest, friendliest, and most peaceful of all, is a big brick home on a residential street a block off the beach just beyond the resort town of Salthill. Catherine Lydon, with the help of her newly retired husband Paddy, rents six big, bright, and comfy rooms with a welcoming living room and a social breakfast table (Sb-£28, Db-£34, family room-£50, eight-minute drive from Galway—follow the beach past Salthill, second right after golf club on Knocknacarra Road, 2 blocks to 1 Burren View Heights, tel. 091/521696). The #2 bus (3/hour, 60p) goes from Eyre Square to the Knocknacarra stop at the B&B's doorstep.

Eating in Galway

Being a tourist and college town, the city is filled with colorful, fun, and inexpensive eateries. People everywhere seem to be enjoying their food. Try these two handy places (one at the top and the other at the bottom of the old town):

McDonagh's Fish and Chips is everybody's favorite chippie. They have a fast, cheap section and a classier restaurant. If you're determined to try Galway oysters, remember that they're in season September through April only. Other times, you'll eat Pacific oysters—which doesn't make much sense to me (£3 cheap lunch, £10 in restaurant, non-smoking, near the river at 22 Quay Street, tel. 091/565001).

The **Galway Bakery Company** is a popular basic place for a quick Irish meal (£3–5 meals in the ground-floor cafeteria, more pricey restaurant upstairs, 9 Williamsgate Street, near Eyre Square).

If you have a car, consider a **Dunguaire Medieval Castle Banquet**, in Kinvarra, a 30-minute drive south of Galway (for more information, see Kinvarra, near end of chapter). The 17:30 banquet can be done very efficiently as you're driving into or out of Galway (B&Bs are accustomed to late arrivals if you call).

Transportation Connections—Galway
By train to: Dublin (4/day, 3 hrs). For **Limerick, Tralee,** and **Rosslare,** you'll need to change in or near Dublin. Train info tel. 091/564-222.

By bus to: Ennis (8/day, 4 hrs), **Doolin/Cliffs** (3/day, 2.5 hrs), **Rosslare** (3/day), **Dublin** (8/day, 4 hrs). Bus info tel. 091/562-000. Nestor Travel runs a cheap and fast bus service from Galway to Dublin and the Dublin Airport (3/day, 3 hrs, tel. 091/797-144 for specifics).

ARAN ISLANDS
The Aran Islands are made up of three limestone islands: Inishmor, Inishmaan, and Inisheer. The largest, Inishmor (8 miles by 2 miles) is by far the most populated, interesting, and visited. The landscape of all three islands is harsh—windswept, rocky fields divided by stone walls, and steep, rugged cliffs. During the winter severe gales sweep the islands and, because of this, most of the settlements on Inishmor are found on the more peaceful eastern side of the island.

There's a stark beauty about these islands and the simple lives its inhabitants lived, and still live today. Precious little of the land is productive, and in the past the people of the islands made a precarious living from fishing and farming. The layers of limestone rock meant that there was little natural soil. Farming soil has been built up by the islanders over centuries of layering seaweed and sand together. The fields are small, divided by more than 800 miles of dry-stone wall. Most of these are built in the Aran "gap" style, where angled upright stones are filled with smaller stones. This allows a farmer who wants to move stock to dismantle and rebuild the walls easily. Nowadays, tourism boosts the local economy.

The islands are a Gaeltacht area, and the islanders speak Irish among themselves but happily speak English for their visitors. Many of them have direct or personal connections with America, and will ask you if you know their cousin Paddy in New York City.

Today the 900 people of Inishmor (literally, "the big island") greet as many as 2,000 visitors a day. The vast majority of these are day-trippers. They'll hop on a minibus at the dock for a 2.5-hour tour to the Dun Aengus fort and spend an hour or two browsing through the few shops or sitting at a picnic table outside a pub with their Guinness.

The other islands, Inishmaan and Inisheer, are smaller, much less populated, and less touristed. While extremely quiet, they have B&Bs, daily flights, and ferry service. For most, the big island is quiet enough.

Kilronan, on Inishmor

By far the Aran Islands' largest town, Kilronan is still just a village. Groups of backpackers wash ashore with the landing of each ferry. Minibuses, bike shops, and a few old men in pony carts sop up the tourists. There are five or six shops and about as many pubs, restaurants, and B&Bs. All of Kilronan is within a few minutes' walk. The Heritage Center, post office, bank (closed Wednesday and Thursday), and best folk-music pub are a few blocks inland. The huge SPAR supermarket, 2 blocks inland from the harbor, seems too big for its tiny community. Several huts rent bikes (about £3 for four hours or £6 for 24 hours).

Tourist Information: The TI is helpful (daily in summer 10:00–18:45, shorter hours March–October, closed in winter, faces the harbor, tel. 099/61263). But don't rely on them for accommodations. The only people who work with them are out of town and desperate.

Getting Around Inishmor

Just about anything rolling functions as a taxi. A trip from Kilronan to Dun Aengus costs about £2 in a shared minibus. Flag them down and don't hesitate to bargain. Pony carts cost about £20 per load for a trip to the west end of the island. Biking is great. Bikers take the high road over and the low road back—fewer hills, scenic shoreline, and, at low tide, 50 seals sunbathing.

Sights—Inishmor

▲**Aran's Heritage Center**—This new little museum, while nothing impressive, offers a worthwhile introduction to the island with displays covering the geology, its archaeological wonders, and the traditional lifestyle (£2, daily 10:00–18:00, tel. 099/61355).

▲**Island Minibus Tours**—There couldn't be more than 100 vehicles on the island and the majority seem to be minibuses. A line of buses awaits the arrival of each ferry offering 2.5-hour, £5 island tours. Tourists complain that the "guides" don't say much. There's really not much to say. I learned that 900 islanders live in 14 villages and have three elementary schools and three churches. Most own a small detached field where they keep a couple of cows (sheep are too much trouble). When pressured for more information, my guide explained that there are 400 different flowers and 19 different types of bees on the island. The tour is a convenient time-saver, zipping you to the end of the island for a quick stroll in the desolate fields, giving you ten minutes to wander through the historic but visually unimpressive "seven churches," and then dropping you for 90 minutes at Dun Aengus (20 minutes to hike up, 30 minutes at the fort, 20 minutes back, 20 minutes in café or shops at drop-off point) before running you back to Kilronan. Ask your driver to take you back along the smaller coastal road (scenic beaches and sunbathing seals).

▲▲▲**Dun Aengus**—This is the island's blockbuster sight. The stone fortress hangs spectacularly and precariously on the edge of a cliff 300 feet above the Atlantic. The crashing waves seem to say, "You've come to the end of the world." Little is known about this 2,000-year-old Celtic fort. Its concentric walls are 13 feet thick and 10 feet high. As an added defense, the fort is ringed with a commotion of spiky stones sticking up like lances called a *chevaux de frise* (literally "Frisian horses," named for the Frisian soldiers who used pikes like these to stop a charging cavalry). Slowly, as the cliff erodes, hunks of the fort fall into the sea. Dun Aengus doesn't get crowded until after 11:00. I enjoyed half an hour completely alone at 10:00 in the tourist season. Be there early or late if you can (free, always open, 5.5 miles from Kilronan).

Inishmor Island

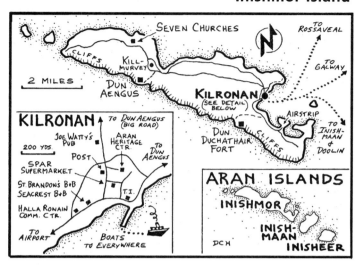

Seven Churches (*Na Seacht Teampaill*)—Close to the western tip of the island, this gathering of ruined chapels, monastic houses, and fragments of a high cross date from the eighth to 11th centuries. The island is dotted with early Christian reminders of how, in the fifth century, Christianity was brought to the islands by St. Enda. St. Edna established a monastery on the island, and many great monks studied under him. Among these "Irish apostles"—who started Ireland's "Age of Saints and Scholars" (A.D. 500–900)—was Columba, who founded the monastery of Iona in Scotland.

Man of Aran—The 1933 movie, *Man of Aran*, offering a good look at traditional island life with an all-local cast, is shown at the town hall (£3, one hour, at 15:00, 17:30, and 20:00). The movie features *currachs* (canoe-like boats) in a storm, fishing for sharks with handheld harpoons, how the fields were made from bare rock, and turn-of-the-century life here, back when bike rental wasn't an option.

Kilmurvey—This is the island's second village which sits below Dun Aengus. With a gaggle of homes, a laid-back hostel (see below), a B&B, a great sheltered beach, and a pub, this (except for the folk music in the pub) is the place for solitude.

Sleeping in Kilronan, Inishmor
(£1 = about $1.60, tel. code: 099, mail: Kilronan, Aran Islands)

Remember, this is a poor island. Nearly all rooms are plain, with facilities down the hall. No one bothers to take credit cards.

St. Brandon's B&B, the only place with real charm, is the best place in town. With a cozy living room behind ivy-covered walls and a breezy garden, Kathleen Tierney rents eight rooms (D-£26, Db-£30, about £5 less outside of summer, save £2 if you settle for a continental breakfast, tel. 099/61149).

Bayview House is the biggest place in town, overlooking the harbor as central as can be above its classy little coffee shop/restaurant (eight rooms, seven with harbor view, D-£34, Db-£36 in July and August, less otherwise, tel. & fax 099/61260).

Doyles B&B is a humble, homey little place with dumpy rooms, but is right on the harbor—down where they pile the nets (D-£24, one family quad with bunks, tel. 099/61280, Mr. and Mrs. Mullin).

Costello's B&B has four plain rooms in a plain home in a fine garden setting (D-£28, Db-£32, tel. 099/61241, Sally Costello).

Aran Islands Hostel, overlooking the harbor above the Joe Mac Pub, is cheap but noisy (beds around £9, tel. 099/61255).

Dun Aengus Hostel is for those who really want to get away from things. It's located near Dun Aengus, 5 miles from Kilronan, surrounded by birds, stone walls, and vast views, and near a pub (with good music) and restaurant and a fine beach (£5 per bed in four- and six-bed rooms, communal kitchen, small shop, free pickup upon arrival if you call 099/61318, run by friendly manager, Ian). The only B&B nearby is the **Kilmurvey House** (tel. 099/61218).

Eating in Kilronan
Kilronan's cafés dish up soup, soda bread, sandwiches, and tea. **Joe Watty's Bar** does good pub grub. Three restaurants do good dinners: the **Aran Fisherman**, **The Bayview**, and the classier **Dun Aengus** (most expensive, tel. 099/61104). The **SPAR supermarket** has all the groceries you'll need.

Pub Music
Several pubs in Kilronan offer live music nearly nightly in summer. Off-season you're likely to find music on Wednesday,

Friday, and Saturday evenings. Joe Watty's Pub (just past the post office) has reliably good Irish folk music. Other pubs offer Irish tunes but with musical detours beyond the tin whistle. The town hall (Halla Ronain) becomes a dance hall on most Saturday and Sunday nights, when from midnight to 2:00 locals have a *ceilidh* (kay-lee), the Irish equivalent of a hoedown.

Transportation Connections—Aran Islands

By ferry from Galway: O'Brien Shipping, with daily departures at 9:30 from Galway (dock is five-minute walk from TI) and 16:30 from Inishmor, offers a reliable and easy passage (90 minutes sailing time, £15 return, tel. 091/67672).

By ferry from Rossaveal: The *Aran Sea Bird* is the most weather-resistant of the ferries sailing from a port 20 miles west of Galway (3/day in summer, 2/day off-season, 35-minute crossing but allow two hours including bus connection from Galway, £19 round-trip including shuttle bus from and back to Galway). Shuttle buses depart from Galway 75 minutes before the boat sails. Summer schedule: from **Rossaveal** at 10:30, 13:30, and 18:30; from **Inishmor** at 9:00, 12:00, and 16:30. Island Ferries office is in an alley 1 block from the Galway TI, tel. 091/561-767.

By ferry from Doolin: This ferry is handy if you're in Doolin but is notorious for being canceled because of wind or tides (for specifics, see Doolin, below).

By plane: Air Aran, a friendly and flexible little airline, makes the ten-minute flight to Inishmor hourly in peak season, four times a day otherwise (£35 round-trip). They fly their nine-seat planes from the Connemara Regional Airport, 20 miles west of Galway (not the Galway Airport). A shuttle bus—£5 round-trip—runs from Galway for each flight. The Kilronan Airport is small (baggage is transported from the plane to the "gate" in a shopping cart). Your ticket includes a free minibus shuttle to and from Kilronan (2 miles from the airport). For reservations and late seat availability, tel. 091/593-034, fax 091/593-238. Ask for a 10 percent discount—they have lots of coupons out.

COUNTY CLARE AND THE BURREN

Those connecting Dingle in the south with Galway, the urban center of the west, can entertain themselves along the way by skipping through the fascinating landscape and tidy villages of

County Clare. Ennis, the major city of the county with a medieval history and a market bustle, is a workaday Irish town ideal for anyone tired of the tourist crowds that plague so many Irish stops these days. The Cliffs of Moher, a series of dramatic cliffs overlooking the Atlantic, offer tenderfeet a thrilling hike. The Burren is a unique, windblown, limestone wasteland which hides an abundance of flora, fauna, caves, and history. And for your evening entertainment, you can join a tour bus in a castle for a medieval banquet at Kinvarra or join traditional Irish music enthusiasts from around Europe at a tin whistler's mecca, Doolin.

Planning Your Time

By train and bus, Ennis is your gateway. You'll need to be more flexible and patient; for many, without wheels the area's charms aren't worth the headaches.

By car the region can be an enjoyable day-long drive-through or a destination. None of the sights have to take much time. But if you hike for an hour or three, both the Cliffs of Moher and the Burren are better experiences. If driving between Dingle/Tralee in the south and Galway/Aran Islands in the north, the following is a rushed and long day but much more interesting than the fast road via Limerick: Drive north from Tralee to catch the Tarbert–Killimer car ferry (avoiding the 80-mile drive around the Shannon estuary, see Route Tips in the Dingle chapter), then drive the scenic coastal route to the Cliffs of Moher for an hour break. The scenic drive through the Burren with a couple of stops and a tour of the caves takes about two hours. There's a 17:30 medieval banquet at the Dunguaire Castle near Kinvarra or you could head straight to Galway for a less touristic evening romp through its old town.

Sights—County Clare and the Burren

▲▲▲**Cliffs of Moher**—A visit to the Cliffs of Moher is one of Ireland's great natural thrills. For 5 miles the dramatic cliffs soar as much as 700 feet above the Atlantic, to the delight of cliff-walking hikers as well as big-bus tourists who stop at the visitor's center for a look. Drivers park at the visitor's center (£1, TI office, shop, and cafeteria; three public buses stop here daily in the summer). From the center, walk 200 yards past harpists and accordion players along a low wall of the local

Liscannor slate (notice the squiggles made by worms, eels, and snails a few years ago when the slate was still mud on the seafloor) to the cliff edge. O'Brien's Tower (1853) marks the highest point. The wonderful trail leads along the cliffs 3 miles south to Nag's Head.

But for the best thrill, read the warning, consider the risk, and step over the slate barrier and down onto the stone platform. Here, there are no crowds. If you're a risk-taking fool, gingerly belly out to look over the ledge and find yourself in a dramatic world where the only sounds are the waves, the wind, the gulls, and your stomach signaling frantically for help. There's a particularly peaceful corner of the platform over on the far right. In the distance, on a windy day, the Aran Islands are wearing their white necklace.

Doolin—This town is a strange phenomenon. Tourists go directly from Paris or Munich to Doolin. It's on the touristic map for its three pubs which feature nightly Irish folk music. A few years ago this was a mecca. Irish musicians came together here to jam and a few aficionados provided the lucky audiences, a necessary element to any music session. But now the crowds and the foreigners are overwhelming the musicians, and the quality of music is not as reliable. Still, Irish as well as European music-lovers crowd the pubs and the bodhran beat goes on.

Doolin has plenty of accommodations (see Sleeping, below), several good restaurants, and a Greek island-without-the-sun ambience. Each pub serves decent dinners before the music starts. The "town" is hard to recognize as a town. It's strung out along a road from the tiny harbor for a couple of miles. Nearest the harbor, the Lower Village (Fisherstreet) has **O'Connor's Pub** (tel. 065/74168) and is the closest thing to a commercial center. A mile farther up the road, the Upper Village (Roadford) straddles a bridge with the other two destination pubs, **McGann's** (tel. 065/74133) and **McDermott's** (tel. 065/74328). Music starts around 21:30 and finishes around midnight. On my last trip I hit Doolin on a mediocre music night. The *craic* is fine regardless.

From Doolin you can hike or bike (rentals in town) up the Burren Way for 3 miles to the Cliffs of Moher. (Get advice locally on the trail's condition and safety.)

The boats from Doolin to the Aran Islands can be handy but are often canceled. Even a balmy day can be too windy (or the tide can be too low) to allow for a sailing from Doolin's crude little port. If you are traveling by car with any time limits, don't risk sailing from Doolin. Without a car you can travel on from the Aran Islands by the bigger boats so Doolin might work for you (one-hour cruise, £20 return, tel. 065/74455 to see what's sailing).

Lisdoonvarna—This little town of 1,000 was known for centuries for its spa and its matchmakers. Today, except for a couple of weeks in September when it celebrates its Matchmaking Festival, it's pretty sleepy. (The bank is open one day a week.) Still, it's more of a town than Doolin and apart from festival time, less touristy. Lisdoonvarna is becoming known for reliably good traditional music in its pubs. I'd stay here rather than Doolin (see Sleeping, below) and commute. Doolin is just a couple miles down the road. (TI tel. 065/74630).

▲▲**The Burren**—Literally the "rocky place," the Burren is just that. The 50-square-mile limestone plateau is so barren a disappointed Cromwell surveyor described it as "a savage land, yielding neither water enough to drown a man, nor a tree to hang him, nor soil enough to bury him." But he wasn't much of a botanist, because the Burren *is* a unique ecosystem with flora that has changed little since the last ice age 10,000 years ago. It's also rich in prehistoric and early Christian sights. The first human inhabitants of the Burren came about 6,000 years ago. Today this "Limestone Land" is littered with over 2,000 historic sites including about 500 stone forts from the Iron Age.

Botany of the Burren in Brief: The Burren supports the greatest diversity of plants in Ireland. Like nowhere else, Mediterranean and Arctic wildflowers bloom side by side in the Burren. It's an orgy of cross-pollination that attracts more insects than Doolin does music-lovers—even beetles help out. Limestone, created from layers of sea mud, is the basis of the Burren. (This same basic slab resurfaces 10 miles or so out at sea making the Aran Islands.) The earth's crust heaved it up. The glaciers swept it bare, dropping boulders as they receded. Rainwater cut through weak parts in the limestone, leaving crevices on the surface and Europe's most extensive system of caves below. These puddles grew algae which dried into a powder. That, combined with bug parts and rabbit turds (Irish hares abound in the Burren), creates a very special soil. Plants which do well in dry, nearly soil-less terrain fill the cracks in the limestone. Flowers appreciate the chemicals in the limestone. Grasses and shrubs don't do well here, and wild goats eat any trees which try to grow, giving tender little flowers a chance to enjoy the sun. Different flowers appear at different months, sharing space rather than competing. Flowers are best in June and July.

Sightseeing the Burren: The drive from Kilfenora to Ballyvaughan offers the best quick swing through the historic Burren.

Kilfenora (5 miles SE of Lisdoonvarna) is a good starting point. Its humble but hard-working community-run Burren Centre gives a quick tour of its one-room museum followed by an intense 12-minute video explaining the geology and botany of the region (£2.20, daily 9:30–18:00 in summer, tel. 065/88030). You'll see copies of a fine eighth-century golden collar and ninth-century silver brooch (now in Dublin's National Museum). The ruined church next door has a couple of 12th-century crosses but isn't much to see. Mass is still held in the church which claims the Pope as its bishop. (In the 16th century, when the Anglican English were taking over Ireland, the Pope defended the town as best he could—by personally declaring himself its bishop.) The Burren Centre lunch room is handy.

At the Leamaneh Castle, a ruined shell of a fortified 17th-century house not open to anyone these days, turn north on R480 (direction Ballyvaughan). After about 5 miles, you'll hit the start of the real barren Burren and see a stone table a couple hundred yards off the road (to the east, toward an ugly gray metal barn building).

This is the **Portal Dolmen** (also called the *Poulnabrone Dolmen*—"dolmen" means stone table). Two hundred years ago, locals called this a "druid's altar." Four thousand years ago it was a grave. Wander over for a look. Wander farther afield for some quiet time with the wildflowers. (It's crowded in midday with tour buses, but it's all yours early or late.)

The **Cahercommann** ring fort (one of 500 or so in the area) can be seen on the crest of a hill just off the road about a half-mile south of the Portal Dolmen. (You can park at the intersection and walk up the gray farm's driveway and through the gate marked "stone fort" for a look, but there's really not a lot to see.) The stretch from the dolmen north to Ballyvaughan offers the starkest Burren scenery.

The **Aillwee Caves** are touted as "Ireland's premier show-cave." I couldn't resist a look. While fairly touristy and not worth the time or money if you've seen a lot of caves, they are impressive and offer your easiest look at the massive system of caves that underlie the Burren. Your guide will walk you 300 yards into the plain but impressive cave, giving you a serious 30-minute geology lesson. During the Ice Age, underground rivers carved countless caves like these. Brown bears, which became extinct a thousand years ago, used this cave, for hibernating. At a constant 50 degrees it may have been ideal for a sleeping bear, but I needed my sweater (£4, £10 family deal, daily 10:00–18:00; it's clearly signposted just south of Ballyvaughan; tel. 065/77036).

Kinvarra—This two-pub town, between Ballyvaughan and Galway (half an hour from each), is waiting for something to happen in its minuscule harbor. It faces the Dunguaire Castle, a 4-story towerhouse from 1520 standing a few yards out in the bay. (For B&Bs, see Sleeping, below.)

The **Dunguaire Medieval Castle Banquet** is Kinvarra's most tourist-worthy sight. The 500-year-old Dunguaire Castle hosts a touristy but fun medieval banquet (17:30 and 20:00, tel. 091/37108). The evening is as intimate as 70 tourists (two tour groups and a few travelers) gathered under one time-stained barrel vault can be. For £30 you get a mediocre three-course meal with wine served amid an entertaining evening of Irish tales and folk songs. It's a small and multi-talented cast: one harpist and three singer/actors who serve the "lords and ladies" between tunes. The one-hour medieval stage show that comes with dessert is the highlight (the Ruthin banquet in Wales is much better).

Ennis—This simple little market town, the main town of County Clare (pop. 15,000), provides those relying on public transit with a handy transportation hub (good connections to Limerick, Dublin, and Galway; see Transportation Connections, below) and a chance to wander around a workaday Irish town which is not reliant upon the tourist dollar.

The town has its history, but apart from the friary, it's best simply wandered through. If you're spending the night (see Sleeping, below), you'll find plenty of live music in the pubs. In fact, Ennis is emerging as the next "Doolin" on the traditional music scene.

The Franciscan monks arrived here in the 13th century. The town grew up around their friary. The Ennis Friary, from 1300, with some fine limestone carvings in its ruined walls, is worth a look (£1 includes a personalized tour, daily in summer

9:30–18:30). Ask the guide to fully explain the crucifixion symbolism in the 15th-century Ecce Homo carving.

Sleeping in Country Clare and the Burren
(£1 = about $1.60)

Sleeping in Doolin
(tel. code: 065)
Harbour View B&B is a fine, modern house a mile from the Doolin' fiddles overlooking the valley. Mrs. Cullinan keeps the fire on in the guests' living room (which is stocked with touring books and games) and serves a classy breakfast (Sb-£18, Db-£32, larger family room-£54, on the main road halfway between Lisdoonvarna and the Cliffs of Moher next to the Statoil gas station, tel. 065/74154). **Doolin Hostel**, right in Doolin's Lower Village, caters creatively to all the musical needs of backpackers (£7 dorm beds, £8 private rooms, Lower Village, tel. 065/74006).

Sleeping in Lisdoonvarna
(tel. code: 065)
Each of these three places is on the main "Galway" road near the center square and church: **Marchmont B&B** rents two large twin/family rooms and two small doubles in a fine old house (Db-£32, just past the post office, tel. 065/74050, Eileen Barrett). **Banner County Lodge** (D or Db-£28, tel. 065/74340) and **St. Genevieves B&B** (D-£26, Db-£30, tel. 065/74074) are closer to the square but bigger, scruffier, and less personal.

Sleeping in Kinvarra
(tel. code: 091)
Cois Cuain B&B is a small but stately house with a garden overlooking the square and harbor of the most charming village setting you'll find. Mary Walsh rents three super-homey rooms for non-smokers (Db-£34, The Harbour, tel. 091/637-119).

Sleeping in Ennis
(tel. code: 065)
These three places are clustered a block toward the town center from the train/bus station: **Greenlea B&B** is a charming little place with three spacious and comfy rooms run in a

simple way by Mary Conway (S-£13, D-£26, £1.50 less per person with a continental breakfast instead of a full fry, Station Road, tel. 065/29049). **Grey Gables B&B**, just across the street, is a bit more upscale and has four rooms run by Mary Keane (two small D-£30, two large Db-£36, Station Road, tel. 065/24487). **St. Judes B&B** rents three sleepable rooms in a bunker-like annex (Db-£30, twin room is much better than the cramped doubles, around the corner from Grey Gables, tel. 065/42383, Catherine Quinn).

Transportation Connections—Ennis

By train to: Galway (6/day, 70 min), **Limerick** (6/day, 1 hr), **Dublin** (7/day, 4.5 hrs). Train info tel. 065/40444.

By bus to: Galway (5/day, 1 hr), **Dublin** (4/day, 4 hrs), **Rosslare** (1/day, 5 hrs), **Limerick** (4/day, 70 min), **Doolin/Lisdoonvarna** (2/day), **Tralee** (5/day). Bus info tel. 065/24177.

NORTHERN IRELAND

Ireland was once part of Great Britain—a colony made more distant from London than its Celtic cousins, not so much by the Irish Sea as by its Catholicism. Protestant settlers from England and Scotland were planted in Ireland to help assimilate the island into the British economy, but the Catholic Irish held strong to their culture.

Over the centuries, British rule was never easy. But in the beginning of this century the sparse Protestant population could no longer control the entire island. Ireland won its independence but the northern six counties (the only ones with a Protestant majority) voted to stay with Britain.

With 94 percent of the Republic of Ireland Catholic and only 6 percent Protestant, there was no question who was dominant. But in the north, the Catholic minority was a sizable 35 percent that demanded attention. Discrimination was considered necessary to maintain the Protestant status quo in the North and that led to "The Troubles" which have filled headlines since the late 1960s. It is not a fight over Catholic and Protestant religious differences. It's whether Ireland will be free or part of Britain. And the indigenous Irish, who generally want a free, united, and independent Ireland, happen to be Catholic.

When Ireland won its independence (a 1921 treaty gave it dominion status within the British Commonwealth—like Canada) the issue of unity with the North had to be dealt with. It was uncertain what the final arrangement would be. In the North the long-established Orange Order and the newly mobilized Ulster Volunteer Force (UVF) worked to defend the union with Britain. The UVF became the military muscle of the "Unionists." This would be countered on the Catholic side by the Irish Republican Army (IRA). With the Republic's neutrality and the North's enthusiastic support of the Allied cause in WWII, Ulster won a spot close to London's heart. After WWII, the split seemed permanent, and Britain invested heavily in Northern Ireland to bring it solidly into the United Kingdom fold.

With the Civil Rights movement of the 1960s, Irish rights issues needed to be addressed. Extremists polarized things and demonstrations became violent. As Protestants and Catholics clashed in 1969, the British Army entered the fray. They've been there ever since. In 1972, a watershed year, combatants moved from petrol bombs to guns. A new, more violent IRA emerged. In the most recent 25-year chapter in the struggle for an independent and united Ireland, over 3,000 people have been killed.

A 1985 agreement granted Dublin a consulting role in the Northern Ireland government. Unionists bucked this and violence escalated. In that same year, the Belfast City Hall draped a huge and defiant banner under its dome proclaiming "Belfast Says No."

In 1994 the banner came down. In the 1990s, with Ireland's membership in the European Union, the growth of its economy, and the weakening of the Catholic Church's influence, the consequences of a united Ireland are less threatening to the people of the north. A strong movement toward peace seems to be underway.

In 1994 the IRA declared a cease-fire. The Protestants followed suit and talks are underway. The Republicans want British troops out of Ireland and political prisoners released. The Unionists want the IRA to turn in its arms and figure their prisoners are terrorists and jail is where they belong. Major hurdles to a solid peace persist. But the "Belfast Says No" sign is down. The downtown checkpoints are history, "bomb damage clearance sales" are over, and more tourists than ever are venturing up to Belfast.

Terminology

Ulster consists of nine counties in the north part of the island of Ireland. Six of those make up Northern Ireland (while three of those counties remain part of the Republic). Unionists want the North to remain with Britain. Republicans (and Nationalists) want a united and independent Ireland ruled by Dublin. Sinn Fein is the political wing of the Irish Republican Army (IRA). In 1996, Sinn Fein (whose leader is Gerry Adams) got its best election ever with 15 percent of the vote in Northern Ireland. Orange, and the red, white, and blue of the Union Jack, are favored colors of Unionists. Green is the color of the Republicans.

Northern Ireland is a Different Country
When you leave the Republic of Ireland and enter Northern Ireland you are crossing an international border. You change money, stamps, and phone cards, and your Eurailpass is no longer valid. The Irish punt (while worth almost exactly one British pound sterling) must be changed. Northern Ireland issues its own Ulster pound and also uses English pounds. Like the Scottish pound, Ulster pounds are interchangeable with English pounds. But it's best to change your Ulster pounds into English ones before returning to England (free at any bank in either region).

Safety
Tourists in Northern Ireland are no longer considered courageous (or reckless). Traveling there is as safe as traveling in England. You have to really look for trouble to find it here. Just don't seek out spit-and-sawdust pubs in working-class Protestant neighborhoods and sing Catholic songs. July 12 is Orange Day, the day Protestants parade and flex in favor of remaining separate from the Republic of Ireland. Catholics have their similar days in mid-August. Lay low if you stumble onto any big green or orange parades.

BELFAST

Seventeenth-century Belfast was only a village. With the resettlement, or "plantation," of Scottish and English settlers and the success of the local linen, rope-making, and shipbuilding industries, it boomed. The Industrial Revolution took root with a vengeance in Belfast. While the rest of Ireland remained rural and agricultural, Belfast earned its nickname "Old Smoke" and built many of the brick buildings you'll see today. In 1888, Queen Victoria gave city status to Belfast (which had a population of 300,000). Its citizens then built the town's centerpiece, City Hall.

Belfast is the birthplace of the *Titanic* (and many ships that didn't sink). The two huge, mustard-colored cranes (the biggest in the world, nicknamed Samson and Goliath) rise like skyscrapers above the harbor as a reminder of this town's shipbuilding might.

It feels like a new morning in Belfast. Security checks, once a tiresome daily routine, are now rare. What was the traffic-free security zone has shed its gray skin and is now a bright and bustling pedestrian zone. On my last visit, the children dancing in the street were both Catholics and Protestants. They were part of a community summer camp program giving kids from both communities reason to live together rather than apart.

Still, it's a fragile peace and a tenuous hope. The pointedly Protestant billboards and the helicopter that constantly hovers over the Catholic end of town remain reminders that the island is split, and about a million Protestants prefer it that way.

Planning Your Time

Big Belfast is thin on sights. For most, a day of sightseeing is plenty.

Day trip from Dublin: With the handy new 90-minute Dublin–Belfast train (and its cheap £15 day-return tickets) you could make Belfast a day trip: catch the early train from Dublin; 10:30, city hall tour, browse the pedestrian zone, lunch, ride a shared cab up Falls Road; 15:00, Ulster Folk and Transport Museum; return to Dublin in the evening.

Two days in Northern Ireland from Dublin: Take the train to Portrush for two nights and a day to tour the Causeway Coast (castle, whiskey, Giant's Causeway, resort fun), then follow the Belfast-in-a-day plan above.

Two days in Belfast: This allows time to splice in the Living History tour, a city walking tour, the Botanic Gardens and Ulster Museum, and some low or high after-dark culture.

Orientation (tel. code: 01232)

For the first-time visitor in for a quick look, Belfast is pretty simple. There are three zones of interest: central (Donegall Square/City Hall/pedestrian shopping/TI), southern (Ulster Museum/Botanic Gardens/university/accommodations), and western (working-class sectarian neighborhoods over the freeway). Belfast's "Golden Mile"—stretching from the Europa Hotel to the university district—connects the central and southern zones with many of the best dinner and entertainment spots. To call Northern Ireland from the Republic of Ireland, dial 08, then the city code (for Belfast: 01232), then the local number.

Tourist Information: This modern center has an enjoyable bookshop (in summer Monday–Saturday 9:00–19:00, Sunday 12:00–16:00; in winter, closes at 17:15 and all day Sunday; on the north edge of the city center at 59 North Street, tel. 01232/246-609). Get the fine free city map and the weekly entertainment guide, *That's Entertainment* (covering pub music, concerts, theater, movies, restaurants, and cultural news). Refer to this for your evening fun.

Arrival in Belfast: Arriving by fast train, you'll go direct to Central Station. Slower trains arc through Belfast, stopping at several downtown stations including Central Station, Great Victoria Station (most central, near Hotel Europa and Donegall Square), Botanic (close to the university and

Botanic Gardens), and Adelaide (near several of my recommended accommodations).

Getting Around Belfast

If you line up your sightseeing logically, you can do most of the town on foot.

By Bus: Handy buses with friendly drivers go from Donegall Square East to Malone Road and all recommended accommodations (#70 and #71, 80p/ride, all-day £2.10 pass). A free Rail-Link bus loops from Central Station to Donegall Square and around town, stopping near the TI on North Street (free, 4/hr, not Sunday).

By Taxi: Taxis are reasonable and should be considered. Rather than use their meters, which lots of locals don't trust, many cabs charge a flat £2.50 rate for any ride up to 2 miles. It's £1/mile after that. Use a shared cab if you're going up Falls Road (explained below).

Tours of Belfast

▲**Walking Tour**—A 90-minute Town Walk introducing you to the historic core of town leaves from the TI (£3, daily at 14:00, call TI to confirm schedule, tel. 01232/246-609).

▲**Bus Tours**—The "Belfast: A Living History" bus tour offers the best introduction to the city's recent and complicated political and social history. You'll cruise the Catholic and Protestant working-class neighborhoods with a commentary explaining the political murals and places of interest—mostly dealing with "The Troubles" of the last 25 years. You see things from the bus and get out only for a tea break (£7.50, Tuesday, Thursday, and Sunday at 13:00 throughout the summer, 3.5 hours, from Castle Place, tel. 01232/458-484).

Sights—Belfast

▲▲**City Hall**—This grand structure, with its 173-foot-tall copper dome, dominates the town center. Built between 1889 and 1906, with its statue of Queen Victoria scowling down Belfast's main drag and the Union Jack flapping behind her, it's a stirring sight. In the garden you'll find memorials to the *Titanic* and the landing of the U.S.A. Expeditionary Force in 1942—their first stop en route to Berlin. Take the free, 45-minute tour (summer Monday–Friday usually at 10:30 and 14:30, less off-season, call 01232/320-202, ext. 2346, to check

Belfast

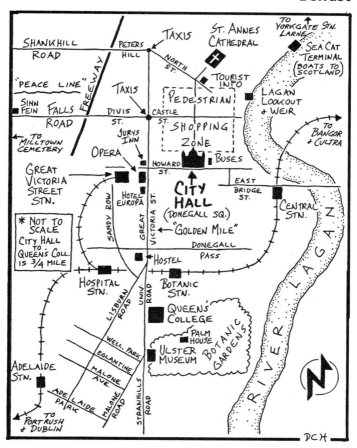

The following labels appear on the map:

SHANKHILL ROAD · PETERS HILL · TAXIS · ST. ANNES CATHEDRAL · TO YORKGATE STN. LARNE · SEA CAT TERMINAL (BOATS TO SCOTLAND) · "PEACE LINE" · NORTH ST. · TOURIST INFO · LAGAN LOOKOUT & WEIR · SINN FEIN · FALLS ROAD · FREEWAY · TAXIS · DIVIS ST. · CASTLE ST. · PEDESTRIAN · SHOPPING ZONE · TO MILLTOWN CEMETERY · JURYS INN · OPERA · HOWARD ST. · BUSES · TO BANGOR & CULTRA · GREAT VICTORIA STREET STN. · SANDY ROW · HOTEL EUROPA · GREAT VICTORIA ST. · CITY HALL (DONEGALL SQ.) · "GOLDEN MILE" · EAST BRIDGE ST. · CENTRAL STN. · RIVER LAGAN · *Not To Scale City Hall to Queen's Coll. is 3/4 mile · DONEGALL PASS · HOSTEL · HOSPITAL STN. · LISBURN ROAD · UNIV. ROAD · BOTANIC STN. · QUEEN'S COLLEGE · PALM HOUSE · ULSTER MUSEUM · BOTANIC GARDENS · WELL. PARK · EGLANTINE · MALONE AVE. · ADELAIDE STN. · ADELAIDE PARK · MALONE ROAD · STRANMILLIS ROAD · TO PORTRUSH & DUBLIN · DCH

schedule and book). If you can't manage a tour, at least step into the interior, with its marble swirl staircase. (Politely ask the receptionist for the free City Hall booklet and postcard that tour-takers get.)

The tour gives you a rundown on city government and an explanation of the decor that makes this an Ulster political hall of fame. Queen Victoria and King Edward VII look down on city council meetings. The 1613 original charter of Belfast granted by James I is on display. Its Great Hall— bombed by the Germans in 1941 and its stained glass blown out by the IRA in 1991—looks as great as the day it was made.

Across the street, the 200-year-old Linen Hall Library welcomes guests (17 Donegall Square North, tel. 01232/321-707). It has a fine hardbound ambience, coffee shop, royal newspaper reading room, and a top floor of documents and posters documenting "The Troubles" (top floor by tour only—call for schedule).

Golden Mile—This is the overstated nickname of Belfast's liveliest dining and entertainment district which stretches from the Opera House to the university district.

The **Grand Opera House**, originally built in 1891, bombed and rebuilt in 1991 and bombed and rebuilt again in 1993, is extravagantly Victorian and *the* place to take in a concert, play, or opera (closed to sightseers, for ticket information tel. 01232/240-411). **Europa Hotel**, next door, while considered the most bombed hotel in the world, feels pretty casual.

Across the street is the museum-like **Crown Liquor Saloon**. Built in 1885, it's now a part of the National Trust. A wander through its mahogany, glass, and marble interior is a trip back into the day of Queen Victoria (although the privacy provided by the snugs—private booths—allows for un-Victorian behavior).

Lagan Lookout Visitors Centre—This center shows off the fruits of the city's £650 million investment in its harbor. The tidal River Lagan left the town with daily unsightly mud flats. The weir, built in 1994, controls the tides, making the harbor much more functional. It also doubles as a free pedestrian bridge over the river, affording walkers a fine view of the harbor area including the big cranes and the new convention center. The visitor's center, while mildly entertaining and enthusiastically "interactive," is not really worth the £1.50 entry fee (Monday–Friday 11:00–17:00, Saturday 12:00–17:00, Sunday 14:00–17:00, a short walk from the TI, just past the town clock tower).

▲▲**Falls Road**—It would have been a happy day when the sectarian neighborhoods of Belfast had nothing to be sectarian about. For a look at what was one of the home bases for "The Troubles," explore the working-class Catholic Falls Road neighborhood.

At the end of Castle Street, you'll find a square filled with old black cabs—and the only Gaelic-language signs in downtown

Belfast. These shared black cabs efficiently shuttle residents from outlying neighborhoods up and down Falls Road and to the city center. Any cab (except those in the "Whiterock" line) goes up Falls Road, past Sinn Fein headquarters and lots of murals, to the Milltown Cemetery (65p, sit in front and talk to the cabbie). Easy-to-flag-down cabs run every minute or so in each direction on Falls Road. They do one-hour tours for £12 (cheap for a small group of travelers).

At the Milltown Cemetery walk past all the Gaelic crosses down to the far right-hand corner (closest to the highway) where the IRA "Roll of Honor" is set apart from the thousands of other graves by little green railings. They are treated like fallen soldiers. Notice the memorial to Bobby Sands and the 11 other hunger strikers who starved in protest for a united Ireland in 1981.

The Sinn Fein headquarters is near where Divis Road becomes Falls Road (look for the protective boulders in the sidewalk and the Irish Republic flag on the roof). The adjacent bookstore is worth a look. Page through books featuring color photos of the political murals which decorate the buildings. Money raised here supports families of imprisoned members of the IRA.

A sad corrugated wall called the "Peace Line" runs a block or so north of Falls Road separating the Catholics from the Protestants in the Shankill Road area.

Sandy Row—While you can ride a shared black cab through the Protestant Shankill Road area, the easiest way to get a dose of the Unionist side is to walk Sandy Row. From the Europa Hotel, walk a block down Glengall Street, turn left and enjoy a ten-minute walk through a working-class Protestant street. A stop in one of the many cheap eateries here may give you an opportunity to talk to a local. You'll see a few murals filled with Unionist symbolism. The mural of William of Orange's victory over the Catholic King James II (Battle of the Boyne, 1690) stirs Unionist hearts. (From the south end of Sandy Row, it's a ten-minute walk to the Ulster Museum.)

▲Ulster Museum—While mediocre by European standards, this is Belfast's one major museum. It's free and pretty painless: Ride the elevator to the top floor and follow the spiraling exhibits downhill with a cheery café halfway down. You'll find an interesting "Made in Belfast" exhibit just before an arch which proclaims "Trade is the golden girdle of the globe." The history section is given an interesting British slant (such as the implication that the famine was caused by the Irish population doubling in 40 years—without a mention of various English contributions). Top things off with soggy bits of gold, silver, leather, and wood salvaged from the Spanish Armada's shipwrecked *Girona* (lost off the Antrim Coast north of Belfast in 1588) and a pretty darn good mummy (free, Monday–Friday 10:00–17:00, Saturday 13:00–17:00, Sunday 14:00–17:00).

▲▲**Ulster Folk and Transport Museum**—This 60-acre two-museum complex is straddling the road and rail at Cultra, midway between Bangor and Belfast (8 miles out of town).

The Folk Museum is an open-air collection of 30 reconstructed buildings from all over the nine counties of Ulster designed to showcase the region's traditional lifestyles. After wandering through the old town site (church, print shop, schoolhouse, humble Belfast rowhouse, cyber café, and so on), you'll head off into the country to nip into cottages, farmhouses, and mills. Each house is warmed by a wonderful peat fire and a friendly attendant. The sight can be dull or vibrant, depending upon your ability to chat with the attendants. Drop a peat brick on a fire.

The Transport Museum (downhill, over the road from the folk section) consists of three buildings. Start at the bottom and trace the evolution of transportion from 7,500 years ago—when people first decided to load an ox—to modern times, with intriguing sections on the local Gypsy culture and the sinking of the Belfast-made *Titanic*. In the next two buildings you roll through the history of bikes, cars, and trains. The car section rumbles from the first car in Ireland (an 1898 Benz) through the "Cortina Culture" of the 1960s to the local adventures of John De Lorean with a 1981 model of his car. (£3.60, £8.50 for families, April–September Monday–Saturday 10:30–17:45, Sunday 12:00–17:45; closes daily at 16:00 in winter; check schedule for any special events on the day of your visit, allow three hours minimum, tel. 01232/428-428.)

From Belfast reach Cultra by taxi (£8), bus #1 or #2 (2/hr, 30 minutes from Oxford Street), or train (2/hr, 15 minutes, from any Belfast train station or Bangor). Trains and buses stop right in the park. Public transport schedules get skimpy on Saturday and Sunday. There's a complete schedule on the wall at the bottom building in the Transport section. Drivers can drive from one section to the next.

▲**Botanic Gardens**—This is the backyard of the Queen's University. On a sunny day, you couldn't imagine a more relaxing park setting. On a cold day, step into the Tropical Ravine for a jungle of heat and humidity. Take a quick walk through the Palm House, reminiscent of the Palm House in London's Kew Gardens, but smaller (free, Monday–Friday 10:00–12:00 and 13:00–17:00, weekends 13:00–17:00).

Sleeping in Belfast
(£1 = about $1.60, tel. code: 01232; to call Belfast from the Republic of Ireland, dial 08-01232 before the local number)
Sleep Code: **S**=Single, **D**=Double/Twin, **T**=Triple, **Q**=Quad, **b**=bathroom, **t**=toilet only, **s**=shower only, **CC**=Credit Card (**V**isa, **M**asterCard, **A**mex).

Belfast's best budget beds cluster in a comfortable area just south of the Ulster Museum and the university. Two train stations (Botanic and Adelaide) are nearby, and buses zip down Malone Road every few minutes (#70 and #71). Any red-and-white bus on Malone Road goes to Donegall Square East. (For the first three places, get off the bus immediately after the green BP gas station or ride the train to Adelaide.) Taxis, cheap in Belfast, will take you downtown for £2.50 (your host can call one). Belfast is more of a business town than a tourist town, so business-class room rates are lower or soft on weekends.

Queen's Elms Halls of Residence is a big brick Queen's University dorm renting more than 300 rooms to travelers during summer break (mid-June–mid-September). While the rooms, all singles and twins, are indestructibly basic with showers down the hall, they come with a free laundry service and a self-serve kitchen (S-£13, D-£21, cheaper for students, 78 Malone Road, tel. 01232/381-608).

Ulster People's College Residential Centre rents 30 beds in ten cheery, un-dorm-like rooms year-round on a quiet street near the stop for the bus into town (S-£15, D-£30, £2 per bed cheaper with a continental rather than Irish breakfast, free laundry, 30 Adelaide Park, tel. 01232/665-161, fax 01232/668-111).

Malone Lodge Hotel provides slick, modern, business-class comfort and professionalism in a charming environment on a quiet, leafy street. Its 33 bright rooms have a contemporary French feeling and are discounted on weekends. The lounge and dining room are sumptuous (Sb-£70 weekdays, £40 on Friday, Saturday, and Sunday, Db-£88/£56 on weekends, Tb-£98/£74, elevator, CC:VMA, 60 Eglantine Avenue, Belfast BT9 6DY, tel. 01232/382-409, fax 01232/382-706).

Camera House Guest House is newly renovated with large smoke-free rooms and an airy, hardwood feeling throughout (Sb-£35, Db-£45–52, CC:VM, 44 Wellington Park, Belfast BT9 6DP, tel. 01232/660-026, fax 01232/667-856, Paul Drumm).

Malone Guest House is a classy stand-alone Victorian house fronting the busy Malone Road. It's well-run by Mrs. McClure with two spacious singles and six large, pastel twins (Sb-£32 or £25 on Friday, Saturday, or Sunday, Db-£47 or £39 on weekends, 79 Malone Road, Belfast BT9 6SH, tel. 01232/669-565). Breakfast comes with a puzzle.

Windermere House rents eight rooms in a large Victorian house including several small but pleasant singles (S-£20, Sb-£28, very small D-£32, D-£38, Db-£42, T-£44, CC:VM, 60 Wellington Park, tel. 01232/662-693, Ms. Murray).

Liserin Guest House rents six new-feeling rooms (S-£20, Sb-£23, Db-£40, 7 Eglantine Avenue, tel. 01232/660-769, Sid and Ina Smith). **East Sheen Guest House** rents five basic rooms (S-£17.50, D-£35, 81 Eglantine Avenue, tel. 01232/667-149, Mrs. Davidson). **The George B&B** (D-£35, Db-£42, 9 Eglantine Avenue, tel. 01232/683-212, Colette McGuinness) and the **Eglantine Guest House** (21 Eglantine Avenue, tel. 01232/667-585) are on the same street.

Belfast International Youth Hostel is big, basic, and creatively run with 40 twins and quads. It's located near the Botanic train station in the heart of the lively university district and close to the center. Features include free lockers, left luggage, laundry service, cheap cafeteria, elevator, and no curfew (S-£15, D-£24, beds in a quad-£8, CC:VM, 22 Donegall Road, tel. 01232/324-733, fax 01232/439-699).

Jurys Inn, the latest in this popular chain, is a huge American-style place that rents its several hundred identical modern rooms for one simple price in downtown Belfast (up to three adults or two adults and two kids for about £55, 2 blocks from City Hall on Spires Mall, Dublin reservation board tel. 01/454-3363).

Sleeping in Bangor
(£1 = about $1.60, tel. code: 01247, mail: Bangor, Co. Down)

For a laid-back seaside hometown—and more comfort per pound—sleep half an hour south of Belfast by commuter train in Bangor. Bangor, formerly a slick Belfast seaside escape, is now sleepy and almost residential-feeling. But with elegant old homes facing its newly spruced-up harbor, not a hint of big-city Belfast, and easy train connections to downtown Belfast (2/hour, 30 minutes), Bangor appeals. From the station, walk five minutes to the harbor. The first two listings face the sea a few blocks to the right. The third faces the harbor on the left.

Pierview House B&B is a chandeliered winner with three of its five spacious rooms overlooking the sea (D-£30, grand Db-£32, family room, CC:VMA, 28 Seacliff Road, tel. 01247/463-381, Mr. and Mrs. Watts). **Sea Crest B&B** is homey and friendly with no lounge but four fine rooms (D-£30, CC:VM, 98 Seacliff Road, tel. 01247/461-935, Irene Marsden).

Battersea Guest House, one of a row of tall stately homes overlooking the yacht basin, rents four rooms (small D-£32, grand seaview double-£35, 47 Queen's Parade, tel. 01247/461-643, Rene and John Brann).

Royal Hotel is a fine old place right on the harbor with good weekend rates on its 34 rooms (Db-£70 weekdays, £50 on weekends, view rooms pricier, CC:VMA, 26 Quay Street, BT20 5ED, tel. 01247/271-866, fax 01247/467-810).

Eating in Bangor
Your hosts can direct you to their favorite eatery. The bar at **Royal Hotel** (facing the harbor) serves great £6 dinners in a welcoming atmosphere. The **Steamer Bar** (next door, upstairs from the pub) is also good. **Dragon House** provides a tasty Chinese break from all the pub grub (76 High Street, tel. 01247/459-031).

Transportation Connections—Bangor
By train to Belfast: Trains go from Bangor station (the end of the line, don't use Bangor West) into Belfast via Cultra (Ulster Folk and Transport Museum). The journey (2/hr, 30 min) gives you a good close-up look at the giant Belfast harbor cranes. Belfast Central has a free Rail-Link shuttle bus to the

town center (4/hr, not Sunday). Stay on until the Botanic train station for the Ulster Museum, Golden Mile, and Sandy Row.

Transportation Connections—Belfast

By train to: Dublin (12/day, 1.5 hrs), **Larne** (hrly, 1 hr), **Portrush** (7/day, 2 hrs). Train info tel. 01232/230-671.

By bus to: Larne (hrly, 1 hr), **Portrush** (2/day, 3.5 hrs), **Glasgow** (3/day, 8 hrs), **Edinburgh** (3/day, 9 hrs), **London** (2/day, 12 hrs). Ulsterbus tel. 01232/337-003.

By plane: British Air flies to **Glasgow** (3/day, 45 min, £62 one day in advance) and **London** (5/day, 1 hr, £77 one-way, but you can buy a £55 round-trip ticket and forget to return—it's allowed).

By ferry to: Liverpool (tel. 01232/779-090) and **Stranraer, Scotland** (via "Sea Cat" catamaran, tel. 0345/523-523, or Stena Line ferry, tel. 01232/747-747). The P&O Ferry goes from **Larne** (20 miles north of Belfast) to **Cairnryan, Scotland** (tel. 01574/274-321).

ANTRIM COAST AND PORTRUSH

The Antrim Coast—the north of Northern Ireland—is one of the most interesting and scenic coastlines in Britain and Ireland. Within a few miles of the train terminal of Portrush you can visit some evocative castle ruins, tour the oldest whiskey distillery, and hike along the famous Giant's Causeway—a World Heritage Site.

The homely seaside resort of Portrush used to be known as "The Brighton of the North." While it's seen its best days, it retains the atmosphere and buildings of a genteel, middle-class seaside resort. Portrush fills its peninsula with family-oriented amusements, fun eateries, and B&Bs. Summertime fun-seekers promenade along the toy harbor and tumble down to the sandy beaches which extend in sweeping white crescents on either side.

Superficially, it has the appearance of any small British seaside resort, but its history and the fact that many students from the University of Coleraine choose to live here give Portrush a little more personality. There are the usual arcade amusements, but also nightclubs, restaurants, summer theater in the Town Hall, and convivial pubs that people from Belfast travel for. At the end of the train line and just a few miles from several important sights, it's an ideal base for exploring the highlights of the Antrim Coast.

Planning Your Time
You need a minimum of a full day to explore the Antrim Coast, so allow two nights in Portrush. An ideal day might be

a bike tour of the castle, distillery, and Giant's Causeway followed by nine holes on the Portrush pitch-and-putt course. Consider this side trip north from Dublin:

Day 1: 11:00–16:00, Train to Portrush.

Day 2: All day for Antrim Coast sights and Portrush.

Day 3: 8:00–10:00, Train to Belfast, all day in Belfast; 19:00–21:00, Train back to Dublin.

Orientation (tel. code: 01265)

Portrush's pleasant and easily walkable town center features sea views in every direction. On one side is the harbor and restaurants, and on the other are Victorian townhouses. The tip of the peninsula is marked by a lighthouse and a park filled with tennis courts, lawn bowling greens, and putting greens.

The city is busy with students during the school year. July and August is beach resort boom time. June and September it's laid-back and lazy. Families pack Portrush on Saturdays and revelers from Belfast pack its hotels on Saturday nights.

Tourist Information: The tourist office (more generous and helpful than those in the Republic) is in the big, modern Dunluce Centre (daily 9:00–17:00, until 20:00 in July and August, tel. 01265/823-333). Get their fine 20p Antrim Coast handout and a free Belfast map if you're Belfast-bound.

Arrival in Portrush: The train tracks stop at the base of the tiny peninsula which Portrush fills. (The small station has no bag check.) The TI is 3 long blocks from the train station (follow signs down Eglinton Street and turn left at the fire station). All listed B&Bs are within a five-minute walk of the train station (see Sleeping, below). The bus station is 2 blocks behind the train station.

Getting Around the Antrim Coast

By Bus: In the summer, open-top buses connect Portrush, Dunluce Castle, Old Bushmills Distillery, and the Giant's Causeway every two hours (maybe hourly in summer). You could spend two hours at Bushmills and the Causeway, but you'd be bored at the castle (£2.80 round-trip, buy ticket from driver, pick up a schedule at the TI).

By Car: Distances are short and parking is easy. Don't miss the treacherously scenic coastal route down to the Glens of Antrim.

By Taxi: Groups go cheaper by taxi, which costs only £5

Portrush

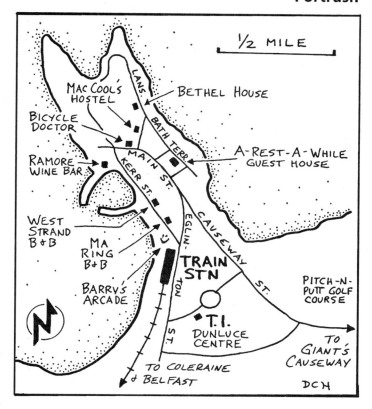

from Portrush to Giant's Causeway. (For £10 the cabbie may wait and bring you back.)

By Bike: The laid-back **Bicycle Doctor** shop rents sturdy bikes (£3.50/6 hours, £7/day, £5 deposit, borrow a clip for your pants, open daily with a dinner break 9:00–21:00 in season, in town center at 104 Lower Main Street, tel. 01265/824-340, run by William and Jackie). See "Causeway Coast Bike Ride" in Sights, below.

Sights—Portrush

Barry's Old Time Amusement Arcade—This is a fine chance to see Northern Ireland at play. Just below the train station on the harbor, it's filled with candy floss (cotton candy) and little kids learning the art of one-armed bandits—2p at a time. Get £1 worth of 2p coins from the machine and go wild.

Pitch-and-Putt at the Royal Portrush Golf Course—Like those in Scotland, Irish courses are highly sought after for their lush but dry greens—lots of rain with grass on porous, sandy soil—in glorious settings. While serious golfers can get a tee time there, rookies get a dose of this wonderful golf setting at the same course's "Skerry 9 Hole Links" pitch-and-putt range. You get two clubs and balls for £4.50, two can golf for £9, and they don't care if you go around twice (daily April–September 8:30–19:30, five-minute walk from the station, tel. 01265/823-335).

Sights—Antrim Coast

▲**Dunluce Castle**—The romantic ruins of Dunluce Castle, perched dramatically on the edge of a rocky headland, are a testimony to this region's turbulent past. During the Middle Ages, it resisted several sieges. But on a stormy night in 1639 dinner was interrupted as half the kitchen fell into the sea, taking the servants with it. That was the last straw for the lady of the castle. The Countess of Antrim packed up and moved inland and the castle "began its slow submission to the forces of nature." While one of the largest castles in Northern Ireland and beautifully situated, there's precious little to see among the broken walls.

Expansion of the castle was financed by the salvaging of a shipwreck. In 1588, the Spanish Armada's *Girona*—returning home after an abortive English mission and laden with sailors and valuables of three abandoned sister ships—sank. More than 1,300 drowned and only five washed ashore. The shipwreck was excavated in 1967 with a bounty of golden odds and silver ends ending up in Belfast's Ulster Museum.

Castle admission includes a little impromptu guided tour of the ruins and a 15-minute video which is interesting for its effort to defend the notion of "Ulster, a place apart—facing Scotland, cut off from the rest of Ireland by dense forests and mountains . . ." (£1.50, daily April–September 10:00–19:00, less on Sunday, 10:00–16:00 in winter, tel. 01265/731-938).

▲▲**Old Bushmills Distillery**—Bushmills claims to be the world's oldest distillery. While King James I (of Bible fame) granted their license to distill "Acqua Vitae" in 1608, whiskey has been made here since the 13th century. Distillery tours

Northern Ireland's Antrim Coast

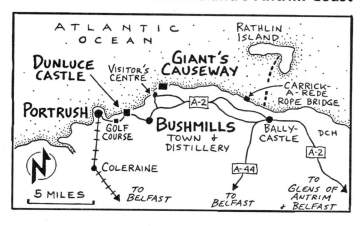

take you through the process, making it clear that Irish whiskey is triple-distilled while Scotch whiskey is only double-distilled. The 45-minute tour starts when the mosh pit is filled with a porridge that eventually becomes whiskey. (The left-overs of that porridge are fed to the county's particularly happy cows.) You'll see thousands of oak casks—the kind used for Spanish sherry—filled with aging whiskey including special "millennium whiskey" from 1975, aging until the year 2000 when those who paid £4,000 for each will be delivered 250 very special bottles for their celebration. (In an uncharacteristically shrewd move, Goldie Hawn bought one before they sold out.) The finale, of course, is the tasting in the Potstill Bar—the former malt kilns. When your guide asks for a tasting volunteer, go for it. Two volunteers per tour get to taste test six different whiskeys (Scotch vs. Irish). Everyone else gets a single glass of their choice. Non-whiskey enthusiasts might enjoy their special spicy (cinnamon and cloves) hot toddy. To see the distillery at its lively best, visit when the 100 workers are manning the machinery—Monday morning through Friday noon (weekends tours see a still still). Tours are limited to 25 and book up. In summer, call in your name to get a tour time before you arrive (£2.50, daily March–October, tour departures on the half-hour from 9:30 with last tour at 16:30, closed winter weekends, tel. 01265/731-521). The distillery is a sign-posted quarter mile from Bushmills town center.

▲▲▲**Giant's Causeway**—This 4-mile-long stretch of coastline is famous for its bizarre basalt columns. The shore is covered with hexagonal pillars that stick up at various heights as if someone was offering God his choice of 37,000 six-sided cigarettes.

Geologists claim the Giant's Causeway was formed by volcanic eruptions 60 million years ago. As the lava surface cooled, it contracted, cracking into hexagonal shapes. As the layer of hardened but alligatored rock settled, it broke into its many stair steps.

In actuality, the Giant's Causeway was formed by an Ulster warrior giant named Finn MacCool who wanted to reach his love on the Scottish island of Staffa. The causeway once did stretch to Scotland, way back when the two lands were connected. Today, while settled, the formation still extends undersea to Staffa, just off the Scottish coast. Finn's causeway was ruined (into today's "remnant of chaos") by a rival giant. As the rival fled from ferocious Finn back to his Scottish homeland, he ripped up the causeway so Finn couldn't chase him.

For more information on Finn, as well as details on the ridiculous theories of modern geologists, start your visit in the visitor's center. The slide presentation is more relaxing than interesting (£1, 25 minutes, on the half hour). The real information is on the walls of the exhibition. There are, of course, a gift shop and cafeteria standing by.

A minibus (40p each way, 4/hr) zips lazy ones a half mile directly to the Grand Causeway, the highlight of the entire coast. But consider walking the mile along the cliff tops to the steep stairs down, and then back up to the visitor's center. Or, you could walk the entire 5-mile Giant's Causeway trail and see the entire honeycombed coastline. The most commanding view of the causeway is from a clifftop perch called Hamilton's Seat. The 75p hiking guide points out the highlights named by 18th-century guides (the Camel's Back, the Giant's Eye, and so on). The causeway is always free and open (visitor's center open daily 10:00–17:00, until 19:00 in July and August, £2.50 to park, tel. 01265/731-855).

Causeway Coast Bike Ride—It's an 8-mile, one-hour pedal from Portrush past Dunluce Castle and Bushmills to the Giant's Causeway Visitors Centre. From Portrush to Dunluce Castle, allow 20 minutes: bike along the Royal Portrush Golf Course and past some beautiful beach scenery (a bike-friendly sidewalk keeps timid riders away from traffic). It's another 20 minutes to Bushmills; the distillery is a quarter-mile detour inland from the town square. Bushmills is a good place for a lunch break with the fancy Bushmills Inn, several cheap and cheery pantries, and a happy chippie called Hip Chip. From Bushmill, the Giant's Causeway is 20 minutes farther. The hills are gentle and traffic's not bad. See Getting Around, above, for info on bike rental.

▲**Carrick-a-Rede Rope Bridge**—For 200 years fishermen have strung a narrow 80-foot-high bridge (planks strung between wires) across a 65-foot-wide chasm between the mainland and a tiny island. The bridge (not the original) still gives access to salmon nets, which are set during the summer months to catch the salmon turning the coast's corner. The island affords fine views and, especially during nesting season, great chances to see seabirds (free, strung from April–September, 20 minutes' walk from the 50p car park).

▲**Antrim Mountains and Glens**—Not particularly high, never more than 1,500 feet, the mountains are cut through by a series of large glens running northeast to the sea. Glenariff, with its waterfalls, especially the "Mare's Tail," is the most beautiful of all the nine glens.

Sleeping in Portrush
(£1 = about $1.60, tel. code: 01265, zip code: BT56 8DG)
Sleep Code: **S**=Single, **D**=Double/Twin, **T**=Triple, **Q**=Quad, **b**=bathroom, **t**=toilet only, **s**=shower only, **CC**=Credit Card (Visa, MasterCard, Amex).

Portrush's many B&Bs all seem well-worn. But small-town well-worn is better than big-town well-worn. August and Saturday nights can be tight. Otherwise it's a "you take a half a loaf when you can get it" town. Rates vary with the view and season—probe for softness. Each listing faces the sea, though seaviews are worth paying for only if you get a bay window. Ask for a big room (some doubles can be very small; twins are bigger). Lounges are invariably grand with bay window views. All places listed have lots of stairs but are perfectly central and within a few minutes' walk of the train station. Parking is easy.

A-Rest-A-While Guest House overlooks a seaside park with a grand strand view. Margaret and Ross Torrens keep their old ten-room house tidy, completely smoke-free, and promise to honor these prices throughout 1998 (two tiny view S-£13, D-£26, Db-£36, ask for one of their four huge seaview

£26 doubles—a great value even with the plumbing down the hall, one huge view family room, 6 Bath Terrace, 3 blocks from the station on the quiet side of town, tel. 01265/822-827).

Ma Ring B&B rents 14 well-worn but decent rooms (S-£15, Sb-£20–25, D-£25–30, Db-£30–40, family room, self-service kitchen, CC:VMA, 17 Kerr Street, facing the harbor a block in front of the station, tel. & fax 01265/822-765). Call Jim or Eveline to get their best price; then ask for a 10 percent cash/direct booking discount for readers of this book.

West Strand Guest House has 15 tidy tree-house rooms, none with private bathrooms (S-£13–15, D-£26–30, fine view lounge, 18 Kerr Street, tel. 01265/822-270, Muriel Robinson).

Bethel House B&B is a cozy, completely smoke- and alcohol-free Christian-run place overlooking the sea on the quiet side of town. Request the bigger or view rooms. Some doubles, especially on the top floor, are tiny but all are nicely refurbished (S-£16, Sb-£18–20, D-£30, Db-£36, elevator, big homey lounge used nightly in the summer for a 30-minute hymn-singing fellowship, 7 Lansdowne Crescent, tel. 01265/822-354, Tom and Marie Graham).

MacCool's Portrush Youth Hostel is a friendly and laid-back place with 20 beds in four rooms (two, four, six, and eight beds each, £6 per bed, one tiny £12 double, one all-girls' room, lockers, guests' kitchen, book- and game-stocked lounge, 5 Causeway View Terrace, halfway between the station and the tip of the peninsula in the center of Portrush, tel. 01265/824-845).

Drivers may want to stay just out of town at **Glenkeen Guest House** (ten rooms, Sb-£25, Db-£37, some smoke-free rooms, CC:VM, 59 Coleraine Road, seven-minute walk from the station, tel. 01265/822-279, Mrs. Little) or at **Summer Island House** (five rooms, Sb-£20, Db-£36, family room, 14 Coleraine Road, five-minute walk from station, tel. 01265/824-640, Mrs. Armstrong).

Eglinton Hotel, the only real big normal hotel in town, is central but noisy and impersonal. It's a dark place with small doubles and bigger twins (Db-£50–70 with demand, CC:VMA, 49 Eglinton Street, across the street from the train station, tel. 01265/822-371, fax 01265/823-155).

Eating in Portrush

Being a university town and a get-away-from-Belfast town, Portrush has more than chips joints. Eglinton Street is lined with cheap and cheery eateries. The place for dinner is definitely the **Ramore Wine Bar**. While the upstairs restaurant is an exclusive and pricey place, the much-loved bar below is bursting with happy eaters enjoying the most inviting menu I've seen in Ireland with huge £7 meals ranging from steaks to vegetarian and a good £1.50 glass of red wine—a nice break after all the Guinness. Come early for a table or sit at the bar (£4.50 lunch specials, dinner 17:30–21:30, closed Sunday, tel. 01265/824-313).

Transportation Connections—Portrush

By train to: Coleraine (2/hr, 12 minutes, sparse on Sunday), **Belfast** (7/day, 4/Sunday, 2 hrs), **Dublin** (7/day, 4/Sunday, 5 hrs, several tight but easy connections, £18 one-way, £24 round-trip with Belfast stopover).

By bus to: Belfast (along scenic coast, 2/day, 3.5 hrs, £6).

APPENDIX

BRITAIN

What's So Great About Britain?

Regardless of the revolution we had 200 years ago, many American travelers feel that they "go home" to Britain. This most popular tourist destination has a strange influence and power over us.

Britain is small—about the size of Uganda (or Idaho)—600 miles long and 300 miles at its widest. Its highest mountain is 4,400 feet, a foothill by our standards. The population is a quarter of the U.S.A.'s. Politically and economically, Great Britain is closing out the 20th century only a weak shadow of the days when it boasted that "The sun never sets on the British Empire."

At one time Britain owned one-fifth of the world and accounted for more than half the planet's industrial output. Today the Empire is down to token and troublesome scraps such as the Falklands and Northern Ireland. Great Britain's industrial production is about 5 percent of the world's total, and Italy has a higher per-capita income.

Still, Britain is a world leader. Her heritage, her culture, and her people cannot be measured in traditional units of power. The United Kingdom is a union of four countries—England, Wales, Scotland, and Northern Ireland. Cynics call it an English Empire ruled by London, and there is some tension between the dominant Anglo-Saxon English (46 million) and their Celtic brothers and sisters (10 million).

In the Dark Ages, the Angles moved into this region from Europe, pushing the Celtic inhabitants to the undesirable fringe of the islands. The Angles settled in Angle-land (England), while the Celts made do in Wales, Scotland, and Ireland.

Today Wales, with 2 million people, struggles with a terrible economy, dragged down by the depressed mining industry. A great deal of Welsh pride is apparent in the local music and the bilingual signs—some with the English spray-painted out. The Welsh language is alive and well.

Scotland is big, accounting for one-third of Great Britain's land area, but sparsely inhabited, with only 5 million people.

Only about 80,000 speak Gaelic, but the Scots enjoy a large measure of autonomy with their separate Church of Scotland, their own legal system, and Scottish currency (interchangeable with the British).

Ireland is divided. Most of it is the completely independent Catholic Republic of Ireland. The top quarter is Northern Ireland, ruled from London. Long ago the Protestant English and Scots moved into the north—the Catholic, industrial heartland of Ireland—and told the Catholic Irish to "go to hell or go to Connemara." The Irish moved to the bleak and less productive parts of the island, like Connemara, and the seeds of today's "Troubles" were planted. There's no easy answer or easy blame, but the island has struggled—its population is only one-third (3 million) of what it used to be—and the battle continues.

As a visitor today, you'll see a politically polarized England. The Labor and Liberal parties, currently in charge, are attempting to shore up a social service system undercut by years of Conservative rule (Thatcher, Major). While in charge, the Conservatives (who consider themselves proponents of Victorian values—community, family, hard work, thrift, and trickle-down economics) took a Reaganesque approach to Britain's serious problems. England is still recovering.

Basic British History for the Traveler

When Julius Caesar landed on the misty and mysterious isle of Britain in 55 B.C., England entered the history books. The primitive Celtic tribes he conquered were themselves invaders who had earlier conquered the even more mysterious people who built Stonehenge. The Romans built towns and roads and established their capital at "Londinium." The Celtic natives, consisting of Gaels, Picts, and Scots, were not subdued so easily in Scotland and Wales. The Romans built Hadrian's Wall near the Scottish border to consolidate their rule in the troublesome north. Even today, the Celtic language and influence are strongest in these far reaches of Britain.

As Rome fell, so fell Roman Britain, a victim of invaders and internal troubles. Barbarian tribes from Germany and Denmark, called Angles and Saxons, swept through the southern part of the island, establishing Angle-land. These were the days of the real King Arthur, possibly a Christianized Roman general fighting valiantly, but in vain, against invading barbarians. The island was plunged into 500 years of Dark Ages—wars, plagues, and poverty—lit only by the dim candle of a few learned Christian monks and missionaries trying to convert the barbarians. The sightseer sees little from this Saxon period.

Modern England began with yet another invasion. William the Conqueror and his Norman troops crossed the English Channel from France in 1066. William crowned himself king in Westminster Abbey (where all subsequent coronations would take place) and began building the Tower of London. French-speaking Norman kings ruled the country for two centuries. Then followed two centuries of civil wars, with various noble families vying for the crown. In one of the most bitter feuds, the York and Lancaster families fought the War of the Roses, so-called because of the white and red flowers the combatants chose as their symbols. Battles, intrigues, kings, nobles, and ladies imprisoned and executed in the Tower—it's a wonder the country survived its rulers.

England was finally united by the "third-party" Tudor family. Henry VIII, a Tudor, was England's Renaissance king. He was handsome, athletic, highly sexed, a poet, a scholar, and a musician. He was also arrogant, cruel, gluttonous, and paranoid. He went through six wives in 40 years, divorcing, imprisoning, or beheading them when they no longer suited his needs. Henry also "divorced" England from the Catholic Church, establishing the Protestant Church of England (the Anglican Church) and setting in motion years of religious squabbles. He also "dissolved" the monasteries (around 1540), leaving just the shells of many formerly glorious abbeys dotting the countryside and pocketing their land and wealth for the crown.

Henry's daughter, Queen Elizabeth I, who reigned for 45 years, made England a great trading and naval power (defeating the Spanish Armada) and presided over the Elizabethan era of great writers (such as Shakespeare) and scientists (Francis Bacon).

The long-standing quarrel between England's "divine right" kings and nobles in Parliament finally erupted into a civil war (1643). Parliament forces under the Protestant Puritan farmer Oliver Cromwell defeated—and beheaded—King Charles I. This civil war left its mark on much of what you'll see in England. Eventually, Parliament invited Charles' son to take the throne. This restoration of the monarchy was accompanied by a great colonial expansion and the rebuilding of

London (including Christopher Wren's St. Paul's Cathedral), which had been devastated by the Great Fire of 1666.

Britain grew as a naval superpower, colonizing and trading with all parts of the globe. Her naval superiority ("Britannia rules the waves") was secured by Admiral Nelson's victory over Napoleon's fleet at the Battle of Trafalgar, while Lord Wellington stomped Napoleon on land at Waterloo. Nelson and Wellington are memorialized by many arches, columns, and squares throughout England.

Economically, Britain led the world into the industrial age with her mills, factories, coal mines, and trains. By the time of Queen Victoria's reign (1837–1901), Britain was at the zenith of power with a colonial empire that covered one-fifth of the world.

The 20th century has not been kind to Britain. Two world wars devastated the population. The Nazi blitzkrieg reduced much of London to rubble. The colonial empire has dwindled to almost nothing, and Britain is no longer an economic superpower. The "Irish Troubles" are constant as the Catholic inhabitants of British-ruled Northern Ireland fight for the independence their southern neighbors won decades ago. The war over the Falkland Islands in 1982 showed how little of the British Empire is left, but also how determined the British are to hang on to what remains.

But the tradition (if not the substance) of greatness continues, presided over by Queen Elizabeth II, her husband Prince Philip, and the heir-apparent Prince Charles. With economic problems, the turmoil of Charles and the late Princess Diana, the Fergie fiasco, and a relentless popular press, the royal family is having a tough time. But the queen has stayed above it all and most British people still jump at an opportunity to see royalty. With the death of Princess Diana and the historic outpouring of grief, it's clear that the concept of royalty is alive and well as Britain enters the third millenium.

Britain's Royal Families

802–1066	Saxon and Danish kings
1066–1154	Norman invasion, Norman kings (William the Conqueror)
1154–1399	Plantagenet
1399–1461	Lancaster
1462–1485	York
1485–1603	Tudor (Henry VIII, Elizabeth I)

1603–1649	Stuart (with civil war and beheading of Charles I)
1649–1659	Commonwealth, Cromwell, no royal head of state
1660–1714	Stuart restoration of monarchy
1714–1901	Hanover (four Georges, Victoria)
1901–1910	Edward VII
1910–present	Windsor (George V, Edward VII, George VI, Elizabeth II)

Architecture in Britain

From Stonehenge to Big Ben, travelers are storming castle walls, climbing spiral staircases, and snapping the pictures of 5,000 years of architecture. Let's sort it out.

The oldest ruins—mysterious and prehistoric—date from before Roman times back to 3000 B.C. The earliest sites, such as Stonehenge and Avebury, were built during the Stone and Bronze Ages. The remains from this period are made of huge stones or mounds of earth, even man-made hills, and were created as celestial calendars and for worship or burial. Britain is crisscrossed with lines of these mysterious sights (ley lines). Iron Age people (600 B.C. to A.D. 50) left desolate stone forts. The Romans thrived in Britain from A.D. 50 to 400, building cities, walls, and roads. Evidence of Roman greatness can be seen in lavish villas with ornate mosaic floors, temples uncovered beneath great English churches, and Roman stones in medieval city walls. Roman roads sliced across the island in straight lines. Today, unusually straight rural roads are very likely laid directly on ancient Roman roads.

As Rome crumbled in the fifth century, so did Roman Britain. Little architecture survives from Dark Ages England, the Saxon period from 500 to 1000. Architecturally, the light was switched on with the Norman Conquest in 1066. As William earned his title "the Conqueror," he built churches and castles in the European Romanesque style.

English Romanesque is called "Norman" (1066–1200). Norman churches had round arches, thick walls, and small windows; Durham Cathedral and the Chapel of St. John in the Tower of London are typical examples. The Tower of London, with its square keep, small windows, and spiral stone stairways, is a typical Norman castle. You'll see plenty of

Norman castles—all built to secure the conquest of these invaders from Normandy.

Gothic architecture (1200–1600) replaced the heavy Norman style with light, vertical buildings, pointed arches, soaring spires, and bigger windows. English Gothic is divided into three stages. Early English (1200–1300) features tall, simple spires, beautifully carved capitals, and elaborate chapter houses (such as the Wells Cathedral). Decorated Gothic (1300–1400) gets fancier, with more elaborate tracery, bigger windows, and ornately carved pinnacles, as you'll see at Westminster Abbey. Finally, the Perpendicular style (1400–1600, also called "rectilinear") goes back to square towers and emphasizes straight, uninterrupted vertical lines from ceiling to floor with vast windows and exuberant decoration, including fan-vaulted ceilings (King's College Chapel at Cambridge).

Through this evolution, the structural ribs (arches meeting at the top of the ceilings) became more and more decorative and fanciful (the most fancy being the star vaulting and fan vaulting of the Perpendicular style).

As you tour the great medieval churches of England, remember that nearly everything is symbolic. For instance, on the tombs, if the figure has crossed legs, he was a Crusader. If his feet rest on a dog, he died at home; but if the legs rest on a lion, he died in battle. Local guides and books help us modern pilgrims understand at least a little of what we see.

Wales is particularly rich in English castles, needed to subdue the stubborn Welsh. Edward I built a ring of powerful castles in Wales, including Caernarfon and Conwy.

Gothic houses were a simple mix of woven strips of thin wood, rubble, and plaster called wattle and daub. The famous black-and-white Tudor, or half-timbered, look came simply from filling in heavy oak frames with wattle and daub.

The Tudor period (1485–1560) was a time of relative peace (the War of the Roses was finally over), prosperity, and renaissance. Henry VIII broke with the Catholic Church and "dissolved" (destroyed) the monasteries, leaving scores of England's greatest churches gutted shells. These hauntingly beautiful abbey ruins surrounded by lush lawns (Glastonbury, Tintern, Whitby) are now pleasant city parks. York's magnificent minster survived only because Henry needed an administrative headquarters in the north for his Anglican church.

Although few churches were built during the Tudor

period, this was a time of house and mansion construction. Warmth was becoming popular and affordable, and Tudor buildings featured small square windows and often many chimneys. In towns where land was scarce, many Tudor houses grew up and out, getting wider with each overhanging floor.

The Elizabethan and Jacobean periods (1560–1620) were followed by the English Renaissance style (1620–1720). English architects mixed Gothic and classical styles, then Baroque and classical styles. Although the ornate Baroque never really grabbed England, the classical style of the Italian architect Palladio did. Inigo Jones (1573–1652), Christopher Wren (1632–1723), and those they inspired plastered England with enough columns, domes, and symmetry to please a caesar. The Great Fire of London (1666) cleared the way for an ambitious young Wren to put his mark on London forever with a grand rebuilding scheme, including the great St. Paul's and more than 50 other churches.

The celebrants of the Boston Tea Party remember England's Georgian period (1720–1840) for its lousy German kings. Georgian architecture was rich and showed off by being very classical. Grand ornamental doorways, fine cast-ironwork on balconies and railings, Chippendale furniture, and white-on-blue Wedgewood ceramics graced rich homes everywhere. John Wood, Jr. and Sr., led the way, giving the trend-setting city of Bath its crescents and circles of aristocratic Georgian rowhouses. "Georgian" is English for " neoclassical."

The Industrial Revolution shaped the Victorian period (1840–1890) with glass, steel, and iron. England had a huge new erector set (so did France's Mr. Eiffel). This was also a romantic period, reviving the "more Christian" Gothic style. London's Houses of Parliament are neo-Gothic—just 100 years old but looking 700, except for the telltale modern precision and craftsmanship. Whereas Gothic was stone or concrete, neo-Gothic was often red brick. These were England's glory days, and there was more building in this period than in all previous ages combined.

The architecture of our century obeys the formula "form follows function"—it works well but isn't particularly interesting. England treasures its heritage and takes great pains to build tastefully in historic districts and to preserve its many "listed" buildings. With a booming tourist trade, these quaint reminders of its—and our—past are becoming a valuable part of the British economy.

British TV

British television is so good—and so British—that it deserves a mention as a sightseeing treat. After a hard day of castle-climbing, watch the telly over a pot of tea in the comfortable living room of your village bed and breakfast.

England has four channels. BBC-1 and BBC-2 are government regulated, commercial-free, and traditionally highbrow. ITV and channel 4 are private, a little more Yankee, and they have commercials—but those commercials are clever and sophisticated and provide a fun look at England. Broadcasting is funded by an £80-per-year-per-household tax. Hmmm, 35 cents per day to escape commercials.

Whereas California "accents" fill our airwaves 24 hours a day, homogenizing the way our country speaks, England protects and promotes its regional accents by its choice of TV and radio announcers. Commercial-free British TV is looser than it used to be, but still careful about what it airs and when.

American shows (such as *Baywatch*) are very popular. The visiting viewer should be sure to tune their television to a few typical English shows including a dose of English situation and political comedy fun, and the top-notch BBC evening news. Quiz shows are taken very seriously (unlike in the U.S.A.). For a tear-filled slice-of-life taste of British soap dealing in all the controversial issues, see the popular *Brookside*, *Coronation Street*, or *Eastenders*.

Benny Hill comedy has become politically incorrect but is rumored to be coming back. And if you like Monty Python–type comedy, you've come to the right place.

IRELAND

Irish History

One surprising aspect of Ireland is the richness of its history. While the island is not particularly well-endowed with historic monuments, it is soaked in history. Here's a thumbnail overview.

The story of Ireland can be broken into four sections:
500 B.C.–A.D. 500   Iron Age

500–900	"Age of Saints and Scholars"
900–1900	Age of invasions and colonization
20th century	Independence and the question of a united Ireland

The Celtic people left the countryside peppered with thousands of ancient sights from the Iron Age. While most of what you'll see are little more than rockpiles and take a vigorous imagination to reconstruct (ring forts, wedge tombs, monumental stones, and so on), just standing next to a megalith that predates the pharoahs while surrounded by lush Ireland is evocative. The finest gold, bronze, and iron work of this period is in the National Museum in Dublin.

The Romans called Ireland Hibernia "Land of Winter"— apparently too cold and bleak to merit an attempt to take over and colonize. The biggest non-event in Irish history is that the Romans never invaded. While the mix of Celtic and Roman contributes to what makes the French French and the English English, the Irish are purely Celtic. If France is boules and England is cricket, then Ireland is hurling. This wild Irish national pastime (like airborne hockey with no injury timeouts) goes back to Celtic days, 2,000 years ago.

Celts worshiped sun. Perhaps St. Patrick had an easy time converting the locals because they had so little sun to worship. Whatever the case, a former Roman slave boy, Patrick, helped Christianize Ireland in the fifth century. From this period on, monks established monastic centers of learning which produced great Christian teachers and community builders. They traveled, establishing monastic communities all over Ireland, Britain, and Europe. One of them, St. Brandon, may have even sailed to America.

While the collapse of Rome left Europe a mess, it meant nothing to Ireland. Ireland was and remained a relatively cohesive society based on monastic settlements rather than cities. While Europe was rutting in the Dark Age mud, the light of civilization shone brightly in Ireland through a Golden Age lasting from the fifth through the ninth centuries. Irish monks—such as those imported by Charlemagne to help run his Frankish kingdom in A.D. 800—actually carried the torch of civilization back to Europe. Perhaps the greatest art of Dark Age Europe are the manuscripts (such as the ninth-century Book of Kells, which you'll see in Dublin) "illuminated," or richly illustrated, by Irish monks. Impressive round towers dot the Irish landscape—silent reminders of this impressive age.

Viking invasions of the ninth century wreaked repeated havoc on the monasteries and shook Irish civilization. Vikings established trading towns (such as Dublin) when before there were only Celtic settlements and monasteries.

The Normans, who invaded and conquered England after the Battle of Hastings (1066), were Ireland's next uninvited guests. In 1169, the Anglo-Normans invaded Ireland. These invaders, big time organizers, ushered in a new age in which society (government, cities, and religious organizations) was organized on a grander scale. Individual monastic settlements (the basis of Irish society in the Age of Saints and Scholars) were eclipsed by monastic orders just in from the Continent such as the Franciscans, Augustinians, and Cistercians.

The English made a concentrated effort to colonize Ireland in the 17th century. Settlers were "planted" and Irish society was split between an English-speaking landed gentry and the local Irish-speaking landless or nearly landless peasantry. During the 18th century, English Ireland thrived. Dublin was Britain's second city. Over time, greed on the top and dissent on the bottom required colonial policies to become more repressive. The Enlightenment provided ideas of freedom and the Revolutionary Age emboldened the Irish masses. (Even the non-Catholic Dubliner, Jonathan Swift—dean of St. Patrick's cathedral in the early 18th century—declared "Burn all that's British, except its coal.") To counter this Irish feistiness, English legislation became an out-and-out attack on the indigenous Gaelic culture. The harp, symbol of Irish culture, was outlawed. Written and unwritten laws made life for Catholics and Irish-speakers very difficult.

The potato famine of 1845–1849 was a pivotal event in Irish history. The stature of Ireland and its language never recovered. In a few years Ireland's population dropped from 8 million to 5 million (3 million either starved or emigrated). Ireland's population has not changed since. Britain's population, on the other hand, has grown from 12 million in 1845 to around 60 million today. (During this period, Ireland's population, as a percent of England's, dropped from 65 percent to 8 percent.)

While the English are likely to blame the famine on overpopulation (Ireland's population doubled in the 40 years leading up to the famine), many Irish say there actually was no famine—just a calculated attempt to starve down the local population. In fact, there was plenty of food grown on the island for export. It was only the potato crop which failed . . . and that happened to be what the Irish subsisted on.

The average farmer grew fancier export products for his landlord and was paid in potatoes which, in good years, he grew on the side. (If this makes you mad at the English landlords, consider American ownership of land in Central America where the landlord takes things one step further by not growing the local staple at all. He devotes all the land to more profitable cash crops for export and leaves the landless farmer no alternative but to buy his food—imported from the U.S.A.—at plantation wages, in the landlord's grocery store.)

The famine was a turning point in Irish history. Before the famine, land was subdivided—all the boys got a piece of the family estate (which grew smaller and smaller with each generation). After the famine the oldest son got the estate and the younger siblings, with no way to stay in Ireland, emigrated to Britain, Australia, Canada, and the U.S.A. Today there are 40 million Irish-Americans.

After the famine, Irish became the language of the peasant. English was for the upwardly mobile. Because of the huge immigration to the U.S.A., Ireland faced west and American influence increased. (As negotiations between Northern Ireland and the Irish Republic continue, American involvement in the talks is welcomed and considered essential by nearly all parties.)

The tragedy of the famine inflamed the nationalist movement. Uprising after uprising made it clear that Ireland was ready to close this thousand-year chapter of invasions and colonialism. Finally, in 1919, Ireland declared its independence. While the northern six counties (the only ones without a Catholic majority) voted to stay with Britain, the independent Republic of Ireland was born. (For a review of the ongoing "Troubles" between the North and the Republic, see the Northern Ireland chapter.)

The Irish Pub

When you say "a beer, please" in an Irish pub, you'll get a pint of Guinness (the black beauty with a blonde head). If you want a small beer, ask for a half-pint. Never rush your bartender when he's pouring a Guinness. It takes time—almost sacred time. If you don't like Guinness, try it in Ireland. It doesn't travel well and actually is better in its homeland. Murphy's is a very good Guinness-like stout but a bit smoother and milder.

In an Irish pub, you're a guest on your first night; after that you're a regular. Women traveling alone need not worry—you'll become part of the pub family in no time.

It's a tradition to buy your table a round and then for each person to reciprocate. If an Irishman buys you a drink, thank him by saying, "Guh rev mah a gut." Offer him a toast in Irish—"Slahn chuh!" A good excuse for a conversation is to ask to be taught a few words of Gaelic.

Craic is the sport that accompanies drinking in a pub. *Craic* (crack) is the art of conversation. People are there to talk. If you feel a bit awkward, remind yourself of that.

Here's a goofy excuse for some *craic*: Ireland—small as it is—has many dialects. People from Cork are famous for talking very fast (and in a squeaky voice). So fast that some even talk in letters alone. ABCD fish? (Anybody see the fish?) DR no fish. (There are no fish.) DR fish. (There are fish.) CDBD Is? (See the beady eyes?) OIBJ DR fish. (Oh aye, be Jeeze, there are fish.) For a possibly more appropriate spin, replace the fish with "bird" (girl). This is obscure but your pub neighbor may understand and enjoy hearing it. If nothing else, you won't seem so intimidating to him anymore.

You might ask if the people of one county are any smarter than the next. Kerry people are considered by some of their neighbors to be a bit out of it.

Traditional Irish Music

Traditional music is alive and popular in pubs throughout Ireland. "Sessions" (musical evenings) may be planned and advertised or impromptu. Traditionally, musicians just congregate and jam. There will generally be a fiddler, flute or tin whistle, guitar, *bodhran* (goat skin drum), and maybe an accordion. Things usually get going around 21:30 or 22:00. Last call for drinks is around 23:30.

The *bodhran* is played with a small two-headed club. The performer's hand stretches the skin to change the tone and pitch. The wind and string instruments embellish melody lines with lots of improvised ornamentation. Occasionally, the fast-paced music will stop and one person will sing an *a capella* "lament." This is the one time when the entire pub will stop to listen as sad lyrics fill the smoke-stained room. Stories—ranging from struggles against English rule to love songs—are always heartfelt. Spend a lament enjoying the faces in the crowd. A *ceilidh* (kay-lee) is an evening of music and dance . . . an Irish hoedown.

The music comes in sets of three songs. Whoever happens to be leading determines the next song only as the song the group is playing is about to be finished. If he wants to pass on the decision, it's done with eye contact and a nod.

A session can be magic or lifeless. If the chemistry is right, it's one of the great Irish experiences. The music churns intensely while the group casually enjoys exploring each others' musical style. The drummer dodges the fiddler's playful bow with his cigarette sticking half-ash straight from the middle of his mouth. Sipping their pints, a faint but steady buzz is skillfully maintained. The floor on the musicians' platform is stomped paint-free and barmaids scurry artfully through the commotion gathering towers of empty cream-crusted glasses. With knees up and heads down the music goes round and round.

Make yourself right at home, drumming the table or playing the ten-pence coins. Talk to your neighbor. Locals often have an almost evangelical interest in explaining the music.

Let's Talk Telephones

Smart travelers use the telephone every day—for making hotel reservations, calling tourist information offices, and phoning home. In Europe, card-operated public phones are speedily replacing coin-operated phones. Each country sells telephone cards good for use in its country. Get a phone card at any post office. To make a call, pick up the receiver, insert your card in the slot in the phone, dial your number, make your call, then retrieve your card. The price of your call is automatically deducted from your card as you use it. If you have a phone card phobia, you'll usually find easy-to-use "talk now, pay later" metered phones in larger post offices. Avoid using hotel room phones, which are major ripoffs for anything other than local calls and calling card calls (see below). For more information, see the Introduction: Telephones and Mail.

Calling Card Operators

Calling home from Europe is easy from any type of phone if you have a calling card. From a private phone, just dial the toll-free

number to reach the operator. Using a public phone, first insert
a small-value coin or a British or Irish phone card. Then dial the
operator, who will ask you for your calling-card number and
place your call home. You'll save money on calls of three minutes
or more. When you finish, your coin should be returned (with a
card, no money should have been deducted). Your bill awaits you
at home (one more reason to prolong your vacation).

	AT&T	**MCI**	**Sprint**
Britain	0800-89-00-11	0800-89-02-22	0800-89-08-77
Ireland	1800-55-00-00	1800-55-10-01	1800-55-20-01

Dialing Direct

Calling Between Countries: First dial the international access
code, then the country code, the area code (if it starts with
zero, drop the zero), and the local number.

Calling Long Distance Within a Country: First dial the
area code (including its zero), then the local number.

Some of Europe's Exceptions: In Spain, area codes start
with 9 instead of zero (just drop or add the nine instead of the
zero). A few countries lack area codes, such as Denmark, Norway, and France. You still use the above sequence and codes to
dial, just skip the area code.

International Access Codes

When dialing direct, first dial the international access code of
the country you're calling from.

Austria: 00
Belgium: 00
Britain: 00
Czech Republic: 00
Denmark: 00
Estonia: 800
Finland: 990
France: 00
Germany: 00
Ireland: 00

Italy: 00
Latvia: 00
Lithuania: 810
Netherlands: 00
Portugal: 00
Russia: 810
Spain: 07
Sweden: 009
Switzerland: 00
U.S.A./Canada: 011

Country Codes

After you've dialed the international access code, dial the code
of the country you're calling.

Austria: 43
Belgium: 32
Britain: 44
Czech Republic: 42
Denmark: 45
Estonia: 372
Finland: 358
France: 33
Germany: 49
Ireland: 353
Italy: 39

Latvia: 371
Lithuania: 370
Netherlands: 31
Norway: 47
Portugal: 351
Russia: 7
Spain: 34
Sweden: 46
Switzerland: 41
U.S.A./Canada: 1

Telephone Directory
For train info anywhere in Britain, dial 0345/484-950.

Britain	Tourist Info
Bath	01225/477-101
Blackpool	01253/621-623
Cambridge	01223/322-640
Cardiff	01222/227-281
Chipping Campden	01386/841-206
Coventry	01203/832-303
Durham	0191/384-3720
Edinburgh	0131/557-1700
Hadrian's Wall	01434/605-225
Inverness	01463/234-353
Ironbridge Gorge	01952/432-166
Keswick	017687/72645
London	0181/846-9000
Oban	01631/563-122
Ruthin, N. Wales	01824/703-992
Stow-on-the-Wold	01451/831-082
Stratford	01789/293-127
Wells	01749/672-552
Windermere	015394/46499
York	01904/621-756

Ireland	Tourist Info	Train Info
Dingle Town	066/51188	————
Dublin	1-550-112233	01/836-6222
Galway	091/563-081	091/564-222
Kilronan, Inishmor	099/61263	————

Other Useful Numbers in Britain

Emergency (police and ambulance): 999
Operator Services: 100
Directory Assistance: 192 (free from phone booth,
    otherwise expensive)
International Information: 153
U.S. Embassy: 0171/499-9000
Eurostar (Chunnel Info): 01233/617575
Train and Boats to Europe Info: 0990-848-848

London's Airports and Airlines

Heathrow

General Information: 0181/759-4321
Terminal 3: 0181/745-6375
Terminal 4: 0181/745-4540
Air Canada: 0181/897-1331
American: 0345/789-789
British Air: 0345/222-111
British Midlands: 0345/554-554
SAS: 0171/734-4020
United Airlines: 0800-888-555

Gatwick

General Information: 01293/535-353 for all airlines—except
British Airways at 01293/567-000.

Climate Chart

The chart below gives average daytime temperatures and average number of days with more than a trickle of rain.

	J	F	M	A	M	J	J	A	S	O	N	D
London	43°	44°	50°	56°	62°	69°	71°	71°	66°	58°	51°	45°
	15	13	11	12	11	11	12	11	13	14	15	15
S. Wales	45°	45°	50°	56°	61°	68°	69°	69°	65°	58°	51°	46°
	18	14	13	13	13	13	14	15	16	16	17	18
York	43°	44°	49°	55°	60°	67°	70°	70°	65°	57°	49°	45°
	17	15	13	13	13	14	15	14	14	15	17	17
Edinburgh	42°	43°	46°	51°	56°	62°	65°	64°	60°	54°	48°	44°
	17	15	15	14	14	15	17	16	16	17	17	18
Dublin	40°	41°	44°	47°	52°	57°	60°	59°	56°	50°	45°	42°
	13	10	10	11	10	11	13	12	12	11	12	14

Numbers and Stumblers

•Europeans write a few of their numbers differently than we do. 1 = 1 , 4 = 4 , 7 = 7. Learn the difference or miss your train.

•In Europe, dates appear as day/month/year, so Christmas is 25-12-98.

•Commas are decimal points and decimals commas. A dollar and a half is 1,50 and there are 5.280 feet in a mile.

•When pointing, use your whole hand, palm downward.

•When counting with fingers, start with your thumb. If you hold up your first finger to request one item, you'll probably get two.

•What we Americans call the second floor of a building is the first floor in Europe.

•Europeans keep the left "lane" open for passing on escalators and moving sidewalks. Keep to the right.

•And please . . . don't call your waist pack a "fanny pack."

Weights and Measures

1 British pint = 1.2 U.S. pints
1 imperial gallon = 1.2 U.S. gallons or about 5 liters
1 stone = 14 lbs. (a 175-lb. person weighs 12 stone)
28 degrees Centigrade = 82 degrees Fahrenheit
Shoe sizes = about .5 to 1.5 sizes smaller than in U.S.

British–Yankee Vocabulary

advert advertisement

afters dessert

"A" levels advanced high school exams

anorak parka

anti-clockwise counterclockwise

aubergine eggplant

Balloons Belgians

banger sausage

bangers and mash sausage and mashed potatoes

bank holiday legal holiday

bap hamburger-type bun

ben Scottish for mountain

billion ten of our billions (a million million)

biro ballpoint pen

biscuit cookie

black pudding sausage made from dried blood

bloke man, guy

bobby policeman ("copper" is more common)

bomb success

bonnet car hood

boot car trunk

BR British Rail

braces suspenders

bridle way path for walkers, bikers, and horse riders

brilliant cool

BTA British Tourist Authority

bubble and squeak cold meat fried with cabbage and potatoes

bum bottom or "backside"

candy floss cotton candy

car boot sale temporary flea market with car trunk displays (a good place to buy your stolen goods back)

caravan trailer

cat's eyes reflectors on the road

ceilidh Scottish informal evening of song and folk fun (kay-lee)

cheap and nasty cheap and bad quality (pay monkeys, get peanuts)

cheeky (or saucy) smart alecky

cheerio goodbye

cheers thanks (also, a toast)

chemist pharmacist

chips french fries

chock-a-block jam-packed

cider alcoholic apple cider

clearway road where you can't stop

coach long-distance bus

concession discounted admission

cotton buds Q-tips

courgette zucchini

courier tour escort or guide

craic (pron: crack) good conversation (Irish and spreading to England)

crisps potato chips

cuppa cup of tea

dear expensive

dicey iffy, risky

digestives round graham crackers

dinner lunch or dinner

diversion detour

donkey's years until the cows come home

draughts checkers

drawing pin thumbtack

dual carriageway divided

highway (four lanes)
estate agent   realtor
face flannel   wash cloth
fag   cigarette
fagged   exhausted
faggot   meatball
fanny   vagina
fell   mountain, hill, or high plain
first floor   second floor
flat   apartment
football   soccer
force   waterfall (lake district)
fortnight   two weeks
Frogs   French people
gallery   balcony
gallon   1.2 American gallons
gangway   aisle
gaol   jail (same pronunciation)
garden   yard
Geordie   from northeast England (Durham), coal mining culture/accent
give way   yield
glen   Scottish for narrow valley
goods wagon   freight truck
grammar school   high school
half eight   8:30 (not 7:30)
heath   open land without trees
holiday   vacation
homely   likeable or cozy
hoover   vacuum cleaner
hundredweight   112 pounds
ice lolly   popsicle
interval   intermission at the theater
ironmonger   hardware store
jelly   jello
Joe Bloggs   John Doe
jumble   sale, rummage sale
jumper   sweater
keep your pecker up   be brave

kiosk   booth
kipper   smoked herring
knackered   exhausted (Cockney: cream crackered)
knickers   ladies' panties
knocking shop   brothel
knock up   wake up or visit
ladybird   ladybug
lead   leash
let   rent
lip salve   chapstick
loo   toilet or bathroom
lorry   truck
mac   mackintosh coat, raincoat
mate   buddy, friend (boy or girl)
mean   stingy
mews   courtyard stables, often used as cottages
minced meat   hamburger meat
motorway   highway
nappy   diaper
natter   talk and talk
neat   a straight drink
neep   Scottish for turnip
nosh   food or eat
nought   zero
noughts & crosses   tick-tack-toe
off license   liquor store or a place selling take-away liquor
take away   to go
pasty   crusted savory (usually meat) pie
pavement   sidewalk
petrol   gas
pissed (rude), paralytic, bevvied, sloshed, wellied, popped up, ratted, "pissed as a newt"   drunk
pillar box   postbox
pitch   playing field

plaster Band-Aid
poppers (or press studs) snaps
pram baby carriage
publican person who runs a pub
public convenience public toilets
public school private "prep" school (Eton)
put a sock in it shut up
queue line
queue jump crowd in line
queue up line up
quid pound (money, worth about $1.60)
randy horny
redundant, made fired or laid off
Remembrance Day Veterans' Day
return ticket round-trip
ring up call (telephone)
rubber eraser
sanitary towel sanitary napkin/pad
sausage roll sausage wrapped in a flaky pastry
Scotch egg hard-boiled egg wrapped in sausage meat
self-catering accommodation with kitchen facilities, rented by the week
sellotape scotch tape
serviette napkin
single ticket one-way ticket
sleeping policeman speed bumps
smalls underwear
snogging kissing and cuddling
solicitor lawyer
starkers buck naked

starters appetizers
stone 14 lbs. (weight)
subway underground pedestrian passageway
surgical spirit rubbing alcohol
suss out figure out
swede rutabaga
sweet dessert
sweets candy
ta thank you
taxi rank taxi stand
tea towel dish towel
telly TV
theater live stage (not "cinema")
tick a check mark
tight as a fish's bum cheapskate (water-tight)
tights panty hose
tipper lorry dump truck
tin can
to let for rent
top hole first rate
topping excellent
top up refill a drink
torch flashlight
towpath path along a river or canal
tube subway
twee quaint, cute
underground subway
VAT value added tax
verge grassy edge of road
verger church official
wellingtons, wellies rubber boots
wee urinate
whacked exhausted
witter on gab and gab
yob hooligan
zebra crossing crosswalk
zed the letter "z"

Faxing Your Hotel Reservation

Most hotel managers know basic "hotel English." Faxing is the preferred method for reserving a room. It's more accurate and cheaper than telephoning and much faster than writing a letter. Use this handy form for your fax. Photocopy and fax away.

One-Page Fax

To: _____ @ _____
           hotel   *fax*

From: _____ @ _____
             name   *fax*

Today's date: ____ / _____ / ____
                day *month* *year*

Dear Hotel _____,

Please make this reservation for me:

Name: _____

Total # of people: _____   # of rooms: _____   # of nights: _____

Arriving: ____ / _____ / ____   My time of arrival (24-hr clock): _____
           day *month* *year*   (I will telephone if I will be late)

Departing: ____ / _____ / ____
             day *month* *year*

Room(s): Single___ Double___ Twin___ Triple___ Quad___

With: Toilet___ Shower___ Bath___ Sink only___

Special needs: View___ Quiet___ Cheapest Room___

Credit card: Visa___ MasterCard___ American Express___

Card #: _____

Expiration date:_____

Name on card: _____

You may charge me for the first night as a deposit. Please fax or mail me confirmation of my reservation, along with the type of room reserved, the price, and whether the price includes breakfast. Thank you.

_____
Signature

_____
Name

_____
Address

_____
City   *State*   *Zip Code*   *Country*

Road Scholar Feedback for
GREAT BRITAIN & IRELAND 1998

We're all in the same travelers' school of hard knocks. Your feedback helps us improve this guidebook for future travelers. Please fill this out (attach more info or any tips/favorite discoveries if you like) and send it to us. As thanks for your help, we'll send you our quarterly travel newsletter free for one year. Thanks! **Rick**

I traveled mainly by: ___ Car ___ Train/bus tickets
___ Railpass   Other (please list _____)

Number of people traveling together:
___ Solo ___ 2 ___ 3 ___ 4 ___ Over 4 ___ Tour

Ages of traveler/s (including children):

_____

I visited _____ countries in _____ weeks.

I traveled in: ___ Spring ___ Summer ___ Fall ___ Winter

My daily budget per person (excluding transportation):
___ Under $40 ___ $40–$60 ___ $60–$80 ___ $80–$120
___ over $120 ___ Don't know

Average cost of hotel rooms: Single room $_____
Double room $_____   Other (type _____) $_____

Favorite tip from this book:

_____

Biggest waste of time or money caused by this book:

_____

Other Rick Steves books used for this trip:

_____

Hotel listings from this book should be geared toward places that are:
___Cheaper   ___More expensive   ___About the same

Of the recommended accommodations/restaurants used, which was:

Best _____

    Why? _____

Worst _____

    Why? _____

I reserved rooms:

____from USA   ____in advance as I traveled

____same day by phone   ____just showed up

Getting rooms in recommended hotels was:

____easy   ____mixed   ____frustrating

Of the sights/experiences/destinations recommended by this book, which was:

Most overrated _____

    Why? _____

Most underrated _____

    Why? _____

Best ways to improve this book:

_____

I'd like a free newsletter subscription:

___ Yes   ___ No   ___ Already on list

_____

Name

_____

Address

_____

City, State, Zip

_____

E-mail Address

Please send to: ETBD, Box 2009, Edmonds, WA 98020

INDEX

Rick Steves' Phrase Books

Unlike other phrase books and dictionaries on the market, my well-tested phrases and key words cover every situation a traveler is likely to encounter. With these books you'll laugh with your cabby, disarm street thieves with insults, and charm new European friends.

Each book in the series is 4" x 6", with maps.

RICK STEVES' FRENCH PHRASE BOOK & DICTIONARY
U.S. $5.95/Canada $8.50

RICK STEVES' GERMAN PHRASE BOOK & DICTIONARY
U.S. $5.95/Canada $8.50

RICK STEVES' ITALIAN PHRASE BOOK & DICTIONARY
U.S. $5.95/Canada $8.50

RICK STEVES' SPANISH & PORTUGUESE PHRASE BOOK & DICTIONARY
U.S. $7.95/Canada $11.25

RICK STEVES' FRENCH, ITALIAN & GERMAN PHRASE BOOK & DICTIONARY
U.S. $7.95/Canada $11.25

Books from John Muir Publications

Rick Steves' Books

Asia Through the
Back Door, $17.95
Europe 101: History
and Art for the
Traveler, $17.95
Mona Winks: Self-
Guided Tours of
Europe's Top
Museums, $18.95
Rick Steves' Europe
Through the Back
Door, $19.95
Rick Steves' Best of
Europe, $18.95
Rick Steves' France,
Belgium & the
Netherlands, $16.95
Rick Steves'
Germany, Austria &
Switzerland, $15.95
Rick Steves' Great
Britain & Ireland,
$16.95
Rick Steves' Italy,
$14.95
Rick Steves' Russia
& the Baltics, $9.95
Rick Steves'
Scandinavia, $13.95
Rick Steves' Spain
& Portugal, $14.95
Rick Steves' French
Phrase Book, $5.95
Rick Steves'
German Phrase
Book, $5.95
Rick Steves' Italian
Phrase Book, $5.95
Rick Steves'
Spanish &
Portuguese Phrase
Book, $7.95
Rick Steves' French/
Italian/German
Phrase Book, $7.95

City•Smart™ Guidebooks

Albuquerque, $12.95
(avail. 4/98)
Anchorage, $12.95
Austin, $12.95
Calgary, $12.95
Cincinnati, $12.95
(avail. 5/98)
Cleveland, $14.95

Denver, $14.95
Indianapolis, $12.95
Kansas City, $12.95
Memphis, $12.95
Milwaukee, $12.95
Minneapolis/
St. Paul, $14.95
Nashville, $14.95
Portland, $14.95
Richmond, $12.95
San Antonio, $12.95
St. Louis, $12.95
(avail. 5/98)
Tampa/St. Peters-
burg, $14.95

Travel✦Smart™ Guidebooks

Alaska, $14.95
American South-
west, $14.95
Carolinas, $14.95
Colorado, $14.95
Deep South, $17.95
Eastern Canada,
$15.95
Florida Gulf Coast,
$14.95
Hawaii, $14.95
Kentucky/
Tennessee, $14.95
Michigan, $14.95
Minnesota/
Wisconsin, $14.95
Montana, Wyoming,
& Idaho, $16.95
New England, $14.95
New York State,
$15.95
Northern California,
$15.95
Ohio, $14.95 (avail.
5/98)
Pacific Northwest,
$14.95
Southern California,
$14.95
South Florida and
the Keys, $14.95
Texas, $14.95
Western Canada,
$16.95

Adventures in Nature Series

Alaska, $18.95
Belize, $18.95

Guatemala, $18.95
Honduras, $17.95

Kidding Around™ Travel Titles

$7.95 each
Kidding Around
Atlanta
Kidding Around
Austin
Kidding Around
Boston
Kidding Around
Chicago
Kidding Around
Cleveland
Kids Go! Denver
Kidding Around
Indianapolis
Kidding Around
Kansas City
Kidding Around
Miami
Kidding Around
Milwaukee
Kidding Around
Minneapolis/St.
Paul
Kidding Around
Nashville
Kidding Around
Portland
Kidding Around
San Francisco
Kids Go! Seattle
Kidding Around
Washington, D.C.

Ordering Information

Please check your
local bookstore for
our books, or call
1-800-888-7504
to order direct and to
receive a complete
catalog. A shipping
charge will be added
to your order total.

Send all inquiries to:
John Muir
Publications
P.O. Box 613
Santa Fe, NM 87504